Before the Anzac Dawn

Before the Anzac Dawn

A military history of Australia to 1915

Edited by
CRAIG STOCKINGS & JOHN CONNOR

NEWSOUTH

A NewSouth book

Published by
NewSouth Publishing
University of New South Wales Press Ltd
University of New South Wales
Sydney NSW 2052
AUSTRALIA
newsouthpublishing.com

© in this edition Craig Stockings and John Connor 2013

© in individual chapters is retained by the chapter authors
First published 2013

10 9 8 7 6 5 4 3 2 1

This book is copyright. Apart from any fair dealing for the purpose of private study, research, criticism or review, as permitted under the Copyright Act, no part of this book may be reproduced by any process without written permission. Inquiries should be addressed to the publisher.

National Library of Australia Cataloguing-in-Publication entry
Title: Before the Anzac dawn: a military history of Australia to 1915/ edited by Craig Stockings and John Connor.
ISBN: 9781742233697 (pbk)
ISBN: 9781742241616 (ePub/Kindle)
ISBN: 9781742246604 (ePDF)
Notes: Includes index.
Subjects: Australia – History, Military – 19th century.
 Australia – Armed Forces – History.
Other Authors/Contributors:
 Stockings, Craig, 1974– editor.
 Connor, John, editor.
Dewey Number: 355.00994

Design Josephine Pajor-Markus
Cover design Nada Backovic Design
Cover images Top image: Shutterstock; bottom image: Charles Hammond, *Australians and New Zealanders at Klerksdorp, 24 March 1901*, 1904, oil on canvas 77 x 127.6 cm, Australian War Memorial (ART19564)
Printer Griffin Press

All reasonable efforts were taken to obtain permission to use copyright material reproduced in this book, but in some cases copyright could not be traced. The author welcomes information in this regard.

This book is printed on paper using fibre supplied from plantation or sustainably managed forests.

Contents

	Acknowledgments	vii
	Contributors	viii
	Introduction *John Connor*	1
1	Traditional Indigenous warfare *John Connor*	8
2	Frontier warfare in Australia *Jonathan Richards*	21
3	British soldiers in colonial Australia *Peter Stanley*	39
4	The battle for the Eureka Stockade *Gregory Blake*	62
5	Australian naval defence *Greg Swinden*	90
6	Australians in the New Zealand Wars *Damien Fenton*	118
7	The rifle clubs *Andrew Kilsby*	148
8	Australia's boy soldiers: The army cadet movement *Craig Stockings*	174
9	Australians in the wars in Sudan and South Africa *Craig Wilcox*	204

10 Radical nationalists and Australian invasion novels *Augustine Meaher IV*	230
11 Edwardian transformation *Craig Wilcox*	255
12 The capture of German New Guinea *John Connor*	283
Notes	304
Index	338

Acknowledgments

First and foremost we must acknowledge the authors of the various chapters of this book. The quality of their scholarship was matched by a spirit of co-operation which made the job of editing – without exaggeration – a pleasure. We are personally and professionally indebted to them. Thank you for being part of this project.

I would also like to express my gratitude once again to the team at UNSW Press. The continuing vision, expertise, skilled and friendly support provided was invaluable.

Further thanks to the long list of others who have assisted in any way in this project. I trust the product matches your faith and expectations.

Craig Stockings and John Connor

Contributors

Greg Blake has been a secondary school teacher since 1977 and taught in schools in Victoria, the Northern Territory and the ACT. Greg has had a lifelong interest in military history and contributed articles on the subject to a variety of UK and US publications. Greg is the author of *Eureka Stockade: A Ferocious and Bloody Battle*, the first account of Eureka that examines the event as a military engagement in a detailed manner. Greg is continuing his postgraduate studies and in addition to secondary school teaching has tutored at the University of New South Wales, Canberra. Greg is an accomplished artist and has contributed to magazines and instructional texts both in Australia and overseas. Greg currently lives in Canberra.

John Connor is a senior lecturer in History at the University of New South Wales, Canberra. His books include *The Australian Frontier Wars 1788–1838* (2002) which was shortlisted for the Royal United Services Institute's Westminster Medal for Military Literature, and *Anzac and Empire: George Foster Pearce and the Foundations of Australian Defence* (2011). He is currently writing a history of the British Empire in World War I, and, with Peter Stanley and Peter Yule, a history of Australia during the Great War.

Damien Fenton is a senior historian at the Ministry for Culture & Heritage in Wellington, New Zealand. His interests include Australian and New Zealand military history and he has worked in this area as an academic and a public historian in both countries. He was a member of the organising committee responsible for the conference 'Tutū te Puehu – New Zealand's Wars of the Nineteenth Century' held in Wellington, February 2011, the first military history conference ever held on the subject. His latest publication is *To Cage a Dragon: SEATO and the Defence of Southeast Asia* (2012) and he is currently working on an illustrated history of New Zealand and World War I. He is also the editor of the Ministry's World War I website: www.firstworldwar.govt.nz.

Andrew Kilsby is an independent historian and author of *Lions of the Day* (2008), *The Bisley Boys* (2009), *Fallen Leaves* (2010) and, with Greg Swinden, *HMAS Melbourne 1913–1928: The Forgotten Cruiser* (2013). He has further authored a number of articles and other commissioned histories. Andrew is also executive officer for Military History and Heritage Victoria Inc, and operations and marketing manager for the National Vietnam Veterans Museum. Andrew has acted as convener at military history conferences, including '1942: Australia in the Shadow of War' (Melbourne, 2012) and produced a number of military history exhibitions, including 'Saluting their Service' (2010), 'Citizen Soldiers of Oakleigh' (2011) and most recently, the centenary exhibition 'Fear God and Honour the King: HMAS *Melbourne* 1913–1928' (2013).

Augustine Meaher IV is the director of the Department of Political and Strategic Studies at the Baltic Defence College in Tartu, Estonia. His areas of academic interest are diplomatic and Australian military history, especially civil military relations. He has recently published *The Australian Road to Singapore: The Myth of British Betrayal* (2010) and is the author of several articles on Australian military and diplomatic history. He is presently editing a collection of essays on invasion novels due for publication in 2014. His current research project is a study of Australian diplomatic policy towards the Baltic States during the Soviet period.

Jonathan Richards worked as a fruit-picker, gardener, public servant, postman, telephonist and school groundsman before enrolling as a part-time university student during the 1980s. After completing a Bachelor of Arts in Australian and comparative studies in 1995, he was awarded the degree with honours in history in 1997. His doctoral thesis on Queensland's infamous Native Police Force was accepted in 2005, and published in 2008 as *The Secret War: A True History of Queensland's Native Police*. He has taught a number of historical and social science courses at undergraduate level since. His research interests include frontier policing and violence, Indigenous and community history, and more recently archival explorations of death in Queensland. He is particularly interested in the general lack of interest shown by academic historians in Australia's frontier history, and how this vacuum has been filled by popular writers and amateur historians.

Peter Stanley is a professor of History at the University of New South Wales, Canberra. He was previously the principal historian at the Australian War Memorial, where he worked from 1980 to 2007, and headed the National Museum of Australia's Research Centre from 2007 to 2013. He has published 25 books on Australian military social history, British imperial and medical history, and environmental history, and is a prominent commentator on Australian war history. His books include *Bad Characters: Sex, Crime, Mutiny, Murder and the Australian Imperial Force*, which jointly won the 2011 Prime Minister's Prize for Australian History. His most recent book is *Black Saturday at Steels Creek* and his next will be *Lost Boys of Anzac*.

Craig Stockings is an associate professor of History at the University of New South Wales, Canberra. His areas of academic interest concern general and Australian military history and operational analysis. He has published a history of the army cadet

Contributors

movement in Australia entitled *The Torch and the Sword* (2007), and a study of the First Libyan Campaign in North Africa 1940–41: *Bardia: Myth, Reality and the Heirs of Anzac* (2009). He has also edited *Zombie Myths of Australian Military History* (2010) and *Anzac's Dirty Dozen: 12 Myths of Australian Military History* (2012). His current research project (with associate professor Eleanor Hancock), concerning the Axis invasion of Greece in 1941, will be published this year.

Greg Swinden joined the RAN College in 1985 and graduated from the Australian Defence Force Academy in 1987 with a Bachelor of Arts. He subsequently served in HMAS *Swan*, Navy Office, HMAS *Creswell*, HMAS *Melbourne*, Naval Support Command and as a divisional officer at the Defence Academy. During 2000 he served for a three-month period in East Timor, before further operational deployments to the Solomon Islands, the Persian Gulf and on border protection patrols. In 2003–04 he served as the RAN liaison officer in Singapore. During late 2011, Commander Swinden served in the Middle East and Afghanistan as a senior logistics officer. He is currently the deputy director at the Sea Power Centre, Australia.

Craig Wilcox is a historian who lives and writes in Sydney. His most recent scholarly book, published by Cambridge University Press is *Red Coat Dreaming: How Colonial Australia Embraced the British Army* (2009). He is currently writing two illustrated books on collections in the National Library of Australia, and exploring Sydney's Hunter Street in collaboration with the Brisbane artist Phil Tamblyn.

Introduction

JOHN CONNOR

'Australia', claimed Prime Minister Billy Hughes soon after the end of World War I, 'was born on the shores of Gallipoli'.[1] If this were true, Australia has no military history – or any other history to speak of – before the first Anzac Day, and it will have been a waste of your time and money to buy and read this book. Hughes, however, was mistaken.

The 12 chapters in this book – covering topics from traditional Indigenous warfare to the capture of German New Guinea in 1914 – reveal that warfare and martial culture had a significant role in the lives of Australians long before soldiers landed on an obscure Turkish beach on 25 April 1915. With Anzac Day becoming the *de facto* national day – described in more recent prime ministerial speeches as a day for 'Australians of all heritages and walks of life' marking 'the first time that a fledgling nation got a real sense of itself'[2] – it is inevitable that this pre-1915 history has been neglected. This period of history does not provide the simple, linear narrative of Australian identity that so many crave. Instead, it often reflects Australia's origins as a collection of British colonies and is discarded for being 'too British', and 'not sufficiently Australian'.

It must be remembered, however, that the Gallipoli campaign was fought by Australian soldiers who saw themselves as both Australian and as part of the British Empire, with no contradiction between these seemingly separate identities.[3] The organisation they enlisted in was called the 'Australian *Imperial* Force'.

When the troops arrived in Egypt and had access to British Army uniform stocks, most discarded their slouch hats and started wearing peaked 'patrol caps' so they would look more like British soldiers. Photographs show that most Australians who landed at Anzac Cove on 25 April were wearing these British caps, and in 1919, when the Australian Government commissioned artist George Lambert to produce the large painting entitled 'Anzac, the landing 1915', his initial pencil sketches showed the Australians ascending the ridge wearing their British caps.[4] Perhaps at the instigation of official historian Charles Bean, Lambert later re-drew these soldiers, changing their headgear from 'British' caps to 'Australian' slouch hats.[5]

If the real image of the Gallipoli landing required the 1920s equivalent of extensive 'photoshopping' to make Anzac Day appear more 'Australian', then remembering these earlier military campaigns will be even more problematic. Postage stamps provide the perfect example of this difficulty. Australia Post regularly issues stamps to commemorate significant historical events. It released stamps to mark the centenaries of New South Wales troops going to fight in Sudan in 1885 and the larger Australian commitment to the South African War from 1899 to 1902 (for both campaigns, see Chapter 9), but chose to portray the events in such a vague and ambiguous manner that most people would not realise they were commemorating Australian involvement in nineteenth-century overseas conflicts. The 1985 stamp issue, entitled 'Colonial military uniforms', consisted of five different stamps designs, each featuring illustrations of soldiers from a unit formed in the Australian colonies before Federation. One of the units portrayed was the New South Wales Contingent to the Sudan, and the stamp shows a soldier kissing a woman goodbye with a sailing ship in the background. There is nothing to indicate his destination in Sudan, and nothing to explain that

Introduction

the issue is commemorating the centenary of the first Australian military unit to be deployed to an overseas war.[6]

In the same way, five stamps issued in 2000 marked the centenary of the first Australian to be awarded the Victoria Cross (VC). Three stamps featured portraits of the three surviving Australian VC recipients, the fourth had an illustration of the medal itself, while the final design bore a portrait of Neville Howse, who became the first Australian to receive the VC after an act of gallantry on a battlefield in South Africa in 1900. Nowhere on the stamps is there any indication of who or why the Australians were fighting in South Africa in 1900. By commemorating Howse and his bravery under fire, the Australian role in South Africa is remembered, but without mentioning the war.[7]

It is not surprising that Australians find it difficult to mine their past and unearth examples of national identity that can be directly linked to the contemporary independent Australian nation. This is a problem shared with other post-colonial states, including, for example, the Republic of Ireland. The reason for this is that so much of Australian (or Irish) history has been shaped not by internal actions, but by external political, cultural and economic factors. These external factors are often global in nature, such as British imperialism, mass migration, economic globalisation or the world-wide impact of World War I.[8]

But Australians need to know and understand their own history, and part of this understanding must be the realisation that Australian history is often not theirs alone, but is a transnational history shared with other people in other parts of the world. Australia is now a fully independent nation, but it was not always the case. For much of the continent's history since 1788, its non-Indigenous population saw Australia as a component within a 'British World'. Any attempt to look into the past to identify narrowly 'Australian' characteristics in people who had a much wider view of the world will, at best, be incomplete. At worst, it will be a deliberately misleading portrait, much like the slouch-hatted Australian soldiers in Lambert's Gallipoli painting.

The aim of this book is to tell the more complicated but still important stories of how both Indigenous and non-Indigenous Australians experienced war and thought about war *before* the landing at Anzac Cove. These people of the past dressed, ate and lived differently to current-day Australians; what is most important to realise is that they thought differently as well. Most Australians today abhor violence in any form, and many oppose Australian participation in overseas wars. As we will see, many Indigenous and non-Indigenous Australians of the past approved of martial values, and even saw them as central to their cultures. The contributors in this book – all experts in, and passionate for, their topics – will explain why this was the case, and the impact these events and beliefs have had in the development of modern Australia.

In line with this aim, *Before the Anzac Dawn* begins with the form of Australian warfare that has existed longer than any other: the traditional warfare of Aborigines and Torres Strait Islanders that began when these peoples first arrived on the Australian continent at least 60 000 years ago. Many people believe that Indigenous Australians did not fight 'wars', as they had nothing that resembled the conflicts between modern nation states. John Connor in Chapter 1 argues that how societies fight wars is a reflection of their culture. It is true that Aboriginal and Torres Strait Islander warfare was different to modern state-versus-state conflicts, but it came out of the nature and values of Indigenous societies, and was warfare nonetheless.

From the end of the eighteenth century until well into the twentieth, Aboriginal warriors also fought British settlers, soldiers and police on an ever-shifting frontier for the control of the continent. In Chapter 2, Jonathan Richards describes the frontier wars by which British institutions and cultures were established in Australia, and whose outcome still determines the relationship between Indigenous and non-Indigenous Australians to this day.

With the establishment of British colonies came the arrival of British Army garrisons. As Peter Stanley shows in Chapter 3, when these soldiers first arrived in Australia, they were mostly kept busy guarding convicts, fighting Aborigines and chasing bushrangers. By the 1860s their role in maintaining public order had become the responsibility of the colonial governments, and the British regiments farewelled Australia in 1870.

The most famous action that British soldiers conducted in the Australian colonies was their attack on the Eureka Stockade in Victoria in December 1854. In Chapter 4, Gregory Blake argues that the events surrounding this skirmish on the Ballarat goldfields have been misunderstood. What is generally seen as a military massacre of defenceless miners was in fact a regular military engagement, in which the men holding the stockade (including Californians who had fought in the Mexican–American War of 1846–48) held their ground for some time.

As the Australian colonies developed in the second half of the nineteenth century, they began creating military institutions of their own, although based on British models. In Chapter 5, Greg Swinden charts the similar development of Australian colonial naval forces, from their early reliance on Royal Navy squadrons, to the rather haphazard establishment of colonial naval forces, and eventually the creation of the Royal Australian Navy in 1911.

In 1860, the Victorian warship *Victoria* sailed across the Tasman Sea to New Zealand and fought alongside British and New Zealand colonial forces against Māori tribes in the Taranaki. In the subsequent Waikato War that began in 1863, the New Zealand Government recruited about 2500 men from the Australian colonies to fight the Māori. In Chapter 6, Damien Fenton recounts the experiences of these first Australians to fight in organised military units in an overseas war.

British martial values and what the British historian Ian Beckett has described as the 'amateur military tradition' naturally spread to the Australian colonies. In some cases, as Andrew Kilsby shows in Chapter 7, rifle clubs were created in Australia in direct imitation of the National Rifle Association in the United Kingdom. As Craig Stockings similarly demonstrates in Chapter 8, the school cadet movement in Australia developed in parallel to its British counterpart. In both cases, the organisations reflected the widely held belief of that period that the inculcation of martial values in boys and men was beneficial, even necessary, to society in general.

As mentioned earlier in this Introduction, the first Australian military unit to serve in an overseas war was the New South Wales contingent to Sudan in 1885. This would be followed on a larger scale by the many contingents from the six Australian colonies and, following Federation, from the Commonwealth of Australia, which fought in the South African War between 1899 and 1902. In Chapter 9, Craig Wilcox investigates why Australians of this time so eagerly volunteered 'as patriots and as pragmatists' to fight in the British Empire's wars in Africa.

The late nineteenth century saw the development of a new literary genre in Britain: the invasion novel, which imagined a surprise and generally devastating enemy attack on one's homeland. The invasion novel soon appeared in the Antipodes, but as Augustine Meaher points out in Chapter 10, the Australian version differed from the British original. Australian invasion novels envisaged a massive Asian invasion that is eventually overcome by Australian civilians who are 'natural soldiers' – an idea

Introduction

which would later become central to the Anzac legend.

In 1901, the six Australian colonies came together to form the Commonwealth of Australia. In Chapter 11, Craig Wilcox examines how federal governments in this period created military institutions such as the Royal Australian Navy, compulsory military training or government rifle factories as a form of nation-building. When Britain declared war on Germany in 1914, this defence structure meant that Australia was immediately able to despatch an expeditionary force northwards to German New Guinea. As John Connor explains in Chapter 12, the prompt capture of that enemy colony in September 1914 and the prevention of its use as a base for German warships removed a real threat to Australia and its trade during World War I.

Over six months before the landings at Anzac Cove, six Australian sailors and soldiers were killed during the capture of German New Guinea. At the time, these men were remembered as the first Australians to die in World War I. As that war continued, and 60 000 Australians died at Gallipoli and Palestine and on the Western Front, these first six men slipped from the public mind, as did the short but successful campaign in which they fought. The same can be said of all the conflicts, organisations and ideas discussed in the chapters of this collection. The brightness of the legendary Anzac dawn has blinded us to all the events that occurred before it. This book illuminates these hidden stories.

1

Traditional Indigenous warfare

JOHN CONNOR

The Australian War Memorial in Canberra and the Canadian War Museum in Ottawa have much in common. Both buildings have a prominent position in their nation's capital. Both attract large numbers of visitors: 1.2 million people went to the Canadian War Museum in the 2011–12 financial year and 835 000 people attended the Australian War Memorial.[1] Both display exhibits on the South African War, World Wars I and II, the Korean War, peacekeeping operations and the war in Afghanistan. There is, however, one significant difference between the two institutions. The first gallery in the Canadian War Museum, entitled 'Wars on our soil: Earliest times to 1885', begins with displays on the traditional warfare of the Canadian indigenous peoples.[2] The Australian War Memorial has no equivalent exhibition.

Australians are more reluctant than Canadians to acknowledge the traditional warfare among their nation's first inhabitants. There is a common view that Australian Aborigines and Torres Strait Islanders did not fight wars. This is partially a reaction to nineteenth-century settler stereotypes that falsely portrayed Aborigines as violent savages in order to justify their expropriation and subjugation, and partially a reflection of a current widespread belief that pre-contact Aborigines lived in an idyllic society in which armed conflict did not exist. So much evidence contradicts this assertion that it is clear that – in common with most other peoples throughout history – Aborigines and Torres Strait Islanders did have traditions of warfare. These ways of war combined violence and ceremony, and were a significant part of life for the 60 000 years that the first Australians have lived in this land.[3] This chapter briefly introduces this large topic by examining the broad forms that traditional Aboriginal warfare took, and by describing a fraction of the thousands of different types of weapons made and used by Aborigines and Torres Strait Islanders.

It is true that some settlers during the 1800s exaggerated the level of violence in traditional Aboriginal warfare. Newspapers abounded with descriptions of the 'disgusting ferocity' and 'savage passions' with which Aborigines fought each other.[4] It was convenient to claim, as former Premier Sir Arthur Palmer stated in the Queensland Parliament in 1880, that 'the native black of Australia was essentially a treacherous animal',[5] because this supported the belief that the settlers had more right to the land than its Indigenous owners, and that it justified colonial governments' use of draconian measures to control their Aboriginal populations.

It is partially in response to this prejudice of the past that some recent historians have attempted to downplay the level of warfare in pre-contact Aboriginal society, or even to argue that such conflict did not occur at all. Michael Martin in *On Darug Land: An Aboriginal Perspective* asserts that 'traditional Aboriginal society was not an internally hostile one' and, in the caption to an illustration of a Sydney Aboriginal man, brings the reader's attention to the figure's woven possum hair belt and hair band – ignoring the club, spear and shield he also carries.[6] When Australia Post issued a series of stamps featuring 'Aboriginal crafts' in 1987, the designs included close-up details of a Western Australian spear-thrower and a New South Wales shield. Both were described as 'hunting implements'. It is true that spear-throwers were used for hunting as well as warfare, but shields were clearly never used for hunting.[7] According to the entry on 'weapons' in *The Encyclopaedia of Aboriginal Australia*, 'The primary use of many weapons is for hunting or in ceremonies, and their use as weapons is only secondary'.[8]

A related argument made, for example, by Ian Howie Willis in the same encyclopaedia's entry on 'warfare', accepts that 'there were undoubtedly wars between groups', but he stresses the difference between the causes of traditional Indigenous warfare and 'the causes for which nations make war: territorial expansion, securing economic advantage, differences in political and religious ideologies, and the urge to devastate and annihilate'.[9] This is a valid point, but it can lead some to argue that, because Aboriginal warfare was different to the conflicts fought by modern nation-states, it cannot be defined as 'war'.[10]

This is an unsustainable proposition. Human societies fought wars for thousands of years before the development of the modern state. The American historian John Lynn points out that how wars are fought depends on the 'values, beliefs, assumptions, expectations, preoccupations and the like' of the societies that fight them. This means that as societies have developed and changed throughout history, so too has war. As Lynn puts it:

> War demands endurance, self-sacrifice, and heroism, but conceptions of cowardice and courage, or brutality and compassion are hardly constants across human societies; one culture's bravery is another's bravado and one's mercy is another's meekness. Neither are those values and identities that compel and inspire warriors in combat consistent across age and place.[11]

Traditional Indigenous warfare

The traditional warfare of Aborigines and Torres Strait Islanders must be understood in its own terms and not according to ideas of 'war' specific to other societies. Aboriginal society was organised in small, non-hierarchical kinship groups, and this structure was reflected in the scale and scope of their warfare. As Richard Broome has written: 'Internal conflict was managed by these kinship systems, and while violence was part of their world, as with any society, kinship acted to contain it'.[12] Aborigines fought to protect their kinship group and to uphold their group's status in relation to neighbouring groups. Prussian military thinker Carl von Clausewitz's famous definition of war – 'an act of force to compel our enemy to do our will' – can certainly be applied to traditional warfare in Australia.[13]

Traditional Indigenous warfare was a significant component of Torres Strait Islander and Aboriginal societies because both were warrior cultures. Many groups presented young males with weapons as part of the initiation ceremony of becoming a man. Darug youths were given spears which had special designs to identify their group, and Darug men were rarely seen without their spear.[14] In north Queensland, youths were given a blank shield which they would paint immediately after their initiation.[15] Some forms of traditional warfare, especially the concept of 'payback' and non-lethal spearings, remain part of Aboriginal customary law in some regions today. Phyllis Batumbil, a Yolngu elder from Mata Mata in Arnhem Land, stated that it took the Japanese air attacks on the Northern Territory in 1942 to cause a temporary truce in Yolngu traditional warfare. Once the Yolngu had played their part in the Allied war effort to 'get rid of the Japanese ... they got back again' to traditional warfare.[16]

Traditional Indigenous warfare may have been limited but it was also universal. It was limited in the number of combatants because the groups involved were small, and limited in the duration of fighting because warriors always had to stop campaigning in order to resume food gathering. This form of warfare was universal because entire communities participated in it. Every initiated male became a warrior, and boys learnt to fight by playing with toy spears, shields, clubs and boomerangs. In some cases, Indigenous women also engaged in warfare.[17] All members of every group could become a victim of war.

Horatio Hale, an American scientist who visited the colony of New South Wales in 1840, identified four main types of traditional Aboriginal warfare. Hale's classifications offer a generally useful introduction to a complex topic. These four forms are: formal battles, ritual trials, raids for women, and revenge attacks.[18]

Formal battles, in which two groups of Aborigines fought each other and ended hostilities after a few participants had been killed or wounded, have often been compared to ceremony or sport rather than true warfare. This type of combat with limited casualties, however, had a practical purpose. For groups with only a few hundred, or even only a few dozen members, one or two deaths in every raid or battle added up to a sizeable percentage loss if warfare was constant, and could threaten the group's very existence. It was impossible to control casualties in impromptu raids and ambushes, but it was possible to limit losses in formal battles to the benefit of both sides.[19] Daniel Paine, a settler living in Sydney in the 1790s, recognised the logic in this aspect of the local Darug's formal battles when he commented that had these actions been 'attended with those fatal consequences which result generally from the Battles of those Nations who are stiled Civilized and Christian the race would soon be extirpated from the country'.[20]

Formal battles were usually fought to settle grievances between Aboriginal bands, and generally required days of preparation while the protagonists assembled. The Darug limited the duration of their formal battles by beginning them late in the afternoon and ending them soon after dusk. Darug women did not take part in the actual fighting of formal battles, although Captain David Collins observed that the signal for the commencement of one formal battle between a Darug and a Darawal group from south of Sydney was an old Darawal woman striking the Darug man Colbee with a club. As well, women participated in the formal battles by, as sailor Daniel Southwell wrote, making 'noisy expostulation' from the sidelines which could be heard over 'the Clashing of Spears and the strokes of lances'.[21]

Ritual trials, like formal battles, had an established structure and were a punishment for murder, assault and perhaps other crimes in which a man was required to stand his ground and accept any wounds he might receive. Some may quibble with Hale's classification of these as warfare, but if one accepts Margaret Mead's definition of 'war' as any 'organized and socially sanctioned violence ... not regarded as murder',[22] then trials carried out under Aboriginal customary law can certainly be included within this meaning. The weapons used in ritual trials varied: the Waka Waka north of Brisbane threw spears; the Wiradjuri on the Macquarie River in New South Wales used clubs; while the Kurnai of Gippsland in Victoria preferred boomerangs.[23]

Raids for women are a form of traditional Aboriginal warfare that is frequently misunderstood. To prevent inbreeding, Aboriginal society recognised the need for men to marry women from outside their small kinship group. Sometimes women were 'abducted' only after they had given prior consent and her group's resistance 'was only simulated'.[24] Historian Shino Konishi has argued that early European accounts of raids for women, and the use of these sources by authors in recent writing, give a false impression of Aboriginal men's 'sexual savagery'.[25] In fact, raids for women are best understood not as examples of sexual violence, but as a form of economic warfare. The late economic historian Noel Butlin pointed out that in traditional Aboriginal society, women's food gathering and child-bearing abilities were economic resources which were fundamental to the group's survival. Some Aboriginal men held property rights over the women in their group, and Butlin argued that these property rights were at least 'very important', and were probably 'basic to Aboriginal order'.[26]

Some Aboriginal raids for women were therefore aimed at transferring property from one group to another, and they must be considered warfare in the same way that fighting for economic reasons would be considered warfare in other societies.[27] When Aboriginal men first met British men, they believed that, like rival Aboriginal groups, the British wanted to take their women. Wiradjuri elders hid their women before they met New South Wales Governor Lachlan Macquarie and his entourage at Bathurst in 1815, and the King Ya-nup men of south-west Western Australia did the same in the 1820s and 1830s whenever they encountered members of the small British garrison at King George Sound (now the site of Albany).[28]

Revenge attacks, the fourth type of Indigenous warfare, were carried out by one group on another group in retaliation for a death in the group. Traditional Aboriginal societies believed all deaths were caused by the evil conduct of others: violent deaths were recognised as being the result of a person's action, while non-violent deaths were believed to be the result of a person's sorcery. Accordingly, as historian Tiffany Shellam has written, 'Even natural deaths needed to be avenged'.[29] For instance, Darug funerals included a ceremony in which the corpse would be asked who had caused the death, a person or a group would be 'named' as responsible, and they would be attacked in revenge.[30]

The level of violence in revenge attacks varied across the continent. For the King Ya-nup people, Shellam argues that 'the target was an individual who represented the "tribe", rather than a particular person', and the retaliation was a spearing intended to wound rather than kill (the spear was aimed so as to avoid hitting vital organs).[31] For the Darug of Sydney, revenge attacks were also sometimes non-lethal spearings, but on other occasions they resulted in the victim's death.[32] On the Murray River, revenge attacks involved two or three men stealing silently into campsites at night and strangling their victim, sometimes with such stealth that the victim's group did not know about the killing until they discovered it in the morning. These war parties were grimly referred to as 'the ones who take you by the throat'.[33]

As suggested by the different outcomes for which these four main forms of traditional warfare were waged, Aborigines and Torres Strait Islanders used a wide variety of weapon types and design. Innumerable designs were created, refined and abandoned over the 60 000 years of Aboriginal occupation of Australia. The famous Bradshaw Aboriginal rock paintings of north-west Western Australia, for example, depict types of spears that have long since been superseded.[34]

The most common types of weapons were spears and clubs, produced, as *The Australian Encyclopaedia* put it in 1925, in 'endless varieties' of designs.[35] Spears were manufactured as either thrusting or throwing weapons. Thrusting spears were shorter, generally between 1 and 1.5 metres long. Tasmanian Aborigines had a thrusting spear around 1 metre in length; the Darug of Sydney named their spear of this type the *dooull*.[36]

Throwing spears were generally longer: some as much as 4 metres in length.[37] Solid wooden spears were heavy – those used by the Tiwi of Melville and Bathurst Islands weighed up to 1.8 kilograms[38] – and were hard to throw. The wood used to produce spears was therefore carefully chosen. Many were made from particular varieties of acacia tree, because they offered both strength and the ability to resharpen the spear point with a combination of heating and scraping without the wood cracking. In the central Western Desert, the wood of the wonga-wonga vine was used to make spears because of its flexibility. This plant was named for a group of mythological women with slender and pliable bodies.[39]

In order to make throwing spears lighter, increasing their range and accuracy, some Aboriginal groups developed composite designs. These used a hollow reed or grass-tree stalk for the spear body, joined with gum to a short spearhead of solid wood. The Darug's composite spear had a main body constructed from the stalk of the grass tree *Xanthorrhoea*.[40] The material used to provide the deadly tip of the spear varied according to local availability. Darug living on Sydney Harbour used sharpened shells or fish bones, while those living inland tipped their spears with stone or kangaroo bone.[41]

Thrusting spears had unbarbed spear heads so the warrior could easily extract it from the victim's body for further stabbing. Throwing spears often had serrated or barbed heads because they inflicted more serious wounds – what the *Sydney Gazette* described in 1805 as an 'incurable laceration'. These were also harder to remove, impeding the target's movement in battle. A hand-thrown spear had a maximum range of about 60 metres.[42] To enable spears to be thrown more accurately and over a longer distance, Aborigines invented spear-throwers. The Darug word for spear-thrower is *woomera*, and it is by this word that this weapon, in all its regional varieties, is known in the English language.[43] These were a length of wood that acted as an extension of the warrior's arm: the warrior held one end in his hand, the base of the spear was placed in the other end. As the Māori Te Pahi commented when he saw one in use during his visit to Sydney in 1805, woomeras added 'much additional velocity' to the spear.[44]

The Aborigines of Tasmania, south and central Queensland and the Tiwi in the Northern Territory did not use woomeras. In the rest of the country, woomeras came in three main designs: broad and heavy, so they could also be used as clubs or shields made in central and western Australia; a narrower lath type used in northern and south-western Australia; and a narrow stick-like design used in northern and south-eastern Australia. The 'gooseneck' spear thrower of the north-west Northern Territory and far eastern Kimberley was 1.5 metres long, thin and light with a large gum peg to hold the spear. The 'goose' spear weighed only 50 grams and when launched from a woomera had a range of over 100 metres.[45]

The second common type of Aboriginal weapon was the club. Generally between 60 and 90 centimetres in length, the club head was normally made of stone or wood. Like spears, clubs came in a wide variety of designs. Tiwi used a club about half a metre in length and a kilogram in weight, with a grooved handle to provide a better grip. The Darug made one club which had oyster shells attached to the head.[46] Sometimes the club handle was pointed so it could be used as a stabbing weapon, or in some parts of eastern Australia, the handle was curved to facilitate throwing.[47]

Throwing sticks were similar to throwing clubs but manufactured outside eastern Australia: Tasmanian throwing sticks were pointed at both ends; in the Kimberley they were pointed at one end and rounded at the other; while the Tiwi made sticks that were blunt at both ends. Throwing sticks were usually between 60 and 70 centimetres in length. Most were straight, but some were curved like boomerangs except with a circular rather than flat cross-section.[48]

Boomerangs are the best known Aboriginal weapon, but they were not used in large areas of Australia, including Cape York, parts of Arnhem Land, the Kimberley coast, Tasmania, and the region of South Australia west of Lakes Eyre and Torrens.[49] The word 'boomerang' comes from the Darawal language from south of Sydney, but those used in warfare were generally of the non-returning type.[50] When Bungaree of the Darug used a boomerang in a ritual fight in 1804, the *Sydney Gazette* breathlessly wrote that he threw the boomerang:

> 20 or 30 yards distance, [it] twirled round in the air with astonishing velocity, and alighted on the right arm of one of his opponents, actually rebounded to a distance of not less than 70 or 80 yards, leaving a horrible contusion behind, and exciting universal admiration.[51]

The Aboriginal peoples of central Australia produced hooked boomerangs, designed to catch on a shield and spin around to hit the warrior behind it.[52]

Women engaging in warfare often used their digging sticks as weapons. In some areas men also used fighting sticks, such as the Tharrgari inland from Carnarvon in Western Australia who made a 2-metre long fighting stick called a *wana*. Knives were used in close combat. Generally these had a stone blade, although on the west coast of Cape York, knives were made by attaching shark teeth to a wooden handle. In central Australia, fighting picks, consisting of a stone point attached at right angles to a long wooden handle, were manufactured.[53] In Tasmania, stones were the main projectile weapon, and could be effective especially if thrown from high ground onto an enemy below.[54]

Shields were used mostly in formal battles. Large, light shields were used in most parts of Australia, except Tasmania, to deflect spears. In the rainforest areas of north Queensland, broad shields were carved out of fig trees. In south-eastern Australia, smaller shields were also used in hand-to-hand fighting. These were generally small, circular and up to 15 centimetres thick so as to absorb the shock of blows from a club. These small shields generally had no decoration or were decorated by paint. This was because carved designs would soon be defaced in close combat.[55]

The main Torres Strait Islander weapons were bows and arrows, and stone headed clubs. Both the bow and bow strings were made from bamboo. The Aboriginal groups on the northeast coast of the Cape York Peninsula were in regular contact with the Torres Strait and were the only Aborigines to adopt these weapons.[56]

Aboriginal and Torres Strait Islander warfare should be acknowledged as making a uniquely Australian contribution to the history of armed conflict. It may also have a role in encouraging future Australian sporting success. In 1999, Senator Aden Ridgeway, a Gumbaynggir man from the north coast of New South Wales, noted that Aboriginal culture played a smaller role in Australian public life compared to Māori culture in New Zealand: 'We can measure it by the way we play rugby. The New Zealanders get out there and do the haka and the Australians get out and huddle.'[57] Ridgeway proposed that whenever the Wallabies play the All Blacks at an Australian venue, men from a local Aboriginal community should perform a war dance to answer the challenge of the Māori *haka*. If this could be implemented, it would provide due recognition to Indigenous culture and imbue the Australian players with the warrior spirit which has been part of this land for 60 000 years.

Further reading

W Arthur & F Morphy (eds), *Macquarie Atlas of Indigenous Australia*, Macquarie Library, Sydney, 2005

C Barker, J Mulvaney & N Green (eds), *Commandant of Solitude: The Journals of Captain Collet Barker 1828–1831*, MUP, Melbourne, 1992

R Broome, *Aboriginal Australians: A History since 1788*, 4th edn, Allen & Unwin, Sydney, 2010

J Connor, *The Australian Frontier Wars, 1788–1838*, rev edn, UNSW Press, Sydney, 2005

—— , 'Traditional Aboriginal warfare', in P Dennis *et al* (eds), *The Oxford Companion to Australian Military History*, 2nd edn, OUP, Melbourne, 2008

D Horton (ed), *The Encyclopaedia of Aboriginal Australia*, 2 vols, Aboriginal Studies Press, Canberra, 1994

J Mulvaney & P White (eds), *Australians to 1788*, Fairfax, Syme & Weldon, Sydney, 1987

T Shellam, *Shaking Hands on the Fringe: Negotiating the Aboriginal World at King George's Sound*, UWA Press, Perth, 2009.

2

Frontier warfare in Australia

JONATHAN RICHARDS

Conflict between Aboriginal people and European settlers began soon after the arrival of the First Fleet in Sydney Cove. As the perimeter of settlement expanded inland and along the coast, further clashes occurred. Some fights were about land, while others began over alcohol and women. Despite attempts by colonial authorities to treat both groups as equals before the law, there was little punishment of colonists for violence against Aborigines. While it is not possible to fully account for this subject in one brief chapter, this overview strives to show the importance, complexity and persistence of racial conflict on the Australian frontier, and to introduce the growing number of recent studies in this important field.

Frontier warfare varied considerably in style and intensity across Australia. In Tasmania, soldiers and settlers combined in an attempt to sweep Aboriginal people from the landscape, while in Victoria some Aboriginal men joined the Native Police and helped colonisers crush resistance. In Western Australia, conflict over land soon led to sporadic conflict which lasted from 1834 until the early decades of the twentieth century. In New South Wales seven Europeans were hanged for massacring Aboriginal men, women and children at Myall Creek in 1838, but far from stopping violence this simply caused reprisal parties to become more secretive. Squatters and their workers often surrounded Aboriginal camps at night, attacked at dawn and killed indiscriminately. In South Australia and Queensland, the complex struggle continued for decades. Resistance continued in some districts, while in other areas settlers and Aboriginal people negotiated and began to build relationships that would last for generations. When the opposition proved too strong, Native Police troopers or private reprisal parties delivered death and injury.

Eventually, after the majority of Aboriginal people died from disease, starvation or violence, colonisers' attitudes changed. A belated recognition of their status as 'British subjects' emerged, although it was never really fully realised until the end of the twentieth century. Labelled 'our Aborigines', the survivors of frontier warfare in the nineteenth century were rounded up by police and officials and removed to church missions and government reserves. The violent conflict that had largely but not completely characterised the first 150 years of European occupation is now called by Aboriginal people 'the shooting time'.

The violence that occurred between European colonisers and Indigenous peoples in the frontier regions of Australia has not usually been accepted as a form of warfare. In order to justify its inclusion in this military history it is therefore important to clarify a few key concepts. To start with, 'frontier' is an elusive term with multiple meanings, and some academics, including numbers of historians, prefer the concept of 'contact zone' as a more accurate description of an insidious and gradual, but almost always incomplete, process of colonisation in settler societies such as Australia.[1] 'Contact zone' conveys the meaning of two cultures meeting, or even just touching each other, while 'frontier' implies a distinct line or border separating two countries.

'War' has been defined as 'armed conflict' between two 'recognizable political entities', usually sovereign nations or peoples.[2] However, the sort of violence mainly precipitated by Europeans during the lengthy and widespread process of colonial annexation and imperial expansion is called different things in different parts of the world. Resistance by indigenous peoples, or other forms of sovereign entity, has also been given a complete range of specific terms. Clashes between Europeans and indigenous nations in North America tend be referred to as 'Indian Wars'. Conflicts in most parts of Africa are usually named after the people opposing colonisation, such as the Zulu War (now the Anglo-Zulu war), the Hausa War, and so on; or after the location of the conflict (for example, the Sudan campaign). The protracted Māori resistance in New Zealand, previously referred to as the 'Māori Wars', is now more often described as the 'New Zealand Wars'.[3]

Yet 'war' is not a very flexible term. Conflicts that took place during the creation of empires, often downplayed as 'frontier' or 'colonial' affairs, were usually seen as being somewhat lesser events than 'real' wars between European powers. They were, in the words of British army officer Colonel Charles Callwell, 'small wars'.[4] Britain was constantly involved in small wars for most of the nineteenth century.[5] Sometimes these conflicts were called 'frontier wars' or 'internal policing'. The locations were (and are) familiar: South Africa (in the 1840s, 1870s and 1900s), India and New Zealand (1860s, 1880s and 1890s), Afghanistan (1880s and 1890s). The term 'frontier war' peaked – in Australian newspaper references at least – during the decade between 1890 and 1900, with a sharp spike in 1897 when it appeared especially in reporting events on the North-West Frontier of British India. In contemporary times, such 'small wars' or 'frontier wars' are termed 'low-intensity conflicts' or 'border skirmishes'.[6]

Frontier conflict in Australia has received similarly varied descriptions. Early references in both colonial newspapers and official documents mentioned 'war', but some of the first published histories seemed intent on dismissing violence between colonisers and indigenous peoples as insignificant, something that only took place in other parts of the world.[7] Attempts have recently been made to revive this uninformed misunderstanding.[8]

From about the mid-twentieth century, the idea that Australia was the least violent of Europe's outliers was replaced by an obsession with organised resistance, large-scale massacres and genocide.[9] As one writer noted, many of the 'less scholarly' books published during the 1970s tried to 'ride the wave of popularism' in their focus on frontier violence and attempts to show 'Aboriginal people as warrior heroes engaged in a patriotic battle to defend their country'.[10]

This in turn has given way to a more complex and informed understanding, reflecting the growing number of studies at the local and regional level which have uncovered the range of Indigenous responses to, and experiences after, the arrival of Europeans. Archival records generally confirm historian Richard Broome's statement that 'only a minority of settlers actually practised violence against Aboriginal people'.[11] Yet it also seems that most settlers were largely indifferent to inter-racial violence, although media and politicians could easily whip up fear, hysteria and racial antagonism. The same records also show that a small number of colonists actively defended Aboriginal people from the aggression of others.

So European colonisation in Australia was not 'a simple, dualistic process involving two isolated, opposing entities'.[12] Some Aboriginal people welcomed the colonisers and used their presence in attempts to extend their own power over other Indigenous groups. As Patrick Wolfe argues, settler colonial invasion in Australia, and elsewhere, was 'globally complex'.[13]

The newly colonised were not the only people to respond in

a variety of ways. Colonisers were not homogenous, and settlers transported ideas about race and colonising practices across the settler world. Some European settlers, who feared and hated 'others', shot first and asked questions later. Historian Bruce Vandervort convincingly argues that frontier conflict originated 'as much by turmoil on the periphery as by plans for expansion made by governments'.[14] More recently, both Lisa Ford and Kristyn Harman have traced the 'criminalisation' of indigenous peoples in North America and Australia, effectively and conclusively connecting sovereign settler statehood with concepts of criminal law in different colonial settings.[15] The difficulties that Europeans faced enforcing sovereignty and their concepts of law on Aboriginal people have also recently been carefully examined by Heather Douglas and Mark Finnane, who argued that 'at different points around the Australian continent Indigenous peoples used force tactically, and negotiated terms of engagement with invading settlers where they could'.[16]

Some still maintain that European colonisation in Australia was benign and peaceful, but such arguments about the level of violence on Australian frontiers are intrinsically linked to debates over the differences between the British and other European empires. As writer Richard Gott notes, many apparently still believe 'the British Empire was obtained and maintained with a minimum degree of force'.[17] It was always easier to point the finger at other empires as examples of oppression than to acknowledge the violence that British colonists routinely deployed.

European settlers, and their allies – which might or might not include indigenous assistants – fought and often killed native peoples wherever they established colonies. The success of empires relied upon a 'fiscal-military' state with strong links between bankers, traders and armies. As Michael Grewcock has noted, 'The colonial empires of the European states were forged and sustained by full-scale military mobilisations', and that violence became 'a precondition for nationhood'.[18] Some have extended this analysis and argued that 'settler imperialism may be described as a process ... that is genocidal in itself'.[19] Colonisation – like genocide – is by definition inherently violent.[20]

Certainly, many settlers described the native people they shot and killed as 'sub-human', and so justified their actions to themselves and to others. Colonists believed in violence, and justified its use against indigenous people. They may have seen their actions as 'progressive' and 'natural', but they usually did not claim religion or nationality as excuses. Instead, historical 'evidence' of racial inequalities was used as grounds for colonial violence. The colonisers felt no guilt, as they nearly always ascribed the blame for escalating conflict and the savage conduct of wars in colonial locations to the 'other side'.

Those who argue that frontier violence did not happen in Australia ignore the fact that European empires expanded over the last five centuries or so as the outcome of a combination of technology, ideology and skills.[21] Specialists made weapons, and alliances or plans, while others applied these techniques in the colonial field of conflict. The various arts of warfare, and the military successes that emerged from this modern combination allowed Europeans and their allies to dream of even greater gains, and further expansion.

One of the most useful and important strategies for growing empires was 'divide and rule': the practice of using a select indigenous group as the shock troops for the colonisers. This was the tactic that worked well in Africa, in India and Ceylon (Sri Lanka), and 'without Indian soldiers, Britain could never have conquered and controlled the Indian subcontinent'.[22] The use of 'native forces' to assist the invader was as old as the concept of empire itself. Just as the Greeks and the Romans recruited local soldiers, so too did Britain, France, Spain and the other European powers.²³

Yet, triumph in colonial warfare was not always guaranteed, regardless of the colonisers' more sophisticated weapons and strategies. The settlers who arrived in Australia during the eighteenth and nineteenth centuries knew that in other parts of the world indigenous peoples had shown great resistance to imperial expansion and occasionally, albeit temporarily, had reversed the European colonial tide. They knew that victory in a new colony was never absolutely or easily assured. Colonisers knew that it was best to be on guard from the outset. The Māori of New Zealand, the Zulu nation on the edges of the Cape Colony, the Native Americans and numerous other 'martial tribes' were all fierce and formidable warriors. The tribal fighters on India's North-West Frontier and the pirates of the South China Sea could never be completely defeated, only held at bay.

Native resistors held one great advantage over the invaders: their knowledge of the landscape and resources: in other words, they enjoyed better 'military intelligence'. The use of local forces (and their knowledge) by the coloniser dramatically changed the odds: 'When a body of Natives is attached it should invariably be employed in examining bush or rugged ground offering concealment to an enemy, before any European body is ordered to advance'.²⁴ Armed indigenous forces, such as the Malay Corps in Ceylon and the Cape Regiment in South Africa, provided security for settlers and traders, and opportunities for victory.

As European settlement in Australia expanded from the first beach-head of Sydney and other secondary landing places around the continent and on offshore islands, the amount of country under the control of colonists increased.²⁵ Colonial authorities often referred to territory as being either 'inside' or 'outside the settled districts' (the limits of European power), with implied connotations about law, culture and sovereignty. A similar expression, 'within' or 'beyond the pale', had been the dividing line between 'civilised' and the 'uncivilised' in Ireland, England's first overseas colony.[26] The fact that so many early administrators were former military officers was another common factor between these two colonial situations.

We now understand that responses to colonisation varied throughout the colonial world. What might be termed 'resistance' in one setting could be seen as mild 'disapproval' or 'passive non-cooperation' in another part of empire.[27] In Australia, sustained resistance to colonisation, often termed by Europeans as 'depredations', 'troublesome', 'outrage' or simply 'bad', proved that Aboriginal people were capable of conducting guerilla warfare.[28] Tactics included burning crops, killing animals, attacking isolated settlements and travellers, and ambushes. As a result, Aboriginal groups in some parts of Australia, especially the continent's north, successfully managed to hinder but never completely halt European expansion.

However, Australian history lacks a specific title for this sustained and widespread colonial violence. This was and still is often justified by an argument that the level of conflict in this country was 'not really war' but localised violence or internal 'policing'.[29] Australian frontier conflict was apparently not deemed to be of a sufficient intensity or organisation to be called the 'Aboriginal Wars'. Historian Bill Thorpe has argued the opposite: that this was no 'police action' and that 'to suggest that Aboriginal and non-Aboriginal combatants were not in a state of war trivialises the people and the processes responsible for the invasion and colonisation of this continent'.[30]

This semantic disjunction arises from an apparent serious gap between 'frontier' and 'military' historians in Australia. For example, a recent book on Australia's mounted soldiers makes only fleeting reference to the tactical impact of horses on the frontier, and none at all to the state-sanctioned violence perpetrated by mounted police.[31] One of the few efforts to cross this line investigated Queensland's early colonial militia and rifle clubs, and usefully explored the connections between colonisation, militarism and violence on the frontier.[32]

Although British soldiers served as the colony's first police, and participated in much of the early inter-racial conflict, for many decades the connection between penal guards and orchestrated violence remained largely unacknowledged.[33] This disconnect is aptly illustrated by the history and impact of the various Native Police forces, which were specially created military units to smash Aboriginal resistance. Widely ignored by military historians (who apparently considered these forces as 'unsoldierly'), these paramilitary units operated at the vanguard of European colonisation in four Australian colonies.

Callwell's sentiments regarding 'small wars' would have been appreciated by the Europeans who established the colony of New South Wales, the convicts and guards of the First Fleet. Although early books often mentioned the conflict between these forces and local Aboriginal peoples, many later historians simply glossed over this period's violence. From the 1970s, new understandings of the fraught relationship between Aboriginal Australians and the first 'boat people' began to emerge. Keith Willey, Jan Kociumbas, Inga Clendinnen and Grace Karskens, among many other historians, refocused attention on the punitive expeditions authorised by Governor Phillip which largely set the tone for later relationships between Aboriginal people and European settlers throughout Australia.[34] Some writers considered the violence as a form of genocide.[35] Individuals such as Bennelong, Bungaree and Pemulwuy slowly began to emerge from the records as significant communicators and colonial warriors.[36]

Among the growing number of regional studies, John Ferry's *Colonial Armidale* discusses the violence that often accompanied Aboriginal dispossession.[37] He particularly notes how violence and masculinity became interconnected in colonial Australia. Ferry's work on the New England frontier is complemented by David Kent's insightful writing on racial violence in adjacent districts. He concludes that 'under-recording and misrepresentation' of frontier violence, in those areas at least, 'were systemic and characteristic'.[38]

Karskens relates how the violence began in May 1788, four months after the arrival of the First Fleet. In *The Colony* she also explores the arguments over the smallpox outbreak of 1789 and the possibility that the disease was deliberately used as a weapon to defeat Aboriginal resistance (a topic previously discussed by Kociumbas).[39] Biological warfare is not a subject that most Australians associate with frontier history.

The most detailed account of these early clashes (and others) can be found in John Connor's *The Australian Frontier Wars*.[40] This was one of the first (and still is one of the few) scholarly books to carefully and effectively assess frontier conflict in Australia by considering the specific weapons and tactics used in this new antipodean struggle. Connor covers areas including the coastal rivers and plains of New South Wales, the Bathurst district across the Great Dividing Range, and early clashes in Tasmania, Victoria and Western Australia. Connor shows how Europeans and Aboriginal fighters struggled to control access to water, food and other resources. In assessing the guerilla warfare that developed during the late eighteenth and early nineteenth centuries, he concludes that the arrival of horses gave the invaders an immense advantage on the rolling plains of the Australian inland. Mobility, technology and communication soon allowed the colonisers to gain the upper hand on the open grasslands and lightly wooded forests.

Unauthorised occupation or 'squatting' took place beyond the original Nineteen Counties surrounding Sydney ('the limits of location') from the earliest days of European colonisation. Eventually, squatting was legalised and pastoral districts were created to facilitate the rapid selection of Crown Land by colonists, but in 1839 a parliamentary committee examined a proposed Bill 'to restrain the unauthorized occupation of Crown Lands'.[41]

Soon afterwards Governor Sir George Gipps approved the establishment of the Border Police, a force intended to enforce the law 'beyond the boundaries' of European colonisation. The colony's Mounted Police Force operated within the limits of settlement while the troopers of the Border Police, attached to Crown Land Commissioners in each pastoral district, would establish British law and authority 'beyond the limits of location'.[42]

There was no doubt that Europeans saw their acquisition of land as lawful, right and proper. One squatter, commenting on the governor's new Act, said the 'native blacks' were 'hostile to the whites' but added he could 'assign no satisfactory reason for the hostility'.[43] One observer noted at the same time that a war was 'going on throughout the Murrumbidgee frontier': 'Not an open fight, but a regular guerrilla warfare'.[44] A number of serious clashes occurred in the colony's southern districts, as well as sporadic 'collisions' in the west.

As settlement spread the conflict extended to the colony's northern limits, and it was here that military officers investigated clashes with local Aboriginal people. When colonists complained about Aboriginal attacks, Gipps said they 'exposed' themselves to this when they 'go beyond the limits with which it is possible for the Government to protect them'. As governor he was 'bound to protect [the Aboriginal people] as much as any other'.[45]

It was in 1838, on the Liverpool Plains, that the massacre at Myall Creek took place. RHW Reece's *Aborigines and Colonists* examined the Myall Creek killings within a broader context of racial conflict across inland New South Wales.[46] The colony's first northern unit of Native Police, under the command of Frederick Walker, was deployed 11 years later, in 1849, supposedly to 'prevent' violence on the frontier. Subsequent events proved that these Native Police in fact achieved the opposite result.[47]

The second British colony was established in 1803 in Tasmania, then known as Van Diemen's Land. The struggle between Europeans and the Tasmanian Aborigines has become known around the world as a classic case of almost complete ethnic cleansing.[48] When losses of stock and supplies, coupled with an increasing rate of settler fatalities, became too serious, soldiers, convicts and free settlers formed the so-called 'Black Line' in 1830 across the island's south-east corner in an attempt to clear the settled districts of further resistance. This was the only frontier conflict in Australia usually deemed worthy of the title 'war'.[49]

Many historians have written about the struggles to defend and conquer Tasmania. More recently Lyndall Ryan and Henry Reynolds have been the main figures in a debate involving violence-denier Keith Windschuttle, and their work provides an excellent understanding of colonial warfare in that part of Australia.[50] Ryan has recently reassessed the importance of the Black Line, arguing that it was an effective way to break Indigenous resistance.[51]

In Victoria, recent estimates place the number of Aboriginal deaths from frontier violence in the region of 1000 people. This was the location of the original body of paramilitary Native Police in Australia. First established in 1837, the force only lasted until the 1850s. Conflict continued throughout this period. Good accounts of early settlement history in Victoria, including frontier violence, can be found in Richard Broome's *Aboriginal Victorians*.[52] Conflict, including massacres, is also dealt with by Jan Critchett and Ian Clark.[53] Critchett's work assesses the complex relations, including violence, that developed on all Australian frontiers. Although Marie Fels' book on the Native Police, *Good Men and True*, is the best known, and Michael Cannon's *Who Killed the Koories?* is well-written and very readable, recent work by Ian Clark is more reliable.[54] Bruce Pascoe presents a well-researched examination of frontier warfare in Victoria, and Lyndall Ryan builds on Broome's and Clark's work to argue that the term 'massacre' is not over-used.[55] She utilises a range of secondary sources to argue that settler massacre, not disease, reduced the Aboriginal population of Victoria by 80 per cent in 15 years.[56]

Although the Victorian recruitment of Native Police ended soon after it began, that colony's police force continued to use Queensland trackers for many decades. Gary Presland's book on the experiences of these men is an excellent study of the complexities of Aboriginal–European relations in early twentieth century Australian police forces.[57] Armed troopers from Queensland's Native Police, brought to Victoria during the 1870s in an unsuccessful attempt to track and capture the members of the infamous Kelly Gang, were the first example of this intercolonial collaboration.[58] It is worth noting that volunteers for this task eventually became harder to find.

The first European settlement in Western Australia was a small military outpost established at King George Sound (now Albany) in 1825. When Perth was founded on the Swan River in 1829, conflict between colonists and Nyungar people began almost immediately. Neville Green's and Tom Austen's work on frontier warfare in this area is particularly useful.[59] As Austen notes, clashes occurred in Western Australia, as they did elsewhere, when 'colonists killed for food or drove inland the animals which the old occupiers were used to eating to survive'. He also reminds us that 'many Aborigines did not want to fight', preferring to watch the newcomers instead, but he concludes that European colonisation constituted an invasion nonetheless.[60]

One 'collision' between colonists and Indigenous people, at Pinjarra in late 1834, has become a topic of fierce debate. While primary sources referred to this event as a 'battle', later historians have called it either a 'massacre' or an 'encounter'.[61] Regardless of the words used, European soldiers, police and squatters in Western Australia were responsible for the killing or jailing of hundreds of Aboriginal men and women.[62] Simon Adams, for example, explores the circumstances surrounding the execution of Richard Bibby in 1859, the first European hanged for the murder of an Aboriginal person in Western Australia.[63]

In that state's northern districts, work by Gill, Lewis and others documents the level of conflict in the Kimberley and other remote parts of Western Australia.[64] *Jandamarra and the Bunuba Resistance*, by Howard Pedersen and Banjo Worunmurra, is significant because of the level of research involved and because it is the first assessment of frontier violence co-authored by a European historian and an Indigenous story custodian.[65]

South Australia, the only Australian colony established without the transportation of convict labour, was nevertheless created in the same spirit of industrious colonisation as the rest of the nation. British reformers' hopes that the violent excesses of other colonies might be avoided here were proved wrong as Aboriginal people were displaced and dispersed by both government and settlers.[66] Colonists feared they would be outnumbered, particularly in the colony's isolated northern parts which later became the Northern Territory. Conflict in South Australia has most recently been examined by historians Robert Foster, Rick Hosking and Amanda Nettelbeck.[67] Using primary material, they assess the many clashes that took place from the earliest years of the colony's foundation. Violence on the frontier is, as they and other scholars carefully and persuasively argue, remembered in different ways according to the versions of stories transmitted through time.[68] Their work reveals how history, memory and myth have become entangled in popular histories and oral accounts of frontier warfare.

Hundreds of Indigenous people were killed in central and northern Australia, where a small formation of Native Police was briefly deployed with fatal consequences.[69] Richard Kimber estimates that over 650 Aboriginal people were killed by police in central Australia from 1881 to 1891, a total that he contrasts, on the basis of oral evidence, with the official figure of just 44 deaths.[70] Peter Vallee's detailed and comprehensive research into central Australian history is a good introduction to this part of the nation's most recent 'frontier' province.[71] Similarly, Tony Roberts' excellent work on conflict around the Gulf of Carpentaria provides useful, well-researched information on racial violence straddling colonial boundaries, while Nicolas Grguric provides good insights into one settler response to Aboriginal resistance: the construction of fortified homesteads.[72] The exploits of William Willshire, who led a Native Police unit during the 1880s and was tried for the murder of two Aboriginal men in 1891, are dealt with in Nettelbeck and Foster's *In The Name of the Law*.[73]

When the colony of Queensland was established in 1859, it quickly also gained the Native Police.[74] Based on similar formations in Victoria, India, Ceylon and the Cape Colony, this unit was not like a modern police force. It had only one function: to crush any Aboriginal resistance to European colonisation. The Native Police were deployed in mounted detachments (usually consisting of about six Aboriginal troopers led by a white officer). When aspiring settlers complained about 'attacks' or 'depredations', the force went into action, 'punished the offenders', and made the country 'safe' for Europeans. The killings were supposed to be kept secret, so the bodies of their victims were usually burnt.[75]

Excellent work by Noel Loos and others clearly illustrates the extent of frontier violence in the colony's northern half.[76] Careful and thorough research into the activities of the Native Police reveals the level of violence associated with that force, as well as the huge exaggerations in many so-called 'historical' accounts.[77] For example, primary records prove that the clash near Cloncurry in 1884 – called 'Battle Mountain' by Hudson Fysh in 1970 – was a routine frontier 'collision'. Although still violent, there is absolutely no evidence to support the claim that Aboriginal men formed into ranks and fought a military-style battle.

After the 1880s, as colonisation spread north and west, ordinary (white) police stations gradually replaced the Native Police across Queensland. Unarmed Aboriginal 'trackers' were often attached to each station to care for horses, to cut wood, and to assist in the location of missing persons, stolen livestock or wanted criminals. Sometimes, the troopers of the few remaining Native Police detachments in north Queensland were referred to in public statements as 'trackers'. Mounted and fully armed, these Indigenous men were sent on bush patrols into the colony's rugged and isolated tropical districts. These 'Black trackers' were really 'Aboriginal troopers'.

Frontier conflict in Australia started soon after European colonisation began, and continued for at least 150 years. Colonists and Aboriginal men fought over land and resources, and alcohol and women. European colonisation in Australia was not a simple process, however, but complex and continuous. In some districts, Indigenous peoples sometimes slowed or prevented European annexation. Indigenous opposition even caused colonists to abandon their holdings. Settler reprisal parties were secretive affairs, often involving dawn attacks on Aboriginal camps. Men, women and children were killed indiscriminately. Few settlers were punished for this violence, but soldiers, police and settlers often tried to remove Aboriginal people from the landscape by whatever means possible. Complicating matters further, Indigenous fighters sometimes joined the colonisers as Native Police troopers. Others starved to death or died from introduced diseases. And yet in other places, small numbers of settlers negotiated with local Aboriginal people, and bartered food for labour. They built good and enduring relationships with Indigenous families. Records clearly show, however, that violence was common on the Australian frontier, and that Aboriginal people were largely the victims.

Further reading

B Attwood, *Telling the Truth about Aboriginal History*, Allen & Unwin, Sydney, 2005

B Attwood & SG Foster, *Frontier Conflict: The Australian Experience*, National Museum of Australia, Canberra, 2003

T Austen, *A Cry in the Wind: Conflict in Western Australia 1829–1929*, Darlington, Perth, 1998

R Broome, *Aboriginal Australians: A History since 1788*, Allen & Unwin, Sydney, 2010

I Clark, *'That's my country belonging to me': Aboriginal Land Tenure and Dispossession in Nineteenth-Century Western Victoria*, Heritage Matters, Melbourne, 1998

J Connor, *The Australian Frontier Wars*, UNSW Press, Sydney, 2005

J Critchett, *A Distant Field of Murder: Western District Frontiers 1834–1848*, MUP, Melbourne, 1990

L Ford, *Settler Sovereignty: Jurisdiction and Indigenous People in America and Australia 1788–1836*, Harvard University Press, Cambridge, 2010

R Foster, R Hosking & A Nettelbeck, *Fatal Collisions: The South Australian Frontier and the Violence of Memory*, Wakefield Press, Adelaide, 2001

R Foster & A Nettelbeck, *Out of the Silence: The History and Memory of South Australia's Frontier Wars*, Wakefield Press, Adelaide, 2012

G Karskens, *The Colony: A History of Early Sydney*, Allen & Unwin, Sydney, 2009

M McKernan & M Browne (eds), *Australia: Two Centuries of War and Peace*, AWM, Canberra, 1988

AD Moses (ed), *Genocide and Settler Society: Frontier Violence and Stolen Indigenous Children in Australian History*, Berghahn Books, New York, 2004

AD Moses (ed), *Empire, Colony, Genocide: Conquest, Occupation, and Subaltern Resistance in World History*, Berghahn Books, New York, 2008

A Nettelbeck & R Foster, *In The Name of the Law: William Willshire and the Policing of the Australian Frontier*, Wakefield Press, Adelaide, 2007

H Pedersen & B Worunmurra, *Jandamarra and the Bunuba Resistance*, Magabala Books, Broome, 1995

RHW Reece, *Aborigines and Colonists: Aborigines and Colonial Society in New South Wales in the 1830s and 1840s*, Sydney University Press, Sydney, 1974

J Richards, *The Secret War: A True History of Queensland's Native Police*, UQP, Brisbane, 2008

T Roberts, *Frontier Justice: A History of the Gulf Country to 1900*, UQP, Brisbane, 2005

L Ryan, *Tasmanian Aborigines: A History since 1803*, Allen & Unwin, Sydney, 2012

LE Skinner, *Police of the Pastoral Frontier: Native Police 1849–1859*, UQP, Brisbane, 1975

3

British soldiers in colonial Australia

Peter Stanley

On New Year's Day, 1810, men of the 73rd Regiment of Foot clambered from boats onto the Government Wharf in Sydney Cove as the transports that had brought them from Britain fired 15-gun salutes. Assembling on the wharf, no doubt swaying uncertainly as they adjusted to solid ground after their seven-month voyage, they formed into column of companies and marched off, up Sergeant Major's Row (later George Street), between lines of the New South Wales Corps – men who felt apprehensive after their officers' coup against Governor William Bligh three years before. At the military barracks the rest of the New South Wales Corps awaited them, presenting arms as the 73rd marched in. After they had waited in the mid-summer sun for half an hour, New South Wales's new governor, Lachlan Macquarie, appeared and inspected them. Macquarie read his commission before the officers of the two corps and the principal gentlemen of the colony, and the 73rd wheeled into line and marched the two miles south to its camp at Grose Farm, roughly where Sydney University lies today. Ensign Alexander Huey complained to his diary that evening that he had had 'nothing to eat this day but potatoes'.[1] It was the first day that a line regiment of the British army spent in Australia, the first of 60 years in which

British troops formed the garrison of the Australian colonies.

The 73rd was only the first line infantry regiment to arrive in Australia. Red-coated British soldiers' association with Australia goes back to the very origins of British settlement, and even beyond. The complement of James Cook's *Endeavour* included 13 Royal Navy Marines, who may have been among the first Europeans to step ashore when he landed near present-day Sydney in 1770. Three companies of Marines later served as the garrison of the colony from 1788, but this expedient soon proved to be a failure. The Marines refused to act as convict guards, and proved recalcitrant over the hardships of the settlement. Even before departing from Britain, Marines made clear that they were 'sorely aggrieved' at learning that their rum ration was not guaranteed after their arrival in Botany Bay.[2] At Sydney Cove, Marines worked alongside convicts, although they struck over pay rates. In March 1788, Private John Easty recorded, 'the Battalion of marines Turned out and Said they could not work any longer without being Paid for itt' (sic). Captain Arthur Philip, the colony's governor, was repeatedly exasperated by the Marine officers' demands and misconduct.[3]

In response, British authorities decided to recruit a military unit raised specifically for service in the colony: the New South Wales Corps. The first contingents arrived in 1790 and the corps went on to serve around Sydney, Parramatta and Newcastle, on the frontier of settlement on the Hawkesbury, in Van Diemen's Land and on Norfolk Island. Its troops faced Aboriginal resistance (see Chapter 2) and convict uprising, sharing the hardships of the Sydney settlement's early years. Reinforced by further drafts from Britain, and the local enlistment of convicts and emancipists, the corps' men lived what must have been among the easiest life of any British soldiers at the time. Many acquired land and engaged in trade, most living not in barracks but in huts around

Sydney. Their officers, many marginal gentlemen whose commissions represented commercial investments, profited even more from enterprise. Their increasing confidence and independence brought them into conflict with a succession of governors, culminating with a coup against Bligh in 1808.

The New South Wales Corps was at last recalled, and in 1810 the 73rd arrived to form the garrison of the Australian colonies, the first of a succession of British line regiments governed by military officers who also acted as the commanders-in-chief of the military force in their respective colonies. They remained until 1870, with 25 regiments serving across the continent in total, and up to five at any one time between the mid-1830s and the mid-1840s.

Despite its impressive arrival – the regiment had been given new uniforms and kit as their transports neared Sydney – the 73rd soon encountered the tensions that afflicted soldiers serving in a convict society. Its officers bemoaned the higher cost of living in the distant colony, and found the social politics of free, emancipist and bond a trial. The officers of the regiments that followed, the 46th and 48th, were scandalised by Macquarie's toleration of emancipists. Their men, partial to the fiery East India rum so easily obtained in Sydney, became less tractable than their superiors wished. Macquarie bemoaned the fact that the soldiers formed 'matrimonial or less proper connexions with the Women of the Country', and that they consequently 'lose sight of their military duty and become ... identified with the lower class of inhabitants'.[4] Macquarie's complaint echoed down the decades. Twenty years on, an officer wrote to *Colburn's United Service Journal* of the disruption of Australian service. Regiments, he claimed, were 'completely cut up and disorganised', broken up into drafts on convict ships, 'separated at embarkation, and never again meeting as a regiment until ... they proceed to India'. What could be expected, he asked, 'after an intercourse of such long standing with the culprits and malefactors committed to their charge'?[5]

The soldiers' 'military duty' in the convict colonies of New South Wales and Van Diemen's Land involved actively operating against armed opponents of British authority, notably against convict and other armed rebellion, bushranging and resistance by Indigenous people. Throughout the period, as Jonathan Richards shows elsewhere in this book, part of the army's task was to meet and suppress Aboriginal resistance. While this intermittent conflict flickered off and on across the frontier of settlement, for most of the period soldiers in Australia contended only occasionally with overt threats to order. For the most part, they coped with tiresome guard duties (a wicked combination of the uneventful and harassing) and with the threat that long service in a convict colony would undermine and erode the subordination that was the basis of the British army's effectiveness.

As the only uniformed and armed agents of government, soldiers were useful and versatile symbols of officialdom. Until the 1860s, every colonial capital had a military force, and for the first 50 years of settlement every town of any size in the south-eastern colonies – Parramatta, Bathurst, Goulburn, Newcastle, Launceston – had a garrison. For much of the convict period military detachments were posted to the many outstations of settlement, the convict colonies such as Norfolk Island or Port Arthur. Military settlements also placed an official stamp on some even more remote parts of the continent. The possibility of French encroachment in Australia periodically alarmed colonial secretaries and prompted military settlements in north and western Australia, at King George Sound (1826), Melville Island (1824) and Port Essington (1837). In the 1840s troops were posted to settlements in outposts on the frontiers of settlement, such as Helidon on the Darling Downs, or Port Lincoln at the foot of Eyre Peninsula in

South Australia. Soldiers were therefore a constant presence in many parts of Australia in the decades after 1788, and were the ultimate arbiter of legitimate political authority.

Between 1810 and 1870, what did British soldiers do in colonial Australia? What purpose did they fulfil? What relationships did they forge with the people and the land in which they served?

On 20 March 1831, Captain George Mason of the 4th (King's Own) Regiment was leading his grenadier company along a country road in East Anglia, one of the many 'changes of station' that military detachments made in the course of home service. At one of the periodic halts which Mason called to relieve his men, a cavalryman trotted up and handed him a message. He smiled and remarked to his subaltern, Ensign Fortescue, 'A change of route, no doubt'. The company had just come from standing by at the assizes at Nottingham, a response to the 'Captain Swing' riots afflicting rural England at the time, and Mason surely expected to be sent to assist magistrates elsewhere. He broke the seal on the paper and read 'you will proceed to Chatham … and embark on board of a transport ship in readiness for Sydney, New South Wales'.

Mason, an officer with private means and no need to soldier in remote and uncomfortable foreign parts, later admitted that he felt 'thoroughly disgusted' with this order. But the teenaged Fortescue saw only the prospect of adventure. He turned to the men, standing or sitting by the roadside, and impulsively called out 'Huzza, my men, for Botany Bay!' The men responded three cheers, and another for their captain. Moved by his men's loyalty, Mason tossed a coin to decide whether to sell his commission or accompany them to New South Wales. Within a week, Mason and his men had embarked on the convict transport *Jane*, and almost exactly a year later he was himself sworn in as a magistrate of the colony of New South Wales.[6]

Mason's orders were a surprise, but they did not reach him by chance. The British garrison of the Australian colonies served as part of a global system. Line regiments were posted to Australia as part of several well-defined 'trooping routes'. After serving for a few years at home (recruiting, training, and often supporting public order in disaffected parts of Britain and Ireland), they were sent off for long periods of foreign service. Regiments on the 'overseas roster' selected for Australian service went for an average of about six years, then moved on to India for a further seven. Some regiments experienced even longer postings: the 99th Foot served longest in Australia, from 1842 to 1856, including seeing service in New Zealand against Māori resistance to British settlement.[7]

As Mason's reaction suggests, a posting to Australia was not always popular. When Thomas Bunbury's regiment, the 80th, was ordered to New South Wales in 1837, he recalled it as 'a calamity'. His colonel queried the order and enlisted the aid of influential friends to change it. Unsuccessful, he sold his commission instead. It is likely that this prejudice against Antipodean service influenced the composition of the officers who did serve in Australia, although detailed prosopographical research remains to be undertaken.

While red-coated military detachments were visible, the most pervasive sign of military force in the eastern colonies between 1825 and 1850 was the detachments of military Mounted Police. The force's troopers, the *Sydney Herald* declared, 'operated as a powerful preventative against bushranging, and combinations of armed depredations'. The Mounted Police's colony-wide divisional structure imposed a ramshackle regime of surveillance and pursuit across the settled areas. Dressed in cavalry-style blue or Rifles-style green uniforms, they effectively suppressed widespread bushranging outbreaks and rounded up absconding convicts, including 200 from January to May 1835 alone. The colonies' prosperous settlers welcomed their energy and persistence: 'If once set on the ... print of a bushranger's foot', the *Sydney Herald* gushed, 'they have never quitted it till they have secured their prey'.[8]

Their officers saw the dispersed detachment of their most energetic and reliable men more ambivalently. Thomas Bunbury spoke for many when he described the loss of such men as 'a great evil', not least because they also generally remained in the colonies after their regiments departed.[9] The Mounted Police gave rural magistrates, and the wealthier settlers whose interests they represented, an armed and mobile force, whose members developed considerable expertise in the bush. They often acted without the co-operation of the lower status shepherds, small-holders and, of course, assigned convicts, but they succeeded remarkably, one of the most impressive but still unregarded achievements of British soldiers in the colonial empire. One bushranger, 'Buchan Charley', supposedly admitted to a victim that his life was 'wretched beyond conception', largely because he had been 'hunted day and night by the mounted police, prevented from sleeping, or even taking a meal ... they were always on his track'.[10] That soldiers became bushmen confounds the usual stereotype of the redcoat as automaton lacking initiative. The basis of civil police forces in several colonies, the Mounted Police's role in imposing order has been rarely been acknowledged, certainly not recently.

Soldiers also formed a highly visible part of colonial society, especially in their small capitals. When the lawyer Roger Therry arrived in Sydney in 1829, he found that a 'considerable regimental force, with a large commissariat establishment, imparted quite a military aspect to the place'.[11] Sydney's huge military barracks, on George Street, was for a time the largest barrack block in the empire. (The present Victoria Barracks, smaller and less imposing, housed a smaller force when it opened in 1848.) The economic significance of the commissariat – the army's local supply system – was locally valuable, but has largely been overlooked, and remains to be thoroughly investigated.

Colonial authority primarily needed soldiers to maintain order among the convict population, both directly over the minority labouring in irons and, indirectly, the majority living and working on assignment to individual settlers. In the mid-1830s, about one in ten of New South Wales's 27 000 convicts laboured either in iron gangs on the colony's roads or in separate penal settlements: the rest were assigned as labourers to settlers, mainly on farms in the country. The largest single penal settlement, Norfolk Island – despite its healthy climate and beautiful situation – remained a place of degradation and hopelessness for convicts. Many of its military guards, continually alert for rebellion, treated convicts brutally. As one former convict testified, they were 'relentless in the extreme'. In the aftermath of the 1834 rebellion on the island, he saw soldiers 'stabbing, kicking and knocking them down'. The tension made a posting to the island harassing for the island's garrison. Officers and sergeants remained vigilant over the recurrent risk of soldiers trading tobacco or grog with convicts or, more ominously, allowing convicts to escape or even deserting and escaping with them.

The second major site at which soldiers served guard duty was on convict iron-gang stockades, and this also exposed small detachments to the privations of the bush – with mosquitoes the least of the irritations. The Quaker James Backhouse inspected several stockades while touring New South Wales in 1835. The Wollongong stockade he thought 'remarkable for its cleanliness [and] order', but he was less pleased by Junction Stockade near Mount Victoria in the Blue Mountains. There he found a small detachment of soldiers living in huts alongside their convict charges, and this proximity embittered relations between the two. Backhouse heard the soldiers use 'irritating language, mixed with curses', and saw them knock convicts down, something he thought degraded and hardened the convicts, and brutalised both parties.[12] Thomas Bunbury, having seen how the discipline and cohesion of the 80th suffered from being scattered across nearly 20 stations in the late 1830s, recalled that it was 'difficult to conceive of any employment more calculated to destroy the discipline of a corps'. Bunbury's chief concern was that young officers in charge of isolated detachments fell into the company of socially inferior settlers, and 'insensibly acquire their habits'.[13]

In a period of rapid and profound social and political change in which unrest occurred in the British Isles – unrest which often resulted in convicts being transported to Australia – it is not surprising that relationships within the army were correspondingly dynamic. The New South Wales Corps has been portrayed as being, as a General Order put it in 1796, chronically 'turbulent beyond example'.[14] Although often portrayed as loyal automatons, ferociously disciplined, soldiers' dealings with authority often reflected tensions in contemporary British, Irish and indeed, colonial society. Throughout this period, British soldiers engaged in frequent negotiation and small-scale protests, on ships voyaging to Australia, at out-stations and in capital city barracks. In 1839, for example, men of the 80th Foot protested on Norfolk Island over the removal of some vegetable gardens that they had taken over (on payment) from men of the departing 50th.[15] In 1845, men of the 99th Foot occupied Sydney's barrack square, and 'armed themselves for resistance', protesting at the reduction in their grog ration.[16] In what a soldier recalled nearly

50 years later as a 'calamitous and ignominious mutiny', they expressed 'menace towards the General and his officers, compelling them to leave the barracks; to their deep humiliation and disgust'.[17] (This so-called 'grog mutiny' ended when detachments of the 11th Foot arrived from Hobart to intimidate the protesters.) Regiments posted to Australia displayed many of the signs of the reforms through which the army passed in both the period between Waterloo and the Crimea – in the reduction in flogging, and the establishment of schools and savings banks – as well as the better known post-Crimean reforms in the soldiers' conditions of service.

External threat was neither serious nor taken seriously, despite periodic scares such as when two ships of the American Wilkes exploring expedition arrived undetected in Sydney Harbour at night in 1839, or during the Crimean War of 1854–56. While governors and military officers dutifully planned and erected defences, from the earliest months of settlement these fortifications often fell into disrepair. William Charles Wentworth thought that the Dawes Point battery was so badly designed and in such a poor state that 'a single broadside of grape would sweep off all who had the courage or temerity to defend it'.[18] Even so, the apprehension of threat sufficed to ensure that by 1870 every colonial capital had some form of fortification, the most elaborate being built in Sydney, culminating in the erection of the classic Martello tower of Fort Denison, completed in 1857. Detachments of Royal Artillery manned these defences between 1856 and 1870.

Such fortifications were certainly not the only military constructions, and if the military presence in colonial Australia has been largely forgotten, some of its physical reminders are still standing. Military engineers – both as individual officers and, from the arrival of George Barney in 1835, as professional Royal

Engineers – designed many official buildings such as military and convict barracks, offices and prisons, and numerous other structures such as bridges, culverts, wharves and water supplies.

Actual foreign threats remained non-existent, even imaginary. Rather, the real threats to the security of the British colonies, especially in the first 50 years of settlement, came from internal causes: from Aboriginal resistance, bushranging and convict rebellion. Another chapter in this volume deals with British soldiers' role in the intermittent war of conquest waged across the frontier of colonial Australia from its beginnings around Port Jackson from the first months of settlement to the complete subjugation of Indigenous Australia, which continued long after the departure of British soldiers from the Australian colonies. While military force delivered only a part of the violence directed at Indigenous resistance, for at least 70 years it was the only force able to contest organised criminality or popular uprising.

Soldiers routinely countered the threat posed by bushrangers, arguably the most serious demand made upon them. Bushranging became a particular problem in Van Diemen's Land in the 1810s and 1820s, and in New South Wales in the 1820s and 1830s. In Van Diemen's Land in 1814 the increasingly severe depredations of what were already called 'bushrangers' saw large parties of soldiers scouring the island's interior, fighting skirmishes with parties of runaway-convicts. Although not dressed, equipped or trained for prolonged patrols in the bush, the troops' campaigns succeeded. Their persistence and bushcraft seem extraordinary when measured against the training they had received. In 1816, Corporal Justin McCarthy and seven privates of the 46th fought a 90-minute gun battle with the notorious gang led by Peter Geary, a deserter from the 73rd. McCarthy's men mortally wounded Geary, and a month later captured or slew the entire gang.[19] Men of the 73rd, 48th and 46th Regiments patrolled for weeks through the Tasmanian bush, repeatedly demonstrating the kind of initiative and independence supposedly not seen in British soldiers for over a century. Their fight was also markedly savage: one ensign, thinking it necessary to prove that his party had killed three bushrangers, cut off the heads to bring them to Hobart.[20] Although alarming to settlers on isolated properties, bushranging rarely extended to political consciousness or action.

British soldiers in Australia faced open rebellion only a handful of times: at Vinegar Hill in 1804; near Bathurst in 1830; at Eureka in 1854; and (arguably) at Lambing Flat in 1860. Each reflected a different aspect of the use of troops and the changes through which colonial societies were passing.

The rebellion of Irish convicts assigned to properties northwest of Sydney in March 1804 presented the infant colony with its most serious challenge to established order. The battle at Vinegar Hill, which ended the rebellion in a scrappy and one-sided fire-fight on the Toongabbie Road on 5 March 1804, might be seen as a refutation of the many calumnies directed at the New South Wales Corps, its venal officers and unruly rank-and-file. The rebellion came two-thirds of the way through the corps' service in New South Wales, when its early recruits were entering middle-age and when it had acquired many men who had been dismissed as ex-convicts, military criminals and those disregarded as poor material at a time of competition for volunteers as the Napoleonic Wars entered their most intense phase. Long service in a convict colony did expose its members to the temptations of corruption, inefficiency and indiscipline, but on the one occasion when officialdom called on the corps to do the job for which it existed, Major George Johnston led a detachment of 28 men of its Parramatta garrison who routed and suppressed the only serious popular rebellion the colony ever faced.

Recalling the Vinegar Hill uprising 15 years later, William

Charles Wentworth acknowledged in his *Statistical, Historical and Political Description of New South Wales* in 1819 that 'much anxiety is felt ... by the generality of the inhabitants'.[21] The possibility of similar outbreaks was similarly never far from the minds of the authorities in convict colonies. The 1830 outbreak of the 'Ribbon Gang' around Bathurst, in the central-west of New South Wales, straddles the boundary between bushranging (essentially criminal, even if infused by an element of Hobsbawnesque 'social banditry') and outright political rebellion. While bushranging gangs rarely numbered more than ten, the Ribbon Gang, led by Ralph Entwistle, numbered around 80 and possibly over 130 runaway convicts. They therefore presented a serious challenge to local authority. A force of soldiers from the 39th Foot, plus Mounted Police and civilian volunteers, tracked them down to the Abercrombie River, south of Bathurst, fought and killed or arrested them. In November 1830 Entwistle and nine of his men were hanged in Bathurst (on a site now remembered as Ribbon Gang Lane).[22]

The Eureka rebellion, on the Victorian goldfield of Ballarat in December 1854, has by contrast attracted a massive historiography in its own right. Much of it focuses on the character, motives, ideas and actions of the diggers: very little on the soldiers. Gregory Blake has argued persuasively that the fight at the stockade needs to be understood as a battle (see Chapter 4), and that protagonists' actions on both sides were influenced by contemporary military practices, weapons and tactics. The soldiers at Eureka, notwithstanding that at least seven of them died as a result of the attack, have barely figured in the existing historiography. Virtually the only serious treatment of the part played by soldiers in the storming of the Eureka stockade comes in Blake's *To Pierce the Tyrant's Heart*, also the only work on the episode by a writer identifying as a military historian.[23]

With the granting of representative government in the 1850s, colonial politics became more populist and volatile, and troops in Sydney were often called out to maintain order during election protests. The last substantial use of British troops in support of the civil power occurred in 1860. After anti-Chinese riots occurred on the goldfield of Lambing Flat (now Young) in New South Wales, troops twice marched from Sydney to re-impose order and support the civil police. The presence of these troops succeeded in deterring assaults on Chinese miners. Several companies operated further inland (375 km) than any comparable body in what became the final military operation undertaken by British troops in Australia.

By the time of the Lambing Flats riots, British troops were often referred to as 'Imperial', to distinguish them from locally raised volunteers. In the political context of increasingly assertive local legislatures, and increasingly strident colonial patriotism, however, it was – and is – too easy to assume that the British soldiers were foreign to Australian society, simply outsiders sent by a domineering superpower. This was never the case. In a group of colonies in which a large proportion of the population were recent arrivals from Britain, the British soldiers had far more in common with their civilian neighbours than they had differences.

The early authorities' forebodings about the possibility of convict or popular uprising, and the possibility that the military force might not be altogether reliable, rested on the fact that soldiers and convicts came from fundamentally the same strata of British and Irish society. Convicts, whether criminal or political, had often committed offences as a direct or indirect consequence of the broader industrial and economic changes through which the British Isles were passing. While it is no longer possible to accept the traditional stereotype that soldiers came from the poorest or most degraded sections of the labouring poor, it is feasible to argue that men enlisted under the same sorts of influences – poverty, unemployment or economic disruption – that impelled others to crime. Soldiers and convicts, as well as emancipist labourers and small-holders, therefore shared backgrounds and interests that understandably made their officers and colonial rulers nervous.

In Australia, the soldier's essential duty pitted him against emancipists and the growing native-born population, adding to the tensions imported from Britain resentment of the troops' role in enforcing order. As one British officer observed in 1838, 'here anything with a red coat is hated', and he described the native-born as 'insubordinate blackguards'.[24] The resultant mix was volatile, and the picture complex. Reports in the Sydney press in 1833 describe friendly cricket matches between soldiers and colonists, but also brawls and assaults in streets and pubs. In that year the *Sydney Herald* described the mutual animosity often expressed in the streets of Sydney. As the 4th Regiment returned to the George Street barracks after a field day, a man named Patrick Quinn danced ahead of the column – very possibly Captain Mason's grenadiers – teasing the leading ranks as the regiment's band played. The *Herald* described how Quinn 'wheeled in merry circles' to the tune of 'The British Grenadiers' until he was at last arrested.[25]

Despite the severity of discipline in iron gangs and places of secondary punishment such as Norfolk Island, soldiers often regarded convict transportation as an easy option – compared to their own enforced servitude. Privates, for instance, enlisted for the same period as many convicts' sentences: seven years – with no time off for good behaviour. The majority of convicts worked as assigned labourers before receiving a ticket-of-leave, after which many lived better than they could have expected in Britain. In the eyes of many soldiers and civilians, Australia was where, as a taunting popular song put it:

> They feed you and they clothe you
> Better than a working man or soldier
> There's a lot of jolly living over here.[26]

While convict guards at iron gangs and penal settlements might doubt that their charges enjoyed 'jolly living', military corporal punishment seems to have been more severe than in all but the harshest convict regimes, and soldiers did desert (both subjects deserving greater scrutiny). This view seems to have been influential in impelling soldiers in India in the late 1840s to commit offences to be transported.[27] Incidents reported in newspapers and memoirs – such as the private of the 80th who shouted through the bars of a lock-up in Port Philip in 1841, 'You buggers, why don't you break out? I won't prevent you' – suggest that the constant rotation of companies and detachments between headquarters and out-stations was prudent.[28] The several thousand military convicts sent to Australia have at last recently become the subject of scrutiny, in Philip Hilton's recent doctoral thesis, 'Branded D on the Left Side'.[29] Joseph Anderson, the commandant of Norfolk Island in the mid-1830s, found a hundred former soldiers among his 1700 charges. Telling them that 'I consider you are still soldiers', he treated them as trustees.[30] In New South Wales, ex-soldiers re-recruited from convict ranks formed the inefficient and corrupt Border Police in the 1840s, and ex-soldiers also often became constables.

The arrival and departure of infantry regiments over the decades can suggest that soldiers were birds-of-passage, and similarly add to the impression that they remained marginal to the broader themes of colonial life and history. In fact, several thousand men posted to Australia stayed permanently after their service had ended. In addition, a small steam of military settlers trickled into Australia throughout the period. In the aftermath of the Napoleonic Wars and the retrenchment of the army, large numbers of officers on half-pay arrived as hopeful settlers and officials. As Christine Wright shows in her *Wellington's Men in Australia*, their fortunes varied: some establishing official or pastoral dynasties and rising in prosperity and influence; others falling as properties or businesses failed.[31] Men from the lower ranks who arrived as part of contingents of 'military pensioners' and as 'invalids' often enjoyed less happy outcomes. Colonel Geoffrey Mundy evoked the poignant spectacle of two old soldiers, known only as 'Waterloo' and 'Albuera', who in their seventies lived in caves on Sydney Harbour, eking out a living making and selling brooms.[32]

Military life, which often sapped personal initiative and responsibility, left many former soldiers ill-fitted for the challenges of settlement. In the 1840s, Joseph Byrne looked back over 25 years of military settlement schemes and dismissed discharged soldiers and pensioners as 'good for nothing dissipated and worthless characters'.[33] Byrne, an Irish entrepreneur who botched emigration schemes in South Africa and Australia, knew failure when he saw it. More responsible observers, however, endorsed his opinion. John Dunmore Lang, for example, judged that 'soldiers make but indifferent farmers'.[34] James Backhouse described the uproar among the group of Chelsea pensioners he accompanied to Hobart, who three times threatened to throw the vessel's captain overboard. Backhouse sorrowfully observed that 'from having been long-accustomed to act in obedience ... these men are incapable of taking care of themselves', and when faced with temptation they acted 'as children'.[35] Their military background left many ex-soldiers unfitted for farming or business. While Christine Wright advances knowledge of officers' lives, work on other ranks remains to be done. No one has yet surveyed in detail the numbers of those who took their discharge in Australia, but it is clear that many did so, especially from the mid-1850s, whether by gaining a discharge or by deserting.[36]

The army's tenure in Australia reflected the wider history of the British army, in the gradual spread of reform and in that broader demands on the force, especially in New Zealand and India, called units away to active service. The nature of military service also changed as colonial society developed. For the first 30 years after the arrival of the 73rd with Lachlan Macquarie, troops experienced constant and often severe pressures as detachments were used to support the convict system, and to serve in the Mounted Police. After 1840, as Maurice Austin's pioneering work showed, the transformation in Australian society allowed the garrison to diminish and to become increasingly marginal to that society.[37] The ending of transportation in convict colonies – New South Wales in 1840, Van Diemen's Land in 1856, and Western Australia in 1868 – led to Australia becoming one of the healthiest and least troublesome stations to which British soldiers could be sent. While under the convict system a colonel had considered New South Wales 'the worst country on earth for a soldier', by the late 1840s a private of the 99th told an officer that 'I would rather be a private in Sydney than a general in India'.[38] The colonel of one of the last regiments to serve in Sydney wrote that it was 'a most delightful quarter'.[39]

By the 1860s, however, Australia had become a military back-water and the imperial government negotiated with colonial counterparts to withdraw its troops. Regular British military forces had become practically irrelevant to the more populous, free, self-governing colonies, which were now forming their own military forces. In 1863 Roger Therry remembered how, after the end of transportation in New South Wales, 'the military aspect of the town that struck me on arrival became quite changed into the appearance of an ordinary city of civil inhabitants'.[40] Only the fortifications and barracks it had built, its traditions and a few officers and non-commissioned officers who took positions in colonial militia and volunteer forces, remained as a reminder of British army's former influence.

What do we know of the history of British soldiers in colonial Australia, and what remains to be discovered? Despite its physical removal, for example, British military influence in Australia would persist for another century, yet no one has traced exactly how that influence operated.[41] On the other side of the equation, the red-brick, Victorian gothic museum of the Prince of Wales's Own Regiment of Yorkshire stands in a street in York, well off the Yorvik-Minster tourist-track. It is pretty typical of British regimental museums: staffed by old soldiers, a little run-down, with some brand-new sections detailing the regiment's service in the Gulf or Afghanistan. It is full of mess silver, relics of obscure colonial wars and more recognisable souvenirs of the Kaiser's and Hitler's wars, all commemorating an uneasy alloy of several Yorkshire regiments now amalgamated and re-amalgamated into one super-regiment covering most of the old county. One showcase displays the most incongruous artefacts of all: a boomerang, a shield and a woomera. Clearly these items originated in Australia, and indeed, the 14th Regiment of Foot, one of the regiments whose history the museum now tells, served there. Then titled the 14th (Buckinghamshire) Regiment of Foot, it served in the Australian colonies for less than three years between 1867 and 1870 – long after troops had ceased being used to suppress Aboriginal resistance on the pastoral frontier. And yet here, amid souvenirs of the regiment's service in imperial and world wars, is a reminder that the British army has Australian associations.[42]

The Aboriginal weapons at York are among a very small selection of items that are recognisably of Australia. A survey of the holdings of 30 British regimental and national military museums disclosed that they are among some 120 such artefacts. Besides these Aboriginal weapons, the only other item that is instantly recognisable as Australian is a powder horn in the Museum of the Royal Highland Fusiliers which is inscribed with a kangaroo, created by a member of the 21st Fusiliers.[43] That the service of some 25 line regiments or other corps and perhaps as many as 30 000 individuals should produce such a dearth of material history is symbolic of the relative neglect to which British soldiers' service in Australia has been subject.

This paucity of material evidence reflects the relative ignorance of the experience of soldiers in colonial Australia, knowledge of which has largely been limited to military historians, and these often of an antiquarian or amateur persuasion. The only general history of the subject – Peter Stanley's *The Remote Garrison* – appeared over a quarter of a century ago, and although based on primary research, it is short, not footnoted and aimed at family historians.[44] Since the late Clem Sargent's 1996 study of the 48th Regiment in Australia, *The Colonial Garrison*, only a handful of new studies of regiments with Australian service have appeared: Geoff Blackburn's *Conquest and Settlement*, on the 21st in Western Australia, and Ken Larbalestier's massive self-published internet-based history of the 12th Foot.[45] While a few archaeological projects have been undertaken – such as Ollie Leckbandt's dig of the remains of the Cox's River Stockade, or Jim Allen's of Port Essington settlement – little substantially new interpretation is likely to emerge from this approach.[46] Few notable books have appeared dealing with the subject in the past decade. Craig

Wilcox's innovative *Red Coat Dreaming*, however, rightly reminds an Anzac-obsessed contemporary Australia that when Australians talked about 'the army' a century ago, they thought of British soldiers in red coats.[47] As this chapter has suggested, much more remains to be explored.

Yet while the British army in Australia has attracted little attention over the past couple of decades, the prospects for further research are now brighter than they have been for some time. Several developments in the available sources, and in the broader evolution of the field, have made new work more rather than less likely. While British military historians are as uninterested as ever in soldiers' Australian experience, the deepening interest in convict and colonial Australia, among both scholars and amateur historians, is promising. The experience of British soldiers in Australia is a classic example of the current fashion for 'transnational' history – history that cannot easily be understood within the national historiographical traditions that still govern much of the way we do history. That Australian historians are more inclined now to look beyond national boundaries, especially for subjects who might be birds-of-passage, augurs well for a new history of the British soldier in Australia and his relationships with convicts, settlers, Aborigines and others. In this Australian researchers are dependent upon the relatively slim primary sources that exist, much of them still available only in manuscript in Britain. The series of soldiers' documents in the United Kingdom National Archives (WO 97), for example, holds much unexploited material on soldiers' individual lives, before and after discharge, but has hitherto been used only by family historians.

New sources also offer the prospect of new perspectives. While the massive lode of official documents made available on microfilm through the Australian Joint Copying Project has still not been fully exploited, new sources are actually or potentially available. Collections in Britain hold little new material, although the possibilities of newly donated material becoming available in regimental, county or national collections makes the need for a new 'Mander-Jones' – the classic guide to Australian manuscripts in British collections. Existing sources, such as Captain George Mason's diary quoted here, are also becoming more accessible through digitisation, in Mason's case through the King's Own Royal Regiment Museum, Lancaster.[48] No doubt other new material will be found through digital guides, enabling researchers to draw upon the vast but otherwise inaccessible products of the work of family historians. Hundreds of family historians have researched both the service careers of soldiers who served in Australia – often based on little more than the official records available through the National Archives and the AJCP – but also often including valuable material on soldiers' lives after discharge obtained from local and family sources. Researchers have already benefited from newly revealed sources, such as the recollections of William Pidcock of the 11th, and in future might be able to collate family history sources to say something fresh about the lives of discharged soldiers in Australia.[49]

The largest potential source of new evidence bearing upon soldiers in colonial society, however, comes through the National Library of Australia's 'Trove' database, and especially its massive collection of digitised newspapers. Trove allows researchers to search dozens of newspapers over as many years in seconds, provided they employ useful search terms and date-ranges. Using Trove's capabilities could provide new insights into soldiers' relationships within colonial society, such as officers' relations with settler families, soldiers' role in the management of convict discipline, or their place in local economies. With this new route into existing sources, we might now hope for more, and more profound, studies of the place of British soldiers in colonial Australia.

Further reading

M Austin, *The Army in Australia 1840–1850*, AGPS, Canberra, 1979

G Blackburn, *Conquest and Settlement: The 21st Regiment of Foot (North British Fusiliers) in Western Australia 1833–1840*, Hesperian Press, Perth, 1999

G Blake, *To Pierce the Tyrant's Heart: A Military History of the Battle for the Eureka Stockade 3 December 1854*, Australian Military History Publications, Sydney, 2009

M Higgins, '"Deservedly respected": A first look at the 11th Regiment in Australia', *Journal of the Australian War Memorial*, no 6, 1985, pp 3–12

J Hopkins-Weise, *Blood Brothers: The Anzac Genesis*, Wakefield Press, Adelaide, 2009

K Larbalestier, *12th Regiment of Foot (East Suffolk) Service in Australia and New Zealand 1854–1867*, private publication, 2010

C Sargent, *The Colonial Garrison 1817–1824: The 48th Foot, the Northamptonshire Regiment in the Colony of New South Wales*, TLC Publications, Canberra, 1996

P Stanley, *The Remote Garrison: The British Army in Australia 1788–1870*, Kangaroo Press, Sydney, 1986

——, '"A horn to put your powder in": Interpreting artefacts of British soldiers in colonial Australia', *Journal of the Australian War Memorial*, Oct 1988, pp 13–29

——, 'Remember me when this you see: Artefacts and records of the British Army in Australia held in British museums', privately published, Canberra, 1996

——, 'Soldiers and fellow-countrymen', in M Browne & M McKernan (eds), *Australia: Two Centuries of War and Peace*, AWM, Canberra, 1988

C Wilcox, *Red Coat Dreaming*, CUP, Melbourne, 2009

C Wright, *Wellington's Men in Australia: Peninsular War Veterans and the Making of Empire c 1820–1840*, Palgrave Macmillan, Basingstoke, 2011

4

The battle for the Eureka Stockade

Gregory Blake

Private Michael Roney of the 40th Regiment of Foot took his place in the skirmish line as it formed and peered into the pre-dawn darkness. Everything was silent, nothing stirred, yet he knew that perhaps not more than 200 paces in front of him, hidden within the deep shadows of the rising ground, there stood a barricade behind which by all reports armed men awaited him and his comrades. To the whispered word of command from his officer, a captain named Pasley whom Roney did not know, he stepped forward looking to his left and right to check his progress against the other soldiers spaced out several arms' lengths from each other to his left and right. His thumb fingered the hammer on his musket, but he did not pull it back to cock his weapon. The orders had been specific – no firing until fired upon – and Roney, knowing the harsh consequences for any soldier who disobeyed a direct order, did as he was told. He had gone only a few paces when, about 150 paces to his front, there was a flash and an eruption of flame and smoke. For an instant, no more than a fleeting moment, Roney recognised the distinctive dull thump of a firearm being discharged. Then his head, struck by a bullet, snapped back, killing him instantly.

A moment later a ripple of flame traced itself out along the

The battle for the Eureka Stockade

lines of a rough palisade of miner's slabs that had been erected as a stockade and a hail of shot ripped into the infantry's ranks. Several more soldiers lurched back, struck down in a bloody tangle of smashed limbs and bone. Somewhere behind their line a bugle sounded a call the redcoats recognised in a heart beat. Instinctively they lifted their muskets as one, pulled back the hammers and fired. A great roar of smoke and flame erupted from scores of muskets, sending a hail of deadly lead balls ripping into the now just visible barricade. It was 4:30 Sunday morning, 3 December 1854, on the Ballarat goldfields in Her Majesty's Australian colony of Victoria, and the battle for the Eureka Stockade had begun.

The Eureka Stockade is an iconic moment in Australian history, yet the most commonly accepted understanding of what occurred at the stockade on that Sunday morning in 1854 has, since the time of the event itself, been subject to fundamental misinterpretation, distortion and gratuitous falsehoods.[1] The story-line is well known and in its detail seldom changes. Innocent gold miners, protesting against the harsh tax regime of a tyrannical government, are without provocation wantonly set upon by hundreds of bloodthirsty soldiers and police. No warning is given, and the aggrieved diggers, lacking proper arms and taken completely by surprise, are routed in a few brief minutes. A fearsome bloodletting then unfolds as the military and police run amok, visiting murder and desolation on any unfortunate they managed to catch. The unwavering tenet of the Eureka legend is that it was a brutal massacre, a slaughter that was, 'most heathenish, Bloodthirsty, disgraceful and cruel'.[2]

It is easy to succumb to anachronistic judgments of what occurred at Eureka, as indeed have many who have told the story since. In Harper Lee's wonderful novel *To Kill a Mocking Bird*, Atticus Finch gives his young daughter some sage advice when he tells her that to get to know someone, you must first 'climb into his skin and walk around in it'. This of course means climbing into the skin of the protagonists on both sides of the Eureka conflict. Without doing so, especially in relation to the military participants involved, it is impossible to reach an informed and objective assessment of what occurred during and following the battle for the stockade. Sadly for our understanding of the battle at Eureka, there have been few modern tellers of the tale who have heeded Atticus Finch's advice. Embark with me, then, upon a journey into a legendary moment in Australia's past. It was a moment when the allure of gold fired the unbounded aspirations of the common people. A moment when those aspirations challenged the entrenched social and political order and resulted in bloody conflict, and when an Australian legend was born.

The historical 'truth' of Eureka matter is, in fact, quite different from the dominant narrative. Far from being a massacre of innocents, Eureka was a conflict that was fought as a military engagement between opponents who were mutually prepared for armed conflict. It was a hard-fought contest of arms during which the defenders of the stockade disputed the ground they occupied with considerable resolve. They did so for as long as they were able with not an insignificant display of military acumen. The consequence of this determined resistance was that the ensuing battle was brutal and, in the customary nature of such combats in that era, merciless. Understanding this enables an appreciation for and a fuller understanding of the action at Eureka for what it actually was, rather than what Eureka mythologist would have us imagine it was.

'Massacre at Eureka ... cowardly massacre' trumpeted the correspondent for the *Geelong Advertiser and Intelligencer*.[3] 'Deplorable massacres' howled speakers at a mass meeting held at the Collins Street Mechanics' Institute in Melbourne on

5 December.[4] Digger leader John Basson Humffray echoed the outrage with a promise to present a true account of the massacre at Eureka.[5] The *Ballarat Times*, in a black-bordered article, announced to the world a spectacle that was 'sufficient to appal the stoutest heart'.[6] The *Gold Fields Advocate* presented its readers with a scene of unambiguous desolation:

> This morning Eureka goldfield presents a piteous scene. Women roam the camp crying aloud for their men, their children at their skirts wailing for their fathers, and in the midst of the desolate and heartbreaking sight a lone dog epitomises tragedy with a continuous mournful howl.[7]

Ballarat digger Thomas Pierson described the military and police who had perpetrated the killings at Eureka as 'most heathenish, Bloodthirsty, disgraceful and cruel'.[8] In following years, stalwart Eureka veterans such as John Lynch, Edward Shanahan, Michael Tuohy and Richard Allan insisted that most of the killing occurred outside the stockade after all resistance had collapsed. It is worth noting, however, that such claims of wanton and widespread massacre of innocent miners were from men who, in the case of Lynch, Tuohy and Allan, were in custody. (Shanahan was hiding in an outhouse, concealed from discovery.) None of these men would have been able to witness what was happening outside the stockade or beyond their immediate surrounds, and even then under conditions of emotional duress. Their recollections were also many years after the event. Yet such were the expressions of public and individual outrage and moral condemnation that accompanied the news of the battle at Eureka, and subsequent memories of it.

These claims of massacre – one of the earliest forms of misappropriation of the Eureka memory – were to some extent understandable as a reaction from a civilian community that had in times of peace suddenly had the horrors of war visited upon it. Yet given the military context in which Eureka actually occurred, such interpretations were ill-informed at best and deliberately untruthful at worst. The fact was that the outcome of the conflict at the stockade followed a well-established precedent for that era in how military engagements were conducted and the character of the consequences of those engagements for the defeated. That the outcome at the stockade was a bloody one was undeniable, but it was directly attributable to the nature of the conflict that was fought and a combination of circumstances that inevitably resulted in high casualties – which as was also usual in such cases – fell mostly among the overcome defenders. The battle for the Eureka Stockade was not at all unique in this regard. Viewed in this context it was certainly no wantonly gratuitous massacre.

The facts and context of what occurred at Eureka did not, of course, matter much for those who had lost family and friends in the battle, or for those who could in the highly charged political environment of colonial Victoria at that time make political capital from the fall-out of the affair. Because of this, the myth of massacre took on a life of its own and was repeated in the press and in public forums until it became a firmly entrenched centrepiece of how Eureka would be publically remembered. Contemporary responses to Eureka like these have similarly provided ample fuel for those who have, over the generations and for their own reasons, wished to continue stoking the furnaces of public and private moral indignation. Many accounts of Eureka written since have reflected such righteous populist anger. Statements such as 'The whole military action was one of deceit and totally lacking in the accepted codes of conduct'; and 'the troops brought disgrace on the Military' are typical examples of this outrage.[9]

Nor have professional historians been immune to the seductive lure and imagery of depicting Eureka in this manner. In 1984 John Molony asserted that what occurred after the fall of the stockade was 'butchery', and that 'The wild scene of destruction, by burning or assault, spared nothing'.[10] Weston Bate accused the police of committing murder.[11] Geoffrey Serle describes the actions of some of the police and military as disgraceful.[12] In *Peter Lalor: The Man from Eureka* (1979), Les Blake categorically states that 'The police went crazy with bloodlust', and that 'Tents, stores and huts were wantonly set on fire'.[13]

This characterisation of the Eureka diggers as noble victims foully cut down in defence of a righteous cause by the murderous agents of the government of the day is the central component of the Eureka mythology. It has been used to reinforce the agendas of a broad range of causes and groups throughout the last century which have adopted the symbols and legend of Eureka as their own. The number and diversity of such groups is legion, as have been (and are) their motivations. Despite its persistent passionate portrayal as such, this depiction of what occurred at Eureka is an inaccurate and incorrect representation that is sorely in need of correction. Indeed, it could well be argued that the story of the Eureka Stockade has become so hopelessly entangled within its own legend that it is impossible to unravel what occurred. Yet, the goal is worthy of the attempt.

In *The Face of Battle*, his seminal study of men in combat, John Keegan begins his account of the battle of Waterloo with a quote from the Duke of Wellington. Responding to requests to describe Waterloo in terms that could enable an historical narrative of the battle to be written, the duke replied that the:

> history of the battle is not unlike the history of a ball! Some individuals may recollect all the little events of which the great result is the battle lost or won; but no individual can

recollect the order in which, or the exact moment at which, they occurred, which makes all the difference to their value or importance.[14]

Such is the case with descriptions of the battle for the Eureka Stockade.

Despite there being a great deal of material related to the Eureka stockade available, it is uncollated and greatly uneven in its reliability. Until recently no single source has been able to offer an informed narrative of the whole story.[15] The real challenge comes, as Wellington observed, when one wants to make sense from what one has discovered. This becomes especially so when we begin to unravel the tangle of half-truth and blatant mythology that has until now sufficed to portray the battle. Where, then, does one turn to begin to tell the authentic story of what happened at Eureka at dawn on that Sunday morning in December 1854?

The most obvious place to begin is the carefully worded official government reports of the day. The methodical military descriptions of what eventuated at Eureka and the dry statistical record of logistics, manpower, timings and expenditure, may appear on the surface to be somewhat uninspiring reading. Such material, however, provides us with a solid foundation from which to begin to construct a coherent understanding of the event.

Having established our base, we then need to build on it, adding the body, soul and passion of the personal experience without which any description of human conflict would become essentially meaningless. For this we turn to the recollections, anecdotes and occasional diatribes of those most intimately involved in the battle. Luckily one does not have to look too far to find sources for such material. Rafaello Carboni's much-vaunted account *The Eureka Stockade* is an obvious place to start.[16] Carboni, a member of the insurgents' inner council, was not inside the stockade during the battle, but he did claim to witness the conflict. He wrote his account a year later, when his passion was still aflame and his memory fresh. Although he is shamelessly bigoted in his opinions of participants, frequently pompous, unreliable with timings, and irredeemably self-serving, Carboni's account is still compelling. His description of the battle occupies only a small part of his book, but he nevertheless provides us with an invaluable resource that more often than not stands the test when compared with the recollections of others.

In the same manner, personal journal entries – such as those of Thomas Pierson and shopkeeper Samuel Lazarus – are of great value.[17] Often written only days after the event, these accounts offer us precious details that, when viewed in the military context of events, provide valuable clues as to what most probably did or did not occur. Letters written in the weeks following the battle by those who attacked the stockade – such as Captain Charles Pasley – are equally revealing.[18] Contemporary newspaper articles, both foreign and domestic – even when written by quite obviously partisan correspondents – help enormously to piece together the jigsaw puzzle of what took place. Of particular note here are the pages of the *Argus* newspaper in Melbourne, which offer invaluable material. Finally the voluminous transcripts of the Eureka state trials and court depositions are another rich source of firsthand material related to the fighting.[19] In these transcripts the men who attacked the stockade recount, under oath and presumably as accurately as they can, their movements and actions during the conflict.

When attempting to construct a military narrative, these accounts provide a great deal of detail on the battle. There are the numerous later reminiscences of those who defended or attacked the stockade, as well as those who watched from a distance. These are mostly accounts from, by then, quite elderly men and women.

Despite in some cases being separated in time from the events by half a century or more, they too provide us with a rich well spring from which we can draw and compare with what we know from other sources closer in time to the event. The many second-hand accounts of Eureka should not be dismissed. Even though those accounts are often flawed, there are gems to be found among them, and careful sifting can reveal details that assist to corroborate the accounts of people much nearer to the event.

Having uncovered the sources that will enable us to tell the human story, we must above all allow that story to tell itself. This is an important consideration if we wish to understand the event in the context of the times in which it occurred. The Ballarat diggings had been unsettled for some time. The persistently arbitrary and coercive manner in which the miner's licence laws were enforced, in an environment of limited economic return for very hard physical labour, had aggravated the diggers. Added to this was the widespread perception among the diggers that the police and the courts, the very people entrusted with ensuring the laws were administered, were irredeemably corrupt and self-serving. A repressed rage simmered in the hearts of many, only waiting for a spark to transform itself into violent fury. That spark came on the night of 6 October, when Scots digger James Scobie was murdered near the Eureka Hotel. James Bentley, the owner of the hotel, was blamed by many diggers. When a coroner's enquiry dominated by Bentley's cronies and acquaintances found that he had no case to answer, the result was an outburst of rage. The Eureka Hotel was looted and burned to the ground, and Bentley fled for his life. Reacting to what it perceived to be breakdown of law and order at Ballarat, the colonial government despatched reinforcements of troops and police.

In this highly charged environment, the more astute among the miners began to organise a political response to the challenges that faced them, and in October 1854 formed the Ballarat Reform League. Mass meetings attended by thousands were called by the league, and the diggers aired their grievances and their demands on the government with boisterous fervour. On 11 November 1854 at a mass meeting attended by at least 10 000 diggers, the league adopted a charter of aspirations that were overtly democratic in inspiration.

The government, frightened by what it saw as a dark conspiracy to awaken the demon of democracy among the population, responded by despatching even more troops and police to Ballarat. On the evening of 28 November, diggers who had been provoked earlier in the day by troops marching through the diggings flaunting loaded muskets and fixed bayonets, attacked an arriving company of soldiers, even though these troops were making no militaristic display. In the ensuing fracas, soldiers were beaten, a cart driver severely injured, shots were fired and a drummer boy was wounded in the thigh. Tensions were at breaking point but even so a little prudence and forbearance from the authorities may well have defused any serious confrontation. This was not to be.

In an act of myopic insensitivity, the authorities ordered a large scale 'digger hunt' for 30 November. This hunt for unlicensed miners would have the most profound consequences. Encountering angry diggers who refused to comply with demands to produce their licences at the Gravel Pits diggings, the police called on the military for assistance. This came in the form of infantry, again with fixed bayonets. The presence of armed police and soldiers provoked a maelstrom of violence from the growing crowd of diggers, and in the riot that followed shots were fired (by exactly who remains unsure) and the military swept all before them at the point of the bayonet.

Word of the riot at the Gravel Pits raced across the diggings.

Rightly or wrongly, news spread that the soldiers had fired on the miners. For many diggers, this was the last straw, and they resolved that only radical direct action could remedy the crisis they were convinced they now faced. That same evening a mass of miners gathered on Bakery Hill atop of which flew their newly crafted Southern Cross flag. Many of the diggers were armed, and kneeling together beneath their flag they swore an oath to defend their 'rights and liberties'. Then in the time-honoured tradition of civilian militias, they began to organise themselves into armed companies. Such a practice mirrored that which occurred prior to the first battles of the American War of Independence at Lexington-Concord in 1775. In a similar vein, British Chartist companies during the 1830s and 1840s were mustered with each man having his name recorded. Alfred Black, the Eureka diggers' 'Secretary of War' did the same. The next day the diggers commenced erecting a stockade and began openly drilling under arms. The die had been cast and what up until then had been an angry yet still mostly civil protest movement transformed inexorably into an unambiguous armed insurrection.

With what they viewed as armed insurgents openly drilling under arms, a 'rebel' fortification now constructed, and fearing that 'a riot was rapidly growing into a revolution', the authorities resolved to act.[20] The moon had not set when, at about 2:30 on the morning of 3 December, 276 soldiers and police began to form ranks near the government camp. They did so without any bugle call, shouted orders, or other sound to divulge their presence. The mustered force included 87 infantry of the 40th Regiment and 65 of the 12th Regiment. There were also 30 men of the 40th Regiment's mounted company, and 24 police on foot. A further 70 mounted police completed the muster (see chapter 2 for a further discussion of such troops). The force was commanded by Captain John Wellesley Thomas of the 40th Regiment, an experienced officer who had seen active service in India and Afghanistan. A further 200 soldiers remained in the government camp to guard against surprise attack from the numerous insurgents known to be outside the stockade that night. The order to march was given. The force moved off into the darkness. Disciplined and under perfect control, the troops moved so quietly that one who was with the column observed that a pin could almost be heard to drop.[21] At some time around 4:00, Thomas's force arrived behind Stockyard Hill, a low feature just to the north of where the diggers had built their stockade.

To the stockade's defenders in the receding darkness, the infantry out to their front had been little more than indistinct shapes, mere shadows in the grey light. Irishman John Lynch, clutching his double-barrelled gun and squatting behind a palisade of thick slabs, recounted how he 'could hardly discern the military force at first'. This changed as the soldiers drew closer, and in the growing light they could be clearly seen at about 150 yards.[22] Californian digger Charles Ferguson was waiting behind the cover of the stockade's palisade and could clearly see the soldiers advancing.

One soldier in particular, whom Ferguson thought to be an officer (mistakenly as it turned out), attracted attention. There had been orders issued among the diggers to shoot at the officers if they were attacked by the military.[23] Robert Burnette, another American and described by fellow defender Henry Sutherland as 'a little fellow formerly a barber',[24] stepped forward and lifted his rifle. Taking careful aim he fired what Ferguson would later call the first shot of the 'Ballarat War'.[25] Burnette's shot was the first at Eureka that hit its mark – in all likelihood Private Michael Roney. (No other military casualties were recorded prior to Roney's death.[26])

Following Burnette's shot, whatever inhibitions the stockade defenders had disappeared, and a fusillade of fire erupted from them, cutting into the ranks of the soldiers. Private Felix Boyle of the 12th Regiment, a veteran of the Sikh Wars, was hit square in the face, the bullet punching through next to his nose.[27] Private William Juniper of the 40th went down, his thigh smashed with a compound fracture by a musket ball.[28] Bullets flew thick and fast. Magistrate Charles Hackett presumed, quite understandably in the circumstances, that at least one of those shots was aimed at him. Likewise Lieutenant Richards of the 40th, who was with another magistrate named Graeme Webster and the overall military commander Captain Thomas on the right of the infantry line, described how a shot from the stockade passed just over Thomas's and his heads. Magistrate Webster recalled that same shot had 'whistled close by'.[29]

As with just about everything to do with the battle for the Eureka Stockade, there are contradictory and dissenting opinions about how, when and what actually happened in those first moments. This apparent ambiguity has been eagerly seized upon by legions of Eureka story-tellers, all of whom could extract what they wished from the tale to suit their own agendas. For example, Constable William Thompson gave a rambling testimony to the Ballarat Police Court, in which he firstly stated that 'The rioters immediately fired … hundreds of shots were fired from the stockade'. He then contradicted himself, and stated that 'The military fired before the rioters opened their fire'. Then, confusingly contradicting himself again, he added that 'The first fire was fired from the stockade'. No reason was asked or given for the discrepancy in Thompson's account, which was officially noted by the court. In the same manner some contemporary journalistic efforts present accounts that add grist to the misinformation mill. Charles Knight, writing in the *Mount Alexander Times*, claimed that the soldiers fired the first volley over the heads of the insurgents, which provoked the reply from the diggers. A report by the Ballarat correspondent of the *Argus* claimed that 'A demand was made for the insurgents to lay down their arms, or a bugle call at 100 yards. When this was either refused or ignored the soldiers fired two rounds of blank cartridges – the Diggers returned the fire'.[30] William Kelly, in his *Life in Victoria*, claims that a government spy inside the stockade fired the first shot.[31]

None of these accounts is credible. None of either Knight, the *Argus* correspondent or Kelly was actually present in the stockade during the battle. None even witnessed it from afar. Knight's account of the shots being fired over the heads of the diggers had its genesis in only the single report in the *Argus*.[32] The *Argus* correspondent's claim of blanks being fired prior to the engagement is not corroborated by any other first-hand account, and appears to be little more than an imaginative invention. Kelly's account is one part of a description of the battle that is replete with inaccuracies and inventive assumptions: he mistakenly places Major General Nickle, who he calls 'Nicol', in the government camp prior to the battle, when in fact Nickle was at the time marching north from Melbourne with reinforcements; and he claims that his General Nicol ordered the move against the stockade, when it was the Resident Commissioner Robert Rede who did so. His description of the battle is ludicrously simplistic, with him claiming that the battle was over before the defenders of the stockade had time to reload.[33]

That the Eureka diggers did not fire first, and that as a consequence they were victims of an unprovoked and dastardly assault by the military, has been a centrepiece of the Eureka story since the earliest times. In a published letter to the *Argus*, Peter Lalor, a leader at Eureka and subsequently a politician who earned much support due to his involvement in events at the stockade, was adamant that the soldiers fired first, and that the stockade's defenders did not fire at all at this stage. Instead, he unequivocally stated that, without warning or provocation from the diggers, 'the military poured in one or two volleys of musketry, which was a plain intimation that we must sell our lives as dearly as we could'.[34] Despite being directly contradicted by both the defenders of the stockade and those assaulting it, and despite also the obvious caveat that Lalor's recollection would of necessity be one that was self-serving and intended to assuage any deleterious perception of the diggers' cause, his account forms the basis of 'proof' that the diggers were victims of a heinous crime. Unfortunately for those who peddle such stories, the evidence to the contrary is compelling.

In his after-action report, Captain Thomas made the point that the 'rebels' had fired upon his force 'without word or challenge on their part'. He was adamant that his men did not fire first, and that a single shot followed by a volley had come from the stockade without warning.[35] Private Neill, of the 40th Regiment, claimed the same.[36] Lieutenant Richards stated that the troops received the order to commence firing after the shot had passed over his and Thomas's head.[37] Stockade defender John Lynch, no friend of the military, recalled that the first shot did come from the stockade, and that only then did the soldiers respond with an 'instantaneous fusillade of musketry'.[38] Prominent Eureka 'rebel' Rafaello Carboni, who had been sleeping in his tent not too far from the stockade, heard a discharge of musketry and then a bugle call. This was followed by the audible command 'Forward' and another discharge of musketry.

Carboni's recollection of a bugle call is of great importance in helping us to determine who indeed did fire first. In the British army of the 1850s, it was the bugle that transmitted orders in the field, especially for troops deployed into open order or skirmishing as were those soldiers leading the advance against the stockade. It would have been most unlikely that those soldiers, members of an army that imposed an iron discipline with the threat of the lash for miscreants, would have fired without orders to do so. This is particularly so given that Thomas had distinctly told them not to fire until they heard the bugle command to do so.[39]

To claim that the order might have been whispered, spoken, or even shouted is unrealistic. No one present that morning from either side reported hearing any sort of verbal order given to the soldiers to open fire. Such an occurrence would have been a problematic method of transmitting orders. Not all of Thomas's men would necessarily have heard it, even if shouted, and the potential for confusion would have been great if firing suddenly erupting from the military on only one part of the field. Confusion is anathema to a commander during battle and Thomas, the experienced soldier, would not have entertained encouraging it for one moment. This was especially so as the success of the operation to capture the stockade against determined resistance, now that this was the case, relied upon quick and decisive action.

Thomas gave the order to fire, the bugler signalled it to the troops, and with a throaty tympany and belch of white smoke several score military muskets sent their 0.753-inch calibre soft lead balls whining across the space between their firing line and the stockade's defenders. The relatively low velocity of the musket balls created a distinct sound as they passed through the air. To the firer, the sound is something like a whine dropping to a hum as the ball flies away. To those at the receiving end of the fire, the sound could be like the 'whizzing of mosquitoes'.[40] One digger some distance from the stockade who heard the volley described it as sounding like a file drawn across the teeth of a saw.[41]

Chips splintered from the stockade's slabs as the balls impacted.[42] One defender claimed he saw nine diggers lying dead as a result of the soldiers' first volley.[43] One could have expected that following such an assault, the diggers – civilian miners to a man – would have turned tail and fled, but they did not. The stockade's defenders struck back.

Another of the deeply entrenched myths of Eureka connected to the massacre fable is that, because the diggers were supposedly so poorly armed and caught unawares, their return fire was little more than an 'intermittent splutter' and 'ragged'.[44] In fact the stockade defenders kept up a heavy fire for some ten minutes.[45] Ferguson described the fire from the stockade as being delivered 'with like effect, as deadly as theirs'.[46] John Lynch concurred, recollecting that the diggers engaging in 'Some sharp shooting'.[47] Samuel Perry, who as a 19-year-old was inside the stockade, recalled that 'we were bosses for about 10 minutes'.[48]

The impression of those on the receiving end of that fire did not dispute these observations. Captain Charles Pasley of the Royal Engineers – who at Eureka was acting as aide de camp to the force commander Captain John Thomas of the 40th Regiment, as well as commanding the forward skirmish line of the 40th Regiment during the assault on the stockade – described the fire from the stockade as 'Sharp and sustained'.[49] Captain Thomas, who in his career had witnessed serious combat in India and Afghanistan, referred to the fire coming at his men as 'rather sharp, and well directed'.[50] Thomas's words are most instructive. By 'sharp' he meant that the fire of the stockade defenders was accurate, and by 'well directed' that the fire was delivered in an organised mass against selected parts of his own line. That a man like Thomas assessed the quality of the fire he faced in this manner indicates that at least some among the stockade's defenders were capable of much more than an amateur defence. The question was, who among the Eureka diggers possessed enough military acumen to behave in such a manner?

One group of defenders who exhibited all of these qualities were the Californians of an *ad hoc* unit self-styled the 'Independent California Rangers Revolver Brigade'. There were 20–30 Californians inside the stockade during the battle.[51] Many of these men were veteran 'Mexican soldiers of 46-48' and 'old soldiers in the Mexican war'.[52] With a significant number of the Californians being veterans, they would have constituted one group who were used to accepting direction in battle and capable of exhibiting the degree of fire discipline necessary to produce the 'sharp and well directed' fire attested to.

The Californians were also better armed than the average digger. As their unit's name implied, they were armed with Colt revolvers of various calibre.[53] The accuracy of Burnette's initial shot indicates it is likely that many were also carrying long arms, such as rifles or double-barrelled guns, as indeed was John Lynch who, although not a Californian, was assigned to the Californian Rangers.[54] They also obviously possessed adequate ammunition, or at least enough to sustain their fire for what would amount to almost ten minutes. The Californians occupied the northwest corner of the stockade, which was in the direct line of the main advance for the military in the opening stages of the battle. Many of the Californians occupied shallow shepherd holes that had been turned into rifle pits. These pits consisted of a square framework of logs, high enough to pack the earth dug up around them.[55] Such positions would provide quite effective shelter from which to fire.

Further evidence of the effectiveness of the diggers' initial fire is revealed by the actual casualty figures suffered by the attackers during the battle. Although it is not possible to state exactly when each of the military casualties occurred, it is possible to make an informed estimate for them as a group. Of 17 officially reported military casualties suffered at Eureka, 13 were definitely due to gunshot wounds.[56] If Private Joseph Wall is included as a gunshot-related casualty – although the killing blow seems to have come from a pike – then the number of military killed and wounded due to gunshot increases.[57] Carboni recalled seeing 'about a dozen' soldiers on the ground behind the skirmish line in front of the stockade early in the battle.[58] Given that Carboni's figure was an estimate, and there may have been less (or indeed more) military casualties, his figure of about 12 at least provides a sense of what occurred. If we take 12 casualties as a reasonably reliable figure, it represents 85.7 per cent of the total known gunshot wounds suffered by the redcoats during the entire battle. It is important to note also that these casualties were suffered in the first part of the battle, when fire from the stockade was the only resistance that the military faced. Knowing that in battle most shots fired actually miss their intended target, it emphasises once again the consistent quality of the 'sharp and well directed' fire from the stockade at that time.[59]

The skill to deliver such fire was augmented by some effective and energetic leadership. According to Carboni an American 'officer' commanded the Californian 'rifle pit men'. Despite being wounded in the thigh, he fought like a tiger.[60] If, like many of his American peers, this man had prior military and presumably battlefield command experience, he could have easily co-ordinated the fire encountered by the soldiers. Throughout the battle this officer, whose name has been lost to history, also remained in close contact with the Canadian Charles (Henry) Ross, who commanded a company of diggers on the north side of the stockade. Perhaps this American 'Tiger' inspired Ross's men to fire in a co-ordinated manner as well.

Whatever its precise source, the resistance encountered by the military in the opening stages of the battle completely contradicts the insistence of the traditional Eureka narrative that those

The battle for the Eureka Stockade

defending the stockade were incapable of doing so. Only collective competence, not random individual efforts, could produce such an effort, and the only identifiable group inside the stockade that morning that could have done so was the Californians. Acknowledging this also redresses a long-standing failure to recognise the significant transnational undercurrent present at Eureka.

As the storm of fire descended upon the advancing soldiers, as the bullets from the stockade cut through their ranks, something utterly unexpected occurred: the men of the 40th Regiment began to fall back in disorder. Carboni recalls seeing the soldiers' line 'swerve from its ground'.[61] Lynch mentions that 'the advance of the infantry was arrested for the moment'.[62] Samuel Huyghue, a clerk in the Ballarat Office of Mines, commented on how the severity of the diggers' fire 'caused the Queen's infantry to waver and many of them held back'.[63] Trained regular infantry, including veterans of conflicts in other wars, wavered in the face of their foe. So much for the spluttering fire of the supposedly unarmed, unprepared and befuddled defenders of the stockade.

When the men of the 40th Regiment wavered, the seed was sown for the contagion of panic among the soldiers which may in turn have led to unforeseen consequences. A shop-keeper inside the stockade said later that he thought he had heard Captain Wise of the 40th Regiment call out 'Fortieth are you going to retreat?'[64] Carboni recalled a bugle boy bravely standing his ground and the men, rallied by the efforts of their sergeant and Captain Wise, formed up on the boy's right.[65] It was about this time that Thomas, no doubt realising that he must intervene and restore the spirit of his men, dismounted and took direct command of the troops in front of the stockade, placing himself in harm's way.[66] Thomas's actions in doing so highlighted just how serious the military situation had become. Rallied once again, the advance continued.

One aspect of the battle for the stockade that seems to have completely eluded any of those who have written about the conflict – perhaps unsurprisingly, considering the basic misunderstanding of what actually did occur – is the time taken by the soldiers to reach the stockade after the first shots were fired. The traditional depiction of the actions of the soldiers during the battle, when it is described at all apart from tales related the horrors they inflicted upon the innocent diggers, has been characterised by a chronic failure to understand the fundamental elements of how trained soldiers behaved on the battlefield in that era. A good example of this military illiteracy can be found in descriptions of the assault, such as in Henry Turner's *Our Own Little Rebellion*:

> After another volley from the soldiers, which sounded like an earthquake in comparison with the dropping fire of the insurgents, the order was given to charge. With a wild cheer the soldiers threw themselves on the flimsy palisades, which readily went down before them.[67]

Turner conflates events here, ignoring the time spent crossing the contested ground and only relating the moment when the soldiers stormed the stockade. By so doing he creates an impression of rushing haste. In more recent times Geoffrey Hocking, in *Eureka Stockade: The Events Leading Up to the Attack in the Pre-Dawn of 3 December 1854*, mimics with minor modifications Turner's ill-informed hyperbole:

> At the sound of the bugle, the troops abandoned their lines, and in skirmishing order surged forward. Several of the soldiers in the front line were hit by fire. It was plain to the officer in charge of the foot soldiers that the men within

the stockade would have the best of the battle if it was to be confined to shooting, so he ordered a bayonet charge.

According to Hocking, with a cry of '40th follow me!' the red-coated troopers dashed for the barricade as Captain Wise led the charge forward.[68]

This depiction is a fantasy which equates in no way with the actual military battlefield tactics of the era. Following standard operational procedure, the leading elements of the British line at Eureka had been deployed into skirmish order. In 1854, the British Army was employing a system of skirmishing based on the 1798 *Regulations for the Exercise and Conduct of Rifles and Light Infantry on Parade and in the Field*. Despite its antiquity, these regulations would form the basis of skirmishing tactics within the British Army until the late nineteenth century. When the order came for the skirmishers to commence fire, the system used to carry out that firing was known as a 'chain'. The man on the right wing of each four-man section would step forward three paces and fire, then step back and load. The next three men would then do the same individually, when the right-wing man would repeat the process. Such a system ensured that fire was always being delivered against the enemy, and that the line always presented a partially moving, extended order target – and was thus much more difficult to hit.

The chain was not intended to hold ground, nor necessarily to advance. When the order did come to move forward, the skirmishers would move and fire in bounds, with each man running forward in a controlled manner, firing in turns and holding the new ground. Working in this way allowed a steady rate of advance to be maintained, as well as ensuring that while one quarter of the line was firing the other three quarters were preparing to do so – an important consideration in an era of single-shot weapons.

Skirmishers were also not necessarily meant to engage their enemies in hand-to-hand combat, and would do so only if compelled to. The normal military consensus of the day held that, when it came to serious bayonet work, closer formations were preferable. Consequently skirmishing troops do not have fixed bayonets, as was the case for Thomas's infantry that morning. If an assault looked to be in the making, or the tactical situation appeared to be unfavourable, the skirmish line supports would be brought up.[69] This is in fact exactly what Thomas did at Eureka as the situation developed into a serious confrontation. The skirmishers deployed and began to advance with Captain Pasley in command (belying Hocking's claim that Wise commanded the leading elements of the assault).[70] With only one exception – when a handful of soldiers broke ranks and rushed forward to scale the palisade for a moment before they were chased out again – the military advance was conducted in the steady, careful manner prescribed by regulation and training.[71]

It was not until about the ten-minute mark when, as we will see later, the mounted police had outflanked the stockade defenders and the defenders' fire was distracted, that the soldiers finally came up to the stockade's palisade. The practical consequence of these timings is that it took the soldiers close to ten minutes to cross the roughly 150 yards from the point where Private Roney was killed to when they arrived at the palisade. The sober reality of these timings was that the rate of advance by the soldiers was something like 15 yards per minute. While this figure is entirely notional, and there would have been moments when it was not achieved or greatly exceeded, it indicates that the advance against the stockade was certainly not the wild surge by excited soldiers that is perpetrated by the myth-makers.

The mounted police had not been idle during the exchange of fire between the stockade's defenders and the advancing infantry.

In the growing light they had been working their way through the surrounding tangle of tents, pits and camp detritus to the western face of the stockade, where eventually they made their presence felt. Due to their depleted numbers that morning, the Eureka diggers had not been able to adequately cover that part of the stockade. As the light improved this had been noticed, and was now exploited by the mounted police. In the words of defender John Lynch, they 'wheeled round, and took us in the rear. We were then placed between two fires'.[72]

With fire now coming in from one side and behind them, the Eureka diggers' position was tactically untenable. In response, and perfectly consistent with military practice throughout history, many of the diggers decided that discretion was the better part of valour. Abandoning their posts they turned and ran.[73] There are conflicting accounts of just how this affected the continuing defence put up by the diggers. Huyghue – who despite being presented by some as an 'eye-witness' to the battle was in fact some distance from the fighting, never saw the stockade and compiled the majority of his account from second-hand stories – mentioned that at this time the fire from the stockade became desultory.[74]

This is, however, directly contradicted by those on the spot who stated that a great deal of firing was still going on up until the time that the order to charge was given, which was after many diggers had fled. Lieutenant Richards of the 40th recalled that 'on both sides the fire was kept up heavily until the stockade was taken'. Magistrate Graeme Webster, present throughout the battle, stated that 'at the moment the soldiers entered the stockade' – that is, after many of the diggers had fled – 'There were so many men killed or wounded there in the course of a moment or two, and the men not seeing exactly what it was, hesitated for half a moment'.[75]

Nevertheless encouraged by the fleeing of numerous insurgents, Thomas ordered up his infantry reserves, including the foot police who had been waiting back behind the skirmish line.[76] The order to fix bayonets was then given. Private O'Keefe of the 40th distinctly remembered he was standing only a few yards from the stockade when the order was given. With this order the soldiers would have known that there was to be no compromise. The bayonet was the ultimate weapon of chastisement and it was about to be put to use. Before this occurred one final volley was fired, mowing down any who showed their heads above the palisade. With muskets now unloaded, and with bayonets fixed, Captain Thomas, still dismounted, called out something like 'Fortieth, follow me!'[77] Only then did the redcoats cheer and rush forward.[78] It was about this time that the officer in command of the assault group of the 40th Regiment, Captain Henry Wise, who had already been wounded in one leg, fell shot through both knees with what would be a mortal wound.[79] Those defenders still holding their ground continued to fire at their attackers. Lieutenant William Paul of the 12th Regiment also fell severely wounded at this time with a bullet in his hip.[80]

The battle now became one of desperate individual combats. Ferguson recalled the fighting as savage and 'the most exciting time of my life'.[81] It was during this wild melee that an extraordinary act of bravado and courage occurred, one that underscores the character and resolve of those who continued to stand their ground among the stockade's defenders. Several of the Californians rushed right up to the soldiers, hoping no doubt that by so doing they might make their remaining shots count.[82] It was also about this time that the leader of the Eureka diggers, Peter Lalor, fell with a shot to the top of his left shoulder. Assisted by nearby Californians, Lalor was hidden out of sight in a hole beneath a pile of slabs and the fighting for the stockade passed over and around him. Also during or before this final assault, Edmund Thonen, a German who commanded a miners' rifle company, was shot down and killed. He was seen to fall 'his mouth literally choked with bullets'. Canadian Charles Ross also fell, hit in the groin, and he would die later in the day from his wound.[83]

With the soldiers surging into the stockade it must have seemed that the diggers' fight was over. Yet this was still not to be. One more deliberate act of armed defiance played out before the stockade defenders finally conceded. Irishman Patrick Curtain's pikemen had been previously posted in the southern upper part of the stockade, facing the Melbourne Road. They had held their ground when those diggers who fled had rushed out of the stockade. As the soldiers came up to and then began to cross the palisade, Curtain's men moved towards the redcoats. Private John Neill of the 40th Regiment recalled that these pikemen 'fought well and fierce, not a word spoken on either side until all was over'. Courageous as it was, the pikemen's efforts were forlorn and casualties among them were severe. One source claimed that they were the hardest hit of all the groups within the stockade.[84]

By this time the soldiers and the police on foot were amongst the tents, pits and battle wreckage littering the interior of the stockade. With the resistance of their enemies effectively broken, and in the manner of soldiers who have overcome a determined foe since time immemorial, they set on their defeated enemy mercilessly. Having met stiffer resistance than expected, and with numerous casualties among their comrades as well as two fallen officers, the redcoats' blood was up and their killing instincts for the moment went unchecked. Those defenders who had not managed to run quickly enough, or who had stood their ground to fight it out, fell under the thrusting, stabbing tide.

The stockade had fallen. Those defenders who had not fled were captured, shot, bayoneted or put to the sword. All about lay corpses and wounded men, many horribly scarred and pierced numerous times.[85] Yet it must be remembered that the multiple wounds inflicted on many of the diggers, even after they had been killed, were entirely consistent with the normal military practice of the time to ensure that a fallen foe was actually dead. This was a lesson learned the hard way by British troops in colonial wars such as in India, where enemies would often feign death before 'resurrecting' themselves behind British troops who had passed over them. Thus the practice of multiple wounding became ingrained into the infantryman's culture. To emphasise that this was not a mindlessly brutal exercise unique to Eureka, it is worth noting that a similar practice was carried out by Australian troops fighting the Japanese during World War II.

The exact casualty figures at Eureka remain uncertain. What is certain is that many more than the 22 diggers on Lalor's list died. There were 21 unidentified bodies, in addition to the 22 on Lalor's list, buried after Eureka, making the number of digger dead at least 43. Military casualties are equally uncertain, despite the common claim of only five killed. In any case, once the fighting was over officers began reasserting control over the soldiery and set the troops to rounding up prisoners before handing them over to the police. The soldiers and police then set fire to some tents and many slabs, charring some bodies – the genesis of later unfounded stories that the soldiers and police has deliberately burned men alive.[86] Finally the bugle sounded 'Assembly'. Discipline reimposed, the redcoats formed their ranks outside the stockade and marched away, dragging the Southern Cross flag as a trophy of war behind them.[87]

At Eureka two parties, equally resolved to prevail over their adversary by force of arms, had clashed. The combat was ferocious and the consequences bloody, but all completely consistent with the military mores of the times. In later years Michael Tuohy, one of the most stalwart of the stockade's defenders, soberly observed that 'anything was fair in war time, and we should take what we get and bear it'.[88] The battle for the Eureka stockade was no massacre of helpless innocents. Yet nor was it an inconsequential civil disturbance to be dismissed and demeaned as of little importance. It remains to this day a unique example within the Australian context of truly contested civilian armed resistance to obnoxious authority, and if for no other reason than that it rightfully deserves the iconic place it holds in the Australian story.

Further reading

Outbreak at Eureka: The Eureka Story from the Pages of the Mount Alexander Mail, 8 December 1854, Ballarat Heritage Services, Ballarat, 1998

J Allan (ed), *The Eureka Uprising, by Eye-witness Richard Allan*, Hobart, 2004

H Anderson (ed), *Eureka: Victorian Parliamentary Papers, Votes and Proceedings 1854–1867*, Red Rooster Press, 1999

G Blake, *Eureka Stockade: A Ferocious and Bloody Battle*, Big Sky, Sydney, 2012

R Carboni, *The Eureka Stockade*, Miegunyah Press, Melbourne, 2004

J Corfield, D Wickham and C Gervasoni, *The Eureka Encyclopaedia*, Ballarat Heritage Services, Ballarat, 2004

G Hocking, *Eureka Stockade: The Events Leading up to the Attack in the Pre-Dawn of 3 December 1854*, Five Mile Press, Melbourne, 2004

W Howitt, Land, *Labour and Gold: Or Two Years in Victoria with Visits to Sydney and Van Diemen's Land*, Lowden, Kilmore, 1972 (orig 1855)

W Kelly, *Life in Victoria: or Victoria in 1853 and Victoria in 1858*, Lowden, Kilmore, 1977

J Lynch, *Story of the Eureka Stockade: Epic Days of the Early Fifties at Ballarat*, Goldfields Heritage Publications, Ballarat, 1999

J Molony, *Eureka*, Viking, Melbourne, 1984

C Turnbull, *Eureka: The Story of Peter Lalor*, Hawthorn Press, Melbourne, 1946

D Wickham, *Deaths at Eureka*, Wickham, Ballarat, 1996

5

Australian naval defence

GREG SWINDEN

The Royal Australian Navy (RAN) has always prided itself on being the 'senior service'. It is equally well known as the 'silent service', getting on with the job of protecting Australia and its interests quietly and unobtrusively. While Australia has benefitted greatly from this, the fact remains that for most Australians the military history of this country remains just that – a *military* history. The role that the colonial and Australian navies played in the protection and development of the nation is scarcely known and even less well understood. Indeed, for a nation where 90 per cent of the population lives on or within 100 kilometres of the coast, it is an oddity that most Australians look inland and cling to the myths of the pioneering bushmen and women, bushrangers and the trench-bound mud and blood imagery of Anzac as the icons of our history. William Morris Hughes, Australian prime minister from 1915 to 1923, claimed that Australia was born on the shores of Gallipoli. Many modern Australians tend to swallow this tale.

The reality of Australian nationhood, however, is a much different story – and one that has more to do with the sea than it does the land. Right from the start, Britain's Royal Navy played a pivotal role in discovery and founding Australia, and few would dispute James Cook's or the early naval governors' equally iconic and vital roles in the creation of a British penal colony at the bottom of the world. The reality was even more subtle than this, for the establishment of a British colony in New South Wales was as much about creating a permanent presence in the South Pacific, to counter French ambitions, as it was about dumping Britain's unwanted felons. For the century and a quarter between the arrival of the First Fleet to the landing at Gallipoli, Australia was of major maritime importance, and the role that various navies, British and colonial, played in developing the country from a loose collection of British colonies into a federated nation is one well worth the telling.

No navy is created overnight. That Australia had a strongly equipped and well trained navy on the eve of World War I was no accident. Instead it was the product of nearly 60 years of hard work by generations of Australian and British seafarers and politicians. In the beginning, for much of Australia's early years, its defence rested solely with the Royal Navy. His Majesty's Ships *Sirius* and *Supply* escorted the First Fleet to Botany Bay in 1788, while Royal Navy Marines guarded convicts once the settlement was established. The first four governors of New South Wales were naval officers, and ships of the Royal Navy regularly visited the east coast colony. In 1821 the 'Australia Station' was formally established with a ship detached from the East India Squadron for service off the east coast at regular intervals. Royal Navy ships were permanently based in Sydney from 1859.

Throughout this early period officers and ships of the Royal Navy also continued exploration of the continent and began the important survey work to chart the coastlines of Australia and New Guinea. Commander Matthew Flinders, for example, circumnavigated the continent in the leaky HMS *Investigator* between 1801 and 1803, produced the first map to show the whole landmass, and famously named it 'Australia'. Captain James Bremer chose the location of the first British settlement in northern Australia, at Fort Dundas on Melville Island in 1824, and Captain James Stirling established the Swan River colony at what is now Perth in 1829. Between 1837 and 1839, the survey vessel HMS *Beagle*, under the command of Captain John Wickham, explored and surveyed Australian waters with the now famous naturalist Charles Darwin on board. On 9 September 1839 Wickham sailed the *Beagle* into what is now Port Darwin, and named it in honour of the naturalist whose later works had such a dramatic impact on natural science. Ten years later, Captain Owen Stanley RN, in command of HMS *Rattlesnake*, conducted the first British survey of the south coast of New Guinea, naming the prominent mountain range after himself. Many of the coastal features and mountain ranges in Australia and New Guinea were named by naval officers conducting similar surveys.

Apart from exploration and the charting of the coastlines to aid in the safe navigation of merchant shipping, during this period British warships were also present to keep an eye on the many French, Russian and American vessels which frequented the southern Pacific Ocean. The visit by five US Navy warships to Sydney in late November 1839 was of particular interest as they arrived under the cover of darkness and anchored in Port Jackson without the knowledge of the local authorities. When they were sighted the next morning there was much consternation, and Commodore Charles Wilkes (commanding the US squadron) stated to the local press: 'Had war existed, we might, after firing the shipping, and reducing the great part of the town to ashes, have effected a retreat before daybreak, in perfect safety'.[1] His words were not to be forgotten. Continuing the military role of British ships in this period, and following the British annexation of New Zealand in 1840, tensions between the increasing number of white settlers and Māori led to the Northern War of 1845–1846. Royal Navy warships were involved in transporting troops to the North Island to put down the uprising, and British sailors were also involved in the fighting ashore.

By 1860 the colonies of New South Wales, Tasmania, Victoria, South Australia, Western Australia and Queensland had been created. In 1855, New South Wales, Tasmania and Victoria were granted responsible government, quickly followed by South Australia in 1857 and Queensland in 1859. Such political developments – along with the discovery of large sources of gold in New South Wales and Victoria in the early 1850s, which caused a dramatic increase in the wealth and population in both colonies, and the outbreak of the Crimean War in 1854 between Great Britain and Russia – were the catalyst for the creation of what was to become the colonial navies, and in due course the RAN. Suddenly the colonies had substantial funds to spend and a potential enemy who might wish to attack them – and the ships carrying the gold to Britain. Russian warships had been regular visitors to the South Pacific and Southern Ocean on voyages of exploration, but it was now thought they might come south for more sinister reasons. Colonial politicians grew concerned that perhaps the ships of the Royal Navy would not always be available to defend the colonies when most needed.

In 1855, as a result of these domestic security concerns, the New South Wales government commenced construction on a fort on Pinchgut, a small barren island in Sydney Harbour. It also built a 62-foot ketch named *Spitfire*, mounted with a single 32-pounder gun and crewed by men of the Sydney Naval Volunteers. While the fort on Pinchgut – later Fort Denison – was under construction, *Spitfire* patrolled the entrance to Port Jackson to deter any enemy warships that might try to enter. Fort Denison was not completed until 1857, a year after the Crimean War had ended, and *Spitfire* went north to Queensland in 1859 to be used by the newly created Queensland government as a pilot vessel. Australia's first locally built warship thus had a short life, and the defence of Sydney was left to a mid-harbour island fortress and coastal shore batteries. The Sydney Naval Volunteers were disbanded, but a few years later in 1863 a New South Wales Naval Brigade was formed and continued as a reserve force until Federation in 1901.

Further south, the Victorian government had grander designs. In July 1854, prompted by their new lieutenant governor, Sir Charles Hotham (another former naval officer), the colonial government ordered the construction in England of a steam sloop to be named *Victoria*. She was launched in June 1855 and arrived in Melbourne in May 1856, heralding the birth of the Victorian Navy. Her Majesty's Colonial Ship (HMCS) *Victoria* carried a variety of muzzle-loading guns and saw active service until the mid-1880s. In 1858 she assisted with surveying work in Bass Strait for the planned laying of the first submarine telegraph cable between Victoria and Tasmania. In July of the same year she sailed on a relief mission to Rockhampton in Queensland to repatriate gold prospectors to Sydney. *Victoria* also took an active part in the Taranaki War in New Zealand in 1860–61 as a 'loan' to the governor of New Zealand. As will be recounted in the next chapter, *Victoria* spent ten months transporting supplies as well as British troops and volunteers from the Australian colonies, who were regularly landed ashore to fight alongside the British Naval Brigade. She also patrolled the coast to prevent arms and ammunition smuggling to support the Māori. *Victoria* returned to her home port of Melbourne in April 1861. (In 2010, some 150 years later, the battle honour New Zealand 1860–61 was awarded to the RAN in recognition of *Victoria*'s role in this campaign.) Quite soon after the conflict *Victoria*'s crew busied themselves in the Gulf of Carpentaria, searching for the missing Burke and Wills expedition. While the explorers were not found, Captain William

Norman did give his name to the Norman River, on which the current town of Normanton now stands.

Victoria's participation in the New Zealand War prompted the Victorian government to pass the *Armed Vessels Regulation Act* 1860, allowing recognition of her crew as having served in war. The British government quickly disallowed this Act, however, but its action raised the question of what was to be done about the colonies raising their own forces. The British government's concern was whether another nation, under international law, would recognise a colonial vessel as a British warship with the right to wage war and capture enemy shipping in Britain's name. (This matter had, in fact, been raised a few years before, for in September 1856 the New South Wales governor, Sir William Denison, had proposed that each colony pay half the cost of maintaining the Royal Navy ships on the Australia Station.) The Admiralty was not amused. It would not be dictated to by the colonies which, if paying half the cost of the ships, might then expect that they had some say in forming naval policy.

The cold hard reality of fiscal policy finally overcame the issue. In 1862, the Mills Committee recommended that each British colony contribute financially to its own defence. The *Imperial Colonial Naval Defence Act* 1865 was passed by the British parliament, authorising each self-governing colony to raise naval forces and legitimising the existing Victorian and New South Wales permanent naval forces – or as one historian put it: 'thus making an honest woman out of HMCS *Victoria* at long last'.[2]

Under these new arrangements, the British government still accepted that it had a responsibility for the overall naval defence of each colony, but it now allowed the legal right for a colony to form its own naval forces for local coastal defence. New South Wales had the luxury of Sydney being the main Australasian port for the ships of the Royal Navy (and thus assured of naval protection), and it was therefore reluctant to spend money on naval defence beyond its Naval Brigade and fixed gun batteries. Victoria, on the other hand, commenced spending to acquire more ships, manned by permanent crews augmented by volunteers of the Victorian Naval Reserve.

In February 1868, the Victorian government acquired the elderly British wooden battleship HMS *Nelson* for use as a training ship. Construction also began in England, in September 1867, of a modern iron monitor to defend Port Phillip Bay from possible enemy attack. Named *Cerberus*, after the three-headed dog that guards the gates of hell in ancient Greek mythology, she was completed in May 1870, and by early October Her Majesty's Victorian Ship (HMVS) *Cerberus* sailed for Australia. Permanently manned by 12 officers and 84 ratings of the Victorian Navy, she arrived in Port Phillip Bay on 9 April 1871 and, while described by some as squat and ugly, she was the most modern warship in Australian waters. *Cerberus* went on to serve in the Victorian Navy, the later Commonwealth Naval Forces (CNF) and the RAN from 1870 until 1921. Upon decommissioning her name was transferred to the newly opened Flinders Naval Depot at Westernport, thereby creating an unbroken lineage of the name from 1870 to the present day. So by early 1871 the Victorian Navy had three vessels, *Cerberus*, *Nelson* and *Victoria*, although the latter was often relegated to survey duties in Bass Strait and Port Phillip Bay.

In the mid-1870s the New South Wales government decided to invest in ships for the defence of Sydney Harbour. By this time Sydney was well defended by forts, manned by the Permanent Artillery, on the headlands at the entrance to the harbour. A war scare – between Russia and Britain in 1877 – and the frequent absence of the ships of the Australian Squadron from their main base, combined to encourage the colonial government to create its own sea-going force. Two second class torpedo boats were built, using a British design, at Pyrmont in Sydney. The *Acheron* and *Avernus* (named after ancient Greek and Roman mythological waterways that led to the underworld) commenced service in early 1878. Volunteers of the NSW Naval Brigade – effectively naval infantry – were based in Sydney and Newcastle, but a special company named the NSW Torpedo and Signalling Corps was raised to operate the new vessels. These vessels were armed with a 62-foot spar torpedo – which required the torpedo boat to get very close to their opponent before firing the weapon! In the 1880s these were replaced by two 14-inch torpedoes, driven by compressed air, which could be launched from the vessels, thus enabling the torpedo boats to mount their attack from a much safer distance.

From this point the New South Wales naval force gradually grew. In 1882 it acquired the old wooden corvette *Wolverine* from the Royal Navy as a sea-going training ship for the Naval Brigade. *Wolverine* spent most of her time at anchor in Sydney Harbour, but did conduct training cruises to Newcastle, Port Stephens and Jervis Bay in the late 1880s and early 1890s. By 1892 she was no longer financially viable and decommissioned. *Avernus* and *Acheron* saw regular service throughout the 1880s and 1890s, but were limited to operations within Sydney Harbour. With Federation in 1901 both vessels were transferred to the CNF, but by this stage they were truly obsolete and were sold in 1902. A number of other auxiliary vessels were intermittently operated by the New South Wales naval forces and Submarine Mining Corps during the 1880s and 1890s, but they were effectively civilian vessels on which guns were installed and operated by Naval Artillery Volunteers during the annual Easter training exercises. A motion to purchase an ironclad monitor, similar to *Cerberus*, was raised in 1878, but with local politicians and the public quite comfortable under the protective naval umbrella of the Royal Navy fleet, the scant defence funds available were directed to the military forces instead. Ultimately the New South Wales naval forces in the late colonial period, comprising 500 men, were very much an adjunct to the military, and devoted almost entirely to the defence of Sydney and Newcastle harbours.

Despite concerns that the Royal Naval squadron, based at Garden Island in Sydney, would not be available to defend the Australian colonies when required, that squadron spent much of its time in Australian waters. Sydney also provided significant logistics support to the Royal Navy, with a major dockyard at Cockatoo Island comprising the Fitzroy graving dock, completed in 1857, and the larger Sutherland graving dock from 1890. The Royal Navy powder magazine and armament depot was built at nearby Spectacle Island (adjacent to the Sydney suburb of Drummoyne), in 1884. Overall, the port of Sydney offered the Royal Navy its best port and logistics facilities in the southern hemisphere. The British were unlikely to forsake Sydney's protection, and by default the protection of the other Australian colonies.

Further north, the Queensland government created a Naval Brigade in 1883 and based detachments at the colony's main ports. The Queensland Marine Defence Force formed the following year and soon acquired a number of vessels. These included the gunboats *Gayundah* and *Paluma*, the second-class torpedo boat *Mosquito* – Queensland's first warship – and the picket boat *Midge*. Like *Mosquito*, *Gayundah* and *Paluma* were also built in England, arriving in Brisbane in early 1885. Originally one Queensland gunboat was to be based at Thursday Island and the other in Moreton Bay, but this soon changed with both operating out of Brisbane. Queensland also used civilian vessels retrofitted as auxiliary gunboats or armed launches when the situation and finances allowed. A mine-laying tender, with the unimaginative name of *Miner*, was also acquired for use by the army for laying submarine mines across the mouth of the Brisbane River.

The Queensland Marine Defence Force stood out from the other colonial navies by the frequency and distance of the training cruises undertaken. Throughout the 1880s and early 1890s, gunboats regularly conducted training cruises to the northern Queensland ports of Maryborough, Bundaberg, Rockhampton, Townsville, Cairns and Thursday Island. They also exercised with the naval brigades in each port. *Paluma* spent several years on loan to the Royal Navy, as a survey vessel in northern Australian waters, before being returned to the Queensland government in 1895. During the lean financial times of the mid-1890s *Gayundah* was laid up, but not decommissioned. Her sister gunboat *Paluma* gained some notoriety in February 1893 when she was washed ashore into the Botanical Gardens in Brisbane during a flood. There she sat, high and dry, for several weeks – until another flood refloated her and she was towed back into the Brisbane River. In 1901 both gunboats became part of the CNF. In the early 1900s the Queensland government also started a naval cadet force of boys aged 12–17. The first in the colonies, this scheme was later introduced in the other states.

A little behind the lead of the eastern colonies, the colonial government in Adelaide grew concerned in the early 1880s that, should the Royal Navy be otherwise engaged, South Australia was at risk from foreign commerce raiders. The government promptly ordered the cruiser *Protector*, which was laid down in Britain in December 1882 and arrived in South Australia in September 1884 – the one and only ship of the South Australian Naval Forces. This situation led to a sarcastic remark from a visiting French naval officer: 'A one ship navy? Then you are in no danger of collisions in your fleet.'[3] South Australia also formed a small naval brigade of volunteers who could augment

Protector's crew, and it invested in coastal forts. *Protector*'s service was for many years quite ordinary: she was based at Port Adelaide and conducted regular patrols in Spencer Gulf. Although what we now know as the Northern Territory was then part of South Australia, until 1911 there was no South Australian naval presence in the north. In 1901, *Protector* also joined the newly formed CNF.

More importantly for the South Australian Navy, and ultimately for the future RAN, was the appointment of a retired Royal Navy officer as *Protector*'s second-in-command in 1885. Lieutenant William Rooke Creswell later went on to command *Protector*, not to mention the South Australian Navy (1893–1900), the Queensland Marine Defence Force (1900–04), the Victorian naval forces from 20 October 1904 and, concurrently, the CNF (1904–11) and finally the RAN (1911–19). Creswell had joined the Royal Navy as a 13-year-old cadet in 1866. After varied service around the globe, including suppressing the slave trade on the east coast of Africa where he was wounded, he retired from the navy with the rank of lieutenant in 1878. He joined his younger brother in Australia where they operated a cattle station in the Northern Territory until joining the South Australian Navy in 1885. While Creswell had his critics, it was ultimately his vision, coupled with a good measure of hard work and stubbornness, that in time saw the creation of the RAN and his well-deserved title as the 'father of the Royal Australian Navy'.

Unsurprisingly, Tasmania had the smallest of the colonial navies. It was not really a navy at all but a Torpedo Corps of soldiers who never numbered more then 70 volunteers. Although the Tasmanian parliament had agreed to purchase a gunboat for the harbour defence of Hobart in 1859, nothing was done until a second-class torpedo boat was ordered from England in March 1883. The vessel was christened *Torpedo Boat Number 191* and she kept the name TB 191 for the rest of her unspectacular career. Housed in a boatshed and launched from a 160-foot slipway, she had a crew of ten and carried out exercises and survey work in the Derwent River, but more often lay dormant due to lack of funds. In 1900, TB 191 was retired, and five years later was sold to South Australia. She was towed to Port Adelaide, but saw little service and was disposed of in 1910.

Of all the Australian colonies, only Western Australia did not purchase any warships, but in 1879 it did form a small unit known as the Fremantle Naval Volunteers. This unit was purely for the defence of the port of Fremantle, but was transferred to the army in 1888. Some Western Australian government ships performed a civil role, charting the rugged West Australian coast.

Alone among these varying efforts, only Victoria truly took to creating its own navy, and by the mid-1880s it was the most powerful and well equipped of them all. While *Victoria* had been relegated to survey duties, and the elderly *Nelson* served as a harbour depot ship, the monitor *Cerberus* guarded Port Phillip Bay. She was to be joined in 1884 by the gunboats *Albert* and *Victoria* (the second ship to carry this name), the first-class torpedo boat *Childers*, and the second-class torpedo boats *Lonsdale* and *Nepean*. Another torpedo launch *Gordon*, named after General Charles Gordon who was killed in the Sudan in 1884, arrived in 1885; and yet another, the *Countess of Hopetoun*, steamed from England to Melbourne in 1892. The Victorian Navy had also created a second naval depot at Williamstown, and the nearby Alfred Graving Dock for warship maintenance was completed in September 1873. Ashore, the Victorian Navy still trained its reservists in seamanship and as naval infantry. The Victorians also employed several vessels as auxiliaries and fitted them with guns and torpedoes when required. The colonial government also purchased mines, and established a mine depot at Swan Island near the entrance to Port Phillip Bay. Minelayers were employed to lay the mines which were stretched in a boom-style fashion across the entrance to the bay and could be electronically detonated.

The Victorian and New South Wales navies' minor involvement in the Sudan campaign in 1884–85 requires further mention, with particular attention on three boats. In February 1884, the Victorian gunboats *Albert* and *Victoria*, and the torpedo boat *Childers*, left England, steaming across the Mediterranean *en route* to Melbourne. After arriving at Malta news was received of heavy fighting in the Sudan, where British forces were attempting to relieve General Gordon and his forces besieged at Khartoum. The Victorian government quickly offered the use of its vessels to Britain, which accepted the offer. All three vessels were directed to sail to Suakin, the main British port on the Red Sea, to join the Royal Navy Squadron operating there. They departed Malta on 8 March 1884 and travelled via Crete and Port Said before arriving at Suakin on 19 March. The warships had encountered rough weather in the Red Sea and, after taking water down her funnels, *Childers* had to be taken in tow by *Victoria*. After all this effort, on their arrival at Suakin the British decided the Victorian ships were no longer required, as the fighting had now moved inland. The three warships departed on 23 March 1884 and proceeded to Aden. They eventually reached Melbourne on 25 June 1884 after a delivery voyage of nearly five months.

Almost exactly a year later, Australian forces were back in the Sudan when a specially raised contingent of 770 men from New South Wales (consisting of infantry, artillery and ambulance personnel) was sent to join the British forces at Suakin where they served from 29 March to 18 May 1885 (see Chapter 9). Several men from that colony's Naval Brigade were allowed to join this army contingent, and upon return to Australia rejoined the Naval

Brigade. Several more went on to serve in the Boxer Rebellion in 1900–01, and few even 'sailored on' into the RAN.

The Australia-wide depression of the 1890s affected all six colonies, and the various navies soon found their activities curtailed. Ships were disposed of, laid up in reserve, or confined to harbour. At the same time, however, the question of the continent's defence, including naval defence, gave impetus to the Federation movement. The perceived threats from the north – from the Dutch (in the Netherlands East Indies); the French in New Caledonia; the Germans in their new colonies in the Pacific and New Guinea; and the Japanese, who had defeated China in the war of 1894–95 – was of major concern to a disparate group of English-speaking colonies far from mother England.

In reality the threat of attack was low, but the Royal Navy was still concerned that the isolated colonial navies would be vulnerable to a determined enemy and could be destroyed piecemeal. The colonial ships were of varying types, of dubious capability, and manned by officers and men whom the Admiralty considered poorly equipped and inadequately trained. The various colonial premiers were still concerned that the Royal Navy ships might be deployed elsewhere if troubles arose in Australian waters. As a result, in late 1884 Admiral Sir George Tryon, who was to command the Australia Station from 1885 to 1887, was directed by the Admiralty to commence negotiations with the colonial governors and premiers regarding naval defence. Tryon put forward the plan for a special Australasian Auxiliary Squadron in addition to the Royal Navy ships already on the Australia Station. The individual colonies were to pay 5 per cent of the ships' construction costs, and 100 per cent of their maintenance and manning costs.

Although these ships were commissioned by the Royal Navy, and under the full control of the admiral commanding the Australia Station, they could not be employed outside of the Station without the consent of the colonial governments. The agreement was to last for ten years, would not affect the existing colonial navies, and two of the seven vessels were to be stationed in New Zealand waters. The colonies agreed, and the *Australasian Naval Defence Act* took effect in 1887. Five third-class protected cruisers of 2575 tonnes, then being built in Britain, were re-named *Katoomba*, *Mildura*, *Ringarooma*, *Tauranga* and *Wallaroo*. Two torpedo gunboats of 750 tonnes were re-named *Boomerang* and *Karrakatta*. Their service was generally mundane, living up to the Australia Station's nickname of the 'social station', although ships from the squadron did see occasional active deployment, such as *Tauranga*'s involvement in maintaining order in Samoa during an outbreak of tribal fighting in 1899, and *Wallaroo*'s dispatch to China in 1900 during the Boxer Rebellion. The last of the Auxiliary Squadron departed Australian waters for Britain in 1906, the *Australasian Naval Defence Act* having expired on Federation. In 1903 a new Naval Agreement was passed, ensuring the continued funding by the Australian government (at £200 000 per annum) for British warships on the Australia Station.

The Royal Navy provided the real defence of the Australian colonies through the colonial and into the early Federation period. Individual colonies continued to invest in local naval and military forces, and by 1901 the Commonwealth had a polyglot of naval and land forces of mixed capability and ability. Australia still hid behind Queen Victoria's imposing apron of world-wide naval strength and red-coated (later khaki-clad) soldiers standing guard in far-flung colonies. The next 12 years, however, saw a watershed for Australian defence, as the British Empire's naval and military forces found themselves stretched to the limit and the calls for Australia to take greater responsibility for her own defence became louder.

By 1900, Britain found itself conducting ongoing constabulary duties and fighting small wars across the length and breadth of the empire, the 'thin red line' becoming increasingly thinner. In 1899 the war against the Boer republics of the Transvaal and Orange Free State broke out in southern Africa, and the British had some difficulty in defeating the irregular forces. Offers from the Australian colonies to provide troops were gratefully accepted, and by war's end in 1902, over 16 000 Australians had served in South Africa (see Chapter 9). Only one Australian naval officer saw formal service in the South African campaign. The 40-year-old Lieutenant William Jarvie Colquhoun of the Victorian Navy was serving onboard the Victorian troopship SS *Medic* in 1899. As the vessel's sea transport officer, he was responsible for overseeing the embarkation and disembarkation of troops, horses and equipment. On arrival in South Africa in late 1899, Colquhoun left the ship and attached himself to a Royal Navy Brigade which had been landed from various warships to provide artillery support to the army. These naval brigades were commonplace in imperial Britain and were formed from ships' crews operating ships' guns on hastily prepared gun carriages. Colquhoun commanded one of the naval brigade 12-pounder field guns, and saw action at Magersfontein (December 1899), the relief of Kimberley (February 1900), Paardeberg (the last major conventional battle of the war, in February 1900), Driefontein (March 1900) and the capture of Bloemfontein, capital of the Orange Free State (March 1900). For his bravery and resourcefulness in keeping his gun in action over several months, despite heavy wear and tear, he was awarded the Distinguished Service Order. After his return to Australia he became the naval aide de camp to the governor-general and in 1904 was granted leave to travel to Japan as the special naval correspondent for the *Times* during the Russo-Japanese war. Colquhuon subsequently became a commander in the CNF, and was in command of *Gayundah* when he died onboard in Sydney Harbour in August 1908.

Colquhoun was not, however, the only Australian in naval uniform to serve in the South African War. Cymberline Alonso Edric Huddart, for example, was born in Melbourne in 1881 and educated in Ballarat. His father, James Huddart, was part-owner of the shipping line of Huddart-Parker and, in 1895 young Cymberline joined the Royal Navy, entering Britannia Royal Naval College as a cadet. By late 1899 he was a midshipman serving in the cruiser HMS *Doris* on the South African Station. Huddart was selected be part of the naval brigade, and on 25 November 1899 he took part in the heavy fighting at Graspan, where he was severely wounded. The 18-year-old Huddart died of his wounds later that day, and was posthumously award the Conspicuous Service Cross in July 1901. He was one of the first Australians to die in South Africa.

It was at the other end of the British Empire, however, and in a conflict which is hardly remembered at all in Australia, that the colonies' naval forces found themselves in a larger-scale action. For many years China had been effectively controlled by a collection of foreign powers, including Britain, the United States, Germany, France, Italy, Austria-Hungary and Japan. The Chinese government was ineffectual and control of most of the country lay either with the foreign powers or brutal local warlords. A strong Chinese nationalist movement formed in the late 1890s, however, and among these was the Society of Righteous and Harmonious Fists – otherwise known as the Boxers. In May 1900 the Boxers commenced a large and co-ordinated uprising across northern China, and the foreign legations at Peking were besieged. With the bulk of its military forces committed to the fighting in South Africa, the British government gratefully accepted an offer of naval forces from the Australian colonies. South Australia sent the gunboat *Protector* (under the command of Captain Creswell) which was commissioned in the Royal Navy in September 1900. *Protector* operated in the Gulf of Chihli and was used mainly to move men and stores between the Royal Navy ships at sea and various Chinese ports, as well as carrying dispatches for the British admiral in command. She returned to Australia in December 1900. Queensland also offered her gunboats *Gayundah* and *Paluma*, but the Royal Navy politely rejected them as 'too old and slow' to be of much use.

Victoria and New South Wales each offered a Naval Brigade for service in China, and the offer of this 'naval infantry' was quickly accepted. The New South Wales contingent comprised 250 reservists, Victoria's a 200-man brigade of both permanent and reserve personnel. These combined naval brigades departed Australia in August 1900, but by the time they arrived in China in mid-September, the siege of the legations had been lifted and the fighting throughout northern China became more sporadic as the Boxers were hunted down and executed. The Naval Brigades saw little fighting and were employed in a variety of peace enforcement and civil administration duties as part of the coalition of foreign forces serving in northern China. After enduring a bleak winter, they returned home in April 1901. In 2010 the battle honour China 1900 was awarded to the RAN for this campaign.

Several of these recently returned men were then granted leave to enlist in military forces for service in South Africa. Among them was Midshipman (later Rear Admiral) Leighton Seymour Bracegirdle, from the New South Wales Naval Brigade, who served in the South African Irregular Horse. He later also saw active service in RAN units in German New Guinea (1914–1915) and Gallipoli (1915), and retired in 1947 as the military and official secretary to the governor-general.

The return of the naval brigades from China also opened a

new stage for the naval defence of Australia. On 1 March 1901, following Federation, the Commonwealth had assumed all responsibility for the naval and military defence of the continent. Captain Creswell, then commandant of the Queensland Marine Defence Force, was selected for daunting position of Director of the Naval Forces. He inherited a mixed bag of ships, about 240 regular personnel, and hundreds more reservists and cadets from the naval brigades. Some ships were clearly obsolete and were quickly disposed of, while others, such as *Cerberus*, *Protector*, *Gayundah*, *Paluma*, *Childers* and *Countess of Hopetoun*, were still useful and retained accordingly.

The Naval Agreement Bill of 1901 confirmed the Australian government's desire for the Royal Navy Squadron to continue to maintain the naval defence of the nation. The Bill still provided £200 000 per year to Britain for the ships and men, and debate commenced in earnest as to whether the former colonial naval forces should become a fully fledged Australia navy or be subsumed into an Australian branch of the Royal Navy Reserve. Each side had its advocates and, as ever, money was the principal driver – could Australia afford to go it alone and provide its own navy? Creswell thought yes, and he wrote several papers on the subject and lobbied his political masters, but his opponents were many both in Australia and Britain. The discussion continued over the next eight years at various imperial conferences. Creswell, however, never swayed in his determination to create an Australian navy, and eventually gained the support of both sides of politics, in particular Alfred Deakin and Andrew Fisher, who both held the prime ministership several times in the Federation period. So too, George Foster Pearce, Minister for Defence in 1908–09 and 1910–13, was another keen advocate for an entirely Australian navy.

Following the 1902 Colonial Conference in London, the

Naval Agreement Acts of 1902 and 1903 committed the Admiralty to provide training facilities in the Royal Navy for a reserve of Australian and New Zealand naval volunteers. It was to comprise some 33 officers and 700 men. This would eventually form a core of trained men who could be accessed by the new Australian navy. Thus the Australasian Naval Force (ANF) was formed and it started recruiting in May 1904. The first recruit, 15-year-old John Clubb, of Balmain, received service number '1'. Over the next ten years, another 1795 boys and men from Australia and New Zealand were enlisted in the ANF. These men were effectively Royal Navy ratings who signed on for an initial period of five years service, and served mainly in the Royal Navy ships of the Australia Squadron. They were also sent to England for training at the various Royal Navy bases. Notably, 35 ANF ratings undergoing training in Britain and one CNF officer on exchange duty were present at the coronation of King George V in May 1911, and they were subsequently awarded the Coronation Medal. In the 1890s the Royal Navy also began to accept selected Australian boys into the naval service to be trained as officers. These boys were from families which could afford the high costs of officer training in England, and many of these men later served in the RAN. By early 1913, hundreds of ANF personnel were still serving in the Royal Navy and when they were formally transferred to the RAN most were allocated as commissioning crews to the RAN's newly built ships and submarines. This was a highly successful scheme as it provided the RAN with a ready source of highly trained Australians just as the first of its modern ships were being commissioned.

Finally the *Commonwealth Defence Act* 1903 came into effect on 1 March 1904 and the following year the Commonwealth Naval Board was formed to oversee the new Commonwealth Naval Forces. The board initially comprised the Minister for

Defence, the Director of Naval Forces and a Finance Member. The activities of the CNF were limited in these early years due to funding, but it still conducted regular training cruises and maintenance when finances permitted. In 1903 *Gayundah* took part in experimental wireless telegraphy communication between a station at Kangaroo Point and the ship which operated in Moreton Bay. This was the first use of wireless telegraphy in an Australian warship. The *Wireless Telegraphy Act* 1905 was enacted to regulate the use of this medium between shore stations and ships at sea. The first military wireless activities did not take place until March 1910 during an annual training camp at Heathcote, New South Wales.

At the April 1907 Imperial Conference on the naval and military defence of the empire, Prime Minister Deakin and Captain Creswell put forward their plans for an independent naval defence force for Australia. They met with substantial opposition from the British government, and in particular from First Sea Lord Admiral Sir 'Jacky' Fisher. Fisher saw little benefit in an independent Australian Navy, and pushed Australia to limit itself to coastal destroyers and submarines, for local defence, and leave the main defence of Australia to the Royal Navy's Australia Squadron. Upon his return to Australia, Deakin was criticised in both the press and political circles for what was seen as giving in to British pressure. Australian nationalism was on the rise and a strong navy was seen by many as part of the nation's rite of passage to being recognised as a strong modern nation.

Deakin further upset the British government in January 1908, when he directly invited the United States' government to send its 'Great White Fleet' to visit Australia later that year as part of a planned world tour. Only after the invitation had been sent did Deakin use 'normal channels' to advise the British Colonial Office of Australia's intentions. The British were not pleased, but it was too late to withdraw the invitation. For today's reader it would seem odd that Australia, after Federation, was still required to gain British approval for such an activity, but the shackles of Empire still bound the nation very closely to Britain. The visit of the American fleet of 16 white-painted battleships took place in August and September 1908, with the fleet visiting Sydney and Melbourne to great pomp and ceremony. Overall the visit was a great success, and further enhanced the debate for Australia to form its own navy. The American visit also came at a time when there were increasing concerns regarding Japanese and German expansion in the Pacific. However, in November 1908 Deakin's government fell and he was replaced as prime minister by Andrew Fisher.

Fisher was also well aware of the national concerns regarding defence, and in early 1909 he allocated funding for the building of three modern torpedo boat destroyers for the CNF, noting this was money already allocated to naval defence by Deakin. Two of the destroyers (*Parramatta* and *Yarra*) were to be built in England while the third (*Warrego*) was to be pre-fabricated and the pieces shipped to Australia for assembly at Cockatoo Island Dockyard. The three ships became the first new vessels built for the Australian Navy in decades, and when her keel was laid in March 1909 *Parramatta* earned the title 'first-born of the Commonwealth Navy'.

The matter concerning the future of the Australian Navy came to a head in July 1909 at the Imperial Conference in London. The outcome was a change of heart by the British government, which had become more concerned about maritime defence of the Pacific region. There had been a growing belief among British policy-makers that each colony in the Empire needed to be part of its general defence. The naval arms race between Britain and Germany was now well under way, and if the Australians were prepared to fund their own navy, as part of the ultimate defence of the British Empire, then they should be allowed to do so. Germany maintained a squadron of six cruisers at her colony in Tsingtao (China), there were also concerns that Japan's naval might was also growing, and that Britain's naval strength in the Pacific might be challenged. In August 1909 discussions between both governments ensued. The end result was the Australian government agreed to fund the construction of a Fleet Unit consisting of a battle cruiser, three cruisers, six destroyers and three submarines at a cost of nearly £4 million. Australia would also pay an additional £750 000 for maintenance, training costs in England, and wages and allowances for personnel loaned from the Royal Navy. In December 1909 orders for the construction of the battle cruiser (*Australia*), two light cruisers (*Melbourne* and *Sydney*) and two submarines (*AE1* and *AE2*) were placed with British shipyards, while one light cruiser (*Brisbane*) and three more destroyers (*Huon*, *Swan* and *Torrens*) were to be built at Cockatoo Island.

The *Naval Defence Act* was passed in 1910 and this was effectively the agreement that the Australian government would assume full responsibility for the naval defence of Australia. All British naval forces would be withdrawn from Australian waters and reallocated to other areas, particularly the East Indies and China Stations. Creswell had won, and the modernisation of the Australian Navy had begun. Manning the ships was going to be a problem, however, and recruiting of officers and ratings (sailors) was a major task. Australian-born personnel serving in the ANF who could be transferred were one source, as were men from the CNF and ex-colonial navies, but recruiting both within Australia and of ex-Royal Navy personnel was going to be required. The use of British officers and ratings on loan, however, continued to be the mainstay of the Australian Navy for some years to come.

Australian naval defence

In June 1910, the Australian government invited Admiral Sir Reginald Henderson to visit and advise on the infrastructure needed to create the new Australian Navy. Henderson travelled widely throughout Australia and proposed a 52-ship fleet, manned by 15 000 personnel and spread right around the Australian coast at 16 bases. This was an extravagant plan that Australia could not afford, but some of his recommendations – a naval college for training Australian officers, a dedicated training depot for ratings, and a major base in Western Australia – were quickly adopted.

After the arrival of *Parramatta* and *Yarra* in December 1910, the pace of naval activity increased exponentially. In April 1911 the torpedo boat destroyer *Warrego* was launched at Cockatoo Island, and Navy Office (the naval headquarters) was opened in Melbourne. On 10 July 1911, King George V formally granted the title Royal Australian Navy to the Commonwealth Naval Forces. The long, hard road to create an Australian navy had reached a major milestone. Further, the *Commonwealth Defence Act* 1909–10 introduced compulsory service under the Universal Training Scheme. The effect was thousands of Australian boys and young men were obliged to serve in the Citizen Forces (Navy or Army) as cadets (12–18 years old) or in the Reserve forces (18 and older). The previous volunteer cadet and reserve force numbers swelled and in due course provided a steady stream of trained men to the RAN Brigade and sea-going navy.

In early 1911, the new Royal Australian Navy conducted one of its more substantial operations when *Gayundah* was dispatched to north-western Australian waters to investigate reports of illegal fishing by foreign vessels. For many years the perceived threat to Australia had been considered to be one against the major ports in the south, but now the federal government became concerned about its largely unknown northern coastline. *Gayundah*'s commanding officer, Commander GAH Curtis, received special briefings from Creswell and officials from the Department of Trade and Customs before taking his ship to sea. By late May *Gayundah* was searching Scott Reef (300 km north-west of Cape Leveque Western Australia) when she discovered the Dutch schooners *Harriet* and *Fortuna* at anchor, in Australian territorial waters, with a full load of trepang and trochus shell onboard. Curtis informed both masters they were fishing illegally in Australian waters, seized both vessels and escorted them to Broome for prosecution. The special northern cruise was deemed a success and the Departments of External Affairs and Trade and Customs even split the cost of the activity between them as a result of the successful prosecution of the Dutch vessels.

Construction of the main Australian naval training facility at Westernport – the Flinders Naval Depot – commenced in January 1912, but it was to be September 1920 before the base was ready for use. Construction of the base in Western Australia was commenced, in the area now known as Henderson Naval Base, but it petered out in the 1920s. (It was not until 1976 that a fully operational Western Australian base, HMAS *Stirling*, was finally opened.) In April 1912 the training ship HMAS *Tingira* was commissioned in Sydney, and her first batch of 78 boy seamen commenced training in June. Also in June 1912, the old British cruiser *Encounter* was transferred to the RAN as a training ship and was soon training ordinary seaman fresh out of basic training at Williamstown. In January 1913 the first of the RAN's modern cruisers, HMAS *Melbourne*, was commissioned in England and she arrived in Australia shortly afterwards. In March 1913 the RAN also commissioned the old British cruiser HMS *Pioneer*, and that same month the first intake of 28 cadet midshipman began training at a temporary naval college at Osborne House in Geelong. (The college moved to its permanent home at Jervis Bay in 1915.)

Australian naval defence

The battle cruiser HMAS *Australia* was commissioned in May 1913 and was followed a month later by the cruiser HMAS *Sydney*. In early July 1913, all Royal Navy establishments and property in Australia, including the depot ship HMS *Penguin* at Garden Island, were handed over to the RAN. Thus the RAN obtained a working dockyard, ammunition storage depots, stores and victualling warehouses, a hospital, detention quarters, an accommodation ship, barrack buildings and recreational facilities which the RN had built up over the preceding 80 years. Meanwhile, the RAN's two new submarines, *AE1* and *AE2*, were nearing completion in England and would arrive in Australia in early 1914. Finally on 4 October 1913 the ceremonial entry of the first Australian Fleet Unit occurred at Sydney Harbour when the battlecruiser *Australia* led *Melbourne, Sydney, Encounter, Parramatta, Warrego* and *Yarra* into port for the first time. Admiral Sir George King-Hall, commanding the Australia Station, embarked in his flagship HMS *Cambrian*, ordered a return salute to be fired as the Australian ships passed. On 21 October 1913 *Cambrian* departed Australian waters for the last time and the naval defence of Australia was now fully in the hands of the RAN.

Less than a year later, on 4 August 1914, Australia went to war with Germany. The RAN had been advised of this likely eventuality several days before, and the ships of the fleet were already on their way to war stations around the Australian coast. As will be recounted in more detail in Chapter 12, within six weeks the RAN was in action at the successful capture of German New Guinea, where the nation incurred its first losses on 11 September when five RAN Brigade personnel were killed in action ashore at Rabaul. Three days later the submarine *AE1* was lost with her entire crew of 35 men when she failed to return from a patrol off New Britain. Australian warships also supported the capture of other German colonies including Nauru, Ocean

Island and Samoa. For his part, the German East Asian Fleet commander, Admiral von Spee, decided not to attempt to attack Australian shipping as he rightly considered that his force was out-gunned by the RAN. Instead he attempted to return his ships to Germany and steamed away from Australian waters. The Royal Navy destroyed his squadron at the Battle of the Falkland Islands, on 8 December 1914, but once again Australians were present: three RAN ratings served in HMS *Kent* which sank the German cruiser *Nürnberg*.

At the outbreak of war in 1914 the RAN had not been found wanting. Decades of hard political lobbying, ship-building, preparation and training had ensured that the naval defence of Australia was secure when it was most required. On 9 November 1914, while escorting the first convoy of AIF troops across the Indian Ocean, the cruiser HMAS *Sydney* fought the RAN's first action at sea when she single-handedly destroyed the German cruiser *Emden* at Cocos Island. A cartoon published soon after in the Melbourne *Punch* showed an Australian rating on board *Sydney*, with broken German flag in hand, pointing to the battered wreck of *Emden* aground on Cocos Island. The caption read: 'Alone I did it – What price me now?'

Further reading

J Bach, *The Australia Station: A History of the Royal Navy in the South West Pacific 1821–1913*, UNSW Press, Sydney, 1986

J Bastock, *Ships on the Australia Station*, Child and Associates, Sydney, 1998

J Connor, *ANZAC and Empire: George Foster Pearce and the Foundations of Australian Defence*, CUP, Melbourne, 2011

WP Evans, *Deeds not Words: The Victorian Navy*, Hawthorn Press, Melbourne, 1971

TR Frame, *No Pleasure Cruise: The Story of the Royal Australian Navy*, Allen & Unwin, Sydney, 2004

R Gillett, *Australia's Colonial Navies*, Naval Historical Society of Australia, Sydney, 1982

F Glen, *Australians at War in New Zealand*, Willsonscott Publishing, Christchurch, 2011

Australian naval defence

R Hyslop, *Australian Naval Administration 1900–1939*, Hawthorn Press, Melbourne, 1973

J Jeremy, *Cockatoo Island: Sydney's Historic Dockyard*, UNSW Press, Sydney, 1998

C Jones, *Australian Colonial Navies*, Australian War Memorial, Canberra, 1986

NA Lambert, *Australia's Naval Inheritance: Imperial Maritime Strategy and the Australia Station 1880–1909*, Department of Defence, Canberra, 1998

I McFarlane & N Smith, *Victoria and Australia's First War: Mostly Unsung Military History*, Melbourne, 2005

GL Macandie, *Genesis of the Royal Australian Navy*, Government Printer, Sydney, 1949

B Nichols, *Bluejackets and Boxers: Australia's Naval Expedition to the Boxer Uprising*, Allen & Unwin, Sydney, 1986

—— , *The Colonial Volunteers: The Defence Forces of the Australian Colonies 1836–1901*, Allen & Unwin, Sydney, 1988

R Parkin & D Lee, *Great White Fleet to Coral Sea: Naval Strategy and the Development of Australia–United States Relations 1900–1945*, DFAT, Canberra, 2008

LG Wilson, *Cradle of the Navy: The Story of Flinders Naval Depot (HMAS Cerberus) and Naval Training in Victoria 1855–1981*, RAN, 1981

6

Australians in the New Zealand Wars

Damien Fenton

For most of the nineteenth century, Australian colonists saw New Zealand as the 'wild west', metaphorically if not geographically speaking. For those living in Sydney, Hobart and other Australian settlements in the early 1800s, New Zealand was a lawless land inhabited by fierce warlike tribes of cannibals, frequented only by European whalers, sealers and traders who were even more debauched than the natives.

The reality of course was very different: the Māori (the indigenous people of New Zealand) were traditionally a tribal people, they did wage war between tribes, and, yes, they did practise cannibalism (as part of the spoils of war) – as indeed they did slavery. But Māori society was also incredibly complex and relied upon an elaborate body of customary law, hierarchical structures and religious observances, all to maintain and manage relationships at the level of the family (*whanau*), sub-tribe (*hapū*), tribe (*iwi*) and, crucially, between tribes. For all the heat and anger of a particular inter-tribal feud, the fact was Māori shared a common culture, a common religion and a common language from one end of the country to the other. This was a key point of difference between the Aboriginal and Māori worlds before contact with Europeans. In fact Māori tribal society had more in common with the Scottish Highland clans of the seventeenth or eighteenth centuries than it did with the First Australians. Although the obstacles to united action by Māori tribes in the face of external threat were still high, they were not beyond the realms of possibility – given sufficient provocation.[1]

The authorities in Sydney and London recognised very early on that unregulated European contact with the 'New Zealanders' was a potential source of such provocation and a threat to stability in the region. Whalers and sealers were not exactly natural diplomats and their conduct in New Zealand waters often left much to be desired.[2] Such actions invited retaliatory action on the part of the affected *iwi* or *hapu*, even if it had to be delayed until the ship – or any ship – returned the following season. (Māori had long memories and were well-versed in the concept of collective punishment.)

On the other hand, some captains visiting New Zealand waters worked hard to establish and maintain good relations with the local *iwi*. Those who acted like traders rather than pirates quickly found that most chiefs were quite happy for their tribes to provide women, food and other resources in exchange for European trade goods – especially muskets.[3] The trade in these weapons produced a revolution in Māori warfare that wreaked havoc from one end of the country to the other over a 30-year period of inter-tribal fighting known today as the Musket Wars (roughly 1810 to 1840).[4] The immediate devastation was terrible. In fact, at least one modern academic assessment puts the number of deaths during the Musket Wars at 20 000, which would easily make it New Zealand's bloodiest conflict in terms of loss of life.

These wars also had the perverse effect of not only making Māori warriors proficient in the use of firearms, but also giving them the opportunity to adapt their traditional approaches to warfare. Nowhere was this more evident than in the dramatic change in appearance of Māori *pa* (forts). Traditional *pa* were usually built on high ground, with concentric layers of earthen terraces, solid wooden palisades and towers (*puwhara*) which were elevated fighting platforms protected by a low palisade allowing stones and light spears to be thrown down on attackers – much like an Iron Age British hill fort.[5] With firearms this changed, with the towers disappearing, the terraces giving way to or incorporating entrenchments, and the palisades acquiring firing loopholes. Traditional *pa* had given way to 'gunfighter *pa*'.

Māori adoption of firearms was just one more reason for Europeans to tread carefully in Australia's Pacific neighbour. But the rough justice that governed this early phase of contact was broadly acceptable to both British and Māori. Europeans operated in New Zealand on Māori terms. The advent of permanent European trading posts, and even the arrival of Christian missionaries, did not unduly strain the tolerances of this *modus vivendi*. They did, however, herald the next phase of contact that would provoke inter-racial conflict – European settlement.

Until about 1840 the British government had no plans to settle New Zealand, but they were powerless to stop the small but steady trickle of British subjects and others (especially French and Americans) who did so at their own initiative. At first these individuals could only live there with the explicit permission – and protection – of a local chief and his tribe. By 1830 things were changing. The emergence of semi-autonomous European enclaves became possible and, in the case of Kororareka in the Bay of Islands, a disturbing reality.[6] Founded by whalers in the 1820s, Kororareka had a population of several hundred Europeans by the end of that decade including a number of ex-convicts – and reputedly, escaped convicts – from Australia.[7]

The tribal dislocation and upheaval of the Musket Wars, together with the growth of unregulated European settlement at

Kororareka, raised the prospect of a territory descending into anarchy right on New South Wales' doorstep. This forced the British authorities to act. In 1832 the Colonial Office dispatched James Busby, a former resident of New South Wales and self-appointed expert on New Zealand (despite never having been there before), to take up the position of 'British Resident' – a sort of local consul – in Kororareka.[8] Busby's brief was to restore a modicum of order in the town, at least as far as the British subjects living there were concerned, and to act as an intermediary between the Europeans and their Māori neighbours.

Busby's position was completely undermined by the fact that he had no resources with which to enforce his authority: he could do little more than periodically add his reports to those of the missionaries detailing the latest depredations of the denizens of Kororareka – 'the hell-hole of the South Pacific' in the words of one appalled visitor.[9] To make matters worse, the French were now showing signs of interest in the territory, prompting Busby to hastily compose a 'declaration of independence for New Zealand' in 1835 and arrange for several dozen local Māori chiefs to sign it. Although the British government reluctantly recognised the newly independent status of the 'United Tribes of New Zealand', it did little to deter the French, who continued to sniff around the place. On top of this, in early 1839 Edward Wakefield's 'New Zealand Company', a private commercial enterprise to colonise the country, won enough backing from wealthy investors in Britain to dispatch its first group of free settlers (destined to establish a colony at Port Nicholson, modern-day Wellington).

Faced with this impending free-for-all, the British government decided that outright annexation of New Zealand by the Crown was the only option left if it were not to lose complete control of the situation. As an interim measure, Letters Patent were issued in June 1839 expanding the territory of New South

Wales to include all of New Zealand. In August, Captain William Hobson RN was instructed to proceed to the Bay of Islands to negotiate a treaty with the 'United Tribes' to cede sovereignty over New Zealand to Great Britain.[10]

Hobson stopped in Sydney for provisions and a final consultation with the New South Wales governor, Sir George Gipps, before proceeding to New Zealand. Gipps authorised the deployment of a detachment of Mounted Police to accompany Hobson to the Bay of Islands. Ten troopers under the command of Lieutenant Henry Smart were assigned to the mission, although only four troopers and an NCO could actually be assembled in time to embark with Hobson in HMS *Herald*. Hobson and the troopers arrived at Kororareka on 29 January 1840 and landed the next day. Depending on how seriously one treats the temporary territorial extension of New South Wales to include New Zealand – and it certainly meant nothing to Māori – 30 January 1840 is arguably the date on which an Australian colonial military unit was deployed for the first time on an operation overseas. The rest of the detachment and all ten of its horses arrived onboard the *Westminster* on 14 March.[11]

In the interim, Hobson got on with the job, proclaiming the placement of New Zealand under the jurisdiction of New South Wales and his appointment as lieutenant governor the same day he came ashore. With the help of Busby and the missionary Henry Williams, he quickly arranged for the northern chiefs to meet him at Waitangi, a 'neutral' location near Kororareka, to negotiate a treaty assuring their acquiescence to the annexation. The discussions began on 5 February, when Hobson explained the terms of the treaty and why it was in the interests of both parties to agree to it. The next day, after further argument and debate, they signed the Treaty of Waitangi – modern New Zealand's founding document. Over the next six months or so, copies of the treaty were circulated around the rest of the country by missionaries, traders and Hobson's officials for other chiefs to sign. In October a copy of the treaty, which included both Māori and English versions of the text, was signed by Hobson and despatched to the Colonial Office in London.[12]

The authority of Hobson's office was given real heft when an 80-man detachment from the 80th Regiment, under the command of Major Thomas Bunbury, arrived from Sydney on 16 April.[13] But Hobson was loathe to let go of his mounted troopers, who acted as his personal escort, or Lieutenant Smart, who filled the role of aide-de-camp. The prestige of Hobson's office grew as the bureaucratic separation of New Zealand from New South Wales into a fully fledged colony in its own right proceeded apace, culminating in Hobson's swearing in as the inaugural governor of New Zealand and head of his own Legislative Council in May 1841. In November, Hobson won Gipps' approval to retain the detachment in New Zealand, but this prompted the commander of British forces in New South Wales, Major General Sir Maurice O'Connell, to assert his authority over the men and demand their immediate return.[14] O'Connell prevailed and the men left the colony's new capital of Auckland for Sydney on 30 April 1842. So ended the first Australian military 'intervention' in New Zealand. It would not be the last.

The imposition of British sovereignty over New Zealand put an end to unregulated European settlement, but it ultimately failed to prevent the conflict with Māori that Hobson, the Colonial Office and the missionaries hoped to avoid. At best, it simply delayed it. The Treaty of Waitangi had promised Māori that as British subjects they would retain ownership over their lands, but the creation of a local settler population put successive governors between a rock and a hard place. As more and more settlers arrived, Māori became more and more reluctant to sell land. They also grew increasingly suspicious and fearful of the consequences of European settlement – with good cause. At the same time more settlers meant more pressure and political agitation to 'free up' more Māori land. The dynamics of the situation were all but guaranteed to result in war.

The first serious military conflict between Māori and pakeha (Europeans) erupted, ironically enough, in the Bay of Islands in 1845. After Hobson shifted the capital to Auckland – and took most of Kororareka's European trade with him – a faction of the Ngāpuhi tribe under the leadership of Hone Heke, one of the original signatories of the treaty, became disenchanted with the whole arrangement. The 'Northern War' saw Kororareka overrun and sacked by Heke's warriors before the arrival of British troops, and the armed intervention of other Ngāpuhi *hapu* opposed to Heke, ended the fighting in 1846.[15]

The next three decades were marked by a succession of Māori–pakeha military conflicts. Along with the Northern War these are collectively known today as the New Zealand Wars.[16] The violence reached its peak in the 1860s, beginning with the First Taranaki War (1860–61), fought in that province on the west coast of the North Island. It was followed, indeed directly led to, the Waikato War (1863–64) when the largest and most organised confederation of tribes to resist continued pakeha expansion, known collectively as the King Movement (*Kīngitanga*), took up arms, leading to war across the entire central portion of the North Island. The 'Kingites' and their allies were eventually defeated by British imperial and colonial forces in a series of conventional campaigns. This 'conventional phase' was followed by a series of smaller, but arguably more brutal, regional guerilla wars that finally petered out in the 1870s.

The Northern War required both the British 58th and 99th Regiments to be deployed from Australia to bolster the local imperial garrison (at that time made up of companies from the 80th and 96th regiments).[17] This set the pattern for the conflicts that followed, whereby the British garrisons in the Australian colonies were the first to be called upon if imperial reinforcements for New Zealand were deemed necessary. Between 1840 and 1870, a total of 14 British infantry regiments served in New Zealand, of which only four – the 43rd, 57th, 65th and 68th – did not arrive directly from postings in Australia. In 1846 the British government ended this reliance on short-term detachments from regiments in Australia and assigned New Zealand a permanent military garrison of 2000 men in its own right. The British Army thereafter bracketed New Zealand with Australia in its global relief system, with regiments sent to one or the other but often serving in both before rotating on to India or the United Kingdom.

British Army regiments posted to New Zealand 1840–70[18]

12th (East Suffolk) Regiment of Foot	1860–67
14th (Buckinghamshire) Regiment of Foot	1860–66
18th (Royal Irish) Regiment of Foot	1863–70
40th (Somersetshire) Regiment of Foot	1860–66
43rd (Monmouthshire) Light Infantry	1863–66
50th (Queen's Own) Regiment of Foot	1863–67
57th (West Middlesex) Regiment of Foot	1861–67
58th (Rutlandshire) Regiment of Foot	1845–58
65th (Yorkshire North Riding) Regiment of Foot	1846–65
68th (Durham) Light Infantry	1864–66
70th (Surrey) Regiment of Foot	1861–66
80th (South Staffordshire) Regiment of Foot	1840–44
96th (Manchester) Regiment of Foot	1843–46
99th (Lanarkshire) Regiment of Foot	1844–47

The story of the British Army regiments in Australia, and the degree to which they were integrated into the daily life of their colonial host communities, is dealt with in Chapter 3. Since those regiments also recruited in the colonies which they garrisoned, clearly there were individual Australians who served in the ranks of the British imperial forces that fought in the New Zealand Wars. But these men served in British units in an individual capacity, and the focus of this chapter is on the experience of identifiably 'Australian' units in the New Zealand Wars. These began to appear as those wars reached their apex in the 1860s.

The late 1850s witnessed an astonishing Māori response to European settlement with the creation of the King Movement. Championed by the powerful Tainui confederation of tribes in the Waikato, the movement began as an attempt to put aside petty rivalries and tribal politics to present a united front opposed to further land sales. At the heart of this alliance was the Māori King, Potatau Te Wherowhero, who was crowned and anointed with the support of central North Island tribal leaders at Ngaruawahia in June 1858 (and succeeded by his son Tawhaio in 1860).[19] Not everyone, even within Tainui, recognised his status as king, but many *iwi* and *hapu* outside of Waikato supported the movement's stance on land sales and still sought alliance with the Kingitanga even as they withheld their personal allegiance to its self-styled monarch. It was so successful at stopping land sales that the effect was to create a solid wall of Māori territory straddling almost the entire central North Island with the exception of Hawke's Bay on the east coast and a thin strip of European settlement confined to the coast of Taranaki in the west. To the north, the 'Kingite' border began a mere 50 kilometres south of Auckland, the capital of the colony.[20]

The settlers' alarm and frustration towards the King Movement was shared by the colony's leadership. A co-ordinated land-sale embargo was bad enough, but the installation of a Māori 'king' and the adoption of other trappings of statehood – including a fledgling police force, complete with uniforms, at Ngaruawahia – was an act of defiance too powerful for Governor Thomas Gore Browne to ignore. Tensions across the country rose, and the clamour from the settlers for the authorities to do something about the King Movement became deafening. In 1859 a dispute over the attempted sale of a block of land just north of New Plymouth proved to be the catalyst for action. When the chief of a *hapu* from the local Atiawa tribe offered to sell the land he was quickly overruled by senior Atiawa chiefs, but Governor Browne insisted that the sale proceed. Attempts by Atiawa to obstruct Crown surveyors sent to work on the block gave Browne the excuse he needed to send in the troops, and in March 1860 war broke out between the government and Atiawa, who were soon joined by other Taranaki tribes.[21]

On 5 April 1860 the Victorian government offered to send the pride of the Victorian Naval Service, Her Majesty's Colonial Ship (HMCS) *Victoria*, to New Zealand to assist the imperial and colonial New Zealand forces in the conflict. Built in London and launched in 1855, the 580-ton steam sloop *Victoria* had undergone a refit in 1859 which saw its principal armament upgraded to four 56-cwt and four 25-cwt 32-pounder Armstrong guns.[22] The crew consisted of the ship's captain, Commander William Norman, seven other officers and 50 ratings.[23]

The Victorian government made this offer despite the fact that the deployment of a colonial vessel on active service outside of its home waters appeared to violate international maritime law, at least as far as the Royal Navy was concerned. The Admiralty, clearly no great fan of colonial navies to begin with, had warned the Australian colonies that foreign maritime powers were liable to treat such vessels as privateers. (The practice of privateering had been outlawed since the Paris Declaration of 1856, the first international attempt to codify warfare at sea.)

The Victorian government was well aware of these legal obstacles but, adhering to the adage that it's easier to seek forgiveness than seek permission, went ahead and ordered its warship to set sail for New Zealand anyway. To cover their backsides the politicians rushed a piece of retrospective legislation through parliament to smooth over the legalities. The *Armed Vessels Regulation Act* 1860 was gazetted on 8 June, three weeks after the *Victoria* had departed for New Zealand waters.[24] However this was fast enough to foil the anticipated objection from the Admiralty.

It helped that the local authorities, adopting a thoroughly practical attitude towards the matter, greeted Victoria's gesture of solidarity towards its sister colony across the Tasman with open arms. Governor Browne conveyed his heartfelt thanks before the ship had even left Australia, and the commander of British forces in New Zealand, Colonel Charles Gold, did not hesitate to employ this addition to his command as soon as *Victoria* arrived off the Taranaki coast.[25] The settlers in New Plymouth and the rest of the colony made plain their gratitude via the local newspapers which were full of praise for *Victoria*'s contribution to the war effort.

The tangible contribution of HMVS *Victoria* to that effort consisted in the main of transport, supply and coastal bombardment duties, spiced up by the provision of a 30-man shore party to the *ad hoc* Naval Brigade which took part in some of the fighting on land.[26] Naval brigades were a common feature of British colonial wars throughout the nineteenth century, and the New Zealand Wars were no exception. In this case the brigade was formed from Royal Marine detachments and ships' crew from *Niger*, *Cordelia* and *Pelorus* – all Royal Navy vessels on the Australia Station hastily despatched from Sydney on the outbreak of war – as well as the sailors from *Victoria*.

One of this shore party, Able Seaman Henry Serjeant, became *Victoria*'s only casualty of the war when he was accidentally shot on 13 July by a Royal Marine during musketry training. Serjeant died from his wounds on 6 August 1860, and was buried with full military honours at New Plymouth. In doing so Henry Serjeant became the first serviceman in an official Australian colonial military force to die on active service overseas.[27]

While this would appear to indicate that the Victorian sailors were never really exposed to the dangers of combat, it wasn't for lack of trying. At the end of December the *Victoria*'s shore party took part in the capture of Matarikoriko Pa, one of the many *pa* thrown up by Ngatiawa to block the landward approaches to New Plymouth. At the time the local and Australian papers wrote up the action as a fierce battle ultimately won when the Naval Brigade – with the *Victoria*'s men in the vanguard – stormed the Māori stronghold. In fact Matarikoriko's garrison simply abandoned the position on the night of 29–30 December and the British occupied it next morning unopposed.

The build-up to the taking of Matarikoriko Pa had certainly seemed to promise a fight, with the British and settler forces spending weeks methodically digging a sap, redoubts to protect the sap and flanks of approach to the *pa* and other fieldworks as required. After finally reaching a position where guns could be safely brought forward and the sap finished, British artillery began to bombard Matarikoriko in preparation for an all-out assault. The bombardment lasted two days and while the spectacle impressed the colonial and imperial sailors and soldiers present, it appears to have inflicted a total of only six casualties on the defenders (although estimates at the time grossly inflated these figures).[28]

Clearly recognising that a British assault on Matarikoriko was now imminent, its Māori garrison simply slipped away overnight, the position having outlived its usefulness. The Ngatiawa warriors were happy to confront a British frontal assault as long as it was on their own terms and the opportunity existed to inflict a high ratio of casualties upon the pakeha relative to their own. Once the sap was finished and the odds became much more uncertain, staying put was no longer worth the risk. In this regard Matarikoriko is a textbook example of the 'modern *pa*' which Māori employed against British imperial and colonial forces as the New Zealand Wars reached their crescendo in the 1860s.

The modern *pa* took the adaptation of Māori fortification to European firepower to its ultimate conclusion. Exposure to British artillery bombardment in the Northern War had led to further refinement of the gunfighter *pa* developed during the earlier Musket Wars. Extensive entrenchments, utilising rifle pits, anti-artillery bunkers and communication trenches, were the core feature of the new *pa*. Tightly packed solid wooden palisades were reserved for the inner core of the fort, and were replaced in the outer defensive perimeter with much weaker and flimsier versions which were quicker and easier to erect. The outer palisade's role was no longer one of presenting a solid defensive wall but rather to provide cover for the entrenchments and to obstruct a direct assault. The modern *pa* could also be used as a tactical fieldwork, with no intrinsic value of its own other than to entice the British to battle on ground of Māori choosing. They could be built or abandoned at whim. In the case of Taranaki, Atiawa used them to create a defensive belt to shield their villages and cultivations from attack and then, more aggressively, to dominate the hinterland surrounding New Plymouth, effectively placing the town under siege.[29]

As the war dragged on into 1861, General Pratt's insistence on the use of sapping techniques to counter these tactics came in for much criticism from both the settlers and, possibly in an attempt to goad him into a more rash approach, his Māori opponents.³⁰ The latter was a good indication that on a tactical level sapping was actually an effective answer to dealing with a modern Māori fighting *pa*. But at both the strategic and operational level it was a failure, given the realities in Taranaki at that time. Pratt's 'bite and swallow' strategy, built around this use of traditional siege warfare techniques, required far more men and much more time and resources than were available to him if he was ever going to achieve a decisive victory.

Far from teaching the Taranaki tribes a short sharp lesson and restoring the settler's confidence – the usual British objectives when suppressing 'native uprisings' – Browne now found himself embroiled in a war that was an abject failure in both regards. New Plymouth had been pushed to the brink of total economic collapse and many of the townspeople had abandoned it for the safety of Wellington or even further afield. Pratt's methodical sapping approach offered no prospect of a quick end to New Plymouth's plight or of forcing Atiawa to admit defeat anytime soon. The competence of both Browne and Pratt became the subject of increasingly scathing criticism in the New Zealand newspapers. To make matters worse, Pratt was now reporting that the Taranaki Māori war effort was being bolstered and sustained by Kingite war parties (*taua*) arriving from outside of the province. Despite this external support, some Atiawa *hapu* were feeling the strain themselves after a year of war and were willing to negotiate with the government. Browne seized on the opportunity to bring the whole sorry business to an end. The result was the agreement in March 1861 to a shaky peace in which both sides claimed victory without resolving the fundamental causes of the conflict.³¹

Just under a year since departing for war, HMVS *Victoria* and her crew docked in Melbourne on 11 April 1861 to a triumphal home-coming. Met by Governor Sir Henry Barkly and Melbourne mayor, John Thomas Smith, the crew's return was celebrated with a victory dinner hosted by the latter that very evening.[32] An outburst of colonial and imperial patriotic pride swept the city, with the men of the *Victoria* as its focus. The Victorians seemed determined to ignore the grumblings of the New Zealand settler press that in fact the hostilities had ended in a dismal stalemate that amounted to a humiliation of British arms. The citizens of Melbourne were having none of it, and believed – at least for the week or so following the *Victoria*'s return – that their warship had won its war. Victoria had done its bit and proven its mettle.

If the First Taranaki War taught Governor Browne one lesson it was that the King Movement could only be crushed by confronting it directly, not through proxy war against third parties such as Atiawa. Browne therefore set about preparing for war in the Waikato, the Kingitanga's heartland, almost as soon as the truce in Taranaki had been cobbled together. Browne's term in New Zealand ended seven months later when he was appointed to the governorship of Tasmania, but his successor, Sir George Grey, embraced this approach with even more gusto.[33] Grey had already enjoyed a successful term as New Zealand's third governor from 1845 to 1854, and had won a good reputation among Māori and settler alike. But the situation had changed dramatically in New Zealand since his departure, with the emergence of both settler government and the King Movement. Although he continued to sympathise with the plight of Māori in general, he could no more tolerate the emergence of a *de facto* independent Māori state than Browne or any other agent of the Crown. Grey ordered his new military commander, Major General Duncan Cameron, to concentrate his troops in Auckland and prepare to tackle the Kingitanga head on. Those preparations included the extension of a military road south from Auckland all the way to Pokeno, just north of the intersection of the Mangatawhiri Stream with the Waikato River that marked the Kingite border. Cameron also established a series of redoubts to protect his 'Great Southern Road' and the surrounding farms and settlements of the South Auckland region. The Kingite leadership issued a warning that if any imperial troops crossed the Mangatawhiri Stream it would be considered an act of war, and they too began to prepare for the impending clash: stockpiling ammunition, building *pa* and putting the call out to their kinsmen and allies further afield to ready themselves for a call to arms. In the event 15 of the 26 major tribal groups in the North Island contributed war parties to fight in the Waikato War. Even so, the peak strength of Kingite field forces is not thought to have exceeded 4000 warriors at any point during the campaign (out of a total North Island pool of 12 000 effective Māori warriors at the time).[34]

Grey was careful to avoid provoking the conflict until he had amassed enough troops to cross the Mangatawhiri with confidence. He proved extremely able at wheedling imperial reinforcements out of London, convincing his superiors that Auckland, the capital, was under direct threat of Kingite attack, an argument strengthened when impetuous Kingite *taua* began raiding farms along the 'border' in southern Auckland. His case was strengthened even further when sporadic conflict broke out again in Taranaki at the start of 1863. This resulted in the quick despatch of four more regiments, approximately 3000 men, to bolster Cameron's command. This brought the number of British imperial troops in New Zealand to a total of 5245 by June 1863.[35] Even so, Grey knew he needed more. Cameron had enough imperial 'shock troops' to fight his battles and form the vanguard of any invasion of the Waikato. But who would follow up behind them and protect the line of communications back to Auckland, never mind keep the Kingite lands pacified after the invasion was completed and the 'surge' of imperial troops reduced? Having pushed his luck as far as he could in obtaining imperial reinforcements, Grey had to look elsewhere to find these support forces.

The colony itself was the obvious place to start and Grey did what he could to mobilise its full military potential – but in reality this potential was extremely limited. By the end of 1860, the total European population of New Zealand was estimated to be about 84 000, of which 49 000 were male and 35 000 female.[36] All able-bodied male British subjects (but excluding 'aboriginal natives', that is Māori) between the ages of 18 and 65 were technically liable for militia service under an ordinance promulgated by Governor Hobson in 1845. Men were supposed to parade for a total of 28 days of training annually, and the power to 'draw out' (mobilise) a local militia for active service resided with the governor or, in the event of 'imminent danger' to a settlement, the principal local authority. The 1858 *Militia Act* sought to improve this system by dividing the country into eight provincial militia districts and creating a small permanent staff establishment for each (one officer, two NCOs and a bugler). Due to severe financial constraints, however, the implementation of this system was a haphazard affair.[37]

Often armed with the same 'trade muskets' sold to Māori, the standard of training and drill achieved by these militias was entirely dependent upon the personal taste, experience and enthusiasm of the individuals placed in command of them (efforts of the permanent staff post-1858 notwithstanding). As a result the quality of the various militia units was mixed at best. But while far below the standard of imperial regulars, they were still capable of acting as a second-tier force, guarding lines of communication and garrisoning vulnerable settlements: exactly what Grey wanted. Some militia units served in this capacity during the wars, but the full reserve of manpower encompassed by the militia legislation remained largely untapped during the conflict.

The key constraint to the local militia's usefulness in the New Zealand Wars was the provision in both the 1845 Ordinance and 1858 Act restricting men's service to within 25 miles of their local police office.[38] This meant that militiamen could only be mobilised for military operations in defence of their local town and its immediate hinterland. The upshot was that a few North Island units based in 'frontline' settlements, such as the Taranaki Militia, found themselves mobilised again and again, while the bulk of the country's militia was only infrequently called upon, if at all. Indeed, the muster rolls of the South Island, where just over half the settler population lived by 1860, were effectively off limits to governors, settler governments and imperial commanders alike.

Another option was to raise permanent colonial military units. Grey went down this path by creating the Colonial Defence Force Cavalry in 1862. This corps of mounted troops, with an establishment of 500 men, recruited on the basis of a three-year period of service. Officers and NCOs were appointed (or at least approved) by Grey himself, who more controversially insisted that Māori also be eligible for enlistment.[39] Yet even so, the problem remained that Grey and Cameron would need more than 500 men to guard the lines of communication to Auckland, and neither the colony's finances nor its manpower pool were capable of sustaining a 'standing army' of any significant strength. As it was, the professional status of the Colonial Defence Force Cavalry, coupled with its local knowledge, meant that Cameron quickly co-opted its Auckland detachment into his main body alongside his British Army regulars when the fighting began there.

The third source of combatants open to Grey was the use of Māori tribal auxiliaries: the so-called 'Kupapa' forces supposedly loyal to the Crown. (Kupapa were also sometimes called

'Queenites', supporters of Queen Victoria as opposed to King Tawhiao.) Some were, but many were not so much pro-government as anti-Kingite. Their motivations varied from real devotion to the Crown to the pursuit of either ancient inter-tribal grievances and enmities or newer ones born out of the carnage of the Musket Wars. Regardless of their motivation, the Kupapa proved invaluable to government fighting forces, especially in the guerilla-style campaigns that followed the end of the Waikato War.[40] From the 1860s onwards it became convention for the New Zealand government to give Kupapa war parties European style unit names such as the 'Arawa Flying Column'. This effectively awarded their leaders an honorary officer rank of major or captain (often complete with sword, revolver and uniform) and provided a subsidy to the 'commanding officer' to distribute among his men as he saw fit.

Such honours aside, the Kupapa still did not solve the line of communication problem for Grey and Cameron in 1863. For a start they were Māori war parties, geared for aggressive action in the field and temperamentally unsuited to guard duty. The warriors in those *taua* answered to their chiefs, and no one else, and while imperial officers could suggest a course of action or ask for assistance, they could not order Kupapa leaders to do anything. The hysterical response from nervous and suspicious settlers in south Auckland to the prospect of having Kupapa forces stationed in their midst is also easily imagined.

This left Grey with one last option, and that was a military settlement scheme. It would pay for itself by rewarding soldiers with land confiscated from the Kingite tribes and their allies (like Atiawa in Taranaki) following the successful invasion of the Waikato. It would also provide *de facto* garrison settlements to keep the newly conquered areas pacified after the wars' conclusion and the inevitable withdrawal of the bulk of Cameron's imperial forces. The idea had been discussed and championed by newspaper commentators on both sides of the Tasman since the First Taranaki War and it had its supporters in the New Zealand parliament.

Grey had tried soldier settlement before during his first tenure as New Zealand governor in the late 1840s, although with mixed results. As an assisted settlement scheme, the Royal New Zealand Fencible Corps succeeded in bringing out some 700 British veterans and their families between 1847 and 1852 and establishing them on land around Auckland.[41] As a scheme to increase and improve the colony's defence capacity, however, it was a failure. The men recruited were ex-British Army pensioners or men discharged without pension, and clearly their best soldiering days were behind them. As the Fencibles concentrated on their farms or set up business on their town allotment, their military efficiency soon deteriorated to about the same level as the local militia. Despite this experience, Grey backed the promotion of a new scheme, although he sought to avoid the mistakes associated with the Fencibles.

The key difference of the new scheme was that those enlisting would receive their land only after the completion of three years' active service. As well, the New Zealand government did not bother advertising in Britain, as it was too far away (and too expensive) and would take too long to get the volunteers to New Zealand. Instead, they would recruit from the next best source of white British males – the Australian colonies – as well as inside New Zealand itself. Instead of worn-out ex-soldiers, they hoped to recruit a mix of young men of prime fighting age leavened with experienced military veterans and frontiersmen. The New Zealand government had already tried advertising in Sydney for recruits for the Colonial Defence Force Cavalry in mid-May 1863, but had drawn only 20 volunteers across the Tasman for its trouble. This time Grey and the government believed the terms of service were attractive enough to greatly surpass that effort. Some spoke of enticing 20 000 volunteers to leave Australia for war in New Zealand.[42]

Taranaki was chosen as the pilot model for the scheme. The terms of service for military settler service in that province were gazetted on 6 July 1863. Each man was promised two grants of land on completion of the terms of service: a farm of 50 acres for a private (and increasing in size depending upon rank) and a town allotment. The recruits were effectively treated as full-time militiamen during their three years of active duty. A similar set of regulations for would-be Waikato military settlers was issued a month later.[43] Surprisingly both sets of regulations restricted the area of service to the provinces of Taranaki and Auckland respectively.[44] This oversight was hurriedly corrected in a final set of regulations, gazetted on 12 September, that extended service to the entire North Island and also explicitly made allowances for Australian recruits by offering them free passage to a New Zealand port.[45]

The recruits were organised into self-contained companies of 112 men, including two officers and ten NCOs. Ten companies were enough to form a regiment, and in the end the scheme attracted enough volunteers to raise and sustain one Taranaki and four Waikato regiments. The Taranaki Regiment included large numbers of men from Otago, in the South Island, where the discovery of gold in May 1861 had sparked a frenzy that drew men from as far away as California. Otago's population grew by 20 000 during 1863 alone and, together with the Australian colonies, was targeted by the New Zealand government as a key manpower source for the military settler scheme.[46] Although men recruited in Otago were considered New Zealand recruits by the authorities, many had only recently arrived from the goldfields of Australia.

The first official New Zealand recruiting mission to Australia arrived in Sydney in mid-August 1863. It was led by Lieutenant Colonel George Dean Pitt, New Zealand Colonial Militia. Pitt was a good choice, having only recently left the service of the Victorian government where he had helped to organise the local volunteer forces. The first contingent of 80 recruits, including a number of members drawn from the Sydney Volunteer Rifles, left for Auckland on 28 August and were farewelled by a crowd of 500 friends, family and well-wishers.[47] Hundreds more followed, and Pitt got an even bigger response when he moved on to Melbourne. By the time the last New Zealand recruiting mission to Australia was halted in August 1864, approximately 2500 men from the Australian colonies had volunteered to serve in New Zealand.[48] Many, it must be said, had been enticed by the promise of land grants in New Zealand as partial payment for their services. The most enthusiastic colonies were New South Wales, Victoria and Tasmania, followed by Queensland (a separate colony from as recently as 1859) and to a much lesser extent South Australia. Western Australia was the only colony not to raise a group of volunteers.

It was not so much the raw numbers – unprecedented as they were – that was noteworthy about these volunteers: it was the way they were recruited and deployed as identifiable groups and acquired unofficial titles such as the 'Melbourne Contingent', 'New South Wales Volunteers' and so on.[49] The New Zealand government may have been paying their wages, and had literally given them a one-way ticket to New Zealand, but unofficially the Australian military settlers considered themselves the pride of their 'home' colonies while the citizens of Melbourne, Hobart or Sydney thought of them as 'their boys'. Such was the level of local interest stirred by the departure of the first contingents that shortly afterwards both the *Sydney Morning Herald* and the

Melbourne *Argus* sent their own war correspondents to cover the war in general and the exploits of the Australian volunteers in particular.[50]

The Waikato War finally erupted on 17 July 1863, when British troops crossed the Mangatawhiri Stream and began to push south, flanked on their right by the mighty Waikato River.[51] Cameron's plan was to support his field army with a river flotilla that would accompany it all the way down the Waikato and into the Kingite heartland. The flotilla included a number of gunboats and monitors which offered Cameron invaluable fire support for his advance. Three of the river gunboats – *Pioneer*, *Koheroa* and *Rangiriri* – were designed and built in Sydney at short notice for the New Zealand government in 1863 at a cost of £30 000. *Pioneer* began operations on the Waikato River in November 1863, and was joined by her sister ships the following March. The vessels were operated by a specially raised Water Transport Corps (including some Australians), a colonial unit technically under the direct command of the Royal Navy as New Zealand did not have a colonial navy. New Zealand government agents also filled Australian colonial coffers by emptying Australian militia depots of surplus weapons, ammunition and accoutrements. Private business similarly enjoyed New Zealand government contracts to supply everything from uniforms to oxen (used to provide the heavy lift for the Imperial Commissariat Transport Corps). The New Zealand Wars definitely had an economic upside for the Australian colonies.[52]

River boats and barges would also help keep Cameron's land column in supply throughout the campaign, but they could not eliminate the need for good land-based lines of communication. The broken terrain, dense native bush and treacherous swamps of the Waikato region made it tough going on foot or horseback and almost impassable for wheeled transport. The Great

Southern Road therefore had to be extended through this country.[53] An Imperial Commissariat Transport Service was established to build and run this military lifeline.

Kingite forces put up staunch resistance. They pursued a two-pronged strategy of defending a series of fighting *pa* erected to obstruct Cameron's advance into the Waikato, and sending raiding parties to attack supply columns along the Great Southern Road so as to disrupt the lines of communication with Auckland. This strategy succeeded in delaying Cameron's advance for the first three months of the campaign, and proved beyond doubt the necessity of the military settler regiments to the ultimate success of the campaign. Once they had arrived in sufficient numbers to nullify the threat from Kingite raiding parties, Cameron was able to resume his advance, eventually penetrating deep enough to overrun villages and cultivations and destroy the logistical heart of the Kingite war effort.

The elimination of the fighting *pa* in his path led to major battles at Rangiriri (20–21 November 1863) and Orakau (31 March to 2 April 1864). He then followed up this effort with an expedition to attack the pro-Kingite Ngati Te Rangi and Ngati Ranganui tribes in the Bay of Plenty on the east coast. This resulted in a British defeat at the Battle of Gate Pa (28–29 April) before British fortunes were restored with a victory at Te Ranga (21 June) where the British surprised a Ngati Te Rangi force in the middle of building a *pa*. Subsidiary operations to keep the Taranaki tribes in check were also carried out during this period. The victory at Te Ranga effectively brought the war to a close and cleared the way for massive confiscation of 'rebel' land by the New Zealand government in both Waikato and the Bay of Plenty.[54]

The role of the Australian military settlers in the Waikato regiments was to support the advance of Cameron's imperial troops by guarding the Great Southern Road and manning redoubts across the southern Auckland region to deter and react against Kingite raiding parties. The 1st Waikato Regiment was also included in Cameron's expedition to the Bay of Plenty where they fought at Te Ranga, the only major battle where the military settlers played an active role – although it was more of a one-sided massacre than a pitched battle. The Taranaki Regiment's job was also to play second fiddle in support of the operations of the 57th Regiment, the only imperial regiment left in Taranaki for most of the time.

Despite attempts by some newspapers to turn skirmishes and raids involving Australian military setters into actions of epic proportions, there was no disguising the fact that their war was a decidedly unglamorous one compared to their imperial counterparts. The job they did was essential to the military strategy, but it was also one of dull monotonous routine in wet and primitive conditions, punctuated by clashes with Māori raiders just frequently enough to ensure that the tension and paranoia of bush fighting remained a constant companion. It is telling that some of the more gung-ho types among the military settler regiments transferred to the Commissariat Transport Service to better their chances of seeing action.

Australian military settlers suffered 21 deaths related to combat and a further 70 or so died of disease or accident before the regiments were disbanded on August 1867.[55] The first battle casualties occurred on 23 October 1863, when seven soldiers (including four 'Melbourne Contingent' men) belonging to No 9 Company, 1st Waikato Regiment, were killed in action during a Kingite raid on a farm at Titi Hill near Drury in south Auckland.[56] The last was 19-year-old Private Henry Jeffs, also from Melbourne, who was killed in action while serving in No 8 Company, 1st Waikato Regiment, on the east coast on 15 February 1867.[57]

By the time of Private Jeffs' death, the original enthusiasm with which the Australian colonies had supported the war effort had long since dissipated. Australian colonial governments had actively supported the first New Zealand recruiting missions, and while the New Zealanders may have been disappointed not to have wooed 20 000 across the Tasman, the Australian authorities quickly came to the conclusion that 2500 was more than enough. The Australian colonial press also began to grumble about New Zealand 'poaching' Australian settlers. Initially the New Zealand government had targeted single men (by refusing to pay passage or support to wives and families of volunteers), but this policy proved unworkable and was rescinded on both counts by the end of 1863. This made the charge of poaching even more plausible as families followed in the wake of their men.

As early as January 1864 the Victorian premier, James McCulloch, informed a startled Colonel Pitt that he was to cease his recruiting efforts in Victoria. Hastily convened talks with the New Zealand colonial treasurer, Reader Wood – who happened to be in Melbourne on other business – confirmed the gruff premier's stance.[58] Other colonies did not immediately follow Victoria's lead, nor were they all so explicit in their change of heart, but by 1865 the New Zealand government knew its days of large-scale recruiting drives in Australia were no longer politically feasible.

The biggest factor contributing to Australian disenchantment with the New Zealand wars was undoubtedly the problems besetting the military settler scheme by late 1866 and the subsequent poor treatment of many of the Australian volunteers. As the fighting died down, the Waikato regiments were redeployed across the newly conquered territories and ordered to carve new military settlements and farms out of the bush. Problems arose immediately because the government had not provided adequate funds for such ambitious projects.

As the first wave of volunteers completed their three years service they found themselves waiting for land allotments that in many places had not even been surveyed. The lack of infrastructure meant those who did get their land often found it impossible to put to any productive use. Others still serving were put on half-pay as a cost-saving measure, yet were required to work as full-time labourers. Wives and children were left to languish in overcrowded barracks in Auckland as the promised new homes and lives failed to materialise. Arguments over arrears in pay on discharge became common. In time many of these problems were overcome and, within a decade, the military settlements of Cambridge, Hamilton and Tauranga would be busy, bustling frontier towns. But most could not afford to ride out the early hardships and they ended up selling their allotments to speculators for a pittance. Stories emerged of men left destitute, unable to even afford a passage back to Australia. The news of such hardships and apparent injustices did make it back, however, and did much to discredit the scheme – as well as the wider war – in the minds of readers in Sydney, Melbourne and elsewhere.[59]

Grey's success in obtaining a total of ten British Army regiments for service in New Zealand had come largely at the expense of the Australian colonial garrisons. This caused further resentment among the Australian colonial leadership when, in the wake of the Waikato War, Grey did all he could to delay returning these 'Australian' imperial regiments to their original postings, ordering Cameron to redeploy the bulk of his imperial troops to Taranaki in order to crush reinvigorated resistance there before calls for the return of imperial regiments became too loud to ignore.

The war was won, but victory was not necessarily sweet. The authority of traditional tribal chiefs and social structures was badly undermined by the destruction and defeats suffered by the Kingites in 1863–64, and this led to the emergence of much more radical responses to the European threat. Charismatic self-proclaimed warrior-prophets, whose teachings were derived from a blend of indigenous beliefs and Old Testament Christianity, inspired a new wave of armed resistance, smaller in scale than before but more fanatical than anything the pakeha had previously faced in New Zealand. The most powerful of these new movements, the Pai Marire or Hauhau religion, was founded in the Taranaki in 1863 and later spread across the central North Island in the wake of the Waikato War. The renewed conflict in the Taranaki dragged on until 1866, while the East Coast War – as much a civil war between pro- and anti-Hauhau Māori tribal factions as anything else – lasted until 1868.[60]

Grey had to give up most of his imperial troops after 1866, and even the remaining 'peacetime' British garrison was withdrawn in 1870. Plans were made to replace all the colonial forces raised since 1862 with an Armed Constabulary, a 2000-man para-military force modelled directly upon the Irish Constabulary.[61] This was a demonstration of the government's confidence that, despite the best efforts of the Hauhau and other zealots to keep fighting, the backbone of Māori armed resistance had in fact been broken. The *Armed Constabulary Act* came into force on 1 November 1867. Most of its manpower transferred from existing colonial units, including a number of former Australian military settlers. It also led to the last official New Zealand recruiting mission to Australia, with the arrival in Melbourne of Captain William Stack in November 1868. He left two months later with a contingent of 205 men. Premier McCulloch raised no objections on this occasion, perhaps because of the modest number involved and the pains taken by Stack to exclude married men.[62]

The emergence of the Armed Constabulary also sounded the death knell for the military settler scheme. On 27 June 1867 the New Zealand government cancelled the terms under which land had been promised under the scheme. Those who had yet to receive their allotments would now simply miss out. If this betrayal wasn't bad enough, the final nail in the coffin came three months later when all five military settler regiments were officially disbanded.[63] Those on half pay or otherwise subsidised by the regiments' programme of civil works were left to fend as best they could. For many it was the last straw and they left the settlements to find employment in more established parts of the colony or returned to Australia.

It was an ignominious end to a venture that had initially roused such martial passion and pride among the Australasian colonies. The men who had been cheered off in groups as the 'Melbourne Contingent' or the 'Tasmanian Contingent' slunk back in to port as individuals, most with nothing but bitterness and lost years to show for it. (The ones with happier tales to tell were by default the ones who stayed in New Zealand and made a go of it whether as farmers, townsfolk or soldiers. They were also clearly in the minority.) Although the New Zealand Wars ultimately ended in victory for the British Empire it did not feel like much of a victory for most of the Australians who had fought in it, the early endeavours of HMCS *Victoria*'s crew notwithstanding. It is hardly surprising that Australia's first experience of fighting an overseas war was left to quietly fade from collective memory.

An official campaign medal was authorised in 1869 and remained available for claim for 31 years until the rolls were closed in 1900. Despite being available to colonial veterans (the majority of whom were New Zealand enlistments) as well as imperial ones, it speaks volumes that only 2500 New Zealand War medals were issued to the former.[64] Only 20 per cent of the Australians who served in the Waikato regiments claimed the New Zealand War Medal. But of course by then the Australian colonies were enthusiastically engaged in a new overseas war at the behest of the British Empire and no one much cared for dubious old stories of chasing (or being chased) by fierce tribes of cannibals in the wilds of New Zealand. The war in South Africa was a 'real' war, and this time Australians would settle for nothing less than a starring role for 'their boys'.

Further reading

J Alexander, *Bush Fighting: The Māori War in New Zealand*, orig 1873, Capper Press, Christchurch, 1973

A Ballara, *Taua: 'Musket Wars', 'Land Wars' or Tikanga? Warfare in Māori Society in the Early Nineteenth Century*, Penguin, Auckland, 2003

L Barton, *Australians in the Waikato War 1863–1864*, Library of Australian History, Sydney, 1979

J Belich, *The New Zealand Wars and the Victorian Interpretation of Racial Conflict*, Auckland University Press, Auckland, 1986

E Best, *The Pa Māori*, Dominion Museum, Wellington, 1927

J Cowan, *The New Zealand Wars*, 2 vols, Government Printer, Wellington, 1922–1923

R Crosby, *The Musket Wars: A History of Inter-Iwi Conflict 1806–1845*, Reed Books, Auckland, 1999

F Glen, *For Glory and a Farm*, Whakatane Historical Society, Whakatane, 1984

——, 'New Zealand Wars, Australian involvement in', in I McGibbon (ed), *The Oxford Companion to New Zealand Military History*, OUP, Auckland, 2000

——, *Australians at War in New Zealand*, Wilsonscott, Christchurch, 2011

D Green, *Battlefields of the New Zealand Wars: A Visitor's Guide*, Penguin, Auckland, 2010

J Hopkins-Weise, *Blood Brothers: The Anzac Genesis*, Penguin, Auckland, 2009

I Knight, *Māori Fortifications*, Osprey, Oxford, 2009

——, *The New Zealand Wars 1820–1872*, Osprey, Oxford, 2013

R Stowers, *New Zealand Medal to Colonials*, private pubn, Hamilton, 1998

7

The rifle clubs

Andrew Kilsby

Many Australians of the twenty-first century would be surprised to learn that firearms were an integral part of this nation's colonial and early Federation culture. Whether for military purposes – represented by British imperial garrisons and after 1870 by local unpaid volunteers and paid part-time militia – or for policing, for self-defence or game and bird sport, virtually everyone in Australia owned a firearm or knew someone who did. Moreover, in Australia rifle shooting became more than a sport: it became a (predominantly male) national pastime. The growth of the rifle club movement, as it became known by the early years of the twentieth century, was a natural consequence. The first organised rifle club in Australia was raised in Sydney in 1845, and by mid-1911 there were more than 50 600 rifle club members in the country. By 1917, that number peaked at over 100 000. That the significance of the rifle club movement has slipped from currently dominant conceptions of Australia's military past does not make it a tale less worth telling.

The rifle club movement was indelibly interconnected with ideas of national defence. People across the political and social spectrum believed that the pre-Federation colonies and then the new nation should be able to at least contribute to their own defence, if not actually defend themselves against threats.[1] The formation of Australian colonial rifle associations went hand-in-hand with the first formal wave of volunteer units formed by colonists. In fact, the social nature and amateur status of many volunteer units meant they operated as *de facto* rifle clubs. By December 1861, the strength of local forces in the various Australian colonies was only 4002.[2] The volunteer movement in the Australian colonies was to wax and wane as 'war scares' came and went over the years. The level of government support for volunteers also varied accordingly, usually in direct proportion to the size of the alarm and the wealth of the colony. Notwithstanding this, hundreds of volunteer riflemen were recruited or volunteered to join the British regiments fighting the Māori in the New Zealand Wars which spluttered along from 1860 to 1869 (see Chapter 6).[3]

Most of the colonial rifle associations were formed in the 1860s to support the musketry of the volunteer units, and they were controlled and led by volunteer officers. Their evolution reflected the symbiosis between the two main functions of the citizen soldiers of the time: musketry and drill. Musketry took precedence, with annual prize shoots arranged by the associations easily meeting the standard musketry skill requirements of the volunteer units under their imperial instructors. Yet the volunteers' marksmanship was often poor, and they were often seen as figures ripe for parody. The visiting imperial regiments and detachments, understandably, stood somewhat aloof from these developments.

The growth of rifle club movement in Australia also owed much to similar developments in Britain. In 1859 the British National Rifle Association was formed with the support of Queen Victoria and other prominent social and military figures to promote rifle shooting and the volunteers. In 1861, the British association had 1387 members; by 1866 it had 2946.[4] There were by this time over 150 000 volunteers under arms in England. With the Queen's blessing of the British association, rifle shooting in Australia also became both patriotic and popular for volunteers and general citizens alike. Within a year, rifle associations had been formed in New South Wales, Victoria and South Australia, dominated by prominent civic figures, politicians and volunteer officers.[5]

From the early 1870s, some civilian rifle clubs also began to appear, although these were often shunned by the volunteer-dominated rifle associations and companies. When the Victorian Rifle Association (VRA) introduced a rifle clubs match at their annual tournament in 1871, for example, 42 members from seven rifle clubs participated,[6] but civilian clubs remained quite rare even into the 1880s. Rifle associations were largely independent of the formal control of the defence forces, although many of their committee members were either volunteer officers or ex-volunteers. Unlike volunteer companies and later militia, members of rifle clubs were not expected to drill (that is, to practise battlefield manoeuvres). Once the associations began (reluctantly) to admit civilian rifle clubs to annual matches, civilian riflemen soon showed that they were better shots on the range.

From 1870 to mid-1885, an increased concern and effort was being expended on defence matters. Forced in large part by the withdrawal of the British garrisons, permanent and volunteer officers, and their masters in colonial parliaments, began to consider how best to defend their individual colonies. This led to a series of defence reviews by imperial experts, notably in 1877 and 1882, and these in turn led to changes to the defence postures of the colonies. One such change was the start of regular commandants' conferences which began to develop an Australia-wide outlook on defence matters and led directly to the rise of militia forces throughout the colonies in the early 1880s.

The rifle clubs

Victoria, for example, created a Defence Department with its own minister in 1883. The same year Queensland and Tasmania spent more on defence than ever before – although still admittedly as little as possible. While volunteer units continued in some form or other in most colonies, the larger colonies like Victoria and New South Wales, or the more militarised colonies like South Australia, developed robust paid part-time militias and coastal fortifications. Victoria's defences, developed around Port Phillip Bay, became so formidable that they were referred to as the 'Gibraltar of the South'. The impact on, and response to, these developments by the rifle associations across the colonies was not uniform.

A struggle for control of the clubs and associations began from around 1884, between the professional military men, who wanted a greater emphasis on military aspects such as drilling, and the (former volunteer) riflemen who preferred the sporting aspects of rifle shooting. When paid or part-paid militias were introduced in most colonies in the mid-1880s, a good number of former volunteer riflemen refused to join the militia, choosing to join rifle clubs instead (especially in Victoria). Although the local military commandants became *ex officio* presidents of the associations, their councils tended to remain firmly in the hands of the ex-volunteers. Rifle clubs and associations in some colonies, like South Australia, succumbed early to the military demands for their attention. Others, especially those in Victoria, resisted more strenuously for reasons unique to that colony.

By the late 1880s, however, club riflemen had to swear the military oath, serve for three years and complete a musketry course – in the same way as militiamen and regular soldiers – to be deemed 'efficient'. They also had to attend a certain number of military drills. This was the sore point for the riflemen, although in return the clubs were given a grant for each 'efficient' rifleman and free grants of ammunition. Club riflemen could also purchase government-standard rifles and extra ammunition at reduced cost. Accordingly, most rifle clubs quickly agreed to abide by these rules. Riflemen, who were used to working out the odds of hitting a target in all sorts of conditions, didn't take long to work out that the likelihood of a real emergency and call-out was remote. After all, they could still resign on short notice.

With the introduction of paid militia, pressure also grew for the rifle associations to conduct matches which catered more for the needs of the military. With a major war scare in 1885 – this time caused by fear that Russia would go to war with England – riflemen of the South Australian and Tasmanian rifle associations and affiliated clubs, as well as clubs in other colonies, attended the Easter encampments of the militia and took part in their drills. Even in Victoria, a debate erupted from 1886 as to whether rifle clubs were part of the defence forces. This was partly driven by rifle clubs formed from militia units so that they could compete for prizes in the annual matches of the VRA, and partly to allow Victoria to field their best 'civilian' shots in the intercolonial volunteer matches. (Until then rifle club members who were not also 'efficient' volunteers were disbarred from intercolonial matches.)

Now officially sanctioned, from the late 1880s civilian rifle clubs began to boom in numbers. This growth saw civilian clubs gaining seats on rifle association councils, as well as influencing the types of matches being shot and the prizes being offered in those associations' annual matches. Paradoxically, this occurred at the same time as the military began to view rifle clubs as increasingly important – and cheap – potential military assets. The rifle clubs were filled with men who could at least shoot, increasingly armed with the latest service rifles, and amenable to the aims and aspirations of the defence community, albeit a community dominated by militia. In Victoria, these assets were actively mined to create two large new volunteer corps, namely the Victorian Mounted Rifles and Victorian Rangers. In other colonies, like South Australia and New South Wales, rifle clubs were expected to also become more involved with their militia counterparts, both in training and conduct of rifle shooting matches 'under service conditions'.

By 1888, when the rifle associations of the separate colonies finally came together and formed an Australia-wide national council, their collective leadership was in no doubt that they were joined to the defence forces as a reserve force of some kind (albeit still undefined by statute or regulation). The rifle associations were supported by their respective colonial governments with various grants, and by the military with free issues of ammunition and use of service rifles and military ranges. In return the military advisors to the governments asked for more control over the rifle clubs and their operations. This push for more control was led by officers in various colonies, but most notably by imperial commandants in New South Wales, Major General Edward Hutton and then Major General George Arthur French, and followed intercolonial military conferences from the early 1890s. However, at the working end of this relationship there was a growing conflict between the military goals on one side and the rifle clubs on the other.

Imperial defence expert General Sir James Bevan Edwards, appointed by the British government to conduct yet another inspection of colonial defences, delivered his detailed report to the colonial governments in October 1889.[7] Edwards' report led to an Australia-wide inspection tour by colonial military commandants of sites for fixed defences – places like Thursday Island in the Torres Strait and Albany in Western Australia.[8] Edwards' report was the first to consider rifle clubs in any detail. Among the raft of recommendations both general and particular was a specific recommendation that volunteer riflemen become reservists for the militia.

Subsequent to the report, most of the colonies upgraded their military legislation, most regulating rifle clubs in one form or another. In the short term, the report stimulated impetus to considering exactly how rifle clubs met defence needs.[9] The report also highlighted the type of matches being held at the annual meetings of the colonial associations, stirred interest by military officers in the potential resource that rifle clubs seemed to offer them, and raised into prominence over the following years a number of important differences between the way that rifle associations had been developing and how the military officers thought they should be developing. In short, Edwards' report was the first catalyst to what would become a fundamental issue; whether rifle shooting, as managed by the associations, was there to support the training of the military rifleman, or to train civilian marksmen to win prizes.

Relations between the military and the clubs in New South Wales in the 1890s illustrated the growing tension between the military's modernising aims and the conservatism of the rifle club movement. In January 1894, the colony had a new commandant: Major General Hutton.[10] A highly influential officer – he had most recently been an aide de camp to Queen Victoria herself – he had seen recent active service in Africa and Egypt. He had attended meetings of the New South Wales Rifle Association (NSWRA) in October 1893 and now began a series of inspection tours of militia units, defences and rifle clubs throughout the colony. Following the disbanding of the reserve rifle companies in New South Wales in 1893, Hutton recommended a reorganised force structure which recognised civilian rifle clubs – so long as their members swore the oath of allegiance, making them *bona fide* defence force members (although they still managed to avoid drill).

Hutton also proposed to the NSWRA in late 1895 that military and civilian representation on the council of the association be proportionate.[11] While the vice-presidents contained many military men in their number, it was the inner council of the rifle association which actually ran it, and this was an 'old guard' of long-serving, former volunteers and, increasingly, civilians who were also often former volunteers. The council promptly buried Hutton's proposal. When Hutton finished his appointment as commandant in early 1896, he was replaced by another imperial officer, Major General French. Hutton no doubt gave French a good briefing.

French, like Hutton, actively supported rifle shooting, and he showed a keen interest in everything to do with musketry. At French's urging, three new military-style matches were included in the 1896 programme of the New South Wales division of what was now the National Rifle Association (NRA). But when French made his annual report to the colonial parliament in June 1897, it took the association by complete surprise. French directly criticised the association's riflemen as 'pot-hunters' – essentially elitist marksmen who were more interested in competing for trophies that in improving the general military musketry standards for the bulk of the militia or volunteers. Other signs of growing military irritation were becoming evident. In July 1897, for example, military units effectively avoided attendance at the military matches of the Northern Rifle Association meeting because the matches were not made exclusive to them.

French was noticeably absent from the New South Wales association's annual matches in October 1897. A dramatic falling-off in the number of teams entering for the military matches made it apparent to everyone but the association that something was going on. The military were also irritated by the small prize money allocated to the military matches, but these were just the visible signs of a growing military antagonism towards the association. It was not as if this was new. Ever since the first Commandants' Conference in Sydney in 1894, and perhaps even before that, the message had been delivered: the military commandants wanted service conditions for shooting in rifle association matches.

French's frustration at the conservatism of the New South Wales association and its aging leadership of former volunteer officers finally boiled over in early 1898. He established a military committee to investigate the effectiveness of the rifle association which, unsurprisingly, heavily criticised the association and demanded changes. These included the right of the commandant to veto matches and approve association programmes, to have the books audited by the government, and most of all, to change the rifle association council by having 12 officers directly appointed by the commandant. A newspaper war erupted as the rifle association and its allies quickly lined up against French and his supporters.

The New South Wales rifle association appealed for support from other colonial associations and clubs. It even appealed for relief directly to the colonial premier – only to be forced to hand over the three main military matches and half the government subsidy to the commandant. French went further. In early 1899, he established the Defence Forces Rifle Association, with the governor as patron, in direct competition with the colonial rifle association, and he invited civilian rifle clubs to affiliate with it. This conflict in New South Wales was the most dramatic evidence of the growing frustration by military officers that the rifle club men were supported with publicly funded grants, range staff, ammunition and some free railway travel but did not – or would not – concede that for military purposes their men needed to drill to learn how to manoeuvre on a battlefield. (In most circumstances, accurate individual fire was less important to the military than massed fire brought to bear on the right point by manoeuvre.) Underlying the tension was a hubristic disdain by the expert, mostly civilian, rifle club men for the part-time militiamen, a disdain reciprocated by the militia who considered the club men as effete military at best.

In Victoria a different experience manifested itself, with the more military orientation being promoted from within the club structure. In the mid-1880s a highly successful (volunteer) Victorian Mounted Rifles (VMR) was created from rifle club members, especially in the country districts. This was quickly followed by the Volunteer Rifles (soon renamed the Victorian Rangers) in March 1888, also formed from rifle clubs. In 1886 the commander of the VMR even had some explaining to do when he called the Melbourne Rifle Club 'pot-hunters' as they competed for prizes against the militia.[12] The government also began to apply pressure to the sporting shooters, and in June 1885 it recognised only 17 rifle clubs hosting 217 sworn-in members (listed as infantry) and 302 mounted rifles members. There were in Victoria at the time possibly as many as 306 rifle clubs and about 6000 riflemen, but they were not sworn in and so now cut off from government support. Unsurprisingly, within a few months 51 more clubs had been sworn in.[13] By mid-1887, the VMR had 968 men under arms, while sworn-in members of rifle clubs numbered 4736 (against 3595 a year earlier). These civilian shooters consistently outshot the militia in annual Victorian matches.[14]

Unsurprisingly, the tensions between the military and sporting aspects of the clubs continued to grow. Military officers increasingly insisted that, in return for grants and ammunition, the rifle clubs should act more like military units and shoot and drill on the rifle range as if they were in the field. They wanted matches reflecting conditions on the battlefield, such as fire and movement, volley firing and disappearing or moving targets. The rifle clubs, on the other hand, were moving inexorably towards target shooting at longer and fixed ranges, with bigger cash prizes.

Paradoxically exacerbating the divisions between the military ethos and the rifle clubs was the outbreak of the South African War in 1899. The early successes of mounted and mobile Boer riflemen against the regular British Army units seemed to confirm the rifle clubs' view that their members didn't need to drill to be effective. The fact that South Africa's colonial forces used the same type of irregulars and mounted riflemen against the Boers, with equal success, seemed to further vindicate this view.

Regardless of such debates, the start of the war accelerated the activities of rifle shooting around Australia. Thousands joined the existing rifle clubs, and hundreds of new rifle clubs were formed in the years to the end of the war in May 1902. Many hundreds (the exact number is not known) of rifle club members or former members volunteered to join one of the colonial and later Australian contingents to South Africa. A number were killed or died of disease on active service, including two who had been delegates to the federal council of rifle associations.

During the South African War, the growth of civilian rifle clubs across Australia was nothing short of phenomenal, especially in Victoria. By mid-1898, Victoria already had over 1500 rifle club members as part of its defence establishment. (Queensland by comparison had just 500 rifle club men.)[15] But the wartime growth in rifle club numbers, as reported in the VRA report of November 1900, made these figures pale by comparison:

> The stirring events of the year emphasize the wisdom of encouraging rifle shooting as a necessary element of our

The rifle clubs

> National defence ... In particular, Rifle Clubs to the number of 330 have been gazetted, and at the present time Victoria possesses a line of defence comprising some 19 000 riflemen, animated with a desire to qualify themselves as marksmen.[16]

The scene was set for a great post-war debate, with the rifle shooting movement squarely in the middle. By this time, the rifle associations and their national council were in general united by need. The necessity of maintaining their incomes against parsimonious governments and tightening defence requirements meant that they could not ignore their true constituency, the civilian rifle clubs and the growth in their membership. At the same time, the associations also very much needed to placate the military to guarantee continued access to grants, ammunition and travel concessions.

By May 1901, the newly declared Commonwealth Council of the Rifle Associations of Australia (CCRAA) maintained apparently good relations with the defence establishment, despite disagreements over 'ways and means' to support the rifle club movement. From 1902, however, the new commanding officer of the Australian Military Forces was Major General Hutton, the former anti-club commandant of New South Wales, and he was busy reorganising the Australian defence force through regulation and preparing for Australia's first *Defence Act*. New rifle club regulations would follow. In March 1902, at the first CCRAA meeting held for that year, Hutton – also its president – took the opportunity to enunciate his views on rifle-shooting at length to the delegates. The *Argus* reported his strong support for the CCRAA, so long as it was prepared to act according to his views. Hutton was determined to get military benefit from what was, to his mind, a movement hitherto too preoccupied with competitions and the sporting aspect of shooting. If the government was paying to support rifle clubs, then those clubs had a responsibility to provide some return on the investment. In practical terms this meant practising under military conditions and moving targets, not at static bull's eyes.[17]

Hutton followed his comments to the CCRAA meeting with a minute to the federal Parliament on the defences of Australia:

> The rifle clubs at present constituted in some of the States are organised on sound lines, and their members form a reserve to existing military units. In at least one instance, however, rifle clubs form an organisation apart, which, without officers, without military instruction, and without a system of military organisation can at best provide only a certain number of partially-armed men with an uncertain use of the rifle. The military value of such men as an integral part of the defence forces of Australia can be but small under the existing conditions, and this system requires modification.[18]

The NRA in New South Wales had already been largely cowed by the deliberate programme of intimidation by their own president and state commandant Major General French, who had succeeded Hutton in 1896. Rifle clubs were affiliated with local militia units, and service shooting was instigated. At the national level, Hutton now wanted direct control of the rifle clubs and associations. He would attempt to gain this, as French had done in New South Wales from 1896, by using the two great weapons at his disposal: railway passes and ammunition. He, like French, demanded a return for the government aid to the CCRAA while moving against the older, former volunteer officers running the state associations and the CCRAA itself.

Once again, Victoria was a different matter altogether to New South Wales. When Hutton looked at the VRA, he saw an association which, unlike those in most of the other states, was only nominally under the direction of the local commandant. The rifle clubs in Victoria were actually run by a militia staff officer and former volunteer officer who had been appointed by the colonial (later state) Defence Minister. The VRA council was dominated by an 'old guard' of volunteer officers and heavily influenced by an increasing number of civilian rifle clubs. Indeed, as the South African War came to a close in mid-1902, what was perhaps the most galling feature of the Victorian rifle club movement to the senior military officers was that the officer-in-charge of rifle clubs in Victoria (and president of the VRA), actually had far more men under his command than did the state commandant:

> Owing to the great enthusiasm excited by the war in South Africa there has been an enormous increase of membership, and the strength which on the 30th June, 1899, was 2652, is now (on 19 July 1900) 14 200, and many more clubs are in the course of formation ... Members of rifle clubs are not required either to drill or procure uniform.[19]

It is no wonder that Hutton moved against the strength of the movement in Victoria, which was the largest and most independent part of the various states' rifle club movements in Australia. By 18 July 1901, membership in Victorian rifle clubs had leapt to 20 800 (and this out of 29 251 for the whole of the country, to which New South Wales only contributed 1908).[20] Hutton retired the militia officer-in-charge of rifle clubs in Victoria and moved a more junior and compliant officer from New South Wales to act as secretary under the deputy assistant adjutant-general in Victoria. The Victorian members, dismayed at this turn of events, appealed to their representatives and other supporters in Parliament, but without long-term success.

Hutton genuinely supported rifle clubs, but only if they would comply and conform to his plans for them. The resulting tension between the state rifle associations and the CCRAA with General Hutton came to a head in 1904, when the new Defence Bill went before federal Parliament in July. The Bill brought with it a detailed set of rifle club regulations, tying the movement into the new defence structure of Australia and Hutton's vision of the Australian military forces. In January 1904, Hutton circulated a draft of the new regulations for the state commandants to use to gauge the reaction of the associations and clubs.

The result was quickly evident, with resistance from rifle associations in particular and rifle clubs in general, again especially in Victoria. In the face of this resistance, Hutton called a special meeting of the CCRAA. He was as usual determined to get his way, and the opposition of the associations was to no avail. The meeting was conducted behind closed doors, and was notable for its understated outcome. In a single statement to the press, Hutton reiterated his stated plans, and said 'that many useful suggestions been made by the delegates'. His new regulations came into force, unchanged in any way, on 1 March.

By April 1904 the state associations had begun to toe the line, with more service shooting matches, more 'running man' targets at the ranges, and even, in some cases, attendance at drill.[21] In New South Wales, even the Defence Force Rifle Association, formed by French in 1898 as a counter to the local NRA, folded into the state association because of the amount of service shooting now underway in that association. New service rifles – the short magazine Lee-Enfield, SMLE or 'smellie' as they were most popularly known – were also arriving in Australia, and some became available to rifle clubs. However, rail passes were restricted to riflemen within a 50-mile radius of a match, much to the chagrin of those in Queensland in particular, while restricted ammunition issues remained a sore point to many clubs throughout Australia.

As far as Hutton was concerned, the rifle clubs and associations were now part of the military system of defence, so they ought to act like they were. This would always be a frustrated assumption, and by November 1904, Hutton's command of Australian forces was coming to an end. His position was to be replaced by a system comprising a Council of Defence, an Inspector-General and a Military Board, and the processes for that were being put in place with amendments to the *Defence Act* of 1904. Hutton said that 'few of his duties had given him greater pleasure than in making the efforts to place the whole system of rifle shooting upon a general uniform basis'.[22] In a speech before leaving for England, he went on:

> I beg especially to convey my hearty congratulations to
> the riflemen of Australia for the success which the rifle
> club system has already achieved. I trust that the scope of
> its usefulness may still further be extended, and that the
> patriotic movement, so valuable as an auxiliary to the defence
> system of Australia, may be still further developed and
> increased.[23]

His pride was perhaps misplaced. In July 1905 a report on the state of rifle clubs in Australia showed that numbers of rifle club members were dropping: from 32 883 in July 1901 to 30 242. Victoria saw the largest drop, from 21 565 in July 1901 to only 16 283. Queensland and Tasmania saw dramatic falls as well.[24] In Victoria's case, the compulsory retirement of the popular staff officer for rifle clubs and imposition of military regulations on the hitherto independent rifle clubs may have accounted for the decline. In Tasmania, the disastrous effects of Hutton's military reforms on its traditional military culture were also seen to be directly responsible. However the reasons were just as likely practical: a perception that there was less ammunition available for practice, increased bureaucracy around obtaining increasingly fewer railway passes, and the end of the South African War all contributed.

Despite all of these challenges, Hutton's departure saw, in May 1905, a CCRAA delegate from Queensland appointed as a consultative member of the Military Board to represent Australian rifle clubs.[25] The movement now had 'a seat at the table' and thus at perhaps its highest level of influence since it was declared a 'movement' at a public meeting in Melbourne's Town Hall in July 1900. Attending that meeting had been none other than Alfred Deakin. By 1904 Deakin was Defence Minister – and a major advocate of strong Australian defence – and he would go on to be prime minister three times. Coupled with rising concern at growing Japanese power, especially following Japan's victory over Russia in their recently concluded war, and a rising political consensus that Australia needed to be better prepared for its own defence, the rifle club movement was uniquely positioned to capitalise on the sentiment. Yet it failed to do so.

The year 1905 saw new developments. In 1902 Field Marshal Lord Roberts, hero of Kandahar and the war in South Africa, had came out strongly in support of rifle shooting. His major speech on the issue was even circulated to all Australian units by general order.[26] By 1905, however, with his campaign for public support of rifle clubs a relative failure, Roberts began to support a broader objective – mass military training – and openly supported a new, popular organisation formed to promote the idea called the National Defence League (NDL).

From 1905 the NDL quickly spread its message to Australia, where its branch in New South Wales became especially strong. Many rifle club men became involved, such as Lieutenant Herbert

Dakin, secretary of the NRA in New South Wales in 1904, who became the state secretary of the NDL. In August 1906, writing in the NDL's newspaper *The Call*, Dakin called for greater recognition of rifle clubs in the defence system and for them to play a greater role in defence along the lines of the Swiss system, where rifle clubs conducted the militia musketry courses.[27] The most prominent member of the NDL in New South Wales was Lieutenant-Colonel Gerald Ross Campbell, a vice-president of the council of the state NRA.[28] The smaller Victorian division of the NDL was led by newspaper man and former Victorian Mounted Rifles officer Lieutenant Colonel William Thomas Reay.[29] The well-known Victorian rifle shot, delegate to the CCRAA and from May 1906, secretary of the VRA, Philip Fargher, was one of his lieutenants.[30] In the general political atmosphere promoting militarisation in Australian society, the NDL grew in influence.

During 1906 the defence debate continued. As a result of the rifle club representative's advocacy, the Military Board announced in November that captains of rifle clubs could apply for militia commissions as second lieutenants on a ratio of 1:100 to rifle club members in the state of origin.[31] By early 1908, Deakin was developing a scheme for a national guard and three years of military training for every able-bodied male citizen, preceded by service with the cadets where boys would learn the fundamentals of military life like drill and rifle shooting. Sentiment in support of such a universal military training scheme was growing fast. Men who could not join the militia should join rifle clubs. Regardless of what the military men wanted from rifle clubs, the politicians just wanted numbers, and cheap numbers at that.

In England in early 1908, Lord Roberts introduced an imperial cadet rifle shooting scheme, which Australia enthusiastically supported.[32] However, rifle associations continued to resist calls by military men to replace 'pastime' shooting at fixed targets at known ranges with 'service shooting', not because they did not believe service shooting was important, but because they knew sporting riflemen would not join clubs if they did. In short, club revenue was a large motivator in retaining 'pastime shooting', putting aside the very good reasons riflemen advanced to counter the military views on how to best teach recruits how to shoot. Nevertheless, the rifle associations and the military absolutely agreed on one thing – the need to introduce compulsory military service.

Perhaps because of the rising public knowledge of, and interest in, national defence matters, the rifle clubs were on the rise again. At the beginning of 1908, there were 880 rifle clubs with 45 293 members. But as Major General Hoad noted in his first annual report as inspector-general, delivered in March 1908, only 60 per cent of riflemen had completed their musketry course in 1907, indicating that an aversion to military regulations was as strong as ever.[33] State commandants urged riflemen to attend training camps with the militia, but very few did. In Melbourne, after three attempts, 730 men paraded at Williamstown; in Ballarat only 150 out of over 1600 riflemen in the district turned up.[34]

In Western Australia, the state commandant felt such frustration with the attitudes of the rifle club movement towards service conditions that he formed his own Military Rifle Association.[35] Meanwhile, rifle associations bemoaned the small turn-outs by the militia for association service matches. By this time the rifle club movement was suffering from some years of neglect by successive Australian governments. Riflemen everywhere were seeing much talk but little action around issues like replacement of worn-out barrels, provision of uniforms, upkeep of ranges or provision of new ranges for the ever-popular clubs. The new SMLE service rifles were being doled out to rifle clubs in meagre numbers – one rifle per ten men.

The rifle clubs

By late 1909 there were more than 57 000 men in rifle clubs, but the system was creaking at the seams and the number of 'efficients' actually decreasing by 5 per cent over the previous year alone.[36] The struggle for the Australian government to provide for defence needs in a time of rising expectations was matched in rifle shooting by military apathy. Militiamen chose not to compete against civilian riflemen in association competitions, despite the generous funding directed to service shooting matches and prizes, some complaining that the club men invested heavily in tailor-made match rifles and shooting aids.

A new *Defence Act* was passed in September 1909 which introduced universal military training. The Australian government invited Lord Kitchener to visit, in effect to endorse its defence scheme. In a whirlwind trip around Australia from December 1909 into January 1910, Kitchener did just that. One consequence of his report was the recommendation for Australia to be organised around training areas.[37] He also suggested more staff to administer rifle clubs, and Major MM Boam, the secretary of the rifle clubs in Victoria since 1902, was subsequently appointed in early 1911 as the first Commonwealth Director of Rifle Associations and Rifle Clubs (DRA&RC), reporting to the army's adjutant-general. By the beginning of 1910, the rifle clubs were in place as the third tier of defence for those men who had completed their militia service or who were in some other way unable to do training. However, there were major problems in the system.

Until the new rifle factory at Lithgow began manufacturing after its opening in June 1912, there remained a chronic shortage of rifles. The rifle clubs were eventually promised one modern magazine SMLE on loan between five men, while the rest were issued worn-out older 'long' Lee-Enfields from militia service. Rifle ranges were also in short supply everywhere, causing conflicts with militia units which wanted to practise on the same days as rifle clubs. The militia demanded precedence, sometimes on ranges which had been constructed mainly by rifle club effort. The government, always short of money, eked out grants to the rifle associations and the CCRAA as well as to the new directly controlled rifle club districts and unions throughout the states. Meanwhile, at least until the universal training obligations began in 1911, men continued to flock to rifle clubs.

The rapid change in the defence structure had a profound impact on rifle clubs and their associations. Suddenly there were questions about riflemen's fitness levels, mobilisation plans were drawn up, and more pressure was applied to induce rifle club men to wear uniforms, drill and join militia training. Alexander Ferguson, a consultative member of the Military Board representing Australian rifle clubs, had his tenure extended, but some in the rifle club movement wanted more representation. Others pushed for riflemen to be awarded long-service medals. Both requests were refused. A basic tension remained: the government wanted the rifle clubs to be the third line of defence, but wouldn't (or couldn't) give them the resources to become efficient. The associations and rifle clubs demanded more and more money, without which they maintained that they could not wear uniforms or drill.

Despite all the ostensible efforts to conform to the military's desires for 'shooting under service conditions', by this time the programmes of the state association matches were essentially the same as they were 20 years before. There were a few service matches, but by and large the associations remained wedded to their fixed-target competitions and continued to argue vehemently that the marksman was the key to good rifle deployment and success on the battlefield. In a curious move, given the state of relations with Defence, the NRA in New South Wales decided to abolish service matches altogether from its October programme.

It reasoned that since there had been such a dearth of military entries for those matches it could not afford to continue them, despite the fact that they were obliged to devote half of the prize money grants to military matches. As one South Australian military officer was to put it later, the military:

> wants a man who can load and fire rapidly, and fairly accurately, at moving figures as well as almost invisible earthworks. The military shot has to learn to judge distance, how to take cover, and render covering fire … whereas the rifle shot is a bullseye man. He requires the exact range, the exact wind, and plenty of time to sight. So long as they are shooting under such vastly different conditions there will never be any co-operation between the two.[38]

The rifle associations seemed at times oblivious to the growth of feeling against them in military circles. Well entrenched with political and popular support, they felt impervious to criticism. Relations between the rifle club movement and its associations and the military had reached a critical impasse. By this stage the military saw the rifle clubs, by and large, in the same light as tennis clubs, and ignored suggestions that they trained recruits in musketry. The essential failure of the rifle club movement to embrace service shooting meant it became completely unable to influence rifle shooting in the military. It was both an opportunity missed and a vicious circle entrenched, which only the coming war would break.

In 1913 the incoming DRA&RC, Major William Henry Osborne, introduced a set of rifle club regulations, which gave him the power to administer every aspect of both clubs and associations, including the CCRAA. The DRA&RC now also distributed grant money to associations.[39] Military control of the rifle club movement in most states continued to grow tighter as universal training grew apace. Early in 1914, yet another inspection by an imperial officer occurred when General Sir Ian Hamilton came to Australia at the invitation of the federal government. Hamilton, like Lord Kitchener before him, swung through most of the country and provided a high-level report to Parliament. He inspected rifle club parades, and pronounced himself to be happy enough. 'I have noticed that, when being assembled for inspection or to be addressed, they show themselves capable of performing the more elementary military movements', he sniffed. But he also had a more important comment and warning: 'so long as the Rifle Clubs form the only reserve for the active army, Australian defence must rest on too narrow a foundation'.[40]

With war in Europe increasingly looking inevitable, each state prepared mobilisation schemes. Rifle clubs, the 'efficient' members of which were expected to be available in time of war, were allocated to militia units: 3000 to the Light Horse, 15 000 to the infantry, 1500 to the service and medical corps, 120 to be cable guards, and 9000 on stand-by for future allotment.[41] But the rifle club men still had no uniforms, had few modern service rifles, and certainly were not being used in any meaningful way to assist in training the recruits into the militia or cadets with basic rifle skills. In a speech made in July 1914, Defence Minister Edward Millen promised to increase the allocation of modern service rifles to clubs to bring the ratio up to one between every two men, but he still baulked at the cost of uniforms. He noted the antipathy of militia officers to the rifle clubs, but felt that Australia had no choice but to depend on the riflemen as its only ready reserve.[42]

In July 1914, having visited almost every club in Australia over the previous 18 months, Osborne completed his first report to Parliament on the state of the rifle clubs in Australia. He recorded that on 1 July 1914, there were 1142 clubs nationwide, with 48 226 members of whom 35 080 (73 per cent) were graded 'efficient'. He noted that the number of rifle ranges in operation had risen to 798, and that there were a total of 64 district rifle club unions throughout the country. Government grants had been handed out to the CCRAA (£700), state associations (£5000), district unions (£5000), and remote area unions and clubs (£5000).[43] Considering the size of the rifle club movement, this was a cheap defence reserve indeed, even when adding the cost of range construction and maintenance, and salaries of the rifle club supervisors and range inspectors. (The 800 000 rounds of ammunition expended annually was bought by the riflemen themselves at a discount.)

Osborne's report also addressed at length the dramatic falling off of militia riflemen competing in rifle association and district union competitions. There was, he said, no clear reason for this to occur, but he had also noted that in many instances commanding officers of militia units just happened to call their weekly parades when these matches were to be held. It was an interesting insight into the continuing rift between the rifle clubs and militia units. Osborne stated: 'It seems a hard thing to say, but it would seem that the Rifle Clubs are composed of men who can shoot but can't drill, while the Citizen Forces can drill but can't shoot; if they can, they are very modest about it.'[44] This was a damning indictment of the situation just a month before the declaration of war. It comes as no surprise that the rifle clubs were essentially ignored by military planners when that time came.

With the outbreak of World War I, the rifle club movement, by now with almost 50 000 men in formed units, was completely by-passed by the Defence Department. It recognised the weaknesses of the movement and understood that the domestic, socially orientated rifle club structure – despite its theoretical military value – would be more hindrance than help to forming and despatching an expeditionary force to Europe. So the rifle clubs, as formed units, took no part in the war in any meaningful way.

Although numbers in rifle clubs in Australia grew to an astonishing 118000 by 1917, its fit and able members enlisted in the army as individuals. By the end of the war, while thousands of rifle club men had been killed or wounded, this did little to change the professional military officers' view of rifle clubs, especially in the era of industrialised warfare that came to characterise fighting by the end of the war. While it can be said that the rifle clubs movement, which all along had seen itself as an essential reserve for the defence of Australia, was sidelined by the fact that the war was not to come to Australia, the main reasons for this occurring was its resistance to change after Federation, and especially its inability to adapt to the needs of Commonwealth military structures after 1911, or even during the South African War a decade before. Caught between its volunteer military antecedents and its predominantly civilian ethos, the rifle club movement was unable to be useful militarily when such circumstances finally arrived. Yet Australian military history is more than battles won and lost. The importance and influence over time of the rifle club movement on the home front for almost 70 years prior to World War I was substantial, and worthy of recognition.

Further reading

IFW Beckett, *Riflemen Form: A Study of the Rifle Volunteer Movement 1859–1908*, Ogilby Trusts, Aldershot, 1982

JB Campbell, *The Rifle Club Movement: A Distinct Factor in the Defence Problem*, Metropolitan Rifle Clubs Association/Fraser & Jenkinson, Melbourne, 1909

JE Corcoran, *The Target Rifle in Australia 1860–1900*, Dolphin Press, Sydney, 1975

CH Cromack, *The History of the National Rifle Association of New South Wales, 1860–1956*, Utility Press, Sydney, 1956

T Griffiths, *Lithgow's Small Arms Factory and its People 1907–1950*, vol 1, Toptech Engineering, Sydney, 2006

The rifle clubs

AP Humphry and TF Fremantle, *History of the National Rifle Association during its First Fifty Years 1859–1909*, Bowes & Bowes, Cambridge, 1914

DH Johnson, *Volunteers at Heart: The Queensland Defence Forces 1860–1901*, UQP, Brisbane, 1975

AG Leslie, *Rifle Sketches*, George Robinson & Co, Melbourne, 1906

HE Mills, *The National Rifle Association of New South Wales Official Jubilee Souvenir, 1909: A History of the Past 50 Years of Rifle Shooting in New South Wales*, Atkins, McQuitty, Sydney, 1909

B Nichols, *The Colonial Volunteers: The Defence Forces of the Australian Colonies 1836–1901*, Allen & Unwin, Sydney, 1988

LL Robson, *The First AIF: A Study of its Recruitment 1914–1918*, MUP, Melbourne, 1970

C Stockings, *The Making and Breaking of the Post-Federation Australian Army 1901–1909*, Study Paper no 311, Land Warfare Studies Centre, Canberra, 2007

C Wilcox, *For Hearths and Homes: Citizen Soldiering in Australia 1854–1945*, Allen & Unwin, Sydney, 1998

DM Wyatt, *A Lion in the Colony: An Historical Outline of the Tasmanian Colonial Volunteer Forces 1859–1901*, 6th Military District Museum, Anglesea Barracks, Hobart, 1990

8

Australia's boy soldiers: The army cadet movement

CRAIG STOCKINGS

The history or significance of the military cadet movement before World War I is unknown to most modern Australians. It is unlikely that even those few with personal experience or a vague awareness of the contemporary cadet organisation would view its forebear as anything other than a quaint, small-scale collection of uniformed boys playing soldiers. Like so much of the pre-Anzac military history of this country, however, the passage of time and the inexorable evolution of social activities and attitudes obscure a markedly different reality. The early cadet movement in this country was important – very important. It was a large and influential military, social and educational phenomenon. The first organised cadet unit was raised in 1866 and, after a listless beginning, colonial cadet organisations grew to a combined total of around 21 000 members by 1906. By 1911, on the eve of universal military service for all Australian males aged 14–25, there were more than 24 000 active army cadets under a voluntary Commonwealth scheme. By 1915 the organisation boasted 88 300 members. The sheer number of cadets who served between 1866 and 1915, and the importance placed upon the organisation over that time by politicians, military officers, teachers, educational administrators and the public, may seem improbable and anachronistic today, but this does not make it any less true.

The cadet movement grew out of the slightly earlier and then concurrent practice of military 'drill' in schools. School drill was the nineteenth-century version of physical education, in which a whole class simultaneously performed prescribed movements of the body, usually directed by a teacher and often resembling military manoeuvres. Cadet activities – limited to male teenaged students – took the martial aspects significantly further. Cadets were arranged as 'corps', 'units' or 'detachments', they dressed in military uniforms, carried weapons on parade grounds and used them at rifle ranges and in mock battles. They studied and practised military procedures and drill from official army instruction manuals, and carried themselves, in outlook, form and function, in youthful mimicry of adult soldiers. They were formally recognised by the government, and in many cases were actually considered a part of the volunteer defence forces which, after 1870 and apart from the Royal Navy, were the colonies' only means of defence.

Before tracing the history of the cadet movement in the colonial and early Federation period, however, it is worth noting that four fundamental and contextual forces acted to shape its form and character. The first and most obvious player was the army. From military traditions of 'volunteerism' that factored cadets into the defence and mobilisation plans of some nineteenth-century colonies, ideas of cadet contributions to Australian citizen soldiery were well entrenched up to 1915 and beyond. The army always sought to make use of the cadet force for its own purposes – quite understandably, given that it bore most of the cost of the organisation. The second institutional influence on the cadet movement was from 'educationalists', whether in colonial and state Education departments or among other bureaucrats, headmasters, teachers or any union thereof. Educationalists sought to use cadets to further pedagogical, disciplinary or other educational ends. Again, given that the school structure provided the physical setting of the movement, this is no surprise. Superimposed upon these institutional considerations were fluctuating social attitudes of the late nineteenth and early twentieth centuries concerned with the moral, ethical, physical and attitudinal disposition of Australian youth. The cadet movement's early history is steeped in rhetoric from political, religious, military, educational and parental commentators concerning children's character development. The final factor that shaped the course of the cadet system is more mundane: finance. Like the army of the period, the movement remained subject to the whims of economy. When the coffers were full and the government of the day generous, then the organisation thrived; when the fiscal situation was tightened, the movement suffered and, at times, was targeted by its military and educational patrons in the name of cost-cutting. These four forces or factors formed the contextual framework for Australia's boy soldiers.

At its genesis the cadet movement in Australia (unlike the Australian army) did not descend directly from its British counterpart. Although predated by its English equivalent, the Australian cadet movement developed independently, and concurrently, with it. In 1859 several prominent English public schools – including Eton, Harrow, Winchester and Rugby – raised cadet detachments with the idea of supplementing the militia in the likelihood of clashes with the forces of Napoleon III who, it was feared, intended to pick up where his uncle left off at Waterloo. Such developments in England, building also on residual fear of Russian attack inspired by the Crimean War, had a degree of influence on the origins of the movement in the Australian colonies. Indeed, the example of British regiments in Australia (see Chapter 3) and the military deployment of Australians to such conflicts as the New Zealand Wars (Chapter 6) also helped rouse an interest in cadets. Yet equally, more distinctly Australian social developments – such as the popularity of rifle shooting competitions in the colonies (Chapter 7) – also helped encourage the founding of cadet units.

Ultimately, however, the key factor in promoting the establishment of the movement was the introduction of military drill into the curricula of many schools, both elementary and secondary, from the late 1850s onwards. With an active drill program, the step to the formation of true cadet detachments in many schools was a small one. Also of particular importance were the headmasters of some of the most prominent private schools in the colonies, men who believed earnestly in the moral aims of the British public school system 'to produce boys fit to take leadership in a Christian State and Empire'.[1] Such beliefs, tacitly at least, made them more than receptive to the concept of cadets. From the very beginning, therefore, before any cadet units had been raised, three of the four forces that would come to define the movement were active in laying its foundations. Military, social and educational factors converged to facilitate the establishment of colonial cadets.

The first true cadet units appeared in each of the colonies against such a backdrop. The earliest mention of any force potentially resembling cadets appeared in the *South Australian Government Gazette* of 4 December 1862, which gave the results of a rifle shooting competition for units of the South Australian military forces. The entry listed two privates competing for the 'Cadet Rifles'. Unfortunately, no collaborating evidence is available to confirm the existence or nature of this organisation, and the competitors may well have been nothing more than under-aged shooters. The honour, therefore, of being the first unit to be raised formally on Australian soil must go to the St Mark's Collegiate

School (later The King's School), at Macquarie Fields, Sydney. St Mark's headmaster, Reverend GF Macarthur, had previously been an army chaplain, and was the originator and driving force behind the initiative. He had been at the school for six years when one of his masters, William Dalmas, upon returning from an overseas visit, told him of the cadet corps that had very recently sprung up in the private schools of England. Dalmas brought an enthusiasm for cadets back to the school and passed it quickly to his headmaster, and with the approval of the colony's military establishment Macarthur instituted a corps on 29 March 1866.[2]

Reinforcing the social function of the original St Mark's unit – christened 'The Macquarie Fields Corps' – was its first public parade to commemorate the Queen's birthday in 1866, with 39 cadets marching through the streets of Sydney. Bolstering the infant unit's public popularity, in an atmosphere of general lawlessness in the early 1860s, was the belief that cadet training could instil Christian ethics and values in colonial youth. Such an idea was promoted by an incident involving four brothers from Parramatta, aged between 15 and 21, who were subject to a kidnap attempt by Ben Hall's gang for the purpose of coercing a pardon from the colonial authorities. The boys managed to beat off their attackers and became heroes. They had all been members of the Parramatta Volunteers and St Mark's shooting team, and attributed their survival to their military training.[3] This unlikely incident helped to ignite the movement in New South Wales. The creation of the first true cadet unit in Australia was inspired, therefore, by a clear convergence between educational, military and social considerations.

It was not long before these same factors exerted their influence in other colonies. In 1867, a composite cadet unit was raised in Melbourne by Captain FT Sargood, commanding officer of the Victorian Volunteer Artillery, who was given responsibility for raising a body of cadets from Victorian secondary schools to assist in the reception of the visiting Prince Alfred, the Duke of Edinburgh. Sargood's efforts marked the first attempt at an organised cadet force in Victoria. Although All Saints Grammar School and Wesley College were the only schools to respond with enthusiasm, their detachments were well prepared and on the occasion marched to the corner of St Kilda and Sandridge Roads and had the honour of being the first military formation to salute the duke as he entered Melbourne. Although the unit evaporated almost immediately afterwards, for this early initiative Sargood would later be known as 'the father of cadets'.[4]

In Queensland, the first cadet units appeared in 1870: a time when British troops were withdrawing from the colony and as Europe seemed to be heading for a general war. Unfortunately these early detachments languished for want of official sanction or support. The Brisbane Grammar School unit, for example, was disbanded in 1874, and remained dormant until a more determined effort saw it re-raised as a volunteer cadet corps with a strength of 50 in 1878.[5]

In Tasmania, the movement gained a foothold in 1883 when the headmaster of Launceston Church Grammar School requested permission from the military commandant, Lieutenant Colonel WV Legge, to raise a detachment of between 45 and 50 boys. Legge commented in 1886 that this unit 'respond[ed] well to the call of their Commanding Officer, Major Aikenhead, and mustered fifty-five when marched into camp. Their conduct was, on the whole, good and they bore the hardships of camp life very well.'[6]

To the west, following the granting of responsible government to Western Australia in 1890, that colony's military commandant, Lieutenant Colonel WG Phillmore, immediately signalled military support for cadets. In his final report of 1891, Phillmore expressed his conviction 'that the government would do well to encourage, as much as possible, the formation of cadet corps' as he saw such a movement as achieving social ends as well as supplementing the volunteer forces. Despite his call, no units were actually raised for another four years.[7]

In South Australia cadet units did not appear until 1899 as the final consequence of a long history of school-based drill, and stimulated by the patriotic and martial feeling aroused by the South African War. Thanks to the agitation of Lieutenant Hugo Leschen, teacher and a part-time military officer, a small battalion of cadets was organised around a nucleus of Prince Alfred College and St Peter's College students, and officered by old boys of the two schools who accepted volunteer commissions.[8]

Across all the Australian colonies, the degree of harmony between competing military, educational, social and financial forces defined the fortunes of the colonial cadet organisations from their inception. Where it was achieved, the movement thrived; with disharmony came disappointment. In New South Wales, following the establishment of the St Mark's unit in 1866, and buttressed by a continuing environment of positive military, social and educational attitudes, cadets prospered. From 1871 the cadet movement in that colony underwent rapid expansion, with the number of cadets rising from fewer than 200 in 1870, to 850 by the end of the following year. The early 1870s coincided with the premiership of Henry Parkes, and his commitment to public education saw government-run schools also begin to show an interest, with some 2000 public schoolboys enrolled in cadet corps by 1873. In August that year, 240 cadets of this fledgling organisation paraded in Sydney and as a result many more state school units began to spring up in the city and the surrounding areas. The spread of cadet units into public schools in Australia was an important divergence from their British equivalents and reflected, among other issues, the aspirational nature of the migrants arriving in the colonies. The children of such families would not, in England, have had the chance to be cadets, and the symbolism was significant.[9]

The early development of cadets in Victoria was similarly shaped by harmony between military, educational, social and financial pressure. Between 1883 and 1886, Premier James Service was responsible for stimulating a range of military affairs in his colony, including cadets. He set up a Ministry and Council of Defence, and appointed FT Sargood (now holding the rank of lieutenant colonel) to the new post of Minister for Defence. From his earlier cadet experience in 1867, and conscious of developments in New South Wales, Sargood resolved to create a comprehensive cadet system in Victoria. In 1884, as minister for both Defence and Education, he called a meeting of the principals of colleges and prominent head teachers of state schools for this purpose. On the resolution of this committee the Victorian Volunteer Cadet Corps was inaugurated, with its first units gazetted on 23 January 1885. Within six months it boasted 1850 members (40 per cent of the number of adult soldiers in the colony).[10]

It is worth reinforcing the point that in Victoria, illustrative of a wider pattern, that although it was run by the Department of Defence, the movement there was in many ways underpinned by the co-operation of the Department of Education. For example, the Victorian inspectors of education – the key bureaucrats who regularly visited schools to ensure educational standards and governance compliance – were deeply involved from the beginning which minimised friction between the two departments. They regularly acted as cadet battalion commanders, and thereby solved the question of educational versus military seniority for teacher-officers. One of the first, WM Gamble, went on to become the commander of all Victorian cadets when a national cadet system was established in 1906. As far as the cadet movement was concerned, the inspectors were 'all in favour of its extension' and provided a strong and consistent support. Under such circumstances the Victorian cadet force reached a strength of over 4000 by the end of 1891.[11]

The importance of military, educational, social and fiscal harmony was mirrored in the other colonies. The movement stagnated in Queensland until 1889, when educational and military figures at last committed themselves, and by June 1890 it had 597 cadets training in Brisbane and eight regional areas.[12] Similarly, in February 1903 the original military-administered Western Australian cadet system was supplanted by an entirely new and fundamentally different scheme. The Western Australian Public School Cadet Force was raised, again in imitation of the New South Wales model, and again with educational support central to the organisation's success. The force remained vigorous up to 1905, at which time it held 1310 cadets, representing 46 per cent of the eligible male age group.[13]

The specific and critical influence of finance on the colonial cadet movement was well illustrated by the impact of severe drought and economic depression in Australia in the 1890s. Across the board, retrenchments and down-sizing adversely affected colonial military forces, Education departments, general community life and, a result, the various cadet schemes. From 1892, the newly reinvigorated cadet system in New South Wales broke down almost completely, and in 1893 the colonial government withdrew all support on grounds of economy. Disastrous bank failures in New South Wales deepened the depression, and caused the cadet budgetary allocation to fall from £13 483 to just £5869 in only 12 months.[14] Compounding these difficulties, organised sport became a very strong competitor to the cadet movement in the colony. For private schools the athletic competition of the Greater Public Schools (GPS) was established and grew rapidly in popularity, placing schools in direct competition with each other in a range of sports. From the outset it had an enormous appeal and became a central element of school pride and *esprit de corps* – roles previously accorded to the cadet unit. The GPS sporting competitions were mirrored in state schools by the Public Schools Athletic Association, which although established in 1888, began to flourish in the mid-1890s. Unsurprisingly, many teachers and pupils chose to devote their time to school sport rather than become involved in the equipment shortages and rising costs then characteristic of cadet training. Cadet enrolment in New South Wales fell to 3164 by 1896.[15]

With the end of the depression, however, much of the vigour of the various colonial cadet organisations was restored. In Victoria it grew by 1000 members in 1899 alone, while in 1901 steady post-depression growth saw 4425 enrolled. In contrast to New South Wales, the overwhelming majority of cadets in the Victorian force in this period came from state schools: in 1906, for example, 5000 of its 6000 rank and file.[16] In general terms, the cadet movement in Australia weathered the depression and drought of the 1890s and survived, battered but recovering, into the next phase of its history when the Commonwealth Department of Defence assumed control of a new national cadet organisation from 1906.

Aside from exploring the origins and development of the colonial cadet organisations in order to get a fuller sense of the movement, it is useful to investigate the range of cadet activities. Across the country foot and rifle drill, shooting, ceremonial parades, and annual camps formed the bulk of the cadet training. The State School Cadets in Queensland provided a reasonable representation of cadet training across Australia up to 1906. They paraded for one hour, two afternoons per week at school locations, and attended drill on one Saturday afternoon each month. Units regularly participated in ceremonial events, and conducted an annual camp.[17]

In fact, military tradition dominated parade-ground drill for colonial cadets, despite Education Department control of the movement in some colonies. It occupied a significant proportion of training time and, in the context of contemporary military tactics, constituted both ceremonial and combat training. In all the colonies, cadets were trained in the rifle and drill exercises laid down for adult infantry including:

> the rifle in the march, manual exercises in the ranks and piling arms, paying compliments with arms, company on parade drills, firing exercises by numbers and quick time, standing, sitting, kneeling and lying down, volleys and independent firing in single and two ranks, preparing for cavalry, skirmishing, and sentry duty.[18]

Quite removed from the monotony of drill, cadet rifle shooting competitions were without doubt the most popular form of training. Although sanctioned by the military, the driving force behind these contests was the widespread popularity of the sport in the community (see Chapter 7), the acceptance of the place of weapons in society, and a healthy dose of school pride. Units competed in local events, special invitation contests, inter-school challenges and even intercolonial matches. In 1886–87, for example, an annual competition was established between Australian and New Zealand cadets, with the Brisbane Grammar School unit claiming the first four consecutive victories. Indicative of the esteem accorded to rifle matches, in the 1870s and 1880s the New South Wales Minister of Education regularly granted days off school for cadets to compete. Shooting competitions were equally prevalent in Victoria and the other colonies, and were conducted with the full blessing of the various education systems. Representative of an underlying military intent, and with the idea of creating a pool of skilled marksman for the volunteer forces, target shooting was made compulsory for cadets in Victoria from 1885 and in Western Australia from 1903.[19] As in New South Wales, however, it was not these statutory requirements that generally inspired cadets, but rather the representative competition that excited them.

The third significant cadet pursuit in the colonial era concerned ceremony. Although conducted as military events, cadet ceremonial activities fitted comfortably into nineteenth century social expectations and were well aligned with prevailing community attitudes. In Sydney and Melbourne in particular, cadet formations were a central feature of most civic celebrations. As early as 1869, the St Mark's unit in Sydney, in association with Camden College, began a tradition of parading along the streets, with Sydney Grammar and Newington College joining this annual occasion in 1871 and 1872 respectively. The Sydney state schools were included in this event from 1873, and for the next 30 years ceremonial occasions involving cadets – such as the farewell of the New South Wales military contingent to Sudan in 1885 – were a regular occurrence. On 23 August 1890, in one of the largest cadet ceremonial events in the colony, the Public School Cadet Force conducted a massed parade of some 4800 members in Moore Park in front of a crowd of 30 000 spectators who cheered as the governor inspected the parade. Lady Carrington presented the Queen's and regimental colours, made by the Lady Teachers Association, to the assemblage. The same commitment to civic ceremonial activities was replicated in Victoria and the smaller colonies.[20] In 1901, for example, the Duke of Cornwall (later King George V) inspected 4000 Victorian cadets lined up for review at the steps of Parliament House, followed by a 'grand review and march-past' at Flemington Racecourse involving 4900 boys. The scene was described as 'an immense procession of keen, soldierly lads, who bore themselves with the spring and alertness of trained troops'.[21]

The final significant aspect of cadet training in the colonial era were annually conducted cadet training camps, which again highlighted the military influence on the movement. Dating back to the 1870s, the fledgling private school cadet units of New South Wales regularly took themselves to camp, with Sydney Grammar holding its first at Wisemans Ferry in 1872. Illustrating the combined school spirit and martial flavour of these activities, an incident occurred when the Sydney Grammar unit 'encountered the King's School (St Mark's) cadets strongly posted in the Domain'. A small body of Sydney Grammar School cadets, 'by dint of concealing their own weakness and great shouting, drove the enemy back in confusion on their main body ... the enemy was totally surrounded and surrendered'.[22] Early camps also showed the educational importance for private school headmasters, looking to develop collegiate school spirit. Sydney Grammar School recorded that:

> nothing pleased the chief (Weigall) more than to march out with his company a hundred strong ... white canvas, red coats, the buglers, the boy sentries challenging, the night attack by King's School in which both sides always claimed victory ... what a happy memory of boyhood for many a Sydney merchant and barrister.[23]

In Victoria, the military dominance of annual cadet camps was even further pronounced. Camps were held from 1887 onwards, with the first drawing an impressive 843 cadets and 86 officers, participating in battalion movements, drill, camp duties, guard and sentry duties, and limited rifle shooting. A second Victorian camp was held the following year at Langwarrin that included a 'sham fight' in which three battalions were detailed to defend the camp site from five battalions of attackers. In the 1890s most Victorian camps built up to a mock battle fought on the last day – to the delight of the participating cadets. Some interesting variation was introduced in late 1899 when, again illustrating their distinctly military flavour, one cadet battalion was deployed for a full day to give cadets practice in the capturing of defensive positions from which an enemy attacking Melbourne might bombard the city. Cadet camps in the other colonies, where they were conducted, followed these basic patterns.[24]

Beyond cadet training and activities, three common elements of purpose linked the various colonial cadet schemes. In the first instance, cadet units were raised either for direct military purposes or as part of wider recruiting initiatives, usually with the idea of helping keep down the cost of defence. Secondly, considerations concerning the moral education of boys helped to establish and promote the concept of cadets within the schools systems. Lastly, cadet training and activities were deemed likely to produce general community and social benefits. These three ideas rarely stood in isolation and most supporters of the movement felt a mixture of motivations.

In the first instance, real defence issues helped many early colonial cadet units to establish themselves. The last British garrison left Australia in 1870 and traditional fears of the Germans in New Guinea, of the French generally and then of a Russian invasion from Vladivostok in the mid-1860s gave both the volunteer military forces and the cadet movement significant momentum. Many influential thinkers saw cadets as a useful supplement to the citizen forces as an unpaid but partially trained reserve, an idea that meshed comfortably in the 1870s and 1880s within a general imperative in all the colonies to try to create effective defence forces without the expense and social ramifications of the standing armies and conscript forces of Europe. Some insight into such thinking can be gleaned from Reverend Macarthur's 1866 request to the commanding officer of the volunteer force in New South Wales to establish the original St Mark's cadet unit:

> to create in the minds and habits of our youth a desire and aptitude for the service of the country ... the use of rifles in the corps would promote an interest in drill ... a spirit whereby the lads would become valuable members of the Volunteer Force.[25]

Similarly, in building the Victorian cadet organisation, Sargood wished to 'bind together in one patriotic brotherhood the youth of this country so that, should occasion arise, they may be able in after years to defend their country with the most telling effect'. Major General AB Tulloch, the commandant of Victorian military forces in 1894, took the concept of cadets as a semi-trained reserve one step further. He was in no doubt about the military utility of the cadet force, and actually included them in his schemes of defending the colony from invasion. He believed that:

> young fellows ... are being trained to become a valuable addition to the defences. So highly do I think of the quality of these Senior Cadets, that I have appointed them to their place in the scheme of mobilisation for defence in the event of war.[26]

Of course, like Tulloch, many individual cadets saw their efforts linked directly to colonial security. The cadets of the original

Tasmanian cadet unit at Launceston Church Grammar School, for example, wrote in their school magazine, *The Pardophone*, in May 1886 that 'if any quarrel should arise in which Tasmania's help is needed we would be ready to serve'.[27]

As an indirect military outcome, the idea of using cadets as a means to encourage recruiting into the adult forces was also conceived in the colonial era. The Tasmanian commandant revealed in 1884 that he saw cadets as a 'means of increasing the [Volunteer] Force in the colony, and a source of recruiting'. In Victoria, the value of the cadet corps was said to have been in inculcating a 'military not militant spirit in youth', being designed to 'encourage further service in the senior branches of defence'. So too in New South Wales, the *Sydney Morning Herald* describing the Public School Cadet Force in 1890 as 'the foundation upon which to build up our Australian standing army of civilians'.[28]

Apart from these military and pseudo-military objectives, the idea of raising cadet units for educational and moral purposes was imported from England as part of the 'Arnoldian Tradition', in which 'rifle corps' were a fundamental aspect of many of the Great Public Schools. A report on the movement in 1887 by New South Wales' Minister for Public Instruction noted that cadets were 'taught practically the value of discipline ... many boys will be thus kept from forming bad associations and pernicious habits at a critical point in their lives'. Similarly, Weigall, of Sydney Grammar School, wrote in 1870 that 'the first step towards a corporate school life was taken by the formation of a cadet corps'.[29] Such sentiments reflected a firm general conviction that cadet activities formed a medium for moral education.

Even more generally, it was also widely considered that the various cadet systems would, through the effects of physical fitness, discipline and patriotism, have a positive effect on the social fabric of the community. The commander of the original

Tasmanian cadet unit, Major William Aikenhead, commented that it was:

> calculated to improve the physique of the rising generation, and also benefit the young people intellectually, morally and socially. The lessons of order, obedience, submission to authority, smartness and manliness ... must prove of great advantage.[30]

There was a conscious sense that military training contributed to boys' socialisation process, by which they could learn the established values of the society in which they lived: order, obedience and loyalty. Such sentiments were echoed in South Australia in 1900 by the *Adelaide Register*: 'the advantage of a cadet corps cannot be overlooked. Individually, a boy, by a regular course of drill and military discipline is straightened up mentally and physically.'[31] Most commonly, however, those responsible for promoting the cadet movement before 1906 viewed its purpose as a combination of military, educational and social factors. The four objectives of the Victorian colonial cadets, for example, were to benefit the physical development of boys, to improve school discipline, to train future citizens of Victoria and to create a trained service force for defence purposes.[32]

Although fostered by distinctly colonial institutions, the essentials of the cadet movement saw little change after Federation. From 1 January 1901 the defence of Australia became the responsibility of the Commonwealth, although it was a duty the infant federal government came into only gradually. As far as the various colonial cadet corps were concerned, from Federation they fell under the jurisdiction of the Commonwealth Military Forces, then under the command of the military commandant of Victoria. In practical terms, however, each cadet organisation continued to be administered, structured and run along individual state lines.

The first steps towards the introduction of a truly national cadet movement were made during the preparation of the original Commonwealth Defence Bill in March 1901. The military committee drawing up the Bill recommended that boys below the age of 14 receive military training under the control of the Departments of Education in each state, while those aged 14–17 years should be formed into voluntary senior cadet units armed, trained, equipped and commanded by the military.[33] The resulting *Defence Act* (1903–04) made proviso for the establishment of a Commonwealth cadet system. Importantly for the future of the movement, and in response to mounting community concern regarding national security, when the Senate had earlier discussed the Bill it proposed mandatory military training of all boys aged 14–17. The idea received considerable support, particularly from the Labor Party, with a motion to include a scheme of compulsory cadets only defeated by 15 votes to 10. WM Hughes, Labor parliamentarian and future prime minister, was also vocal in his support for universal cadet training, and although defeated at this time, his continuing agitation – and the line of thought it represented – had significant future implications.[34]

Such deliberations formed the backdrop to considerable public support for the concept of cadets and for the establishment of a Commonwealth cadet system. Both ideas enjoyed the general backing of a federal Parliament containing many serving and retired members of the volunteer military. Large public crowds still attended cadet parades, and press support was substantial. Indeed, state government proposals linking a national cadet system to state schools in post-Federation cadet discussions showed considerable philosophical support from educators as well. The only key organisation not generally supportive of a truly national cadet force was the army. Among a range of key military figures, most state commandants feared that their already meagre budget allocations would be wasted on a cadet system likely to drain limited supplies of permanent officers, instructors and equipment. Fortunately, the first General Officer Commanding the Commonwealth Military Forces, Major General Sir Edward Hutton, was a staunch supporter of cadets and overruled such sentiments. In 1902 he recommended that the cadet scheme 'so successful in Victoria under military control, be similarly developed throughout the Commonwealth'.[35]

Despite Hutton's clear intention, four years after Federation no uniform national cadet system had been established. His annual report for 1903 lamented this fact and attributed it to restricted finances and the priority of restructuring and equipping the adult forces. Hutton continued, however, to resist attempts from the wider military to downgrade the intended national cadet force into a school-controlled activity under the auspices of state Departments of Education. In his eyes this would have had the effect of 'lowering the status of military service'. In any case the strength of the still state-based cadet movement in Australia at the end of 1904 was a healthy 20 070 (New South Wales 7500; Victoria 6000; Queensland 2600; South Australia 1870; Western Australia 1200; and Tasmania 900). The situation was, however, becoming an embarrassment to the federal authorities and from March 1904 a string of events began a process of resolution.[36]

The essential elements of what became the Commonwealth cadet movement were derived from the recommendations of two crucial cadet conferences at ministerial and bureaucratic levels in 1904 and 1905. These eventually decided upon a Commonwealth scheme providing for 20 070 school cadets and 3000 senior cadets. Both Commonwealth and state governments accepted the details of the plan in all but the most minor details.[37] Thus, on 1 May

1906, by stroke of the governor-general's pen, a set of provisional regulations established the new Commonwealth Military Cadet Corps which finally integrated the disparate state-based cadet forces into a truly national system. A renewed wave of enthusiasm for cadets swept the country following the organisation's inauguration, fuelling governmental belief that 'under the recently introduced system great expansion is [to be] expected'. Such positivity was replicated, for the most part, in the states. Sir George Strickland, governor of Tasmania, captured the mood when addressing a cadet parade in Hobart in 1907: 'the cadets of today are the foundation of the future army of Australia, a branch of the great imperial system of defence, on which the continuation of the British Empire is dependant'.[38] Parliamentarian and another future prime minister, Andrew Fisher, described cadets in 1903 as 'a very laudable objective' to which he proposed expending no less than 10 per cent of the military budget.[39]

Despite Fisher's sentiments, however, it was limited finance that hamstrung the movement from 1906. On the surface at least, the organisation was not starved of money. Indeed, the cadet force accounted for £20055 of a defence budget increase of £61474 in 1907–08, and absorbed £50429 (7.6 per cent) of a total defence vote in the 1908–09 financial year. These funds, however, represented a relatively large slice of a very small defence pie, one which accounted for less than half a per cent of national GDP. In real terms, in 1909 cadets were funded at around £1 10s per capita, as compared to around £3 10s for cadets of the New South Wales Public School Cadet Force in 1893.[40] The effect of limited finance was clear. The inspector general of Commonwealth military forces, Major General John Hoad, complained in 1907 that there were not enough serviceable rifles to be issued to all cadets.[41] In 1907 the Minister for Defence, GF Pearce, told Parliament that 'the boys have no rifles, no belts, no bayonets, no haversacks, and no capes. They have nothing except their horses, saddles, bridles, and uniforms, all of which they have themselves provided.'[42]

The development of cadet training and activities after 1906 continued to reflect social, military and educational expectations of the movement. Importantly, however, the period up to 1911 represented a gradual but inexorable move away from its traditional military orientation towards an educationalist emphasis on physical fitness. The instigation of a school cadet conference in 1907 by Prime Minister Alfred Deakin, to discuss the nature of future cadet training, was partly motivated by this developing trend, albeit coupled with a desire from the Defence Department to achieve military control and standardisation over emerging schemes of physical training coming out of various state Departments of Education. There is no doubt that the idea also fitted comfortably with Deakin's public desire to see a system of universal military service introduced in Australia, in which cadet training would play a key physical role in preparing boys for their adult commitments. In any case, the proceedings of the 1907 conference signalled the beginning of a formal move away from a military conception of cadets within schools by focusing more on the idea of a uniform system of physical education.[43]

It was not, however, limited funds or a transition in expectations that spelled the final demise of the post-Federation cadet system: it was the new *Defence Act* proclaimed on 1 January 1911, making Australia the first modern English-speaking country to demand universal and mandatory military training in times of peace. As the first decade of Federation drew to a close, there was a discernible souring of the global security environment and this significantly bolstered proponents of the idea of peace-time conscription – a concept that was antithetical to the voluntary cadet system. When mixed with continuing concern over the cost of defence, 'the cadet force, which had owed its colonial origins to defence fears and the belief that it could save the government money, now fell victim to vastly enhanced fears, and the perception that it was an expensive liability'.[44]

The new *Defence Act* was a profound development. With bi-partisan support, the government exacted compulsory service from all males between the ages of 12 and 25. The Act required all boys between 12 and 14 to become junior cadets; and all between 14 and 18 to serve in senior cadets. This was to be followed, by men aged 18 to 25, by compulsory membership in the Citizen Military Forces (CMF).[45] Empowered by the new Act, the military asserted itself immediately over the remnants of the old cadet system. Army authorities ordered registration for compulsory cadet service to commence at the beginning of 1911, although actual training was initially limited to boys turning 17 in that year.[46] In 1911, following an amendment to the Act, compulsory cadet training commenced.[47] Revealing the ambitious scope of the conscript cadet scheme, in January 1911 Lieutenant Colonel JG Legge, now the army's quartermaster-general, began a national lecturing tour to explain and provide advice to military personnel tasked to administer it. He predicted that of the 188 000 eligible senior cadets in the country, 100 000 would be under training when the scheme matured.[48]

In many ways, the compulsory cadet scheme twisted the purpose of the movement by making military objectives central. The whole rationale for senior cadets rested upon a perceived requirement for a stockpile of young men with basic military training that could be fed into the CMF without wasting time on elementary instruction. Although never officially endorsed as a substitute for adult recruit training, the scheme was clearly interpreted by many military figures with this in mind. Lieutenant Colonel NM Brazier, writing in the *Australian Military Journal* in

1914, explained that such cadet training was intended 'to prepare them to take their place in the army, full of life and patriotism and so defend our country from those foreign nations whose eyes are ever on our fertile shore'.[49]

At the same time, however, there remained significant social and educational aspirations for the 'compulsory cadets' of the period. While in Opposition, Pearce had supported the compulsory military training scheme announced by Deakin on 13 December 1907.[50] For Pearce universal military training had more than defence benefits: it was a form of social conditioning for Australian male youth, teaching them responsibility and citizenship. He also viewed it as a way of diverting boys from spectator sport to more active pursuits:

> It would be a blessing to those youths, I do not say to take every Saturday, but to haul them off by force for a few Saturdays, if necessary, from the football grounds, and give them a few manly exercises on the military field, where they could be taught to square their shoulders and to carry out military evolutions.[51]

Pearce also viewed compulsory training as an important social obligation:

> We compel our youths to go to school until they are fourteen years of age, or can pass a certain standard of education. Why do we do that? Simply because we recognise that it is essential in the interests of the body politic that every citizen of the country should be possessed of a certain degree of education. If it is necessary that our youths should be trained in the duties that will fit them to be effective units in the industrial army, it is equally essential that they should be

taught the duties and responsibilities of which I hold to be the defence of their country, and it is certainly one of the duties of citizenship that they should acquire the ability to defend it in the best manner possible.[52]

Yet despite such philosophies, the conduct of compulsory senior cadet training suffered as a result of war-time circumstances. From 1914 many units were stripped of army instructional staff who were called to duty training reinforcements for the AIF. The pressures of war also meant that from July 1915 parade requirements were reduced significantly. Compulsory drills were suspended for three months from November 1915, and yearly training targets reduced from 64 hours to 48 hours. There was a rapid turnover of attached army personnel as they were promoted or posted to meet war-time requirements. An important outcome of these difficulties was a necessary change of focus from purely military training to other forms of instruction not so reliant on army support including physical education, swimming lessons and so forth. This move away from a wholly military emphasis continued after the war, with unit training programs by 1925 regularly describing route marches, physical, signals, sports and 'general' activities: 14 years earlier drill and musketry exercises had dominated.[53]

Nevertheless, the sheer scale of the compulsory scheme made it a considerable social phenomenon. In the six months to July 1911, a total of 102 194 boys were medically examined for cadet service, and by December 155 132 had been registered for training. Even after those granted exceptions were removed, this left more than 89 000 senior cadets in uniform at the end of 1911, a figure which rose steadily to almost 99 000 by 1921.[54] Given the size of this organisation it was not surprising that the first key challenge was finding enough adult officers to man the multitude of new units. Again indicative of widespread initial community support, the fact that the system began to function at all was attributed to 'the patriotic assistance of those citizens who volunteered, not only from the militia and from the old cadets, but from the population generally'. By 1912 the cadet battalions were short only five commanding officers and 804 regimental officers (from an overall requirement of 2712).[55]

Regardless of these structural constraints, it was the overtly military ethos which now pervaded the cadet movement that proved its greatest source or discontent and, subsequently, its greatest weakness. Put simply, the new system was compulsory, its administration was increasingly seen as authoritarian, and perhaps worst of all, it was boring. In the early years of the compulsory cadet system, training activities were designed to focus on the basic combat-related skills of the service to which cadets would graduate. In general this included marching, weapons handling, drill, navigation, and tactical training. Unfortunately, and owing especially to straitened budgets, for the duration of the scheme the bulk of senior cadet training tended to revolve more around parade ground drill, which represented a cheap and easy option for training staff, with musketry training hardly begun and field training not conducted at all in 1912. The Brighton Grammar School's senior cadet detachment reported in that year that its only activities were 'company drill and rifle exercises'. Despite repeated efforts to overcome the allure of the parade ground, nothing came of such suggestions and the over-emphasis on drill remained.[56]

The problem was also one of inflexibility in the formal syllabus. Cadet commanders did not have the authority to vary the programme in accordance with their wishes or the ability of their cadets, and cadets were subjected to the same elementary training schedules regardless of their experience or stage of training. Even if cadets displayed an absolute knowledge of the material within a year, they faced the prospect of three more years of the same training. One cadet officer summarised the situation, noting 'one teaches a child by starting with the alphabet; but one does not expect him to keep at the alphabet for four solid years'. In short, 'any appeal to the intelligent interest of the cadet is outside the syllabus, and the result is proportional'.[57]

This concentration on drill was exacerbated by the persisting civic and military propensity to utilise cadets for public ceremonial occasions. In order to give a practical demonstration of the first year's results of the compulsory system, the governor-general, Lord Denman, suggested a review of senior cadets be held in Sydney. Accordingly, 18 642 metropolitan cadets paraded in Centennial Park on 30 March 1912. Denman afterwards sent a telegram to the prime minister, Andrew Fisher, suggesting that 'the numbers, organisation, and good order maintained on this parade demonstrated the good results achieved after nine months of universal training'. Denman was surely an optimist: 50 per cent of the cadets at the Sydney parade had no rifles, and some did not have uniforms. Nonetheless, similar activities were repeated in Adelaide, Brisbane and Melbourne.[58]

What was boring often became a nuisance, and what was a nuisance became a cause of dissent. One observer in 1914 concluded that 'the present cadet cry of "the same old thing every time" is not only justified but is in itself responsible for more cadet crime (absence from drills) than all other causes put together'.[59] The problem of cadets evading training became apparent almost immediately. In the first quotas of 1911, so many boys presented themselves for registration but then failed to appear for parades that the military turned to the attorney general for advice on the truancy penalties prescribed by the *Defence Act*, which ranged from extra parade time to fines and even confinement.[60]

Subsequently, from the beginning of 1912 until the middle

of 1914, 27 749 court cases were launched for failing to render cadet service, and of these 5732 resulted in confinement. What these numbers represented, in proportion to the size of the overall scheme, should not be overstated. Government statistics note that from 1911 to 1913, 6.9 per cent of boys eligible for training did not appear and were prosecuted, although the real figure was smaller as these numbers included multiple offenders and cases where employers or parents hindered training. In addition, many who were tried were treated with great leniency by the military, which was becoming increasingly sensitive to criticism it was locking up defaulting cadets and made every effort to provide offenders with the opportunity to make up for missed parades. Indeed, some CMF officers complained in 1912 about such 'soft' attitudes, suggesting that the non-enforcement of fines for senior cadets evading drill was having a prejudicial effect on the parade attendance of adult units.[61]

The military's attempts to legally enforce the compulsory provisions of the senior cadet system were consistently frustrated by civil magistrates. A test case in Footscray involving one RA Barkly resulted in the magistrate rejecting the idea that any penalty could be imposed on a defaulting cadet since it could not legally be recovered until the boy turned 18. The attorney general agreed, and declared that 'until the Act is amended, or until the High Court decides the questions raised in this case, different magistrates will give different interpretations of this section'. By mid-1912 the situation forced Senator Pearce to relent on the strict provision of punishments for cadets neglecting to comply with their training requirements.[62]

From 1913, even when penalties were enforced, they were done so reluctantly and gently. The net result of such military and magisterial policies was predictable. Absenteeism was endemic by 1920, and as the decade progressed – even with reduced training quotas – the authorities were increasingly unable to enforce universal training regulations. In 1928, the total number of missing cadets reached a proportional high point of 901 (out of a current total of around 16 000 eligible boys).[63]

Just as surely as community attitudes facilitated the founding of a compulsory cadet scheme, so too did wider changes in the social climate undermine it. The fact that senior cadet training was compulsory did not mean that it was universal, even accounting for those excused for various reasons, and throughout its existence the scheme faced a degree of dissent from cadets, parents and certain other elements of the community. Importantly, however, the traditional acceptance of the view that 'Australians went against compulsory training, almost from the start of it' was not the simple truth of the matter.[64] Such interpretations over-emphasise the immediacy of protest, non-compliance and rejection of the scheme, while according too little attention on its widespread community support, particularly in the early years. It was overwhelming initial enthusiasm for mandatory training that prevented widespread dissent in the early years. While there is no doubt that such attitudes did change, resistance to compulsion was slow to gather momentum and took nearly 20 years to effect change.

Accepted wisdom also suggests that, if not for World War I, the immediate unpopularity of the compulsory cadet system would have seen it dismantled within a decade. This seems to miss the fact that agitation for compulsory cadet training had existed in political circles since the drafting of the original *Defence Act* in 1903; that the concept was supported widely when enacted in 1909; and that the system continued to function for 11 years after the war ended. Some historians point to 'quiet, inarticulate, non-cooperation' as the main challenge to the compulsory system, and that from 1914 'military authorities had to work harder each year to secure an acceptable number of registrations and prosecutions for non-attendance'. While this is substantively true, it is a misrepresentation. There is no question that levels of senior cadet and CMF dissent increased with time, but that is not the same as suggesting that 'general opinion had changed to such a degree by 1914 that only the war prevented the end of the scheme'.[65] The truth of the matter is that the system of universal cadet training was instituted with overwhelming community support which only began to fade during the war and in the aftermath of peace that followed. It was the gradual shift of public attitudes and the slow growth of general dissent against mandatory training that marked important elements of the cadet story in this period.

Although in the very early stages there were some meek voices of opposition to the senior cadet system, complaining that it seemed a little like militarism, there was an almost complete absence of organised resistance in 1911. More serious complaints only found voice when small numbers started protesting the hardships involved as rain and cold made the experience of training all the more disagreeable. Importantly, in April 1912 the Australian Freedom League came into being as the foremost organisation in opposition to compulsory training, and it quickly began to harness the passive discontent generated by the sheer nuisance of compulsory drill. A second type of emergent anti-cadet agitation came from 'international socialists' who dissented on the basis of a rejection of militarism as it affected the working classes. As these forces gathered, opposing organisations like the Defence League, which had been so crucial in convincing politicians to adopt universal training in the first place, began to lose public support.[66]

Eventually, a combination of changing social attitudes and restricted post-war defence spending saw the senior cadet scheme, along with the adult universal training system it paralleled, gradually wound down from 1922 and finally dismantled on 31 October 1929. But the scheme had left an indelible mark.[67] The era of compulsory cadets had ended and would be replaced, once more, with various voluntary schemes throughout the twentieth and into the twenty-first centuries. That this enduring cadet movement is but one of a number of competing youth development schemes in contemporary Australia – and one without much of a public profile outside of the organisation itself – belies the significance of its long history. Taken in total, the cadet organisation in Australia from 1866 to 1915 was a serious and influential military, educational and social institution. The early history of Australia's boy soldiers is an important and under-acknowledged aspect of the pre-Anzac Australian military history.

Further reading

J Barrett, *Falling In: Australians and Boy Conscription 1911–1915*, Hale and Iremonger, Sydney, 1979

PC Candy, *The Victorian Cadet Movement: An Outline History from 1867 to 1969*, priv pubn, Melbourne, 1969

M Crotty, *Making the Australian Male: Middle-Class Masculinity 1870–1920*, MUP, Melbourne, 2001

C Daley, 'The story of the Victorian Junior Cadet Corps 1855–1912', *The Victorian Historical Magazine*, 20(1), June 1943

J Dawes & L Robson, *Citizen to Soldier: Australia before the Great War: Recollections of Members of the First AIF*, MUP, Melbourne, 1977

DL Henry, 'The Victorian cadet system', *Journal of the Royal United Services Institute*, 3(7), December 1894

R Nicholls, *The Colonial Volunteers: The Defence Forces of the Australian Colonies 1836–1901*, Allen & Unwin, Sydney, 1988

B Oliver, *Peacemongers: Conscientious Objectors to Military Service in Australia 1911–1945*, Fremantle Arts Centre Press, Fremantle, 1997

C Stockings, *The Torch and the Sword: A History of the Army Cadet Movement in Australia*, UNSW Press, Sydney, 2007

TW Tanner, *Compulsory Citizen Soldiers*, Maxwell Printing, Sydney, 1980

C Wilcox, *For Hearths and Homes: Citizen Soldiering in Australia 1854–1945*, Allen & Unwin, Sydney, 1998

9

Australians in the wars in Sudan and South Africa

CRAIG WILCOX

By conventional count, there were no Australian deaths in action during the British Empire's clash with Islamic rebels in Sudan in 1885. But as a politician pointed out before the New South Wales military contingent to the war had even left for the front, one Australian was already 'a martyr to the great cause'.[1] Robert Coveny, born four decades earlier above the New Holland Grocery Warehouse in Sydney's Market Street, had left his native city as a boy, studied in England to be a priest, purchased a commission in the Royal Welch Fusiliers, and risen to command a battalion of the Black Watch – one of the British army's most famous regiments. He had hoped to return or even retire to his birthplace. 'I was, in fact, planning an invasion of Sydney this year', he wrote to his family a year before he died, 'but "Monsieur M" [Mahdi, the rebel leader] put an end to all leave for some time'. To one of his many friends, Coveny was 'one of Britain's bravest sons'.[2] To the Sydney *Freeman's Journal* he was a true soldier and a fine Australian.[3]

For what great cause did Robert Coveny die? By the 1980s, a century after his death, many Australians would look back on the British Empire – if they could be bothered to recall it at all – as something antique and immoral: at best irrelevant to their country's rise; at worst an English tyranny demanding a blood tax in the form of colonial troops for imperial wars from Sudan to Singapore.[4] A few of Coveny's contemporaries saw things that way, but not many of them. As Coveny's life and death remind us, there was no clear division between Australian and British identity or interests in the nineteenth century. This was also an age of empires. One encompassed Australians, radiating boldly out from their ancestral homes back in England, Ireland, Wales and Scotland, sometimes astonishing them, sometimes irritating them, occasionally inspiring them. Then there were the rival empires of France, Russia and Germany that seemed to jostle ominously on the sidelines, not to mention the sullen 'vanquished' civilisations of India and China. True, plenty of Australians were simply bored by talk of empire. Some grumbled at the indifference of Westminster to their own ambitions for a Pacific empire, or its embarrassment at their determination to exclude non-white migrants. But almost any nineteenth-century Australian man who forgot or griped about the imperial connection was nevertheless protected by British battalions and battleships, and so securely at first that no contribution to imperial arms was expected of him until the third quarter of the nineteenth century.

Shifts in global power and in imperial relations around that time ended this happy state, prompting a modest colonial engagement in imperial defence that forms the subject of this chapter. Jostling among empires became real, while colonial governments began to speak up more for their citizens. If the British Empire faltered, then its Australian provinces might be exposed to forced annexation, but those provinces could not be to forced pay a blood tax to London – or any other tax, for that matter. Colonial governments settled on making minor military contributions that were as strategically dubious as they were politically prudent. Australians would not follow Coveny by joining the British army or Royal Navy in large numbers. They would not support those forces as British taxpayers did. Nor would they raise a real army or navy of their own. But the colonies would not wash their hands of empire. The despatch of a small military contingent to Sudan in 1885 was followed by further contingents to the South African War from 1899, and also the partial funding of a squadron of British warships. By prefacing greater Australian military contribution in future global wars, and by generating so many debates and documents for future historians to mull over, these acts of official colonial engagement in imperial defence have obscured a myriad of widespread private engagements by individuals such as Coveny which were already in train by 1885 and which also remained significant into the early twentieth century. This chapter notes the persistence of all that ardent but often invisible activity while charting the rise of its official alternative, and the ultimate incorporation of the former by the latter.

Colonial Australia was a scrawny hatchling of empire, bred in an apparently empty nest unclaimed by Britain's rivals. Spain, Portugal, the Netherlands and China were already bloated with rich provinces. France had considered staking out part of the continent, but lacked the naval and economic power to do so. British settlement thus spread unhindered across the antipodes, building six barely populated but economically viable colonies. Their security was unchallenged for a generation or two. Between the fall of Napoleonic France in 1815 and the rise or resurgence of the French, German and Russian empires from the 1860s, London could impose its will neatly and cheaply throughout much of the world. In 1842 the Chinese empire of 400 million people was forced to open Shanghai and Canton to British traders, and to cede Hong Kong to Queen Victoria. In 1858 a subcontinent of 300 million people was forced under direct British rule after the so-called Indian Mutiny was pitilessly crushed.

A brown, black or Irish subject of the queen might question the benefits of British rule. A cruelly overworked Welsh miner or East End seamstress might do the same. But Britons of 'the middling sort', which included most colonists in Australia and New Zealand, in Canada and South Africa, had less cause. They enjoyed military security, relative prosperity, certain rights, even international prestige. In 1850, the Royal Navy blockaded Athens until the Greek government agreed to compensate a single Gibraltar-born man whose home had been ransacked in a riot. The Sydney newspaper *The Empire* commented that, like a Roman citizen of old, the Briton 'has found the name of his country a protection to him in all lands'.[5]

Some colonists helped bolster the *Pax Britannica* that prevailed through so much of the nineteenth century. A few, like Robert Coveny, chose to buy a commission in the British army, but unlike in North America the army chose not to raise regiments in Australia. Far more Australian horses than men went into military life. By the 1860s the provision of cavalry and artillery remounts to India was a profitable sideline for Australian graziers and ship-owners.[6] These personal or profitable contributions to British forces were stirred by private dreams or family tradition. Imperial defence was not yet a public cause, indeed not even a catchphrase until 1859. Colonists inclined to think about such matters spoke, as Britons had long done, of upholding English honour and English rights abroad as at home. 'Englishmen must inhabit India to keep it quiet', a South Australian wrote during the Indian Mutiny, 'and our army must be large enough to keep possession'.[7] 'Shame to England, how can she hold up her head again!' one of Sir Thomas Mitchell's daughters fumed in Sydney on reading that the Chinese had captured some British gunboats while the French army had 'just returned from a brilliant victory over the Austrians, conquering them in every engagement'.[8]

Sentiments like these were about all that anyone expected from Australia if a war broke out – apart from an uninterrupted supply of sturdy remounts. 'Nobody', wrote the English civil servant Henry Thring in his 1865 pamphlet *Suggestions for Colonial Reform*, 'hopes to see Australians or New Zealanders volunteer for service out of their own country'. Yet Thring felt 'that *some* exertion should be made'.[9] Almost everyone agreed the colonists should begin to defend themselves. The army and navy were a significant expense to taxpayers in Britain, and in the mid-1840s troops stationed in the colonies were eating up a third of the entire defence budget.[10] Redcoats and bluejackets might be necessary in Canada, where conflict along the border with the United States remained possible, or in New Zealand, where the land's traditional owners repeatedly challenged their new rulers – but not in Australia. Anyway, as colonial parliaments took charge of their own budgets and domestic policies it seemed only right, as the House of Commons in London resolved in 1862, that 'Colonies exercising the rights of self-government ought to undertake the main responsibility for providing for their own internal order and security, and ought to assist in their own external defence'.[11] The Royal Navy retained its squadron based in Sydney Harbour, but it handed Australian politicians the keys to the stone forts around the coast that pretended to ward off seaborne attack, and advised them to build more. In 1870 British troops left Australia for good, after colonial governments could not get the artillery they asked for at the price they wanted, nor the right to keep the troops at their posts in war if the army chose to deploy them elsewhere. 'Try to establish a good police', the colonial secretary in London advised the first governor of Queensland even before the troops were withdrawn. 'If you can then get the superior class of colonists to assist in forming a Militia or Volunteer corps, spare no pains to do so.'[12]

It would have been impossible to stop them. During real or imagined military emergencies, the gentry and middling classes in Britain had long formed part-time, community-based volunteer corps to defend local soil while the army was off on campaign. A combination of nostalgia for Napoleonic times and nervousness about possible enemy attack generated new and, this time, enduring units from the 1840s. Colonists from the British middling classes who were rising to social and political predominance in Australia did as their cousins back home were doing. By 1862 most towns and suburbs across the continent were supporting a small, amateurish but enthusiastic volunteer corps or two. Inheriting and expanding the powers traditionally granted to English counties, colonial governments held jurisdiction over these citizen soldiers, and used it to consolidate them into volunteer forces or, with a little more pay and discipline, into voluntary militias: perhaps the nucleus of a future Australian army, but bound irrevocably to serve on local soil. Thus was born an innate assumption that official military efforts in Australia must begin – and might even end – with an ardent but unprofessional effort to defend the continent that left at least the smaller, routine imperial wars to an army raised elsewhere and funded by someone else. But colonial governments also came to own a few small warships. Less confined to local service than citizen soldiers, these vessels hinted at some kind of ambition to take a little of the burden of military spending away from British taxpayers one day. When the government of Victoria ordered an ironclad from an English shipyard in 1866, a British government minister hailed the colonial spirit of independence and loyalty as something to be encouraged.[13]

How far did local defence extend? To a colony's border, or into the wider region? War in New Zealand during the 1860s (see Chapter 6) sparked sympathy and prayer across Australia, the despatch of the warship *Victoria* from Melbourne and the construction of a gunboat in Sydney, the export of hundreds of mounts, and the enlistment of 2450 Australian men into the Waikato militia. The fate of two islands across the Tasman seemed significant to many Australians, if only for the economic opportunities that uncontested British possession offered them.

What, then, of other great islands in the south-west Pacific? Perhaps it was prudent to seize these for the British race, or at any rate for Australian businessmen? As early as 1870, colonial premiers were pressing the British government to annex Fiji. In 1879 Queensland claimed the Torres Strait for itself, and four years later it claimed the whole of eastern New Guinea for the British Empire (see Chapter 12). In Sydney, the *Freeman's Journal* hailed what it saw as the first independent act of a colonial son coming of age.[14] But the spirit of independence and the spirit of loyalty could be very different things.

Had London smiled on Queensland's wild gesture it might have hurried the eventual contracting-out of imperial rule in the south Pacific to Australians and New Zealanders that came with World War I. But for British diplomats, New Guinea was a bargaining chip, not a strategic rampart or a new frontier for making money. The island was a token to be traded to keep the peace between the Great Powers. Queensland was first made to surrender its prize, then to share it with Germany. Protests rippled across Australia, hinting at a breach one day between London and Australia on matters of global strategy. There was no breach as yet, in part because Australians could not afford one. The iron hulls of the Royal Navy ultimately guaranteed them possession of their continent. The colour of the flag floating above a weatherboard hut in some obscure portion in the pestilential tropics was a less important matter.

In any case, the New Guinea venture was not sparked only by local geography and colonial ambition. Also in the mix was a brittle, assertive, anxious imperialism spreading among British communities from Aberdeen to Auckland. A few words from a silk-hatted diplomat at a congress in Paris or Berlin, perhaps verified by a few rounds from a Maxim gun or two in Mombasa or Matabeleland, were now sufficient to turn yet another million or so Africans into British subjects. A vision of a vast domain, of power and wealth and potential, inevitably entered the white mind. Australians learned that 'our empire' was the greatest the world had seen; that it conferred unrivalled religious and political liberty; that it was preserved by English courage, that it might be saved one day by colonial patriotism.[15] The vision, harnessing high-minded idealism to a baser lust for supremacy over whole races, was never confined to the right of politics. 'The conquests we make are forced on us' was not an excuse for aggrandisement made by Benjamin Disraeli, Joseph Chamberlain, Thomas Brassey or any other prominent English imperialist, but by a famously liberal newspaper, the *Manchester Guardian*.[16] Nor was the vision confined mostly to an elite. The British army's conquest of Egypt a year before Queensland claimed eastern New Guinea prompted mass popular celebrations in Australia; 'universal rejoicings among Her Majesty's subjects in Victoria', as the colony's premier informed London.[17]

Yet the growth of the empire and of popular pride in it were partly a nervous compensation for the even more astonishing rise of German and American industry, of European conscript armies, of Russian power across northern Asia. The Royal Navy could no longer defend all points at once. *Pax Britannica* was passing. What, exactly, would take its place, and how soon? Fear of sudden attack or even invasion rippled repeatedly across British and colonial communities, along with demands that forts and warships guarantee their own little portion of coastline. Professional strategists pushed a contrary solution: the empire's armed forces should unite in battle against an enemy's fleet or strongest point and fight under the eyes of the best admirals and generals, not try to defend everyone everywhere. The more rapid the concentration, the more skilled the troops and crews, the greater the chance of victory. Whatever the approach, the 'exertion' expected of colonists was likely to increase.

Benjamin Disraeli regretted in 1872 that colonial self-government had been granted without requiring the colonies to slap tariffs on non-British imports and accept 'a military code which should have precisely defined the means and the responsibilities by which the colonies should be defended, and by which, if necessary, this country should call for aid from the colonies themselves'.[18] The call became audible in the 1880s, and not only from the mouths of English politicians, press barons, admirals and generals. 'The defence of Australia begins on the hills outside Herat', a Canadian school principal and ardent imperialist quoted a Melbourne newspaper as saying, 'and there already the attack has begun'.[19] The attack on the British Empire and its Australian provinces would not really begin until the 1940s, but there was logic and justice to the call nonetheless. The people of Britain funded the army and navy, along with people in Ireland and India who sometimes had little love for the empire and certainly few political rights within it. Were the self-governing colonies, as the British strategist John Colomb asked, 'neither to furnish men nor money according to their means'? To continue their curious privileges, he mocked, was to reverse Nelson's famous signal at the battle of Trafalgar until it read 'England does not expect every man to do his duty, but every man expects England to do hers!'[20]

Plenty of Australians would have nodded their heads in agreement, at least until the time came to ponder the fine print. The colonies had begun in helpless dependence on a matronly Mother England, and had no armies or navies of their own. It remained difficult for them to accept that mother might want help from her somewhat scrawny daughters. Why would an army that had fought off Napoleon at Waterloo, or a navy that had won command of the sea in a couple of hours off Cape Trafalgar, need a few thousand barely trained Australians? Such men were 'of little, if any use to anybody', a self-appointed people's champion said at a Sydney meeting denouncing the dispatch of the New South Wales contingent to Sudan, 'for they are not really soldiers'.[21]

Some Australians wanted little or no part in the empire anyway. Old-fashioned liberals loved England but hated the new imperial mood, the noisy patriotism, the casual slaughter of native peoples. Radicals – some of them conscious of forming a labouring class in a new land far from old Europe's strife and oppression – were cooking up a rival patriotism, centred on a lumpen-bourgeois dream of Australia as a white man's fortress. 'We want not to be a part of a conglomeration composed of Americans, Africans, Hindoos, Malays and Chinese', insisted one 'son of the soil', 'This is our land, we want no other, and if the foe comes here then we will know what to do'.[22]

But the most common hesitation to engaging in imperial defence, as Disraeli surely knew, arose simply from colonial self-government. It preserved, indeed strengthened ancient English rights not to be dragged unwilling into the Crown's wars, not to be conscripted into the army or pressed into the navy, not to sail overseas to fight under gold-laced admirals and generals. Self-government also enabled colonial parliaments to assert jurisdiction over their own citizens at the expense of London's ability to do so. There would be no repetition of the New Zealand precedent of actively recruiting Australian men for overseas service. No one, of course, proposed forbidding individuals like Roger Coveny from joining the British army. No one frowned on the barracking for the British army and navy from afar, on the prayers for British victories and defeats, or on the donations given to 'patriotic funds' for British military orphans and widows. But if self-government meant anything at all, it surely entailed the right of those parliaments to create an official contribution to the defence of the empire – and also to limit that contribution. Encouraging the raising of local regiments for the British army would have been cheap and popular, but it risked infantilising the colonies or encouraging their politicians to demand equal representation in some kind of imperial council debating defence and other matters – a hopelessly impractical idea given the disparity in population between metropolis and provinces.

Perhaps the way ahead lay simply in last-minute improvisation, in sentiment rather than system? In George Darrell's popular play *The Forlorn Hope*, first performed in Melbourne on Boxing Day in 1879, England is invaded but the unprepared colonies do their bit swiftly and decisively anyway. A young squatter raises and leads a contingent to fight for the little island at the heart of the empire with a battle cry of 'Advance Australia!' and a bravery that surpasses anything shown by the famous Light Brigade of the Crimean War. Most of the Australians are killed, but England is saved. The survivors, as the historian Ken Inglis has wryly observed, return home in time to watch the Melbourne Cup.[23]

Life almost mirrored art in 1885 after Charles Gordon, a devout and popular British general, was killed by the Mahdi's rebels in Khartoum. A Liberal government in London had sent Gordon to evacuate Sudan, not to die there, and it had supported him tardily. His death roused angry popular demands for a punitive campaign. Citizen soldiers around the empire offered themselves for service. Colonial governments offered official contingents. One hundred volunteers from London had recently helped the army take over Egypt, and General Garnet Wolseley had recruited Canadian boatmen to navigate the Nile.[24] Now, after Gordon's death, the British government accepted one official offer – from New South Wales. 'It is the first time in the world's history', Sydney's Catholic archbishop boasted, 'that the blue flag of Australia, gemmed with the Southern Cross, will take its place on the battlefields of nations'.[25] Critics – and there were plenty of them – said the army hardly needed untrained Australians; that England was in no danger; that the Mahdi was a patriot defending his land; that New South Wales should not waste taxes; or that Australians were now entangled in British militarism.[26] The contingent's even more numerous patrons and supporters strenuously refuted each claim. 'Is the good old country always to be succouring us and not expect succour from us?', mocked Edmund Barton, speaker in the colony's Legislative Assembly. 'I want to ask you whether we regard ourselves as a [genuine] portion of the English nation, or as mere hewers of wood and drawers of water?'[27] Another politician assured his peers that 'Englishmen will never forget the handsome way in which New South Wales offered this small assistance to them in their time of danger'.[28]

Small assistance indeed, and brief too. The 770 men who sailed from Sydney in March 1885 saw no great battles. The British government had little interest in pouring more blood into the sand, and a Russian attack on an Afghan border-post in March raised the prospect of a far more serious war on a different rampart of empire. Would the New South Wales contingent join British troops on their way to India and become, in effect, a temporary regiment within the British army, available for service in any campaign going? Would this be how future military contingents from the colonies would be used? 'Our purpose' in raising the force, the acting premier of New South Wales argued, 'was to assist the arms of England wherever our help was needed'.[29] 'It is true that the men were sent for ... Imperial service', the *Sydney*

Morning Herald agreed, but 'Russia may strike England in all the seas, and England must stand prepared at all points to resist her'.[30]

This was code for a cry, common in newspaper columns and perhaps on the street as well, to bring the boys home. Many of the soldiers themselves were unwilling to go on to India, sometimes because of doubts about their officers' ability to lead them into battle.[31] The contingent slunk home to Sydney. There had been no shouts of 'Advance Australia!', no chance to save Old England. Still, a precedent had been set: modest, inefficient and unsystematic, but a precedent all the same, and a safe and easy answer to the alarming demand for greater exertion. An incident serious enough to rouse popular opinion for war would thereafter spark official offers of colonial troops to join the army for a specified purpose. They would be accepted, of course, by a grateful imperial government, and later praised to the skies by British generals. They would be barely trained. They might be few in number. But they would be enthusiastic, and the world would see that the empire was marching together. No wonder London's *Daily Telegraph* described the arrival of colonial troops in Sudan as an event watched by England with almost maternal interest.[32]

But Mother was not content merely to watch. She would now nudge the colonies towards greater effort, towards system as well as improvisation, sometimes by scoffing at provincial apprehensions of sudden attack, sometimes by exploiting them. More than one official in London saw how the 'terrors of "the Russian Man of War" … that phantom ship' spooked Australians in 1885.[33] Such panics, along with rich tax receipts from a long economic boom, seemed about to prompt the colonies to begin building real navies. Yet this was no longer a comforting prospect in London's eyes: according to the new 'blue water' strategy for concentrating ships in war, it was an alarming one. The Admiralty despatched the affable, intelligent Rear Admiral George Tryon to command its Sydney squadron and to persuade Australians to fund British ships, not their own. Tryon carried a proposal with him for an auxiliary squadron to supplement the Royal Navy's existing ships in local waters, but adapted it to suit the mood he found in Sydney and Melbourne. He told colonial leaders they could strengthen local, not imperial defence by helping to fund an auxiliary squadron dedicated to securing their own coast.[34] Restricting the ships' use hardly fitted with the navy's strategy of concentrating the fleet in war. Still, both Admiralty and colonial representatives accepted the plan at the first Colonial Conference called to coincide with the golden jubilee of Queen Victoria's long reign.

'Union for the purposes of mutual defence', Britain's Conservative prime minister told representatives as they assembled in London in 1887, 'That is the business which the Conference now has before it'. Expert advice was heard from a Colonial Defence Committee, newly formed to nudge the provinces to better local defence and then on to wider responsibilities. Although the Admiralty had reservations, the conference agreed that an auxiliary squadron of five fast cruisers and two gunboats would steam to Australia and not leave its waters again without the consent of colonial premiers. In return the colonies would pay the ships' running costs – a subsidy similar to one the Indian government had long paid to the navy. The decision seemed as portentous as the Sudan expedition. 'Let them once realize that they no longer compete with the British taxpayer, but with those of all the Great Colonies', the Colonial Defence Committee's secretary optimistically expected of Britain's rivals, 'and they will abandon the competition as hopeless'.[35] The squadron entered Sydney Harbour in 1891, its ships bearing nicely chosen names such as *Boomerang* and *Wallaroo*, to be met with excited demands for immediate visits to every Australian port. The happy honeymoon soon ended. The Admiralty regretted conceding a veto over the ships' deployment. Australians came to resent that the ships they were maintaining had British crews, and would not train local men.

Riven by hostile factions in its high command, the British army had no single idea, let alone strategy, for nurturing an imperial martial spirit. Still, its officers who went out to advise or command the colonies' military forces from the late 1870s did their best. Some pushed plans supported in London by amateur imperialists or by the Colonial Office. Reforms urged by the visiting British general James Bevan Edwards in 1889, and partly achieved in the mid-1890s by Edward Hutton as military commandant in New South Wales, aimed to build forces dedicated to defending major ports from attack and forming a federal militia able to campaign in any part of the continent, perhaps in nearby Pacific islands, maybe even in Africa or India. Hutton dreamed of the empire's citizen soldiers forming a united imperial army one day, and believed that new mounted rifle regiments formed in rural Australia could be the decisive arm on future battlefields.[36]

Colonial politicians proved immune to Hutton's dream, not because they carried a rival, defiantly nationalist one in their heads but because they were provincial pragmatists. They wanted only those reforms that would cost little to enact, would not alienate citizen soldiers who were their constituents and sometimes their patrons or fellow parliamentarians, and would not cede power to soldiers or politicians from London or – even more importantly – from any neighbouring colony. A few measures were adopted in the 1890s, from modern khaki uniforms to collectively garrisoning Albany and Thursday Island, but raising a federal militia and deciding whether it might fight outside Australia were put off until the colonies themselves federated. If no plans were made for sending voluntary militia regiments overseas, the new Labor Party emerging out of the trade unions and radical politics was not even sure about allowing men to freely enlist in special units for some distant war. Australia's destiny was 'to be worked out within the boundaries of the island continent, not on the frontier of India', insisted the newly elected Arthur Griffith. 'We do not want any more Soudan contingents.'[37]

Most Australians would have disagreed with him. Affection for England, respect for Queen Victoria, interest in the empire and in the British army and navy were rising in the 1890s in comfortable tandem with pride in Australia and anticipation of federal union. It was in Melbourne, and not its less provincial, more imperially minded sister-city of Sydney, that the newspaper series *Deeds That Won the Empire* celebrated the British army and navy in romantic, stirring words that yielded the best-selling non-fiction book by any Australian author before the 1940s.[38] Thomas Brassey, Victoria's governor on the eve of the South African War, proposed that thousands of his colony's mounted riflemen form a reserve to the British army, training locally in peace and pledged to serve overseas in war. A similar proposal came from the progressive politician James Mackay in New South Wales.[39] There is no reason to assume these reserves would have failed to fill their ranks had they been formed. But as the Colonial Defence Committee pointed out, such reserves defied the logic of self-government, not to mention provincial defence fears. What colonial premier would allow some of his best troops to sail away at the very moment an enemy might attack his shores?[40]

The reserve proposals were unofficial responses to ever clearer calls for help from London. What could be more suicidal, the new and forceful colonial secretary Joseph Chamberlain proposed at a second Colonial Conference in London in 1897, than for the colonies 'either to separate themselves in the present stage from the protecting forces of the mother country, or to neglect themselves to take their fair share in those protective resources'?[41]

The colonies had no interest in separation, but they could tolerate a little neglect if it preserved their rights, their budgets, their power, their quiet enjoyment of a continent destined for them by the eclipse of rival empires in great conflicts fought long ago and far away. In a 'defensive war you will find that sentiment would determine everything', George Reid, the premier of New South Wales, assured Chamberlain. 'Our money would come; our men would come', he promised, 'but it is only in those moments that you can make the people one in the sense of sacrifice'.[42] The Admiralty was told the colonies disliked any nudging to deploy the auxiliary squadron beyond their coasts in war. The War Office that administered the British army was allowed to take a supposed first step toward eventual military co-operation, but so small a one that nothing came of it. An exchange between a British artillery battery and a Canadian one merely opened up disputes over disparities of pay and discipline.[43] James Burns, a Sydney businessman and colonel of the New South Wales Lancers, tried to save the cause by sending a squadron of his voluntary militia regiment to Aldershot to train with the British cavalry for six months. George Reid's government had no influence over the venture, such was the persistent tradition of private engagement in military matters. Perhaps this was just as well. The result was a second fiasco, although masked this time by favourable press reports.[44]

Not all of Burns' Lancers returned directly to Australia. The South African War broke out in October 1899 just as their training ended, and most resolved to steam to the front with the British cavalry. Joseph Chamberlain asked Reid's government to endorse their going[45] – a telling case of London joining with colonial governments to privilege official engagement in imperial defence over the old private involvement. The old ways endured anyway, indeed thrived. About 7000 Australians left to fight in

South Africa, not in contingents sent from their colonies but in temporary, stateless 'irregular' regiments over which their politicians had no control and little interest.

For Australians the conflict indeed began in unofficial mode: amid pre-war unrest among Johannesburg mine-workers and shopkeepers who constituted the prickly core of the 'uitlander' or English-speaking business and mining community in Transvaal, an otherwise rural 'Boer' (a local word for 'farmer') republic bordering British territory in South Africa. Some uitlanders were from Australia, and many claimed to be oppressed by their Boer rulers. During a foolish attempt in 1895 to spark a British annexation of Transvaal, Walter 'Karri' Davies from Western Australia raised a small, so-called 'Australian Corps', and was briefly thrown into gaol for his pains.[46] When war finally began four years later, Davies helped raise the Imperial Light Horse, one of the first irregular regiments to join what turned out to be the long, costly and unexpectedly perilous project of conquering Transvaal and its sister Boer republic the Orange Free State. The vast tide of irregulars that washed individually into the fighting and back home again were merely the most obvious of a deep private engagement in the war. Horse-breeders and food-canners rushed to supply a new military market, while men and women moved by the sufferings of British soldiers donated impressive sums to patriotic funds. Early in 1900 these donors would go into partnership with colonial governments in funding a new wave of contingents sent to the front.[47]

Such enthusiasm was scarce in the war's early days. Australian engagement began cautiously, even reluctantly. There seemed little evidence in 1899 of any 'defensive war' such as George Reid had spoken of at the colonial conference two years earlier: no threat to England or India, no emotional spark like the death of General Gordon, no dangerous enemy the British army seemed unlikely to quickly trounce. The absence of political rights for uitlanders bothered almost no one. Still, the War Office could not, for political reasons, draw on Indian troops, and Garnet Wolseley, now the army's commander in chief, sensed advantages for the future if the colonies were called on now. As war loomed, Chamberlain sent a modest request that each colony send just one or two small units of volunteers to join the army in South Africa.[48] Lurid press reports of uitlander flight from Transvaal were one motive for agreeing to the request. Its modest scale was another, making opposition to it seem a little earnest, eccentric or melodramatic. Thus the colonies eased their way into what became a long and bloody conflict in which more than 20 000 Australians would eventually fight and 1000 would die. Were colonial governments duped into going to war? Three years later, Arthur Griffith said so in a pamphlet entitled *The Facts About the Transvaal*.[49] Two historians in the 1970s agreed with him, and their interpretation remains orthodoxy today.[50] But Griffith and the historians ignored a military emergency late in 1899 that changed the war's nature and therefore its significance for most Australians, marking the real beginning of colonial engagement in the war.

The defeat of three British armies in a single 'Black Week' during December 1899 raised the possibility of one or more of the empire's rivals – most likely Germany or Russia – entering the war on the Boer side. Whether looked at from Manchester or Montreal, from Melbourne or Moreton Bay, the conflict suddenly seemed a defence of vital interests. Even Sydney's *Bulletin* magazine, much given to denouncing Australian entanglement in England's 'nigger empire' as a betrayal of the white race, suddenly rallied readers to a new cause: 'The empire, right or wrong'.[51]

But Black Week also seemed an exciting opportunity for citizens to tip the military balance, to prove their worth to the British army and, perhaps, to themselves. Most Boers rode horses to increase their mobility, but the army's cavalry was small, expensive, and had to be kept in hand for battle. The call went out for hardy, fast-moving mounted riflemen to help the army pin down the Boers. The response came in a human torrent of slouch-hatted, horse-borne patriots: 10 000 from England alone, another 2000 from Canada, 1000 from New Zealand, and 5000 from Australia. Some of these men were clothed, equipped and even paid from public donations. As if offering proof that the war now seemed more one of survival than choice, of defence rather than conquest, another 26 000 Australians rushed to join their home-based volunteer forces, voluntary militias and semi-military rifle clubs. Some even hoped to enforce militia service on every man. A large and rowdy public meeting in Brisbane in February 1900 answered 'No, no' and 'We won't have it' to proposals resembling European conscription, but the sudden popular mood for pushing men into uniform was clear.[52] A newspaper urged Queensland's government not to allow 'the supreme moment to pass'.[53]

The moment passed before the Black Week-inspired contingents saw serious fighting. By the middle of 1900, Boer sieges of frontier towns on British soil had been lifted, and both Boer capitals overrun. News of the relief of Mafeking – the town besieged longest by the enemy and which, thanks to Robert Baden-Powell's mastery of publicity, apparently held out with the greatest pluck – sparked a ripple of rejoicing across the white empire in May. For a day or two Australians of all social classes expressed in cheers and songs and skylarking the bellicose imperial patriotism hitherto most evident in the poorest suburbs of London.[54] There was a further thrill when news came that the first men wearing Australian uniforms had won the Victoria Cross.[55] Priests, poets and politicians lauded Australia's part in rescuing the empire from ruin. The part expanded in August 1900, when New South Wales, Victoria and South Australia sent a gunboat and 500 volunteers to the revolt against European and Japanese intrusion into northern China known as the Boxer Rebellion.[56] In October, Rudyard Kipling's poem 'The Young Queen' hailed Australia as 'Bright-eyed out of the battle', and as 'Daughter no more but Sister'.[57] This was high praise from the unofficial poet laureate of empire, but his words also carried an expectation. After all, most families expect more from adults than from children.

Australia was not yet out of the battle in South Africa. The war still had another 18 months to run, allowing thousands more Australians to enlist in more contingents raised early in 1901, and more again early in 1902. Patriotism now became less evident a motivator than pragmatism for engaging in the war. Businesses with spare capacity used the conflict as a way out of economic doldrums. Under-employed workers found in the British army a generous and undiscriminating employer. Australians were now enlisting, sniffed the Victorian politician Alfred Deakin, 'mainly because they are fond of fighting', or because they sensed a 'better scope for the daring, sporting, venturesome spirit'.[58] In South Africa hundreds of these men took up posts in the civil administrations of conquered territory, or in semi-military police forces such as Baden-Powell's glamorous South African Constabulary.[59] This was far from a principled engagement in imperial defence. It was more mercenary than the older, quieter entry into the army or navy by career officers like Roger Coveny. It was, nonetheless, an unprecedented immersion by Australians in an imperial war and in the imperial military system. Australia's newly minted Commonwealth government, assembling in Melbourne in 1901 with Edmund Barton as prime minister, acquired the colonies' remit over military matters and, a little alarmed by so much private initiative, sought to limit that immersion. The Tasmanian government was prevented from accepting a British proposal to house Boer prisoners on their island.[60] Walter 'Karri' Davies was denied permission to recruit in Australia.[61] The final wave of contingents sent to South Africa sailed as a miniature national expeditionary force, although the war had ended before most of the Australian Commonwealth Horse, as the troops were proudly called, could reach the front.[62]

Australians had joined in the South African War both officially and privately, in contingents and in irregular regiments, as patriots and as pragmatists. This coalition of engagement was mirrored by a coalition of opposition. Provincial or nationalist dislike of England's wars was far less audible than liberal voices raised against 'methods of barbarism' being inflicted on the enemy, from internment camps to the dynamiting of whole towns. Nor was it as significant as radical voices calling to keep clear of a conflict supposedly got up by Jews and capitalists, two standard bogeymen of the day.[63] But the most common (if least obvious) strand of opposition was passive disengagement. By the winter of 1900, it was clear that England, let alone Australia, was in no danger. Most Australians returned to living normal lives as though there were no army, no war, no empire.

The thousands of Australians in uniform in South Africa had no choice but to become immersed in all three.[64] 'Always forcing itself on one's mind', Corporal Jack Abbott later wrote, was 'the consciousness of empire', the 'vague realisation that we, the English, and the Canadians, and the Australians, were a race that overran the globe, and that its inheritance is ours'.[65] But was that good news or bad? The long gangs of coal-black labourers and hectic swarms of brown-skinned hawkers, the supposed red-tapeism of the Admiralty and War Office, the faintly patronising air of some British officers and even ordinary British soldiers: all this encouraged precisely the anti-imperial mood that the *Bulletin* and other critics of empire had so long sought to nurture. Serving as mounted riflemen, most Australians ranged far ahead of the army's slower-moving British infantry. Ignoring the defeats that sometimes befell them, and scoffing at mounted riflemen from England, Australians imagined that colonials like themselves were winning the war unaided. Some nursed a violent anger towards the enemy, and towards the British army too.

Whether in uniform or back at home, Australians expected the army and the War Office to indulge the empire's supposed saviours. They were silent, even supportive, when Captain Charles Cox from Parramatta was sheltered from a murder charge after ordering the execution of an African civilian.[66] They were furious when three Victorian soldiers were given death sentences – immediately commuted to imprisonment – for muttering mutiny against their general.[67] The execution by firing squad in 1902 of Lieutenant Peter Handcock from Bathurst and the bushman balladeer Lieutenant Harry 'Breaker' Morant for murdering unarmed civilians in their custody was accepted, yet there was a brief shiver of unease and a public campaign to secure the release from gaol of one of their accomplices.[68] These incidents were mere pinpricks in the imperial relationship. (There is, for instance, no evidence for the frequent assertion that the famous legislative barrier restricting or preventing the execution of Australian soldiers for military crimes has its origins in the Morant affair.[69]) Yet pinpricks sting nonetheless. These ones also aggravated a dull ache from a war that seemed disappointingly inglorious, and they intensified an itch troubling Australian officers who were often denied field commands because of their inexperience and, sometimes, their ineptitude. Australians would fight the Crown's wars again but, in part to indulge their soldiers and gratify their officers, they would do so at the direction of their own politicians, not those in London. 'We will carry our own flag up to the front', Banjo Paterson predicted accurately in 1900, 'When we go to the wars again'.[70]

But not just any war. At a third Colonial Conference, again held in London as the South African War ended, Joseph Chamberlain warned of the looming consequences to Britain's strategic situation and colonial insouciance towards them. 'The weary Titan staggers under the too vast orb of its fate', he pleaded as the conference opened. 'We have borne the burden for many years. We think it is time that our children should assist us to support it, and whenever you make a request to us, be very sure that we shall hasten gladly to call you to our Councils.'[71] If the patronising reference to children rankled, it was the right time for action. Over the coming decade, the German and French armies would each rise toward a million strong, the Russian army even further. The German navy would grow from one third the tonnage of the Royal Navy to half, and an even more rapid expansion would follow. Europe's and America's industrial capacities were already overtaking Britain's. India, Egypt and South Africa were prestigious and priceless imperial resources, but they were also embittered conquests requiring expensive garrisons, and only slight demands could be made of their inhabitants. Eventually, as one of Chamberlain's colleagues saw, 'We shall be thrust aside by sheer weight'.[72] As it turned out that was to look 50 years into the future. In the meantime, who could say what would come of Britain's loss of precedence, of her inability to stare down the jostling of rivals?

The 1902 conference might have proved a turning point for the British Empire, and for Australia's role within it. Australians had recently mobilised for a cruel, acquisitive conflict to expand the empire, to give it a new and lucrative frontier. They had engaged in the war reluctantly at first; then in a burst of patriotism; and then, as the English and Irish and Scots had long done, as a simple fact of life, as a field of economic or personal opportunity. Colonial governments had surrendered their claims to speak for Australian defence efforts to a new federal government that a few visionaries saw less as a proto-national government than a stepping stone to some future imperial federation, a merging of metropolitan and provincial dominions. What would the Australian delegates say to Chamberlain's plea? Would they keep the white empire marching together?

Britain's Board of Trade asked the 1902 conference for preference for British exports, and that seemed fair enough. But when the Admiralty asked for a free hand to deploy its ships, for more money from the colonies, for Australian sailors to become Royal Navy reservists, it had to be content with part of the money it sought and with permission to deploy the auxiliary squadron in the Pacific and Indian Oceans but no further. A War Office call that a proportion of Australian citizen soldiers, perhaps one in four, be 'absolutely pledged' to serve with the British army in any war sanctioned by the federal government was roundly refused. New Zealand co-sponsored the War Office proposal but, like Canada, Australia was firmly opposed to it. A war for Australia, a war for England, perhaps even a war for the ramparts of empire in India or Africa, would see Australians pull on uniform again, but only then and in their own contingents. Almost everything would be left to the last minute and to individual initiative, to the old private engagement in imperial defence henceforth absorbed into the new official engagement. George Reid's formula, rehearsed on stage in George Darrell's play in 1879 and then in full dress in Sudan in 1885, was ready for its opening night on Gallipoli in 1915.

'I advocated a reasonable Imperialism', Edmund Barton explained when he returned to Australia to face a public suspicious that even the cautious deal done with the Admiralty over the auxiliary squadron had been a little too generous, 'and not a reckless tendency to rush into quarrels and disputes without considering the causes'.[73] Morally it was a fine outcome, insisting on weighing up the significance and likely impact of each war when it came. It was politically prudent, and popular too. Whether it was in the British Empire's best interests, or in Australia's for that matter, was less clear. It would certainly have perplexed Robert Coveny, a colonial Australian by birth and British officer in death.

Further reading

J Beeler, 'Steam, strategy and Schurman: Imperial defence in the post-Crimean era 1856–1905', in K Neilson & G Kennedy (eds), *Far Flung Lines: Studies in Imperial Defence in Honour of Donald Mackenzie Schurman*, Frank Cass, London, 1997, pp 27–54

J Belich, *Replenishing the Earth: The Settler Revolution and the Rise of the Anglo-World 1783–1939*, OUP, Oxford, 2009

D Bell, *The Idea of Greater Britain*, Princeton University Press, Princeton, 2007

P Burroughs, 'Defence and imperial disunity', in A Porter & WR Louis (eds), *Oxford History of the British Empire*, vol 3, *The Nineteenth Century*, OUP, Oxford, 1999, pp 320–45

SJ Clarke, 'Marching to their own drum: British Army officers as military commandants in the Australian colonies and New Zealand 1870–1901', doctoral thesis, UNSW ADFA, 1999

CN Connolly, 'Class, birthplace, loyalty: Australian attitudes to the Boer War', *Historical Studies*, 18(71), October 1978, pp 210–32

M Hooper, 'The Naval Defence Agreement of 1887', *Australian Journal of Politics and History*, 14(1), April 1968, pp 52–74

KS Inglis, *The Rehearsal: Australians at War in the Sudan 1885*, Rigby, Adelaide, 1985

P Kennedy, *The Rise and Fall of the Great Powers*, Fontana, London, 1989 (first published 1988)

JA Moses & C Pugsley (eds), *The German Empire and Britain's Pacific Dominions 1870–1919*, Regina, Claremont, 2000

M Saunders, *Britain, the Australian Colonies and the Sudan Campaigns of 1884–1885*, University of New England, Armidale, 1985

S Ward, 'Security: Defending Australia's empire', in D Schreuder & S Ward (eds), *Australia's Empire*, OUP, New York, 2008, pp 232–58

C Wilcox, *Australia's Boer War*, OUP, Melbourne, 2002

10

Radical nationalists and Australian invasion novels

Augustine Meaher IV

On 27 February 1992, Prime Minister Paul Keating charged that during World War II, Britain had 'decided not to defend the Malayan peninsula, not to worry about Singapore and not to give us our troops back to keep ourselves free from Japanese domination'.[1] In short, Great Britain had betrayed Australia at the start of the Pacific War, and Australian conservatives were complicit in this betrayal. It was an old, radical nationalist storyline: Britain, aided and abetted by Australian conservatives, had happily thrown away Australian lives in imperial wars far from Australia, but was totally unwilling to protect Australian interests and territory. That such a claim had some resonance 50 years after the events, and still to some extent does today, is testament to the endurance of a deep-seated concern in the Australian psyche: that the nation is poorly defended and open to invasion by Asia's teeming multitudes. Such fears had their high-point in the late nineteenth century, and go some way towards explaining the willingness with which ordinary Australians joined military expeditions, volunteer forces and, at the outbreak of World War I, the AIF. But they found their most extreme expression in the genre of the radical nationalist invasion novel, which both flesh out these fears and prescribe a political solution for them.

Radical nationalists and Australian invasion novels

The radical nationalists of the late nineteenth century and Federation period believed that an external threat was an ideal means of alerting Australians to the need for a more self-reliant and assertive nation. Australia, with its small European population concentrated on the south-east coastal 'boomerang' and isolated far from its great and powerful protector, was especially prone to invasion scares. Invasion was a deeply held fear in Australia at the time (and remains so today in some segments of the population). Although influenced by the European invasion genre, these accounts are far from being the simple anti-Asian, racist tracts usually dismissed by scholars. They were and are uniquely Australian, and thus offer an engaging insight into Australian society, domestic politics, and the fears of the population. These novels, and the failure of most Australians to adopt their radical nationalist themes, also help to explain why Australians reacted to the outbreak of World War I as they did, and why the performance of Australian troops was mythologised as it was. Those familiar with Australian invasion novels would not have been surprised by the 'Anzac spirit' that emerged on the battlefields of Gallipoli and the Western Front. Throughout such novels, fictional Australians demonstrated that they were 'natural born' soldiers who would rise at a moment's notice to engage a devious foe, usually Asian, that relied upon overwhelming numbers and either British complicity or duplicity.

Australian radical nationalism was a reaction against British imperialism combined with the utopian belief in a fair society, and embodied by the ideals of a 'fair go' and a living wage. It combined 'aspirations for human progress with an assertive, grass-roots national sentiment'. Furthermore, its anti-British agenda extended beyond British imperialism to Britishness itself:

True working-class Australians had been involved in a constant struggle with the more Anglophile, bourgeois elements of Australian society in an effort to realise Australian 'independence'.[2]

Radical nationalism drew its inspiration from the bush legends of the late nineteenth century and the birth of the Australian Labor Party. Most Australian invasionists were from the left – often with a radical tinge – whereas the British invasion genre was dominated by authors from the right.

The first literary invasion prediction was literally a French farce, written in response to the French annexation of Polynesia. *Sydney Delivered; or, the Princely Buccaneer*, by 'Tasso Australasiatticus', was an 1845 burlesque that was apparently – and fortunately – never performed. It was, however, published in the *Australian*, a pre-Federation weekly. The French were, of course, the traditional enemy of Britain, and there had been French invasion scares during the early colonial period. One early governor of New South Wales, Philip Gidley King, was sufficiently worried about French interests in Tasmania that an Anglo–French confrontation took place in 1802, with the British ceremonially raising the Union Jack – albeit upside-down – to assert their sovereignty over King Island in Bass Strait to forestall any French claims.

Visiting French naturalist and explorer François Péron had actually suggested to Paris in the early 1800s that Sydney be invaded and occupied in a lightning-fast *coup de main*. Péron proposed entering Botany Bay under the cover of darkness, and predicted that Sydney would be under French control within an hour: the ultimate expression of the lightning raid that would terrify Australian invasionists for years to come. Péron confidently predicted a bloodless victory since the forces defending Sydney were small, scattered and cowardly, and because the British did not appreciate Australia's strategic vulnerability or its attractiveness to France.[3]

The non-fictional French plans in the Napoleonic period were based on themes that would become common to many of the invasion novels. Péron's belief that Sydney could be easily captured was based on the assumption that the Irish convicts would flock to the French colours and support the invaders. Péron expected over 3000 Irishmen to greet the French invaders as liberators. Several literary depictions of invasion would also focus on a potential 'fifth column' within Australia.

Péron's plans and assumptions would be echoed by invasionists for decades to come, and the actual Australian reaction to an enemy attack on the mainland in 1942 bears out Péron's prediction of panic. Sir Frederick Shedden remembered that the federal Cabinet behaved 'like a lot of startled chooks' when the Japanese bombed Darwin, an act that was hardly unexpected. There was 'mass panic in the town's small civilian population and within the ranks of its uniformed defenders'.[4] Widespread looting occurred, as many defence personnel deserted following the raid, but even this actual attack on the Australian mainland did not lead to a radical nationalist Australia, or an Australian republic.

The Japanese menaced Australia in 1942 because they had managed, albeit briefly, to acquire naval supremacy in the Pacific: a prerequisite for any invasion of Australia and another frequent theme of invasion novels. The ability of Britain to credibly assert sovereignty – whether over King Island or the whole of mainland Australia – was dependent on the Royal Navy's control of the seas, and this remained the cornerstone of Australian defence policy until the Pacific War. Thus, it is unsurprising that upon hearing that the French were going to invade Sydney, Tasso Australasiatticus warned, 'To Rule Britannia, I fear's but a dream!' Once war erupted, the mayor of Sydney lamented:

To rescue Sydney from this horrid go?
No Bars, no Tars
Nor frigate, sloop, nor gun-boat,
On earth, or air, ashore, afloat.[5]

Lacking a naval defence, in *Sydney Delivered* Australia was forced to rely on an outside power to come to its rescue, this time a literal mistress of the seas: the Queen of Polynesia. Many invasion novels have no rescuer coming to Australia's aid, however, reinforcing the prevalent radical nationalist belief that Britain would abandon Australia's defence and that therefore Australia would be best advised to embrace total independence and become a republic embodying socialist utopianism. While *Sydney Delivered* is by far the most fantastic of the pre-war invasion predictions, it introduced several themes that are found in those that followed: a panicky Australian government, a weak or devious Britain, and an Australian population divided into natural-born, mainly rural soldiers, who instinctively realise the threats Australia faced, and those interested only in material wealth, who were overwhelmingly urban.

The departure of the last British garrison from Australia in 1870 made Australians even more prone to invasion scares, as it meant that if the Royal Navy ever lost naval supremacy, then Australia would be completely on its own. The break in the undersea telegraph cable to the rest of the world in 1872 highlighted Australia's isolation and strategic vulnerability, as many initially believed it indicated the Russians had invaded British India. Ironically, the repair of the cable only made invasion scares increasingly frequent, as Australia was now informed of every imperial and global crisis almost as it was occurring. The Russian advance on Constantinople in the Russo-Turkish War of 1877–1878 and the Anglo–Russian Afghanistan Crisis of 1885 led to further fears of a Russian invasion of Australia, which played on memories of Russian naval visits in the 1820s, when squadrons of the Baltic Fleet had undertaken scientific voyages in Australian waters. These real colonial war scares swiftly abated, however, usually resulting only in a slight increase in militia enlistment or the construction of fortifications, as happened in Melbourne following the visit by the Confederate commerce raider *Shenandoah* during the American Civil War. But these alarms also served to focus public attention on Australia's exposed strategic position, and led to an increased awareness of the importance of Australia's military dependence on Britain and a growing realisation that British and Australian interests, although assumed to be identical, were at times very different. For radical nationalist authors, these war scares, coupled with the publishing success of British invasion novels, provided a new means of attracting supporters to their cause.

The fear that Australian and British interests might diverge led to unilateral Australian action in 1883, when the colonial government of Queensland – in an episode reminiscent of *Sydney Delivered* – annexed the non-Dutch areas of New Guinea in an attempt to forestall German colonial expansion. The imperial government promptly disowned the annexation, to Australia's horror. Britain could obviously not be expected to protect Australia if it did not share Australia's strategic outlook or, even worse, appreciate the threats Australia faced. As if to highlight the threat to Australia, Germany swiftly annexed north-east New Guinea, New Britain – which it renamed New Pomerania – and the northern Solomon Islands.

Australia now needed a protector in the South Seas, but no Polynesian power was available, and German imperialism was anything but farcical. In 1884, Whitehall reluctantly agreed to the annexation of south-east New Guinea if the Pacific colonies, especially Queensland, would underwrite the cost of maintaining a military presence there. The annexation secured Australia's northern flank, but also created a land border with Germany in New Guinea, and long-held fears of foreign intervention in Australia's assumed sphere of interest had been realised. The French war scares of the Napoleonic period, and later ones as France annexed New Caledonia and various South Pacific isles, now seemed to have been a precursor to actual events rather than mere colonial paranoia. Yet, despite being the bogey-men in many British invasion novels, Germans were never the literary invader of Australia.

This omission is interesting as it was, after all, the German victory in the Franco–Prussian War in 1870 that launched the modern invasion novel genre in Britain itself. George Tomykns Chesney's *Battle of Dorking: Reminiscences of a Volunteer* capitalised on the unexpected and remarkably swift Prussian victory. Chesney imagined a successful Prussian invasion of England modelled on the 1870 campaign, revealing how an overwhelming surprise attack was now possible and how devastating military occupation by a hostile force could be. Such a possibility was especially terrifying for Australia, which lacked sufficient naval resources simply to police its vast coastline, let alone to defeat an invading fleet. This strategic exposure had been mocked in *Sydney Delivered*; now it was very real.

While Australia was probably more vulnerable to an invasion than were the British Isles, novels about an invasion of Australia appear to have excited less public debate.[6] In Britain, fears of invasion created a genuine sense of weakness and uncertainty, which infused British politicians and military professionals alike. Such scares deferred indefinitely the otherwise pressing calls for 'retrenchment and reform' in Britain, and led instead to calls to build up the Royal Navy so that it could more effectively fly the flag overseas, and inspired a more belligerent diplomatic policy. Australia, which was genuinely weak, failed to truly appreciate its weakness or to believe that an actual invasion was likely.

Why then were Australians unpersuaded by their local versions of these novels? The answer lies partly in their uniquely Australian characteristics.[7] Far from being simple invasion novels, the Australian sub-genre also served as fertile ground for expounding domestic political fears and radical nationalism. The British reader of invasion literature believed that their most probable enemy was Germany, and that Britain was only protected by the English Channel and the Royal Navy. Australia, on the other hand, faced a multitude of threats both domestic and foreign. Australians were therefore unable to focus on one threat, and chose to do very little in response to either real or imagined threats – a problem in strategic culture that would plague Australian planners until the Pacific War. Australia also lacked a unified national identity to act as a significant rallying call, and so invasionists attempted to create and shape one to serve the purpose. Yet their conception of a national identity held only limited popular appeal, because it was perceived as too radical in the absence of an actual invasion. Australian nationalism before World War I was still waiting for the emergence of an Australian nation. Ironically, this nation would only emerge in an imperial war that would in fact undermine radical nationalism, as Australians became proudly 'British to their bootstraps' and Australia became the most loyal of dominions.

Often the invasionists' true target was not an armed invader, but rather the Chinese already living among them. Earlier colonial fears of an Irish fifth column had largely dissipated with the end of convict transportation and the failure of the Eureka Stockade to precipitate a general revolution. The Chinese population in Australia, however, had exploded during the gold rushes.

Chinese migrants were overwhelmingly male, and were thus seen by some white Australians as a plausible fifth column. The Chinese immigrant population threatened the social cohesion of the Anglo-Celtic colonies, and was accused of bringing diseases and dangerous customs such as opium smoking with which the Chinese would enslave white Australian women. The potential threat posed by Chinese labour was highlighted to the more paranoid and racist white Australians by an official visit of Chinese commissioners investigating the living conditions of Chinese nationals in 1887.

William Lane, a Queensland journalist and utopian trade unionist who had played a crucial role in the creation of the Queensland Labor Party, was also one of the first of the Australian invasionist authors. He believed that these commissioners were Chinese spies, and wrote what was probably the first Asian invasion story: *White or Yellow? A Story of the Race War of AD 1908*, which appeared in serial form in the *Boomerang* in 1888.[8] (Although George Ranken, an earlier invasion novelist writing under the pseudonym WH Walker, had occasionally referred to the Russian invaders as 'Mongols' in *The Invasion* of 1877, he had dwelt on the Nordic origins of many of the invaders, who were far more civilised than the actual Russian officers.[9]) Lane's *White or Yellow?* did not imagine an invasion *per se*, but rather what would happen if Chinese immigration continued unchecked: an invasion of unwanted migrants, a fear to which some Australian politicians still pander. Lane believed the Chinese would inevitably collaborate with the colonial elite, which was already conspiring against average Australians, and this would also lead to miscegenation as they literally climbed into bed with the Chinese fifth column. In *White or Yellow?* the Chinese 'over-ran everything' and 'sat in Parliament, directed State departments, and one had even place upon the bench'; there was also a substantial decrease in white migration, 'as Australia became more and more distasteful to the Caucasian peoples'.[10] Lane had thus set out the 'Populate or Perish!' notion more than half a century before the Australian government would undertake its 'bold experiment' of massive white immigration following World War II, when Australia had again actually believed it faced a realistic threat of invasion.

In *White or Yellow?* the Australian-Chinese are led by Sir Wong Hung Foo, who was engaged to the daughter of the premier of Queensland and planned to rule Australia by creating an Australian-Chinese dynasty. Foo, a prosperous businessman, epitomises what to Lane was the most dangerous sort of Chinaman, because he appears to have accepted Western mores and had been accepted into Western society – at least among the British elite running Australia. Foo is, of course, no gentleman and responds to an anti-Chinese insult from a local farmer by raping and murdering the farmer's daughter, Cissie Saxby. In this Lane played on the fears raised by the recent Mount Rennie rape case, which had horrified colonial Australian society only a year before and had resulted in nine death sentences.[11]

The rapists at Mount Rennie had been Australian 'larrikins' – nineteenth-century urban gang members – but in Lane's Australia it is a Chinese rape that provokes male and female Australians – including, ironically but appropriately given their uniquely Australian attributes, larrikins – to rise up against the Chinese in Australia and against the British colonial elite who consort with them. Australia's ensuing war of independence is thus both a civil war and a race war seeking to answer the question of the title – would Australia be white or yellow?

Foo is eventually lynched and then shot by the widow of the premier in a graphic scene that suggests Lane may have actually witnessed a lynching while in America. The Ku Klux Klan overtones of Foo's lynching are telling, especially as the leading white resisters and Lane's heroes – 'the League' – was a primarily agrarian white nativist movement that wanted a White Australia and was prepared to use violence and intimidation to achieve it. Lang had been in the United States during several violent anti-Chinese outbursts, and the Ku Klux Klan (among others) shared Lane's anti-immigrant, anti-drinking and anti-gambling beliefs. While Lane was in the United States, the White League had seized control of the state government of Louisiana in an action very similar to the seizure of the Queensland parliament described in Lane's novel.

Unusually for an invasion novel, in *White or Yellow?* it is white Australia that emerges victorious and stronger under the leadership of Cissie's father and her fiancé, both of whom instantly become magnificent soldiers as soon as they pick up rifles and rally to the new Australian banner. Most later invasion novels instead portray the invader as victorious, to underscore the folly of relying on Great Britain. Lane did, however, realise that Australia could not defend itself against external threats without a powerful naval ally.

Although Australians' fear of Chinese immigrants was real, there is no indication that colonial governments feared a racial civil war. Indeed, just as *White or Yellow?* was going to press in 1888, the colonial governments agreed to reduce the flow of Chinese immigrants into the Australian colonies at the intercolonial conference. In combination with continuing European migration, this led to a gradual decline in the Chinese population in the Australian colonies. Democracy, not revolution, would eventually answer the question of Lane's title, but neither colonial governments' efforts to curtail Chinese immigration nor the eventual Commonwealth *Restriction of Immigration Act* (1901), which so firmly established White Australia, was enough to convince Lane that Australia was on the right path. He immigrated to Paraguay in 1893 as one of the founders of the Colonia Nueva Australia, a doomed utopian colony, before emigrating from the failing experiment to New Zealand in 1899, where he became a conservative columnist, never to return to Australia.

James Alexander Kenneth Mackay did not need to go to Paraguay or New Zealand to become a conservative: he, unusually for an Australian invasionist, was already one. Although his invasion vision again fed on domestic fears, with Mackay the reader encountered for the first time an external Asiatic invader, albeit one under European control. Mackay's *The Yellow Wave: A Romance of the Asiatic Invasion of Australia* of 1897 thus serves as an excellent bridge between the invasion novels that focused on domestic issues and those that dealt with international affairs.[12]

The Yellow Wave, although also written in response to domestic concern about the Chinese, places an invasion of Australia within an international context. The 'coming of the Mongols' is made possible by a Russian invasion of India and a joint Franco-Russian naval thrust towards Hong Kong. This scenario underscored Australia's exposed strategic position, its utter reliance on Britain, and the possibility that an unexpected lightning strike – as Chesney had envisaged in *The Battle of Dorking* – could also befall Australia. Mackay was simply exploring the consequences of Chesney's predicted swift and unexpected defeat of Britain for the empire.

Once the 'Mongol' invasion begins, Mackay uses anti-Chinese themes similar (although less violent) to those of Lane. He describes the invaders as 'men with the broad yellow faces and coarse black hair of those fierce nomads who followed Genghis Khan' (p 213). Once they landed, 'they began to kill with the indiscriminate hate of wild beasts', and they are in fact only able to mount the invasion because their commander is half-Russian (p 223). The Chinese choose to invade in Queensland because, 'Unable to compete with the cheap labour of the East, the whites never numerous, quickly disappeared' (p 123). There is thus a sizeable Chinese immigrant population ready to assist the Chinese invaders – who, interestingly, treat the Japanese population of Queensland in the same manner that they treated Europeans. Considering that most of China was at the time either under European control or engaged in a civil war, the possibility of an actual Chinese invasion of Australia was extremely remote. The Chinese are ultimately successful in *The Yellow Wave*, but they would soon cease to be a potential invader, defeated by Australian immigration restrictions and the rise of Japan as a Pacific naval power.

The signing of the Anglo-Japanese Alliance in 1902 awoke fears of Japanese expansion and heightened fears that British strategic interests might not place Australia in the preferred position. These fears were only exacerbated by Japan's 1905 victory in the Russo–Japanese War – a victory made ominously possible by an unexpected lightning raid on Russia's Port Arthur. These fears were immediately highlighted in another two invasion novels – *The Coloured Conquest* by 'Rata' (Thomas Richard Roydhouse) and *The Australian Crisis* by 'CH Kirmess' (Frank Fox) – which also tapped into the emergent radical Australian nationalism.

However, to the radical nationalists the main enemy was always the British and their Australian conservative collaborators. For instance Lane's *White or Yellow?* had centred on the Australian bush, and one of the main heroes perfectly encapsulated the then popular romantic notion of the bush:

> I love this Australian land. I love the waves that beat here. I love the skies that are so clear here. I love the very hurricanes that blow up nobody knows how. I love the hills and grass plains and the very sand-banks up North. It is ours.

And who is the true threat to this great land? Not the Chinese, who are the rapacious villains, but rather 'these cursed Imperialistic-plotters have well-nigh lost it for us with their admiration for everything but that which was Australian' (p 25). The white colonists in Australia could not rely on British support, not because the Royal Navy was busy elsewhere – a realistic possibility of which many in London had repeatedly warned Australia for years – but rather because Australia can 'have no hope in England and because her aid will be given to the Chinese' (p 34). The anti-British nature of Lane's work would be found in many radical nationalist tracts over the next century.

In Lane's imaginary world, the British had a long history of betraying Australia. The failure to achieve an Australian federation he blames not on a lack of popular support – which was the real reason that pre-1888 moves for federation had foundered – but on British perfidy. 'With ribbons and titles and false promises Australia had been bought and sold', he claims, articulating a common radical nationalist fear that Australians were being corrupted. Furthermore, he portrays Britain as putting its commercial interests above Australian national interests, and as having actively fought federation by fanning 'the local jealousies [that] kept the colonies apart' (p 34). The belief that Britain was undermining Australian interests was strong in the aftermath of the German annexation of New Guinea, which was blamed especially on the Colonial Secretary, Lord Derby.

Australian invasion novels therefore often aimed at changing not just a policy but also the form of government. (Mackay's *The Yellow Wave* is a noticeable exception, but then Mackay was a member of the New South Wales Legislative Assembly for the Protectionist Party and later Edmund Barton's National Federal Party.) Lane's *White or Yellow?* culminates with a white revolutionary crowd who intend to ethnically cleanse Australia and establish a 'pure' white, republican Australia. *White or Yellow?* is thus an early attempt at giving Australia a radical national identity, and reveals the frustration of such nationalists who were forced to accept a non-violent, non-radical evolution towards self-government. From a radical nationalist point of view, the notion that a foreign threat might be necessary to galvanise Australians into seizing the initiative was logical.

Lane's fictional Australia did indeed grasp its independent destiny, singing the Australian *Marseillaise* and shouting before a fluttering Southern Cross flag, which while not described is apparently very similar to the flag of the Eureka Stockade – the closest Australia ever came to a radical nationalist uprising. In the book the very sight of the new flag even causes a veteran from the stockade to die from joy. Sadly for Lane, radical nationalism never aroused such passion. Lane's Australians spontaneously embrace the radical nationalism he espoused, screaming 'For life or death'. But even in his victorious Australia, the fear of Asia remains palpable, and Australia finds another protector, the United States, whose fleet was 'sweeping the encircling seas' (p 107). Indeed, in *White or Yellow?* the Americans are crucial to the success of the radical nationalist defence. They swiftly recognise the sister republic and force their way into Port Jackson with orders for the American consul to 'take any steps desirable for the ensurance of the success of the rising' (p 106). That Lane's fictionally triumphant nation still needed to rely on the United States simply underscores the naivety of his international outlook. In some later invasion novels, the United States is seen as a natural ally for a newly independent White Australia, while others see it as an economic competitor that cannot be relied on to support Australia in times of crisis.

Lane's work was the only one in which a radical nationalist solution was reached, but all accepted the anti-British views of the radical nationalists. All of the authors lamented that Australian defence policy meekly accepted that 'An invincible British navy is our only safeguard'.[13] Kirmess, in *The Australian Crisis*, depicts Britain failing to come to Australia's aid because 'The White Australia policy robbed them [British capitalists] of profits' (p 34), and because the Royal Navy is not large enough to protect both Australia and the British Isles simultaneously. In *White or Yellow?* Lane similarly described British interests conspiring to ensure that 'the gates of Australasia had been thrown open to the yellow men' (p 1). In Kirmess's invasion novel, the British literally betray White Australia by taking the Northern Territory from the newly formed Commonwealth and allowing it to be settled by Japanese, whom Kirmess depicts as a fifth column which will eventually destroy Australia entirely.

Invasion novels were equally critical of Australian capitalists, who invariably appear as British, even if native-born. Capitalism could not be identified with 'real' Australians if the radical nationalists' vision of Australia were ever to come true. Indeed, radical nationalists were generally critical of the way the Australian 'national type' was developing. Their novels gave them the perfect venue to describe an idealised alternative version of Australian masculinity, one that was striking in its similarity to the character of the Anzacs that emerged during World War I.

George Ranken, writing under the pseudonym WH Walker, lamented in *The Invasion* that:

> A spurious prosperity had for years covered the community with a growth of proud flesh, and the healthy current of national life was clogged. We were becoming a nation of pawnbrokers and publicans. (p 28)

Walker's belief that the national life was 'clogged' was similar to

Lane's, and Lane's chief Australian villain is a former publican. (Lane himself was a teetotaller.) Indeed, the notion that Australians had become self-absorbed is found even in *Sydney Delivered*. One character, upon hearing that Britain no longer ruled the waves, remarks simply 'What's the matter. So long as I get a full platter' (p 7).

The inability of the Australian commercial elite to place their nation's interests above their own left Australia dangerously unable to defend itself, according to Walker. This capitalist class is the main enemy to his Australia in *The Invasion*: they, rather than the Chinese, served as the fifth column that welcomes the Russian invaders: 'business was business, and money was money', and the capitalists think of their country only as something to sell – their main challenge being 'to determine, if they got the chance, to get price for it' (p 86). Walker's main objection to the commercial class in Australia is that they 'were beginning to ignore all colonial ties and to talk of living in England' (p 25). Similarly in Kirmess's *Australian Crisis*, the commercial class hinders the development of a uniquely Australian identity by continuing to identify with Britain. Commercial success thus threatened the Australian identity because 'Commercial Britons have always loved to let others do the fighting for them' (p 51). By contrast, Australians:

> preferred to suffer everything rather than surrender the White Australia ideal and ... included ... people of every political persuasion willing to place fatherland before faction in the hour of national danger, even at the risk of offending British traditions. (pp 51–52)

The invasion novels were at their most nationalistic when they described the Australian traditions that made Australians superior soldiers who could only be defeated by the sheer numbers available to an Asiatic enemy. Tapping into the bush legends that were already firmly entrenched in the popular mind, invasion novels portrayed rural Australians as more politically astute, more loyal to Australia, and better soldiers.

Even Kenneth Mackay, a conservative politician, believed that rural Australians were the best defenders of the country. In the same year in which he wrote *The Yellow Wave*, he personally 'raised the 1st Australian Horse, a regiment of cavalry recruited entirely from country districts'.[14] In his novel Mackay laments that 'the voters of capital seized with insatiable greed acre after acre, never reckoning who should defend their heritage did the spoiler come' (p 231). His rural Queenslanders, however, readily shoulder the burden of defending their homeland, as 'the times had changed the light-hearted Bushman into the resolute, masterful leader' (p 371). The women of the bush are equally resolute, declaring 'let us take off our dresses and put on trousers and coats [and] do our best to help the men' (p 328).

In *The Coloured Conquest*, Thomas Richard Roydhouse (writing as 'Rata') does not extol the virtues of the bushmen, but he does warn against increasing urbanisation which had blinded Australians to the threats posed by the Japanese.[15] This danger is highlighted by the response of the narrator's love, Mabel, to visiting Japanese sailors. The allure of Japan was one that constantly worried Australian men. The recently signed Anglo-Japanese Alliance only increases the Japanese threat in Rata's view, but it also makes many Australians increasingly relaxed towards the Japanese. Even after the Japanese attack, urban Australians are unable to bring themselves to defend their native land. Sydneysiders respond to the arrival of the Japanese by engaging in an orgy of looting and drinking, before firing the city (pp 96–97). When the Japanese arrive they promptly use Australian women

– including Mabel – as 'comfort women', playing on Australian fears of Asian sexual desires: something which had also been graphically portrayed in Lane's *White or Yellow?*

The bushman is also the unquestioned hero of Kirmess' *The Australian Crisis*, in which two bushmen discover the Japanese invaders and immediately attack before attempting to raise the alarm by informing the government that 'an armed invasion had taken place'. In Darwin, complacent officials don't believe their story, and valuable time is wasted before the government finally realises the danger which Australia faces. The treacherous British response, meanwhile, is to express a desire to settle the matter 'quickly and quietly' (p 37).

Such portrayals embody the radical nationalist view that Britain and urban Australia were holding Australia back from its independent destiny. Reviewers of *The Australian Crisis* responded to the book according to their opinion of the nationalism that underpinned it. The *Launceston Examiner* saw it as 'a stirring tale which will appeal very forcibly to the advocates of white Australia', and the Adelaide *Register* recommended that 'every thinking Australian would do well to read this book'. In contrast, the conservative Melbourne *Argus* dismissed it as 'full of improbabilities', while the Adelaide *Advertiser* decried 'the author's fears of the hostile designs of the Japanese, and of the selfish indifference of the Imperial authorities', declaring it unimaginable that the British government would ever 'blockade Australian ports in the interests of the Japanese'.[16]

Unfortunately for the literary Japanese invaders in *Australian Crisis*, 'Far removed from the law-bewitched nerve centres of population, there lived a more offensive type of Australian' (p 83). These rural Australians are determined to protect Australia, and they form the White Guard, 'composed of the sturdy sons of the Australian bush set off by just a dash of a more refined cosmopolitan element made up of a few Americans, Canadians and Australians city bred'. There may be a few non-bushmen in the White Guard, but its elan arose solely because 'daring bushmen made little of natural obstacles in those feverish days. Everybody was acquainted intimately with the terrors of the wilderness and had braved them often before' (p 87).

Again playing to the prejudices of white Australia, in *An Australian Crisis* these bushmen are defeated because the Japanese are aided by Aboriginal collaborators who are the true masters of the bush. The choice of bushmen as the heroes in invasion novels reflected both radical nationalism and also presaged the more populist myth of an 'intrinsic Australian aptitude for soldiering'.[17] As Walker described the Australian forces that rise to meet the Russian invaders in *The Invasion*:

> There were cricket-players, street preachers, gamblers, spiritualists, drunkards, politicians, and in fact, all the most prominent of every eccentric class, but undoubtedly containing men of brains and energy. Most of them went to the front that day, and a good many did not come back. (p 112)

Indeed, the only Australians who do not fight the Russian invaders are capitalists and larrikins: they do not understand that 'the right to shoot Russians [is] an idea [that] was acted upon pretty generally' by almost every Australian who is, of course, a natural born soldier (p 127).

When the Chinese invade in Mackay's *The Yellow Wave*, they find that 'the Australian war officers were little in touch with the national pulse' (p 345) and the only powder factory is 'at a standstill' (p 349). But the population is ready to fight. This readiness is embodied in Lieutenant Jones of the Hughenden Mounted Rifles, who had joined the local militia solely because of his wife's social climbing ambitions and is a 'soft-good man who had no actual experience' (p 304). But when the Chinese charged, 'he fought with the best' and his only regret is that he had not broken his sword over a Chinese invader (p 307). The bushmen also prove themselves as effective cavalry, doing 'all that men may do', and so proving that there was still a role for cavalry in modern combat (p 394).

The most prized possession of Lane's bushman was naturally his polished rifle. The Australian nationalists in *White or Yellow?* are also natural soldiers. Indeed, every farmer and bushman is a willing soldier, and the nationalist movement is centred in the bush: 'every small white farmer' is a natural soldier, a nationalist, and a member of the league that was dedicated to the establishment and protection of a White Australia. The natural combat ability of the white Australians is a necessary plot element, as the scheming and devious Chinese have already formed military units and, coupled with their numerical superiority, this meant that they could only be defeated by the world's greatest soldiers – especially as the world's preeminent sea power would not come to Australia's aid.

Indeed, the invasion novels usually assumed that an invasion would prompt the best traits in the Australian character – mateship, loyalty, courage and self-sacrifice – to come to the fore. The Anzacs would need not go to Gallipoli to be born, they would have been born on the Australian shore had Australia ever been invaded – a convenient argument for later radical nationalists who objected to the glorification of Gallipoli, which they saw (and still see) as an imperial folly.

Given the spontaneous nature of the Australian reactions to these fictional invasions, it is unsurprising that rank meant little in the defending forces, and – as in *The Yellow Wave* – official rank was swiftly disregarded in favour of 'natural leaders' who become the ultimate embodiment of radical nationalism (p 281). When an officer is placed in a difficult position, his first course of action is to go to the nearest pub and have a beer – an image that any number of authors have used in accounts of wars from South Africa to Afghanistan in order to 'Australianise' an officer; the officer's next act is to turn 'to his guide, philosopher, and friend', meaning his working-class sergeant (p 304). The officer 'had the sense not to object to the sergeant's assumption of command' when the battle began (p 307).

The anti-Chinese forces in *White or Yellow?* have only a nominal commander: a small farmer whose only insight into war is the very simplistic 'I'm not a general lads, the Government can beat us hollow I don't doubt, but they can't beat us at hard fighting' (p 66). Given that there was no actual combat in Lane's novel, only a lynching, the leadership qualities of Australian men remain debatable.

When the Japanese fleet enter Sydney Harbour in *The Coloured Conquest*, the only resistance they encounter comes from one soldier who disobeys the orders of his superiors and decides to make the Japanese pay for their invasion by single-handedly sinking several enemy warships (p 100). The courage of such an act is undeniable; indeed, invaders in various novels often laud the courage of the Australian defenders. Australian mateship is another theme that runs through the novels, with soldiers doing everything possible for a mate. In two of the novels, first-hand accounts of the invasion were available only because another soldier had salvaged the diary of dying mate, thus making mateship an essential literary tool as well as a valuable component of the national identity which the authors were intent on creating.

In 1913, a year before the outbreak of World War I, the first Australian invasion movie was released. *Australia Calls* was written by CA Jeffries and John Barr, two Sydney journalists who worked at the radical nationalist magazines *Bulletin* and *Lone Hand*. The Perth *Sunday Times* predicted the film would be 'as foolish as some of the sensational stuff that Jeffries and Barr perpetuate' in their columns. *Australia Calls*, however, with its images of 'the mighty Japanese fleet' steaming into Sydney Harbour 'while airships floated through the sky, dropped fire-bombs into the city and caused the destruction of the capital', with the Asian invasion 'realistically portrayed by real military men and genuine Mongols' caught the public mind.[18] A packed Saturday night audience in Broken Hill responded to the film in the following way:

> The invasion by the Mongols of Australia did not find favour, and the object lesson set forth on the screen seemingly sank deep into the hearts of many of its spectators. The story, as it was unfolded, was followed with bated breath, broken now and again by bursts of appreciative applause. From 'The Warning' right to Aviator Hart's great flight, the picture gripped.[19]

Australia has never been invaded. Even in 1942, the risk (although real) was still extremely low. Yet in the immediate pre- and post-Federation period, fears of an invasion were real and palpable. The government reaction to these fears varied depending on the threat and the world situation. Literary portrayals of possible invasions highlighted Australia's strategic vulnerability and provided the perfect vehicle for early radical Australian nationalists to argue for a stronger and more independent Australia. However, the Australia they advocated did not arise: indeed, when war actually broke out, Australian patriotism produced even closer fealty to the Mother Country. Even Curtin's later 'Look to America' declaration in December 1941 did not indicate a radical change in Australia's relationship with the mother country:

> In a subsequent statement Mr Curtin said that nothing in his statement was to be taken as meaning a weakening of Australia's ties with the British Empire. Australia's nexus with America was that of a military alliance made necessary by geographical considerations. It could be compared with the Entente Cordiale as established by Edward VII between the United Kingdom and France and arose through similar necessities.[20]

However, the radical nationalist traits which authors ascribed to Australian soldiers in imaginary battles were incorporated into the Anzac legend. Some of these ideas, such as that of Australians being natural-born soldiers, continue to dominate the public memory of Australian soldiers, and Australia remains an anxious nation as authors and film-makers continue to depict Australia being invaded. Indeed, more recent popular historians have capitalised on this anxiety by depicting a Japanese invasion of Australia in the Pacific War as having almost occurred – or indeed having actually occurred, as in Baz Luhrmann's wildly inaccurate but popular movie *Australia* (2008), or *Tomorrow When the War Began* (2010). These were simply the latest instalments in the invasion genre, albeit without a radical nationalist tinge, which has long been a staple of Australian literature, and one that is sure to continue.

Further reading

GT Chesney, *The Battle of Dorking*, 1st pub 1871, Read Books, New York, 2011

IF Clarke, *Voices Prophesying War: Future Wars 1763–3749*, 1st pub 1966, 2nd edn, OUP, Oxford, 1992

R Dixon, *Writing the Colonial Adventure: Race, Gender and Nation in Anglo-Australian Popular Fiction*, CUP, Melbourne, 1995

F Krome, *Fighting the Future War: An Anthology of Science Fiction War Stories 1914–1945*, Routledge, London, 2011

W Lane, *White or Yellow? The Race War of 1908*, Little Darling, Sydney, 2011

K Mackay, *The Yellow Wave: A Romance of the Asiatic Invasion of Australia*, 1st pub 1897, reprint, A Enstice & J Webb (eds), Wesleyan University Press, Middletown (CT), 2003

11

Edwardian transformation

CRAIG WILCOX

The first military expeditionary force raised by an Australian government pinned on its 'rising sun' badges and went to war not in western Europe – so long a place of martial dreams and nightmares for the British people and their cousins in the empire's self-governing dominions – but in a strange land of baking summers and freezing winters. They marched against an enemy not quite European, one to whom few Australians had given much thought before the fighting began. The despatch of the Australian Imperial Force to Egypt in 1914 and then Gallipoli the following year simply repeated the earlier despatch of the Australian Commonwealth Horse to South Africa in 1902. The earlier announced what the later affirmed: that Australia would take part in some of the wrenching combats that remade the world during the twentieth century by hastily forming legions of brave and barely trained optimists and shipping them overseas to fight as contingents within the British and, later, the American army.

Yet the greater size, complexity and potential competence of the Australian Imperial Force compared with its predecessor in the South African War, and the escort given the AIF across the Indian Ocean by Australian warships among others, reflected something approaching a revolution in Australia's martial institutions and activity between the Treaty of Vereeniging that ended one war in 1902 and the assassination in Sarajevo that sparked another in 1914. This Edwardian transformation has been frequently narrated,[1] but often as though the new Commonwealth government and its professional military advisers were the sole drivers, and certainly the heroes, of an inevitable, admirable, unchallengeable national project of building an army and navy and keeping both of them from becoming the playthings of imperialists in London. We should not exaggerate the prestige, power and popularity of a handful of men in Melbourne, Australia's temporary federal capital, before World War I. When it came to matters military, these few men stood uncertainly and at times awkwardly on a crowded stage. Equally important, and no less legitimate or more power-hungry, were British politicians, admirals and generals. These men led an empire and its armed forces that had nurtured Australia and still secured it for its people. For all their unexamined and sometimes arrogant privileging of metropolitan security over provincial, their routine criticism of dominion parochialism in defence matters reflected a global strategic view and a vast professional wisdom.

Then there was the vast but rarely harmonious chorus of the Australian people. Australians had grown accustomed during the nineteenth century to being the primary patrons of local defence, having themselves founded the part-time units of citizen soldiers that defended local soil. Many had also cheered the news of British imperial victories in Africa or Asia, and raised donations for orphans and widows of redcoats and bluejackets. They had only recently begun to share with politicians and generals their power to shape military activity. They did so reluctantly at times, eagerly at others. Their preferences and prejudices were as vague and imprecise as they were facts of political and military life. Some supported, indeed agitated for compulsory militia service, but others sheltered their sons from it openly or covertly. Some were cheering the creation of an Australian fleet, just as others were donating handsomely to build battleships for the Royal Navy. The shiver of fear at Japan's victory over Russia in 1905 has deceived some historians into imagining that nearly all Australians had a simple, self-interested defence program, or ought to have had one: better defence of their own soil, and to hell with fighting for a fading British empire.[2] A moment's reflection on the battleship donations, not to mention the broad popular support for Britain after it declared war in 1914, casts doubt, to say the least, on this nationalist fairy tale. Colonial nationalism was real, but it proclaimed a nation within an empire, and an army and navy within their imperial counterparts. Most Edwardian Australians valued the institutions, policies and rhetoric that advertised the emergence of a new society *within* the British world, not outside it: a rising sun in the south, a vigorous daughter of Mother England, a David to Japan's Goliath, and a nephew to Uncle Sam.

When the South African War ended in May 1902, the Commonwealth of Australia was not yet 18 months old. The new federal government was engaged in creating institutions for a wealthy, democratic but thinly populated and ethnically isolated British dominion that everyone expected would grow into a nation one day. Institutions costing little and offering immediate public reward – a tariff wall to prop up local industries, or a dictation test to keep out Asian migrants – were relatively easy to build. Armed forces, on the other hand, required considerable thought and financing. Federal budgets were small at first, the risk of war even smaller, and the rewards of war apparently smaller still. The final contingents came home from South Africa to join their predecessors in bickering over pensions and back-pay. The brutal conflict had yielded no uncontestable vindication of Australian martial ability, but plenty of folk rumour about overbearing British officers, hidebound British military and naval administrators, and an innate military ability among Australian men that must never be crushed by drill and discipline. 'Altogether', smiled the Sydney journalist Frank Fox, 'military glory has lost a good deal of its glamour to Australians in S[outh] Africa'.[3]

Still, the empire had prevailed in battle yet again, and no rival power, not France or Russia, nor Germany or the United States, had dared to intervene. Australians seemed safe, for the moment, behind what Prime Minister Edmund Barton called 'a shield of protection'.[4] Britannia's shield was forged far away on the other side of the globe, by a prestigious British diplomatic service, a small but skilful British army, and the stout ships and men of the Royal Navy. British taxpayers met almost all the cost. Australian funds toward an 'auxiliary squadron' supporting a unit of British warships still based in Sydney were a notable exception, hence the outrage so easily stirred by critics of this 'tribute' paid each year to the Admiralty.[5]

Not that the shield was wide or weighty enough. 'The truth', agreed Britain's leading Liberal politician of the day, 'is we cannot provide for a [truly] fighting Empire, and nothing will give us the power'.[6] Australians in particular worried that a hostile fleet might evade the Royal Navy one day and strike at Sydney or Perth. Despite the frustrations and frictions of the South African War, almost everyone wished to reinforce the British army if a serious war came again. Some said the auxiliary squadron and, behind it, the few tiny, locally manned and sometimes unseaworthy gunboats and torpedo boats then passing from colonial into federal government hands should give way to an Australian navy. Expense ruled this out for the moment, unless the fleet were the shore-hugging mosquito flotilla advocated by William Creswell, Australia's senior naval officer, in a scheme mocked by the Admiralty in London as a useless distraction from the job of concentrating the empire's warships against an enemy's main fleet.[7]

A federal military force seemed cheaper and more obviously

necessary. All English-speaking societies of the day maintained large though scattered formations of part-time, lightly disciplined, highly enthusiastic citizen soldiers, some organised into voluntary militias, others into looser Volunteer forces. The glory of their communities – and the despair of professional officers – such forces existed only to defend local soil in war: both custom and law prevented their despatch overseas. Amalgamating Australia's existing 29 000 citizen soldiers and also, perhaps, its 35 000 rifle club members would not cost much. Excited notions, imbibed from prolonged Boer resistance, that these men could form an untrained guerrilla army promised to cost nothing at all.

Such notions were fading as the South African War receded into history, but the official decision to forge a small, skilled and well-equipped national militia was far from universally popular. Some said it was hatched amid the gold-laced atmosphere that critics detected around Edward Hutton, the socially arch but tactically progressive colonel borrowed in 1901 from the British army to be Australia's first General Officer Commanding. From 1902 to 1904 Hutton tried to forge a crisp military force, much of it mounted on horseback, because the South African War seemed to vindicate the usefulness of mounted riflemen, although he also created static garrisons stiffened by professional gunners and engineers. Hutton's project was doomed by an inadequate budget, by his own impatience and arrogance, by the outrage that cuts and changes provoked among citizen soldiers and local communities, and also by suspicions that he was really assembling a tin-pot army to fight beside British troops on some foreign field.[8] 'So far as can be made out', a Melbourne newspaper warned, Hutton's policy seemed to be 'to create a branch of the Imperial forces in Australia … to be available for action wherever it may be considered best to strike'.[9] The branch was a weak one, however, a paper army according to the secretary of a committee on imperial defence formed in London to advise, or maybe nudge, British and dominion governments on military matters.[10]

Not that Australians meant to turn their backs on the empire. As Edmund Barton said at the 1902 Colonial Conference in London between dominion leaders and British government ministers, his people could be relied on to raise military contingents in an imperial emergency.[11] But they would never allow part of Australia's standing military forces to be committed in peace to some future war of unknown cause, place and likely consequence. Barton's stand was unwelcome to his hosts, all too aware that European rivals were overtaking the empire in industrial and military might and that the British army and navy needed an approximation to the reserve forces of Europe's vast conscript armies. 'We have borne the burden for many years', Colonial Secretary Joseph Chamberlain pleaded. 'We think it is time that our children should assist us to support it.' Barton and his Defence Minister doubled funding for the auxiliary squadron, but plugged their ears to a call that part of their militia be 'absolutely pledged' to reinforce the British army in war.[12]

London's need for allies, and the Royal Navy's wish to concentrate capital ships nearer European rivals, prompted a British alliance with Japan in 1902. The Japanese sinking of a Russian fleet in the straits of Tsushima in May 1905 ended old Australian fears of Russian attack. That it prompted something close to panic about Japan may be a myth that arose later, in the 1940s, to be swallowed by nationalist historians later still.[13] But a shiver of unease clearly chilled many Australian spines in 1905. That Japan had no inclination early in the twentieth century to strike into the South Pacific, and no capability either, was unknown to them. What if the Anglo–Japanese alliance was a mere convenience, or even deception on Tokyo's part? What if Japan made Australia its next object of attack? The new power in the Pacific was, 'so to speak, next door', wrote Alfred Deakin, the Victorian liberal who would dominate federal politics for the next five years, 'while the Mother country is many streets away, and connected by long lines of communication'.[14] Even worse, some whispered discreetly, was the prospect that 'the British navy may not be available to help us in a White Australia quarrel'.[15] Australia's exclusion of Asian migrants was embarrassing in an empire largely populated by black and brown peoples and committed, in theory at least, to giving them the refinements of British civilisation and the protections promised by British law. What if London looked the other way while Japan used force to assert its citizens' right to enter Australia, or if it claimed an unused patch of Australia's notoriously undeveloped north?

William Morris Hughes, a rising star in a Labor Party that emerged from the trade unions to dominate the left-wing of politics, proposed an answer. Only a nation in arms, he said, could repel a Japanese attack.[16] Dr Richard Arthur, a notorious busybody much given to lecturing his fellow man and woman, quantified Hughes's rhetoric by calling for a quarter of a million men to be trained in rifle shooting.[17] Against a number like this, the 20 000 members of the voluntary militia seemed a mere town guard. True, with Hutton gone the force could be steered out of the tactical *cul de sac* of readiness to fight a mounted war in an open, uninhabited countryside unswept by machine-gun fire. Training and arms had begun to reflect developments in British army doctrine rather than the best practice learned in the South African War.[18]

But even the hardest reform seemed unable to compensate for inadequate numbers. Previous military scares – from fear of Russian attack in 1854 to fear of rival European intervention in South Africa in 1900 – had prompted men in their thousands to begin to drill on local parks and race courses, and to press their government to accept them and the units they were forming as new components of the military forces. Tight budgets and scientific recruiting now, for the first time, locked these men out. In compensation, the rifle clubs began to grow (see Chapter 7). During 1900, clubs in Victoria had proclaimed themselves the nucleus of a guerrilla force. Now, five years later, Victorians pushed once again for the clubs to evolve into a nation in arms although not, it was stressed, an armed nation: 'we are conscious of the evils of Militarism, and against Jingoism, for Defence solely, and to inculcate citizen *duty*', explained Marshall Lyle, the mouthpiece for this popular movement, and 'do not see the wisdom of putting in the word so objectionable to Britishers as "Compulsory"'.[19]

Those last words were a dig at a group of rival Sydney-based lobbyists, more disciplined and hard-line, who founded the Australian National Defence League (NDL) soon after Tsushima. Led by William Morris Hughes, Frank Fox and a Colonel Gerald Campbell of a Scottish 'national corps' within the militia, the NDL drew much of its program and methods from a National Service League founded earlier in Britain. But unlike its predecessor, the NDL avoided the mistakes of speaking primarily to political conservatives and of raising the bogey of conscription for foreign service in a professional army. Its aim was solely to expand a domestic militia, and it concluded that compulsion was the necessary means. Through Hughes the NDL spread into the Labor Party, the rising political force. Through Campbell it won over sometimes sceptical citizen soldiers and their families. Through its magazine *The Call*, edited by Frank Fox and illustrated by Norman Lindsay among others, it reached almost everyone else. But Fox won his greatest audience with a popular serial published in the literary monthly *Lone Hand* entitled 'The Commonwealth Crisis', in which Japanese soldier-settlers secretly land in Australia's north (see Chapter 10).[20]

Being a Victorian liberal, Alfred Deakin naturally inclined towards Marshall Lyle's program of mass but not compulsory military activity. Deakin's first Commonwealth government had begun to encourage rifle club membership even before Tsushima, and 54 000 riflemen were shooting at targets by the middle of 1910. But how useful would a swarm of marksmen be on a modern battlefield swept by heavy artillery fire, with railways and motor lorries bringing up reinforcements and ammunition, with zeppelins and perhaps even aeroplanes overhead? They seemed obviously inadequate to professional staff officers such as John Hoad, Gordon Legge and Brudenell White who, after Hutton's departure in 1904 and a government decision not to retain a general officer commanding, were becoming trusted advisers to a rapid succession of sometimes bewildered Defence ministers.

In any case, pointed out Joseph Gordon, the senior professional military officer in New South Wales, Australians were becoming accustomed to compulsion.[21] Most welcomed compulsory education and arbitration of industrial disputes. They would soon accept compulsory voting. Why not compulsory militia service? Compulsion also appealed to older men and women prone to fretting over shiftless youth. 'It would be a blessing', the West Australian Labor politician George Pearce said, 'to haul them off by force for a few Saturdays, if necessary, from the football grounds, and give them a few manly exercises on the military field'.[22] By 1907 Alfred Deakin was won over. In December he announced a scheme for a 'national guard' in which every young man in his late teens or very early twenties would be obliged to serve for 16 days each year.[23] The scheme misjudged the public mood and offended military wisdom. 'Better a real army of 50 000', one Melbourne newspaper sniped, 'than a sham one of a million'.[24] 'I'd rather swallow your scheme for universal service', a Sydney colonel wrote to the NDL, 'which at least possesses the merit of manliness'.[25]

Deakin faltered again when heeding a popular call for an Australian navy, which was 'a course of self-respect as well as of expediency' according to the *Sydney Morning Herald*.[26] Sixteen months after Tsushima, he committed his government to building small warships to secure Australian ports and shipping. 'Of course, the British fleet will still be there to do the actual work of defence', a Tasmanian newspaper laughed, 'and the Commonwealth can have its toy'.[27] Whether the Royal Navy would let the baby splash happily in the bath seemed another matter entirely. Deakin and Creswell steeled themselves to push hard for an Australian navy at another Colonial Conference in London in 1907. They found themselves knocking at an open door. Britain's new Liberal government, which would lead the nation and the empire to war seven years later, was as determined as its predecessors to face down any serious challenge from a rival power. Seeking to contain a rising Germany, it had strengthened ties with France and Russia, and boosted military spending. But it also intended to navigate between military efficiency and political freedom. Britain's citizen-soldiers were made more efficient but not compelled to serve abroad as an army reserve.

The same program was now put to their colonial cousins. At the 1907 conference the dominions were encouraged to continue bringing military training, weaponry and equipment into line with British army practice and merge their staff officers into an empire-wide imperial general staff, but there was no more hustling for offers of troops. As to dominion navies, these were now welcome. Jacky Fisher, Britain's senior admiral, privately rubbished the dominions 'one and all' as prone to 'grab all they possibly can from us and give us nothing back'.[28] But he craved new squadrons based around fast, powerful battle cruisers that could secure imperial communications in war and give pause to other Great Powers while a fleet of capital ships took the fight to the Germans. That meant encouraging, not merely accepting, dominion demands for dominion fleets. 'It means *eventually* Canada, Australia, New Zealand, the Cape ... and India running a *complete* Navy!', he pointed out. 'We manage the job in Europe. They'll manage it against the Yankees, Japs, and Chinese.'[29]

'Eventually' seemed a long time to politicians and journalists worried about Japanese attack – one reason why Deakin ignored imperial protocols in 1908 and initiated an Australian stopover for the Great White Fleet of American warships cruising the globe to advertise Washington's power, especially to Tokyo. Deakin may also have hoped to provoke the Admiralty into sending out a powerful British fleet some day.[30] The American visit proved hugely popular, especially in Sydney where business halted for a week and on one day alone a million tram fares were collected from sightseers. Naval reviews were routine entertainment in the Edwardian age, their beaming searchlights and blazing myriad of electric lamps exhibiting power in every sense of the word.[31] But the visit of the Great White Fleet was more than mere spectacle. It exposed a nagging fear of Japan, and a nagging doubt about British ability to project serious force into the Pacific. During the visit the *Bulletin* carried a cartoon in which Uncle Sam asks The Little Boy at Manly – representing a young Australia – if his father's fleet, the famous Royal Navy, is as powerful as the one he now sees before him in Sydney Harbour. 'Dunno!', the boy responds a little resentfully. 'He never showed it to *me*!'[32]

Plenty of Australians felt the answer to such insecurity was to help the Royal Navy, not build their own ships or look to American ones. In the autumn of 1909 they disrupted official steps towards an Australian navy after news broke that Britain might lag behind Germany in constructing dreadnoughts – the latest (and fabulously expensive) type of battleship. The British government proposed laying down four immediately and another four if needed. 'We want eight, and we won't wait!' was the demand of concerned, sometimes hysterical British patriots. Similar concern rippled throughout the white empire. The New Zealand government offered to pay for one or even two battleships. A new Australian government – a Labor administration under Andrew Fisher – intended to continue Deakin's defence plans, and merely informed London that Australia would play its part by building its own fleet. Thousands of Australians demanded that more be done. The state governments of Victoria and New South Wales vowed to fund a dreadnought between them. The middle-class began to raise the money themselves, from a whopping £10 000 donated by retail store owner Samuel Hordern to a humbler two guineas offered by a self-identified 'Imperialist'.[33] Fisher's government fell partly because it tried to ignore this belligerently imperial mood. Returning to office for the last time, Deakin offered London a dreadnought 'or its equivalent' – a nice phrase allowing politicians to heed public demands or continue towards an Australian navy as circumstances dictated. 'It's not for us to say what form the gift should take', fudged Defence Minister Joseph Cook. 'That should be for our representative, who has gone to England, to discuss.'[34]

Thus it was that an obscure politician from Queensland called Foxton found himself alongside representatives from other dominions at a London naval conference called in the wake of the dreadnought scare. He found the Admiralty keener than ever for an Australian fleet, not the coastal flotilla of Creswell's parochial imagination but an ocean-going squadron based on a battle cruiser that in war could form a Pacific fleet alongside Canadian and British ships. However obscure, Foxton was crafty and stubborn. Backed by Deakin, he agreed to the squadron as outlined, but only if partly funded from British taxes, while the Australian government would reserve the right to pass the ships to Admiralty control in war.[35] An imperial general staff was fine too, provided it had no ability to direct dominion troops or commit dominion governments to any course of military action. There was no questioning at the conference of Australia's – and also New Zealand's – moves towards some kind of compulsory militia service. Indeed Lord Kitchener, the British army's most eminent serving soldier, had already agreed to advise the two dominions in setting up a new military system based on compulsion.

Thus Australia was free, indeed encouraged, to build its own army and navy. Not only was there imperial support for these forces, there would be almost enough money with the lifting in 1911 of a constitutional restraint on federal spending. There would also be firmer hands on the wheel. In 1910 a cool-headed but reformist Labor administration under Andrew Fisher took office. It was the first federal government to have the support of both Houses of Parliament and thus to survive a full three-year term. It created a government savings bank, introduced federal coins and banknotes, enacted maternity allowances and invalid pensions, and founded a permanent federal capital at Canberra. The new Defence minister was George Pearce. The former carpenter was no original thinker, but he had few military prejudices and owed few political favours. He valued expertise and was devoted to his job, taking up smoking to relax while remaining at his desk. Pearce and his Labor colleagues were scarcely the originators of Australia's army and navy, but they were more important than the amateurish Deakin and the faintly ridiculous Creswell in nurturing and shaping them.[36]

Deakin's vision of a national guard had faded even before Kitchener's expertise and Pearce's pragmatism dispelled it forever and conceived a more adult, more formidable mass militia. It would not absorb every man, or anything like it. No one older than 26 would be engaged unless he chose to be. The same was true of most men living outside the cities and large towns, whatever their age might be. Since no one could be made to buy and feed a large and hungry animal, the mounted rifles would remain a mostly voluntary arm. Then again, the new army would not be based on the reckless horsemen of the South African War but on urban infantrymen and gunners trained, armed and equipped just like British soldiers – or so it was hoped. It would be led by the best men risen from the ranks: the era of commissioning officers of social standing or political influence was said to be over. And it would be guided, perhaps even commanded, by professional officers nurtured in a democratic military college being built at 'Duntroon' in Canberra. This army would not be a distinctively Australian institution – New Zealand would raise an almost identical one at the same time – but it would be portrayed as no less redolent of Australia than the stars on its blue ensign, or the kangaroos on its postage stamps. And it would be a mighty force, at least eventually. It was envisaged that in 1920, by which time an eighth annual intake of 20-year-old men would have passed from part-time cadet training to part-time military service, an invader would need to defeat seven infantry divisions and seven cavalry brigades, and this after smashing the coastal fortresses and the Royal Australian Navy.

As Chapter 8 outlines, the first step towards building the army was taken when cadet service became compulsory for thousands of male teenagers in 1911. The intention was to prepare teenagers for militia service. The result verged on farce at first. Thousands failed to register or, if they registered, failed to attend. One lieutenant described the initial muster of his company, only half in jest, as 'an involuntary association of stone-throwing criminals'.[37] Plans for warlike training gave way to a repetitive reality of parade-ground drill. Pearce reduced the hours by a third, permitted cancellations in bad weather, and allowed leave if attendance would cause a youth or his family hardship.[38] It was an unpromising, even troubling rehearsal for the new military system.

In the winter of 1912, as the old bespoke militia marked its demise with parades and the publication of regimental histories, 17 000 cadets born in 1894 were allotted to 32 infantry battalions, 16 field artillery batteries, and other units. Alongside them were thousands of 'VEs' (voluntarily enlisted men) from the old force who had stayed on to fill the ranks of the light horse and garrison artillery – or, if in the infantry, to ride an expected wave of promotions above the heads of the barely tutored mass of 'trainees'. The new militia slogged its way through the equivalent of 16 or more days of basic drill over the subsequent year. Training in the second year, after the absorption of an almost equally unprepared 1895 intake from the cadets, remained simple. Employers were obliged to release trainees for drill, but not VEs – who added this discrimination to resentments they were already feeling at having to put in as many hours as the youths they looked down upon, at being denied rapid promotion after all, and at being forbidden the old comforts of tobacco and alcohol while in camp. At least VEs kept their old pay levels for a time, and their old uniforms. Trainees received a mere half the amount, and their chests were graced with nothing more glamorous or comfortable than a coarse mud-coloured shirt.[39] Young men were supposed not to mind. They were to 'Do it for Australia!', as a marching song crafted by George Taylor of the intelligence corps commanded them.[40]

Doing it for a wise commanding officer was a less abstract incentive, and a more fruitful one. Changing the motivation of trainees from '"I must come" to "I want to come"', and making it seem 'better form to be a good "footslogger" than even a champion footballer', were the aims of Major Richard Crouch as he led the 56th Battalion centred on the working-class Melbourne suburb of Richmond.[41] He assembled his men in the Town Hall to take their oath of allegiance before parents and dignitaries. He collated a patriotic history of military activity in the suburb, applied for a bogus but inspiring battle honour to be sewn onto the battalion's flag, and secured permission to give his unit the romantic title of the Yarra Borderers. He nudged the local brass band to double as regimental musicians, and somehow persuaded the state's popular chief justice to become honorary colonel. These measures were repaid with good attendance, even at a voluntary night march ending in a lecture on why Napoleon lost Waterloo. 'It became a matter of pride, even in such a radical district as we occupied', Crouch later claimed, 'for our men to turn up for the honour of the corps'.[42] Not all men, though. Harry Flintoff, another carpenter but also secretary of the Richmond branch of the Australian Freedom League, resolutely refused to wear uniform. During his third sentence of enforced drill at the Queenscliff forts he agreed to perform non-combat duty in the militia, but soon fled to the Victorian hinterland.[43]

The Freedom League had formed in 1911 to oppose compulsory militia service and, less openly, to aid evaders and resisters. But absence from duty was rarely principled. High attendance at punitive 'supplementary' drills pointed to mostly mundane reasons for missing compulsory sessions: misunderstandings or temporary slackness, family dramas, unco-operative employers. Towards the end of 1912 the Melbourne *Argus* reported that only 384 militiamen, 'a mere nothing in view of the numbers involved', refused to attend any drill at all.[44] Australians, George Pearce later boasted, 'were accepting the compulsory element of universal training in exactly the same spirit in which they accepted compulsory education'.[45] This spirit was fanned by elders such as Walter Murdoch, whose popular school text *The Australian Citizen* lectured readers on their duty to Australia and the empire, on obedience to the will of the state, on the need for a navy, on the vital importance of service in the cadets and militia.[46]

Pearce was hardly alone in thinking drill almost as useful socially as it was militarily. Widespread approval for putting men and boys into uniform and under discipline was indicated by the emergence of the Boy Scouts and the popularity of the Salvation Army. No major political party opposed a compulsory militia. George Kirkpatrick, an acolyte of Kitchener's given a general's rank to guide the new army during its early years, found the Labor troika of Fisher, Pearce and Hughes enthusiastic over Kitchener's plan 'and only criticised it for not going far enough'.[47] Some trade union leaders worried that militiamen might be used to break strikes, obliging Pearce to pronounce that an entire people in uniform could never be made to oppress itself.[48] An anti-military mood was spreading among a new generation of union leaders and Labor politicians, but Chris Watson, Fisher's predecessor as Labor prime minister, assured Gerald Campbell of the NDL that the 'vaporings of a few "one-eyed" people at Broken Hill and Newcastle does not count for much'.[49] Until 1916 he was right.

There was an unintended irony in Pearce's boast that compulsory soldiering was proving as acceptable as compulsory schooling. Some teenagers vented a contempt for military instructors hitherto reserved for their more hapless teachers. Some parents wanted to shield their sons from rough fellows and harsh tutors on the drill square as well as in the school yard. These impulses mingled to form the real obstacle to the new military system. It became clear one warm Saturday in a camp at Liverpool late in 1913, after the 14th Battalion's officers left for dinner in mess dress having forbidden their men from visiting town and posting a picket on a bridge to enforce their confinement. Several hundred men resolved to push past it, fortunately leaving their rifles behind. They threw stones at soldiers and police reinforcing the picket, and pulled a passing woman from her bicycle. Two days later, when sent on a long march, some men griped that they were being punished. The battalion finished camp by making a fiasco of boarding trains to go home. The prime minister tried to shrug off the incident,[50] but a Labor senator condemned the picket as militaristic. Parents protested that their sons were being treated harshly, and some newspapers supported them. No trainee in the 14th Battalion was punished, but the careers of two senior officers were in question for a time.[51] No one seemed to worry about the incident's likely effect on military training and discipline.

'The trouble', an older man protested to Pearce back when cadet service first became compulsory, was that 'you've created a big army of boys who haven't any responsibility, and you've left *me* out'.[52] Plenty of men felt the same. A light horse colonel wanted to raise a mounted force from men too old to be called up into the militia, or who lived outside suburbs and towns. Veterans from South Africa offered to form a military reserve in return for free grants of land. A veteran of the 1879 Zulu war proposed a reserve of former citizen soldiers and British army veterans living in Australia. Local members of the Legion of Frontiersmen, an empire-wide paramilitary force of romantic but harmless reactionaries, lobbied to be accepted as military guides. Scottish and Irish communities, affronted by the disbanding of kilted or harp-badged national corps, demanded permission to re-raise them.[53] All such offers and demands were scorned by the government and its military advisers, none more harshly than the last. We want men to fight for their new country, Pearce made clear in Parliament, not their old one.[54] But it was obvious that the army would need reinforcement, and probably stiffening, if war broke out before 1920. The rifle clubs, having relinquished their dream of evolving into a guerilla army, were given the job, and their fittest members assigned to expand the ranks of local militia units in war. A few riflemen in isolated areas were paid to drill to prepare them to defend the Thursday Island coal depot, and where the telegraph cable came ashore at Darwin to link Australia to the world.[55]

In July 1914 the third annual intake of trainees lifted the army's strength to 62 000 men. Two-thirds of the projected number of infantry battalions were now formed, half of the field artillery batteries, three quarters of the light horse regiments, and nearly all the engineer companies. Fourteen infantry and six cavalry brigades were more or less complete, and the way was clear to begin forming infantry divisions. Looking further ahead, a handful of aircraft and a new flying school constituted the tiny nucleus of a future air force.[56] From June 1913 a new Liberal government under Joseph Cook, with Edward Millen as Defence Minister, planned to remove some of the grievances against the military system by reviving the national corps and dressing militiamen in tailored tunics. Some communities, newspapers and businesses were coming to support the new army as they had long supported the old voluntary forces, praising participation or donating prizes for military competitions. The police reported (a little optimistically) that compulsory drill was having the desired social effect, encouraging respect for authority and refusal to join in larrikin behaviour.[57] But was it building an effective defence? Ian Hamilton, the British army's inspector of overseas forces, enthused about the cadets when he visited Australia early in 1914. He was less admiring of the militia. Part of the new army was ready to meet an invasion, he reported, but only if it outnumbered any attackers by two to one.[58]

The new navy seemed more impressive. Somehow, against all expectations, it was less expensive too.[59] In February 1910 the wife of the British prime minister launched the destroyer *Parramatta*, in her words the 'First born of the Commonwealth

Navy'.⁶⁰ Within 14 months two more destroyers were at sea and the keel laid down for a battle cruiser to be called *Australia*. While the militia was never formally called an army, warships and crews were grandly styled the Royal Australian Navy in October 1911, the same month *Australia* was launched from a Scottish shipyard. Here was a new epoch in the empire's history, the shipyard's director said after the great grey hull settled in the water, one that cemented 'two bed-rock principles of ... Imperial policy ... that we should have an Imperial fleet unsurpassed, unequalled, unconquerable', and that 'we must have absolute autonomy for every component part of our Empire'.⁶¹

The navy began recruiting in 1912 while the new militia was forming. Of the most promising trainees born in 1894, 1500 went not into khaki shirts but into blue bell bottoms, and instead of attending an annual camp they took to sea for 17 days on a gunboat. Thousands more men stayed on from the old naval militia as nautical VEs. A ship had even greater need than a battalion for skilled, disciplined and above all acculturated warriors, so the navy consigned its part-timers to the status of reservists and recruited professional sailors for terms of five or seven years. A few hundred teenagers began a thorough immersion in naval culture by living on the training ship *Tingira* moored in Sydney Harbour. Hundreds of older men, some with a useful trade, went to a training depot at Williamstown then to sea on board a cruiser on loan from the Royal Navy, where they learnt from its British crew. In 1913 two dozen officer cadets entered the naval equivalent of Duntroon, temporarily housed at Geelong – despite money from the dreadnought donors to locate it in Sydney. 'Why, they have a lord's life in the Royal Australian Navy', a recruiter spruiked on a tour of rural Victoria, 'fresh meat, soft bread, and other luxuries ... And the pay! Why if they only knew all about it, the boys in the country towns would rush to join.'⁶²

Even if they did, the navy would have lacked sufficient skilled and experienced sailors for many years, and around 900 had to be borrowed or poached from Britain. Then again, the distinction between a British and Australian sailor was not always clear. Transfer from one service to another was common, and Australian sailors were being sent to England to learn how to crew warships before helping to deliver them from British shipyards to Australian ports. Yet there were doubts about the competence of Australians. Were they sufficiently trained and disciplined? The doubts were brushed aside, not with reforms but with rhetoric. 'We have heard this sort of thing said about us before, in South Africa, for instance', sniffed the journalist Frederic Cutlack, but 'we know what the whole world said in praise of the colonial soldiers'.[63]

In July 1913, the Royal Navy handed over its dockyards and depots in Sydney and prepared to surrender the station. Three months later a new navy symbolically took possession as *Australia*, three cruisers and three destroyers steamed into port: 'a splendid embryo fleet', in the words of a real estate advertisement piggybacking on the event.[64] For Pearce it was 'a concrete illustration of the National Awakening',[65] and for William Morris Hughes evidence that Australia had 'assumed the toga of nationhood'.[66] A strangely silent crowd watched the great ships navigate between decorated yachts to a chorus of booming guns and shrieking whistles. There was more silence three days later as the sailors paraded through the city. 'Perhaps a deep feeling of inexpressive emotion pervaded the crowd', a regional newspaper pondered, but it seemed a disturbing contrast to the welcomes screamed to 'a prominent American boxer when he arrived … a few years ago to box a colored man for the world's championship'.[67] The comparison was an apt one. After all, the new fleet was to be the white race's champion in the South Pacific. Joseph Cook used its arrival to signal to the 'less advanced nations' to Australia's north that a new navy had inherited 'the unconquerable and indomitable spirit of our forefathers'.[68]

At 16 ships in 1914, one of them a battle cruiser, the Royal Australian Navy had a more formidable fleet than Australia would put to sea in 1939, and perhaps has put to sea since. It was nonetheless puny in comparison with the Japanese navy. Worse, the Canadian and British warships that were to complete a Pacific fleet never materialised. At the 1911 Imperial Conference in London, Herbert Asquith, Britain's Liberal prime minister, assured dominion leaders that the Japanese alliance gave them 'a large measure of security'. This left the way open for the Admiralty to lecture everyone on how the empire's navy ought to concentrate to meet Germany's.[69]

It should have come as no surprise when, three years later, Winston Churchill – the young and pugnacious English patriot at the head of the Admiralty – reacted to a massive increase in German ship construction by demanding that all the empire's great ships, including *Australia*, be called home to face their German rivals. The governments of New Zealand and Canada agreed with him. The Pacific fleet could wait, Churchill announced in March 1914, Japan was a British ally, and even if not was unlikely to move against Australia and so risk war with a global empire and the world's greatest navy.[70] Australians were anything but reassured by such arguments. 'To offer us Japanese protection', a Melbourne magazine spluttered, 'is very like telling Mary's little lamb: "Have no fear, small and tender sheep, you are excellently provided for. We have set the wolf to watch over you!"'[71] Such criticism proved short-lived. The outbreak of war with Germany five months later brought the wolf, the sheep and their erratic shepherd together again.

Raising an army and building a navy vastly increased Australian hunger for arms, ammunition and ships. Feeding that hunger might also put food on the table for thousands of workers in new industries – or so federal and state Labor governments planned. Making guns, shells and capital ships was, for the moment, beyond local industry. But government-owned factories in Lithgow and Melbourne began to manufacture and stockpile rifles, explosives, saddlery and uniforms, while Sydney's Cockatoo Island dockyard began to construct destroyers and light cruisers. Three keels were laid on a single hot and dusty day in January 1913, said to be a great moment for Australia industrially as well as militarily. 'We have 1500 men employed here', announced Labor politician and state Minister of Public Works Arthur Griffith, 'and in four months time we will have 3000'.[72] It was certainly a great moment for the trade unions, which had a large say in working conditions on this and other defence sites, and for the Labor Party, which could point to jobs it was creating and industries it was building. But was it value for money? Private companies complained that they could manufacture better items more cheaply. British shipyards and munitions factories could certainly do so, and craft a better product as well. Joseph Cook would soon be objecting that the Labor Party seemed more concerned with 'the cultivation of social experiments' than with 'the fate of the Empire'.[73]

The fate of the empire had been discussed at the 1911 Imperial Conference in London. Edward Grey, Britain's foreign minister, told dominion leaders that Germany was bent on a Napoleonic strategy of forcing rival empires one by one into its orbit. Whatever the truth of the observation, that it was made by the foreign minister was a clear signal that the first great war for nearly a full century was probable, even imminent. Still, the Liberals and Laborites who predominated among the politicians at the conference agreed that there could be no infringement of dominion autonomy, no commitment of dominion governments to a war in advance, no assigning dominion troops to an expeditionary force

– leaving Henry Wilson, the British army's senior draftsman of plans for war, to wish the empire could be delivered up to some 'great man such as Pitt, Bismark, etc'.[74]

Still, the prospect of war with Germany sparked some military planning in Australia, encouraged by the possibility of losing *Australia* to northern seas. Gordon Legge wrote from London that the Japanese navy could send three army divisions towards Australia within a month if they chose.[75] Joseph Gordon, now the chief of Australia's section of the imperial general staff, worried that Japan might indeed seize Australia's undefended, barely occupied north.[76] Then there was the prospect of war with Germany. Picking off the scattered, vulnerable German territories in the Pacific was an obvious, potentially profitable task. But there was no easy benefit accruing from the most serious conundrum of all: how to quickly reinforce a British army embarking on a desperate war with Germany while obeying the unbending stricture not to commit Australia to a foreign war, nor commit Australian men to fighting in it. When a plan for raising an expeditionary force crossed Pearce's ministerial desk, he penned in the clumsy but uncompromising proviso 'as may from time to time be deemed necessary and is voluntarily agreeable so to serve'.[77] Pearce insisted such plans be secret, not to deceive the Australian people[78] but simply because war plans ought to be secret. He may also have wanted to keep in the dark various political colleagues to his left, and to avoid raising expectations in London that Australian troops were virtually on the way.[79]

George Kirkpatrick proceeded speculatively in correspondence with Henry Wilson about an expeditionary force. The two British officers probably reached little more than an understanding that Egypt would be the force's likely initial destination.[80] Talks between Gordon and his New Zealand counterpart established that it might comprise an infantry division and cavalry brigade recruited on both sides of the Tasman. Brudenell White sketched out how to raise the force while waiting vainly for Millen, the new Defence Minister, to concede what his predecessor Pearce would not and allot peacetime units to it, perhaps the national corps.[81] But the national corps remained defunct, the expeditionary force barely existed on paper let alone in reality, and Australia went to war in August 1914 not in obedience to a clear plan but in willing surrender to a powerful popular impulse to resist Germany and defend England.[82] With Japan a dutiful if not exactly enthusiastic wartime ally, Andrew Fisher was free to casually commit the Labor Party and, after returning to government in September, the Australian people, to defending the Mother country 'to the last man and shilling'. The song that caught the popular mood at war's outbreak was 'Australia Will Be There'. Men and women of more elevated tastes would soon swoon over the loftier verses of 'The Bugles of England'. Thousands of men crowded to enlist for the war. Thousands of women formed Red Cross branches. The 40 employees of the Union Shirt Factory in Perth asked to work for an extra day, unpaid, to make shirts for the troops.[83]

However hastily improvised, the Australian Imperial Force had a leaven of veteran sergeants, a cadre of officers accustomed to leading and quartering troops, a rank-and-file almost accustomed to army life and military discipline, and arms and equipment more or less up to scratch. Pre-war planning and the creation of a peacetime army gave Australia's expeditionary force at the start of World War I the same advantages the Australian Commonwealth Horse had had more than two years into the South African War. Starting where its predecessor had left off, the Australian Imperial Force would ultimately become a fine fighting force. It found a real trial by combat that Australians in the previous conflict had not, and the men who fought in their thousands and died in their hundreds at Anzac Cove and in the war's later battles 'got you a tradition', as South Australia's governor would later instruct his citizens.[84] But Australia's first contributions to the war were made before Gallipoli, by the army and navy that had absorbed so much community effort over the past three years — not to mention between a quarter and a third of federal government spending.[85]

The navy steamed north in August 1914 to attack Germany's East Asia squadron, failed to find it — partly because it would not risk a pounding from *Australia*'s powerful guns — and then escorted tiny Australian-New Zealand expeditionary forces leaving Sydney and Wellington to snatch undefended German colonies in New Guinea and Samoa (Chapter 12). Meanwhile thousands of militiamen and rifle club reservists rushed to the metaphorical ramparts, garrisoning ports and cities and securing coaling stations and bridges, wireless stations and undersea telegraph cable landing places. Vigilant gunners fired a warning shot at a German steamer to prevent it leaving Melbourne, proudly claiming to have fired the first British shot in the war. The Kennedy Regiment, a militia battalion recruited across northern Queensland, jostled to join the expeditionary force bound for German New Guinea but was kept back by its inadequate equipment and training, and by the refusal of a ship's crew to leave Australian waters. It was the militia's only brush with war — discounting for the moment the contribution of 20 plain-clothes members of the 82nd Battalion in shooting dead a Broken Hill butcher and ice-cream vendor who had heeded a Turkish *fatwa* to wage holy war on Islam's British enemies.[86] A more dramatic culmination to the decade of effort to secure Australia came in November 1914, with the destruction of the German raider *Emden* by the cruiser *Sydney*. 'They now saw how absurd was the opposition to the creation of the Australian navy', scoffed a performer at a local celebration of the victory, for here was proof that a new branch 'of the old British "sea-lions"' had emerged.[87] Soon Australians would be talking about proof of Australian valour, not British, said to have been established on Gallipoli by men wearing khaki and slouch hats.

Australians went to the aid of Britain and the empire in 1914 as almost everyone had expected. If the aid came in numbers beyond pre-war imagining, it was inefficient nonetheless. The transformation of Australian martial institutions and activity since 1902 had been uncertainly, perhaps unwisely handled. Australia began building its own fleet when aiding the Royal Navy would have been simpler, cheaper and more effective. It raised a mass militia confined to local soil, instead of carefully training a smaller number of troops to take their place within an overseas British army when war came. It built a government munitions industry when private manufacturers and shipyards in Britain were among the best in the world. French colonists living in Algeria before the war, or the sometimes reluctant Bavarian subjects of the German empire, made no such obstacle to the military efficiency of their imperial armed forces before 1914. The Edwardian transformation of Australia's military efforts reflected an ancient British commitment to the right of ordinary men and women to remain almost indifferent to their sovereign's projects, and a new dominion commitment to something like independence within the empire. To elevate custom and rights above efficiency was magnificent in a way, but it was scarcely war.

Then again, Australians were also playing a long game when founding an army, a navy and a munitions industry. They were building national institutions from an almost non-existent base. They were looking ahead in another sense too, to the moment in 1941 when Japan would indeed turn south. It is often said that nations always prepare for the last war. Before 1914, Australia prepared partly for the right war and partly for the wrong one. At least the mistake was one of looking forward rather than back.

Further reading

J Barrett, *Falling In: Australians and 'Boy Conscription' 1911–1915*, Hale & Iremonger, Sydney, 1979

CEW Bean, *With the Flagship in the South*, Werner Laurie, London, 1909

CDC Clark, *No Australian Need Apply: The Troubled Career of Lieutenant General Gordon Legge*, Allen & Unwin, Sydney, 1988

J Connor, *Anzac and Empire: George Foster Pearce and the Foundations of Australian Defence*, CUP, Melbourne, 2011

RA Crouch, 'First steps in battalion training', *Commonwealth Military Journal* (Melbourne), July 1913, pp 395–401

P Dennis & J Grey (eds) *1911: Preliminary Moves*, Big Sky, Sydney, 2011

J Eddy and D Schreuder (eds), *The Rise of Colonial Nationalism*, Allen & Unwin, Sydney, 1988

'C Kirmess' (F Fox), *The Australian Crisis*, Robertson, Melbourne, 1909

N Lambert, 'Economy or empire? The Fleet Unit concept and the quest for collective security in the Pacific 1909–1914', in K Neilson and G Kennedy (eds), *Far Flung Lines: Studies in Imperial Defence in Honour of Donald Mackenzie Schurman*, Frank Cass, London, 1997, pp 44–83

N Meaney, *The Search for Security in the Pacific 1901–1914*, Sydney University Press, Sydney, 1976

D Stevens (ed), *The Navy and the Nation: The Influence of the Navy on Modern Australia*, Allen & Unwin, Sydney, 2005

C Stockings, *The Making and Breaking of the Post-Federation Army 1901–1909*, Land Warfare Studies Centre, Canberra, 2007

C Wilcox, *For Hearths and Homes: Citizen Soldiering in Australia 1854–1945*, Allen & Unwin, Sydney, 1998

12

The capture of German New Guinea

JOHN CONNOR

Six Australians were killed on 11 September 1914 in the fight to capture the German colony of New Guinea. They were the first Australians to die in World War I and the nation mourned their loss. As the war continued, and more than 60 000 Australians were killed at Gallipoli, Palestine and on the Western Front, the memory of these first six men was overwhelmed. These six, and the campaign they and their comrades fought, were forgotten. The New Guinea expedition was a minor skirmish when seen in the context of whole war, but it remains significant. The Australian Naval and Military Expeditionary Force successfully removed a real threat to Australia and its economy by capturing the German radio station at Bitapaka and the excellent harbour at Rabaul, preventing their use by the warships of the German East Asiatic Squadron. The expedition contributed to the British government's strategy to capture all Germany colonies, but it also achieved a long-held Australian 'sub-imperial' ambition to take New Guinea. The campaign was not a universally glorious one. Australian troops in New Guinea were often ill-disciplined and inexperienced. Officers and men committed crimes during the occupation, and the inept Australian commander, Colonel William Holmes, created an international uproar when he ordered the public flogging of four civilians in Rabaul. But these incidents reflected the general lack of training and proficiency of Australian soldiers at the beginning of World War I. Similar behaviour was found among the members of the Australian Imperial Force in Egypt and Gallipoli.

By 1914 Australians had developed long-standing and extensive interests in the Pacific. As soon as the British established their colony of New South Wales in 1788, Sydney became an important trading port for a succession of lucrative and often exotic products gathered in the waters and islands of the South Pacific and exported to the rest of the world. These included whaling from the 1790s to the 1830s for whale oil used in lamps, sandalwood from the 1830s to the 1860s shipped to China as an aromatic incense, and copra (dried coconut) grown on island plantations from the 1870s onwards and used for coconut oil used in candles and soap.[1] Before World War I, at least half a million men,[2] mostly from Solomon Islands and New Hebrides (now Vanuatu), worked on indentured contract in plantations on Pacific islands and Australia.[3] Australians had a significant role in recruiting and transporting this workforce. Some islanders were forced into labour and had to endure harsh conditions, but most willingly agreed to their contracts.[4] Australians also ventured into the Pacific as missionaries and played a major part in the islanders' conversion to Christianity.[5]

The period before 1914 was the age of the great European colonial empires, so it is not surprising that Australians, while part of the British Empire and lacking the power to claim territory in their own right, held their own 'sub-imperial' ambitions in the Pacific. This sub-imperialism manifested itself in two ways. The first was opposition to other European powers, particularly France and Germany, establishing colonies in the region. The second was persistent lobbying to convince the British government to annex particular islands. New Zealand and South Africa, the two other self-governing British dominions in the southern hemisphere, held similar sub-imperial desires on their neighbouring territories in the South Pacific and southern Africa.[6]

Australian colonists opposed the French takeover of Tahiti in 1844 and of New Caledonia in 1853. When Australians established cotton and sugar plantations in Fiji in the 1860s and 1870s, they pressured London to annex these islands, and this played a part in the British government's decision to make Fiji a colony in 1874.[7] Around this time, some Australians began to see potential economic opportunities in the unclaimed eastern half of the island of New Guinea (the western half had been claimed by the Dutch in 1828). In 1874, the British Colonial Secretary, Lord Carnarvon, asked the Australian colonial premiers if they would be willing to match their enthusiasm for annexing eastern New Guinea with financial contributions to fund the proposed colony's administration. No premier was willing to put up any money, so Carnarvon did not go ahead with the proposal. He did however approve making the Torres Strait Islands – which lie between Australia and New Guinea – part of Queensland.[8]

German trading companies first entered the Pacific in the 1850s, and by the 1870s controlled most of the trade in Samoa, Tonga and the islands of Micronesia north of the Equator. They also established trading stations on the islands of the Bismarck Archipelago, near eastern New Guinea.[9] In 1883, the Queensland premier, Thomas McIlwraith, feared this commercial presence might lead the German government to claim all of eastern New Guinea. In order to pre-empt such a move, and force the British government to annex the territory, McIlwraith ordered the nearest Queensland government official, the Thursday Island police magistrate, Henry Chester, to sail to Port Moresby, where he claimed all of eastern New Guinea for Queen Victoria.

McIlwraith's sub-imperial action did not have the result he desired: the British government immediately disavowed his claim and negotiated a compromise with the German government. In November 1884, Britain and Germany partitioned eastern New Guinea. A German protectorate was established in the Bismarck Archipelago and the adjacent north-east portion of mainland New Guinea, which became known as Kaiser Wilhelmsland. A British protectorate was established in the south-east of the island. On 1 September 1906, British New Guinea was renamed Papua and transferred to Australian government administrative control.[10]

German New Guinea became part of the colonial empire that Berlin established between 1884 and 1889. Germany was the last of the European powers to gain overseas possessions and the German colonial empire was much smaller than its British or French counterparts. It consisted of colonies in west, east and southern Africa, the northern China enclave of Kiautchou – centred on the city of Tsingtao (now Qingdao), home port to the German Navy's East Asiatic Squadron – three island groups in the North Pacific, and German New Guinea, Nauru and Samoa in the South Pacific.[11]

Rabaul was the capital of both German New Guinea, known as the 'Old Protectorate', and the more recently acquired North Pacific islands and Nauru, known as the 'Island Territory'. Located at the northern tip of the island of Neu Pommern (now New Britain), Rabaul was overshadowed by mountains and volcanoes and situated on the outstanding harbour of Simpsonshafen. In January 1914, the town had a population of 3271 people, consisting – according to the colonial administration's racial classifications – of 266 whites, 452 Chinese, 79 Malays (mostly from Ambon in the Netherlands East Indies), 27 Micronesians from the North Pacific and 2447 Melanesians from Neu Pommern and other islands. The town was divided on racial lines into three districts. White

Rabaul had tropical bungalows, shady tree-lined avenues and squares, government offices, banks and the offices, wharves and warehouses of trading and shipping companies. Nearby Chinatown consisted of scruffy huts and small businesses ranging from tailors and restaurants to gambling dens and brothels. The Native Compound was on the edge of town and housed the Islander workers on whose labour the colony relied for its existence.[12]

The population of the colony outside Rabaul could not be calculated as accurately. There were 1130 Whites in the 'Old Protectorate' and 2019 Chinese spread across both the 'Old Protectorate' and the 'Island Territory'. German officials estimated the indigenous population of Neu Pommern at 85 000, with perhaps 115 000 people on the other islands of the Bismarck Archipelago. Apart from a few coastal villages, the German portion of the island of New Guinea, Kaiser Wilhelmsland, was entirely unknown to the colonial administration, who admitted in 1914 that it was 'quite impossible to give even an approximate estimate of the population'.[13]

German New Guinea had an area of about 29 million hectares, but in 1913 only 24 190 hectares was under commercial cultivation. Almost all of this land was devoted to coconut plantations, worked by about 17 500 Melanesian labourers and producing 14.5 million kilograms of copra with an export value of 6.1 million Marks. The next most valuable export in 1913 was Bird of Paradise feathers for decorating ladies' hats: the plumage of 16 691 birds earning over 1 million Marks. Total exports from German New Guinea in 1913 totalled 8.5 million Marks, but the colony – like all Germany's possessions except Togo in west Africa – did not pay its way, and required an annual subsidy from Berlin of 1.4 million Marks.[14]

The neighbouring Australian-administered territory of Papua had roughly the same number of white inhabitants,[15] but it provided a stark contrast to German New Guinea. The Australian government did colonialism on the cheap. Its subsidy to Papua in 1915 was only about a third of the amount provided to the German colony. It concentrated on short-term profits rather than long-term development. Papua's main industry was goldmining, and there was little interest in expanding plantation agriculture. Copra exports in 1913 were only one fifteenth of those of German New Guinea. Jens Lyng, a member of the Australian force that captured German New Guinea, acknowledged that there was 'much to admire in what German enterprise has achieved ... and in comparing Papua with German New Guinea we must admit that in some respects the latter is ahead'.[16]

Despite the friction between their rival governments, Australians played a prominent role in German New Guinea as missionaries and plantation owners. Methodist church minister George Brown established the first Christian mission in the region in 1875, ten years before the Germans established their colony. In 1914, the chairman of the Methodist mission in German New Guinea was the Victorian-born Reverend William Henry Cox, who shall appear again later in this story.[17] Australian individuals and companies, including Choiseul Plantations Limited, a subsidiary of the great trading firm Burns Philp, were the main investors developing coconut plantations in Bougainville in the years prior to the war. As the German New Guinea annual report for 1913–14 admitted, Australian business preferred to invest in the colony because labour and other regulations 'favour[ed] the employer' more than in the neighbouring British Solomon Islands or Papua. The German authorities allowed companies to purchase land freehold, unlike the British colonies where only leasehold was available. Labour contracts were for longer periods and wages were 60 per cent lower in German New Guinea than they were in Papua and Solomon Islands. Plantation owners in

New Guinea, unlike their counterparts in the neighbouring British colonies, were even permitted – on the payment of a small annual fee to the German administration – to discipline their workers by hitting them with a cane.[18] The Australian presence even influenced the languages spoken in New Guinea. German missionaries despaired at the 'growing spread of pidgin English' among the indigenous population and the fact that 'German was of no practical use to a black man anywhere in the colony'.[19]

Nevertheless, German New Guinea posed a serious military threat to Australia in the event of war between the British and the German empires. German naval planning before 1914 envisaged that, in such a conflict, the East Asiatic Squadron – based at Tsingtao in China and consisting of the armoured cruisers *Scharnhorst* and *Gneisenau* and the light cruisers *Emden*, *Leipzig* and *Nürnberg* – would probably use Rabaul as a forward operating base to sink merchant ships in Australian waters and 'have a paralysing effect on Australian exports to England'.[20] If such a naval campaign were successful, it would destroy the export-reliant Australian economy and deprive Britain of much-needed commodities such as wool and wheat.

The new technology of radio would enable German warships to communicate with each other and with the German naval command and make their attacks more effective. There were five functioning German radio stations in the Pacific in August 1914: Yap and Angaur in the Karolinen (now Caroline) Islands, Nauru, Apia in Samoa, and Bitapaka, near Rabaul in German New Guinea.[21] The German government may even have encouraged the German radio company Telefunken to construct radio stations at their own cost in Australia in 1910, in Melbourne and on King Island. If Telefunken, rather than its British rival Marconi, had gained permission to develop the Australian radio network, the German navy would have been able to intercept

Australian radio communications in time of war. The positioning of the two Telefunken stations in Bass Strait was significant, as this was a busy shipping route and a proposed wartime area of operations for the East Asiatic Squadron.[22]

As the probability of war between Britain and Germany increased in the years leading up to 1914 the Australian government considered the need to capture German New Guinea. The first plan, drawn up in October 1911, proposed creating an expeditionary force to capture Rabaul consisting of men who had military experience from having served in the South African War.[23] In November 1912, the chiefs of the Australian and New Zealand armies agreed that, on the outbreak of any hostilities, Australia would capture New Guinea and New Zealand would capture Samoa.[24]

When the war began in August 1914, however, the German East Asiatic Squadron did not implement its pre-war plans to attack Australian shipping. Eight months previously, in October 1913, the flagship of the new Royal Australian Navy (RAN), the battlecruiser HMAS *Australia*, had arrived in Sydney with its supporting cruisers and destroyers, and this had dramatically changed the balance of naval power in the South Pacific. The *Australia* was newer, faster and had larger guns than the East Asiatic Squadron's *Scharnhorst* and *Gneisenau*.[25] The squadron commander, Vice Admiral Maximilian Graf von Spee, realised that *Australia* 'by itself, is an adversary so much stronger than our squadron that one would be bound to avoid it'.[26] In order to evade *Australia* – and after Tokyo declared war on Berlin on 23 August, similar modern Japanese battlecruisers – von Spee ordered his ships to sail eastwards across the Pacific away from Australian and Japanese waters.

When Britain declared war on Germany on 4 August (10:00 am on 5 August, Eastern Australian Time), the RAN was already mobilised and the cruiser *Sydney* and the destroyers *Warrego*, *Yarra* and *Parramatta* were positioned off northern Queensland. The Naval Board in Melbourne had been tracking radio signals from von Spee's flagship *Scharnhorst* since 1 August and believed the German squadron was near Rabaul (it was in fact north of the Equator). Acting on this supposition, the RAN Fleet Commander, Rear Admiral George Patey, arrived off Rabaul in HMAS *Australia* on the evening of 11 August and ordered *Sydney* and the three destroyers – which had been painted black at Thursday Island in readiness for a night-time raid – to enter Simpsonhafen and attack the German warships if they were anchored there. The ships were not there, so the next morning the Australian destroyers sailed back into Simpsonhafen in an unsuccessful attempt to identify the location of the German radio station. A landing party went ashore and smashed the telegraph and telephone equipment at the Rabaul post office.[27]

Patey then intended to sail HMAS *Australia* eastwards to Nauru in pursuit of the German squadron. Before he could do this, however, he was ordered to escort the ships carrying the New Zealand and Australian expeditions to capture Samoa and New Guinea. Von Spee's ships continued towards South America, where they fought and sank some obsolete British warships in the Battle of Coronel on 1 November, and then sailed into the South Atlantic where they were met and defeated on 8 December 1914 by modern British warships in the Battle of the Falkland Islands.[28]

On being informed of the British declaration of war on 5 August, the Australian and New Zealand governments immediately implemented their plans to create expeditionary forces to fight with the British army against the Germans in Europe. The following day, the British government asked the two dominions to raise separate forces to take New Guinea and Samoa.[29] The

New Zealand force, consisting of 1374 personnel including six nurses, departed Wellington on 15 August. Escorted by HMAS *Australia* and other warships, it landed at Apia on 29 August and occupied the German colony without any armed resistance.[30]

The creation of the Australian Naval and Military Force (ANMEF) was delayed three days because Colonel Gordon Legge, the new Chief of the General Staff, was on a passenger ship returning to Australia from a secondment with the War Office in London. Legge disembarked at Adelaide on 8 August, caught the overnight train to Melbourne and met the Defence Minister, Senator Edward Millen, the following day. Following this meeting, Millen announced the creation of 'a small mixed naval and military force for service with or without Australia' separate to the Australian Imperial Force (AIF).[31]

The ANMEF consisted of about 1524 soldiers and sailors. To expedite recruiting, training and deployment, the force's military component of an infantry battalion was raised entirely in New South Wales. The naval component consisted of 471 naval reservists, of whom one third were from New South Wales, with the remainder from Queensland, South Australia, Tasmania and Victoria. Colonel William Holmes, the senior militia officer in New South Wales, accepted command of the ANMEF. A veteran of the South African War, Holmes was secretary of the Sydney Metropolitan Board of Water Supply and Sewerage. Commander JAH Beresford commanded the naval contingent.[32]

The ANMEF infantry battalion was similar to the AIF battalions that were being created at the same time. Soldiers in both forces were paid 6 shillings a day.[33] The recruits had similar backgrounds. About 40 per cent of both forces were over the age of 25. Both had significant numbers of men born overseas (mostly in Britain and Ireland): 40 per cent for the ANMEF battalion, and 20 per cent for the AIF's 1st Battalion. After a week's cursory training at the Sydney Showground, the ANMEF embarked on the P&O liner *Berrima*, which had been armed with four 4.7-inch guns, and sailed out of Sydney Harbour on 19 August 1914. Newspapers reported the force's departure, but added 'Their destination is not announced, and only the officers commanding the regiments are permitted to know'.[34]

Berrima sailed northwards and anchored at Palm Island, near Townsville, on 24 August. Patey instructed that the ANMEF should go no further until *Australia* had completed its task in escorting the New Zealanders to Samoa. The troops continued training, and practised landings as they waited for the order to move. This came on 30 August, the day after the New Zealand force occupied Apia. With the cruisers *Sydney* and *Encounter* as escorts, *Berrima* and the supply ship *Aorangi* sailed first to Port Moresby in Papua, arriving on 4 September. About 500 militia soldiers from the 2nd Infantry Regiment (also known as the Kennedy Regiment) were already at Port Moresby. At the beginning of the war these part-time soldiers from north Queensland had been mobilised and transported on the *Kanowna* from Townsville to Thursday Island, where they were to defend the Torres Strait. Here, their commander called for volunteers to join the ANMEF. About half the unit put themselves forward, and these went on the *Kanowna* to Port Moresby. Most were rifle club members (see Chapter 7), some were youths doing their compulsory military training (Chapter 11), all were poorly trained and poorly equipped. Holmes did not want these men as part of the ANMEF, but Patey, who commanded the expedition, decided they should be included. On 7 September the *Berrima* and *Kanowna* and their naval escort departed Port Moresby. The civilian crew of the *Kanowna* had not volunteered to take part in a military operation and refused to sail the ship, so *Kanowna* left the convoy and returned to Townsville.[35]

The remaining ships from Port Moresby fell in with HMAS *Australia* on 9 September at the Louisiades Islands off the eastern tip of Papua. The Australian naval force committed to the capture of German New Guinea was thus substantial: the battlecruiser *Australia*, two cruisers, three destroyers and the two Australian submarines, *AE1* and *AE2*. (On 14 September AE1 would sink with all its crew somewhere off Rabaul. The first RAN ship to be lost, the location of the wreck remains unknown.)[36]

The acting governor of German New Guinea, Doctor Eduard Haber, had made some preparations to defend the colony. The government administration was shifted from Rabaul to the inland village of Toma, about 30 kilometres away. The colonial treasury of gold, silver and banknotes was packed into strongboxes and buried like pirate treasure at three different sites around Toma. The ability to defend German New Guinea was limited, however, because the colony had no formal military organisation, and the ANMEF would face a force, commanded by Captain KGA von Klewitz, consisting of two German regular officers, 59 German reserve officers, non-commissioned officers and soldiers, and about 240 native police. Haber directed von Klewitz to concentrate his force on protecting the Bitapaka radio station. The Germans realised that they would be unable to stop an Australian landing, but buoyed by news of German victories in Europe – which they continued to receive via the radio station at Nauru until 9 September when a landing party off HMAS *Melbourne* took it off the air – they were convinced that Germany would win the war and any Australian occupation would be brief and temporary.[37]

On 11 September 1914, the ANMEF began its operation to take German New Guinea. Around 7:00 am, two parties each consisting of 25 naval reservists – chosen probably because Holmes believed they were better trained than his soldiers –

The capture of German New Guinea

landed at Herbertshöhe and Kabakaul, near where the Australian believed the German radio station was located. The landing party at Kabakaul, commanded by Lieutenant Rowland Bowen and accompanied by army doctor Captain Brian Pockley, started slowly advancing inland through the jungle that lay on both sides of the road leading to the radio station.[38] One Australian would later write that the jungle was so thick 'that half a dozen men would be within a dozen paces of each other and remain quite invisible one from the other', and that 'the bushes were furnished with extremely long and unpleasant thorns, while the places on one's body that were left free from thorn scratches were filled up by mosquito bites'.[39]

Bowen's force came under fire from unseen enemies in trees and in trenches dug beside the road. He stopped the advance and sent a message back to Kabakaul, calling for reinforcements. Around 8:30 am, 59 sailors from *Yarra* and *Warrego*, some armed only with pistols, were quickly put ashore. These were followed by two companies of naval reservists and the machine-gun troops from the ANMEF commanded by Lieutenant Commander Charles Elwell. These men joined the battle and, as the gunfire increased, the native police – who were not trained soldiers – refused to put their heads above the trench and stopped fighting. Around 1:30 pm, a German officer, Lieutenant EE Kempf, raised the white flag and the shooting on both sides stopped. Kempf surrendered his force and guided a group of Australians to the Bitapaka radio station, which they reached around 7:00 pm. The aerials had been brought down, but the radio equipment was intact.[40]

Five sailors – Able Seamen Billy Williams, John Walker (who had enlisted under the name of John Courtney), Harry Street, Signalman Robert Moffat and Lieutenant Commander Charles Elwell – and one soldier – Captain Brian Pockley – were killed in action or died of wounds in the fight to capture the German radio station. Another four Australians were wounded. These casualties could have been higher. The Germans had buried iron pipes filled with dynamite at two places beside the Bitapaka road – what would now be termed Improvised Explosive Devices (IEDs) – but they were not detonated during the ANMEF's advance.⁴¹

One German sergeant and about 30 New Guinean policemen were killed, and a German sergeant and about ten police were wounded. The large number of indigenous casualties in comparison to the Australian and German figures could be due to a number of reasons. The native police had not been trained as soldiers and their deaths may have been due to combat inexperience. Australian soldiers may also have been more likely to shoot dead the black police than the white Germans. Private Jack Axtens wrote in a letter to his father that about '12 niggers were killed' as they fled the battle. It is also possible that Australians shot the New Guinean police after they had surrendered. There are well documented cases of AIF soldiers on the Western Front killing German soldiers attempting to capitulate.⁴²

On 12 September, an ANMEF detachment occupied Rabaul without opposition. The following afternoon they raised the flag and sang the national anthem in the town square. At this time Australia was part of the British Empire, so the flag raised was the Union Jack and the anthem sung was 'God Save the King'. Frederick Burnell, the *Sydney Morning Herald* reporter who accompanied the expedition, wrote that:

> until one has heard [God Save the King] echoing from the lips of a body of men ... triumphant upon an enemy's soil, even in so comparatively small an instance as here at Rabaul, one may safely be said never to have truly to have heard it at all.⁴³

The capture of German New Guinea

The capture of the radio station and the occupation of Rabaul was not the end of the campaign. Having moved his administration from Rabaul to Toma, Governor Haber still refused to submit. On 14 September, the destroyer *Encounter* shelled a ridge near Toma for about an hour – killing and wounding an unknown number of indigenous people – and a detachment of infantry, machine guns and artillery began marching on the village. This show of force was sufficient to convince the governor to commence surrender negotiations. Holmes and Haber signed the terms of capitulation on 17 September, although it would take until 9 December until the ANMEF occupied every major settlement in the colony.[44] Millen marked the end of combat operations in New Guinea by stating:

> Although our losses have been small – and the wish naturally arises that we might have been spared them – at the same time there is cause for congratulation that the accomplishment of so much has been attained at such small sacrifice of life.[45]

With the German surrender, Holmes became the military administrator of the captured colony, a position he retained until 8 January 1915. His short administration was however marred by three poor decisions which contributed to the government's decision to replace him with the more experienced Samuel Pethebridge, the former secretary of the Defence Department.[46]

The first of these decisions occurred during the surrender negotiations, where Haber managed to get Holmes to agree that the Australian government would pay German officials at their current salary for three months and then fund the men's return – via the then-neutral United States – to Germany.[47] When the details of the agreement became publicly known in Australia in

November 1914, it created political controversy. It also caused embarrassment for Senator George Pearce, who had become Defence Minister on 17 September following the Labor victory in the 5 September election. He was initially unaware of Holmes' concessions.[48]

The second was Holmes' decision to send the German flag captured from the main administration building in Rabaul to his employer, the Sydney City Council, where, on 7 October, it was put on display. Prime Minister Andrew Fisher publicly rebuked Holmes, stating 'It was not his to give away'. Pearce told the lord mayor of Sydney, RW Richards, that the flag did not belong to one city but was 'of historical value to the whole of the Commonwealth'. The mayor conceded and presented the flag to the federal government.[49]

The third – and most serious – of Holmes' misjudgments was his decision to publicly flog four civilians in Rabaul on 30 November 1914. The incident arose following an assault on the Australian Methodist missionary William Cox by some Germans and one Belgian man at Namatanai on Neu Mecklenburg (now New Ireland) on 26 October. Cox was visiting the local missionary when a group of armed men came to the house at night, accused him of being a British spy, and hit him 30 or 40 times with a cane. An ANMEF expedition arrested six of the men alleged to have taken part in the attack and brought them to Rabaul.[50]

The ANMEF legal officer, Captain Charles Manning, and the senior German judge, Gustav Weber, advised Holmes to put the men on trial. Instead, Holmes had four of the men summarily flogged in the main square in Rabaul. On 30 November, each prisoner in turn was stretched over the curved lid of a shipping trunk and their hands and feet tied to pegs. Several soldiers, all volunteers, whipped the men with a stick previously used by the Germans to punish natives.[51]

The incident became public in Australia on 13 December when the *Morinda* docked in Sydney, delivering both the flogged men for internment and Holmes' reports for Pearce. The next day, newspapers across the country published accounts of the caning, generally under approving headlines such as 'GERMAN FLOGGERS FLOGGED', 'THEIR OWN MEDICINE' and 'SPEEDY RETALIATION'.[52] Pearce sent a message of congratulations to Holmes for his action, but Governor-General Sir Ronald Munro-Ferguson pointed out to the Defence Minister that the flogging must be condemned, otherwise Berlin could order the flogging of interned British civilians in Germany in reprisal. On 16 December, Pearce told the Senate that Holmes had punished the men without trial and that he would instruct Holmes that his action was 'not to be repeated'.[53]

In January 1915, the German government asked, via the United States government, for a report on the flogging. Munro-Ferguson had already informed British Colonial Secretary Lord Harcourt in a personal letter the true circumstances of the incident in December 1914. To save the British government having to make an embarrassing admission – and prevent the possibility of German retaliation – Munro-Ferguson sent an official telegram to Harcourt on 26 January 1915 stating that the men had been tried before their punishment. The British government forwarded this message to the Americans for transmission to the Germans, although both Harcourt and Munro-Ferguson knew its contents to be untrue.[54]

Holmes' irregular behaviour as military administrator was mirrored in the actions of many members of the ANMEF. The force was ill-disciplined and committed a range of crimes against the civilian population. There were at least two cases of rape,[55] and soldiers openly described in their letters incidents of shooting and flogging indigenous men without justification.[56] The widespread looting of civilian property by officers and men became, as historian Charles Rowley put it, 'a first-class scandal'.[57] In October 1914, five Australian soldiers committed armed robbery on two Catholic priests. The following month, five military policemen stole over 5000 Marks from the safe of a Chinese businessman.[58] When Holmes and the bulk of the ANMEF departed Rabaul on 10 February 1915, Pethebridge – the new administrator who had arrived with the 'Tropical Force'[59] as replacements – requested that all the officers' and men's baggage be inspected for looted items when they disembarked in Australia.[60]

Such a search was carried out and it did find stolen goods. On 24 February, Pearce formed a military court of inquiry that in May recommended that charges arising from looting be laid against five officers and non-commissioned officers – including Lieutenant Colonel John Paton, who had commanded the force that had occupied Rabaul on 12 September 1914. The five were court martialled in May 1915 but were found not guilty on the grounds that the men believed that taking things that did not belong to them was not stealing but was 'souveniring'.[61]

These courts martial juxtaposed the ANMEF's misbehaviour with the first news of the Australians landing at Gallipoli. On 23 May 1915, Reverend WM Madgwick reflected a broader public perception in his sermon at St John's Anglican Church in Heathcote in central Victoria when he argued 'Australia's first efforts had been besmirched by sin at Rabaul, which was a set-off against the brilliancy of our men at the Dardanelles'.[62] This attempt to contrast the behaviour of the ANMEF and the AIF was unfair. Ill-disciplined AIF soldiers had committed similar crimes against the civilian population in Cairo between December 1914 and March 1915.[63]

The occupation of German New Guinea continued for the rest of the war. In October 1914, the *Sydney Morning Herald* had commented – in line with pre-war Australian sub-imperial ambitions – that the capture of New Guinea meant that Australians 'will have to think of the Pacific in terms of extended responsibilities, and of wider spheres of influence'.[64] Most Australians assumed that, having taken German New Guinea, they would be able to keep it. By 1918, the British government had decided that the German colonial empire should be retained by the victorious Allied powers,[65] but United States President Woodrow Wilson initially opposed such imperialism. Australian Prime Minister Billy Hughes began a campaign to ensure Australia kept New Guinea so its resources could be developed and exploited and to provide defence against possible future Japanese aggression. In a speech in New York in June 1918, Hughes stated 'what we have we hold'. At the Paris Peace Conference in January 1919, he made the point that 'as Mexico is to the United States ... so is New Guinea to Australia'. In the end, Hughes got his way. In May 1919 the conference allocated the former German colonies of New Guinea and Nauru to Australian control.[66] New Guinea and Papua would remain Australian territories until they gained independence as Papua New Guinea on 16 September 1975.

The Australian capture of German New Guinea in 1914 remains significant. As the *Sydney Morning Herald* pointed out in November 1914, the ANMEF was 'the first expedition to leave Australian shores that was given work to do with her own men under her own officers'.[67] The ANMEF was Australian, but, reflecting the prevailing views of the time, it was also British. As one soldier wrote: 'Australia's first expeditionary force was a mighty drag-net. It has gathered in the reckless spirits that answer so eagerly when Britain calls.'[68] Another newspaper editorial in

October 1914 promised that the soldiers and sailors killed in this campaign would always be remembered.[69] The scale of carnage that followed in World War I meant instead that these six men were forgotten, but the centenary of World War I provides an opportunity to re-examine this short but successful campaign in Australia's neighbourhood.

Further reading

C Bridge, *William Hughes, Australia: The Paris Peace Conferences of 1919–1923 and their Aftermath*, Haus Publishing, London, 2011

FS Burnell, *Australia Versus Germany: The Story of the Taking of German New Guinea*, George Allen & Unwin, London, 1915

J Connor, *Anzac and Empire: George Foster Pearce and the Foundations of Australian Defence*, CUP, Melbourne, 2011

HJ Hiery, *The German South Pacific and the Influence of World War I*, University of Hawai'i Press, Honolulu, 1995

AW Jose, *The Royal Australian Navy 1914–1918*, vol 9 in CEW Bean (ed), *The Official History of Australia in the War of 1914–1918*, 1st pub 1928, University of Queensland, Brisbane, 1993

WR Louis, *Great Britain and Germany's Lost Colonies 1914–1919*, Clarendon Press, Oxford, 1967

J Lyng, *Our New Possession (Late German New Guinea)*, Melbourne Publishing, Melbourne, 1919

SS Mackenzie, *The Australians at Rabaul: The Capture and Administration of the German Possessions in the Southern Pacific*, vol 10 in CEW Bean (ed), *The Official History of Australia in the War of 1914–1918*, 1st pub 1927, University of Queensland, Brisbane, 1993

R Mallett, 'The preparation and deployment of the Australian Naval and Military Expeditionary Force', in P Dennis and J Grey (eds), *Battles Near and Far: A Century of Overseas Deployment – The 2004 Chief of Army Military History Conference*, Army History Unit, Canberra, 2005, pp 21–32

K Meade, *Heroes before Gallipoli: Bita Paka and that One Day in September*, John Wiley, Brisbane, 2005

C Newbury, 'Spoils of war: Sub-imperial collaboration in South West Africa and New Guinea 1914–1920', *Journal of Imperial and Commonwealth History*, 16(3), 1988, pp 83–106

P Overlack, 'German commerce warfare planning for the Australian Station 1900–1914', *War & Society*, 14(1), May 1996, pp 17–48

——, 'The force of circumstance: Graf Spee's options for the East Asian Cruiser Squadron in 1914', *Journal of Military History*, 60(4), October 1996, pp 657–82

——, '"Bless the Queen and Curse the Colonial Office": Australasian reaction to German consolidation in the Pacific 1871–1899', *Journal of Pacific History*, 33(2), September 1998, pp 133–52

M Piggott, 'Stonewalling in German New Guinea', *Journal of the Australian War Memorial*, 12, April 1988, pp 3–15

CD Rowley, *The Australians in German New Guinea 1914–1921*, MUP, Melbourne, 1958

P Sack & D Clark (trans & eds), *German New Guinea: The Draft Annual Report for 1913–1914*, Department of Law, ANU, Canberra, 1980

D Stevens, '1914–1918: World War I', in D Stevens (ed), *The Royal Australian Navy*, OUP, Melbourne, 2001

R Thompson, *Australian Imperialism in the Pacific: The Expansionist Era 1820–1920*, MUP, Melbourne, 1980

Notes

Introduction John Connor

1. Hughes speech on Anzac Day 1919, in *Courier* (Brisbane), 28 April 1919. This is how this part of Hughes' speech was reported in most Australian newspapers and has appeared in subsequent publications. An alternative – and perhaps more accurate – transcript of Hughes' speech (*Argus*, 28 April 1919) reads: 'Australia's future will be built upon the foundations laid on Anzac Day, when Australia was born. The shores of Gallipoli had made the digger what he is.'
2. Julia Gillard, 'Transcript of doorstop interview, Gallipoli', 25 April 2012, <www.pm.gov.au/press-office/lone-pine-ceremony-gallipoli/>.
3. C Bridge & K Fedorowich, 'Mapping the British World', *Journal of Imperial and Commonwealth History*, 31(2), May 2003, p 6.
4. Photographs of Australians at Gallipoli wearing British patrol caps and Lambert's initial sketches, AWM, WDJ0157, ART11391.279, ART11391.290, <www.awm.gov.au/>.
5. CEW Bean, *Gallipoli Mission*, AWM, Canberra, 1952, p 110.
6. *Australian Stamp Bulletin*, 176, Jan–Feb 1985, p 6.
7. *Australian Stamp Bulletin*, 255, June–July 2000, pp 10–11.
8. I am indebted to David Scott for this idea: see his *European Stamp Design: A Semiotic Approach to Designing Messages*, Academy Editions, London, 1995, p 94.

1 Traditional Indigenous warfare John Connor

1. *Canadian Museum of Civilisation Canadian War Museum Annual Report 2011/2012*, p 30, <www.warmuseum.ca/files/2012/10/arpt1112e.pdf>; *Australian War Memorial Annual Report 2011–2012*, p 29, <www.awm.gov.au/sites/default/files/annual-report-2012.pdf> (both viewed 18 March 2013).
2. <www.warmuseum.ca/event/canadian-experience-gallery-1-battleground/>, (viewed 18 March 2013).
3. B Arthur & F Morphy (eds), *Macquarie Atlas of Indigenous Australia*, Macquarie Library, Sydney, 2005, p 38.
4. *Colonial Times* (Hobart), 12 August 1851; *Empire* (Sydney), 11 May 1852.
5. *Queensland Parliamentary Debates*, vol 33, pp 1137–38, quoted in H Reynolds (ed), *Aborigines and Settlers: The Australian Experience 1788–1939*, Cassell Australia, Sydney, 1972, p 25.
6. M Martin, *On Darug Land: An Aboriginal Perspective*, Greater Western Education Centre, Sydney, 1989, pp 11, 30.
7. *Australian Stamp Bulletin*, vol 191, July 1987, p 3.
8. D Horton (ed), *The Encyclopaedia of Aboriginal Australia*, vol 2, Aboriginal Studies Press, Canberra, 1994, p 1167.
9. Horton, *Encyclopaedia of Aboriginal Australia*, vol 2, p 1013.
10. For example Keith Windschuttle argues that because Aboriginal raids on the colonial frontier did not have a defined political objective it cannot be defined

as 'war': K Windschuttle, *The Fabrication of Aboriginal History*, vol 1, *Van Diemen's Land 1803–1847*, Macleay Press, Sydney, 2002, pp 96–97, 99, 198.
11 JA Lynn, *Battle: A History of Combat and Culture*, rev edn, Basic Books, New York, 2008, pp xiv, xx.
12 R Broome, *Aboriginal Australians: A History since 1788*, 4th edn, Allen & Unwin, Sydney, 2010, p 12.
13 C von Clausewitz (M Howard & P Paret eds & trans), *On War*, Princeton University Press, Princeton, New Jersey, 1989, p 75.
14 D Collins, *An Account of the English Colony of New South Wales, with remarks on the dispositions, customs, manners, etc. of the native inhabitants of that country*, 1798, ed B Fletcher, 2 vols, Reed/Royal Historical Society, Sydney, 1975, vol 1, p 487.
15 Horton, *Encyclopaedia of Aboriginal Australia*, vol. 1, p 985.
16 Interview with P Batumbil, 29 September 2005, quoted in N Riseman, *Defending Whose Country? Indigenous Soldiers in the Pacific War*, University of Nebraska Press, Lincoln (Nebraska), 2012, pp 80–81.
17 Collins, *An Account*, vol 1, pp 466, 485, 488; Ensign F Barrallier, NSW Corps, diary in *Historical Records of New South Wales* (*HRNSW*), vol 5, p 767; *Australian* (Sydney), 14 October 1826; AEJ Andrews (ed), *Hume and Hovell 1824*, Blubber Head Press, Hobart, 1981, p 234; J Bulmer, *Victorian Aborigines: John Bulmer's Recollections 1855–1908*, ed A Campbell & R Vanderwal, Museum of Victoria, Melbourne, 1994, pp 1–2; Horton, *Encyclopaedia of Aboriginal Australia*, vol 2, p 1096; R Atkins, diary, 8 June 1792, National Library of Australia, Canberra, G2198.
18 H Hale, *United States Exploring Expedition during the Years 1838, 1839, 1840, 1841, 1842, Under the Command of Charles Wilkes*, USN Ethnography and Philology, 1st pub 1846, Gregg Press, Ridgewood (NJ), 1968, p 116.
19 LH Keeley, *War Before Civilization*, Oxford University Press, New York, 1996, pp 90–91; D Dawson, *The First Armies*, Cassell, London, 2001, p 57.
20 D Paine, *The Journal of Daniel Paine 1794–1797, Together with Documents Illustrating the Beginning of Government Boat-building and Timber-gathering in New South Wales 1795–1805*, ed RJB Knight & A Frost, Library of Australian History, Sydney, 1983, p 40.
21 A Huey, 'The Voyage of the 73rd Regiment of Foot', SLNSW, Sydney, B1514, p 24; Collins, *An Account*, vol 1, p 486; D Southwell, diary, 7 September 1790, NLA, AJCP, M1538.
22 M Mead quoted in R Broome, 'The Struggle for Australia: Aboriginal–European Warfare 1770–1930', in M McKernan & M Browne (eds), *Australia Two Centuries of War and Peace*, Australian War Memorial/Allen & Unwin, Canberra, 1988, p 94.
23 J Uniacke, 'Narrative of Mr Oxley's Expedition to survey Port Curtis and Moreton Bay, with a view to form Convict Establishments there in pursuance of the Recommendation of the Commissioner of Inquiry', ed G Mackaness, *The Discovery and Exploration of Moreton Bay and the Brisbane River 1799–1823*, Review Publications, Dubbo, 1979, pt 2, pp 35, 37; Hale, *Exploring Expedition*, p 116; J Backhouse, 'Account of a Journey from Parramatta, Across the Blue Mountains to Wellington', in G Mackaness (ed), *Fourteen Journeys Over The Blue Mountains of New South Wales 1813–1841*, Review Publications,

Dubbo, 1978, pt 3, p 19; Bulmer, *Victorian Aborigines*, pp 16, 62–63.
24 Bulmer, *Victorian Aborigines*, pp 8–9.
25 S Konishi, '"Wanton With Plenty": Questioning ethno-historical constructions of sexual savagery in Aboriginal societies 1788–1803', *Australian Historical Studies*, 39(3), August 2008, p 359.
26 NG Butlin, *Economics and the Dreamtime: A Hypothetical History*, CUP, Cambridge, 1993, p 82.
27 As a comparison, see the role of cattle raids in early Irish warfare: TM Charles-Edwards, 'Irish warfare before 1100', in T Bartlett & K Jeffery (eds), *A Military History of Ireland*, CUP, Cambridge, 1996.
28 L Macquarie to Lord Bathurst, 30 June 1815, *Historical Records of Australia*, series 1, vol 8, p 610; T Shellam, *Shaking Hands on the Fringe: Negotiating the Aboriginal World at King George's Sound*, UWA Press, Perth, 2009, p 96.
29 Shellam, *Shaking Hands on the Fringe*, p 104.
30 Collins, *An Account*, vol 2, p 47.
31 Shellam, *Shaking Hands on the Fringe*, pp 91, 90.
32 A Phillip to Lord Sydney, 16 November 1790, *HRNSW*, vol 1, pt 2, p 2012; Collins, *An Account*, vol 1, p 488.
33 Bulmer, *Victorian Aborigines*, p 25.
34 Horton, *Encyclopaedia of Aboriginal Australia*, vol 1, p 149.
35 AW Jose & HJ Carter (eds), *The Australian Encyclopaedia*, Angus & Robertson, Sydney, 1925, vol 1, p 32.
36 Horton, *Encyclopaedia of Aboriginal Australia*, vol 2, p 1013; H Melville, *The History of Van Diemen's Land: From the Year 1824 to 1835*, 1836, ed G Mackaness, Horwitz Publications/The Grahame Book Co, Sydney, 1965, p 38; Collins, *An Account*, vol 1, p 509.
37 Horton, *Encyclopaedia of Aboriginal Australia*, vol 2, p 1013.
38 C Barker, *Commandant of Solitude: The Journals of Captain Collet Barker 1828–1831*, ed J Mulvaney & N Green, Melbourne University Press, Melbourne, 1992, p 119.
39 Horton, *Encyclopaedia of Aboriginal Australia*, vol 2, pp 1195–96.
40 JL Kohen & R Lampert, 'Hunters and fishers in the Sydney region', in DJ Mulvaney & JP White (eds), *Australians to 1788*, Fairfax, Syme & Weldon Associates, Sydney, 1987, p 352.
41 Collins, *An Account*, vol 1, p 488; Lieut D Blackburn to M Blackburn, 15 November 1788, NLA, AJCP M971.
42 *Sydney Gazette*, 8 December 1805; Collins, *An Account*, vol 1, p 486; Horton, *Encyclopaedia of Aboriginal Australia*, vol 2, p 1013.
43 J Troy, 'The Sydney language', in N Thieberger & W McGregor (eds), *Macquarie Aboriginal Words: A Dictionary of Words from Australian Aboriginal and Torres Strait Islander Languages*, Macquarie Library, Sydney, 1994, p 62.
44 *Sydney Gazette*, 22 December 1805; J Belich, *Making Peoples: A History of the New Zealanders from Polynesian Settlement to the End of the Nineteenth Century*, Penguin, Auckland, 1996, pp 141–42.
45 Arthur & Morphy, *Macquarie Atlas of Indigenous Australia*, p 51; Horton, *Encyclopaedia of Aboriginal Australia*, vol 2, p 1167; Horton, *Encyclopaedia of Aboriginal Australia*, vol 2, p 1014.
46 A Campbell, 'Geographic Memoir of Melville Island and Port Essington,

on the Cobourg Peninsula, Northern Australia, with some Observations on the Settlements which have been established on the North Coast of New Holland', *Journal of the Royal Geographical Society of London*, vol 4, 1834, p 156; RJ King, *The Secret History of the Convict Colony: Alexandro Malaspina's report on the British settlement of New South Wales*, Allen & Unwin, Sydney, 1990, p 162.
47 Horton, *Encyclopaedia of Aboriginal Australia*, vol 1, p 203; vol 2, p 1071.
48 Horton, *Encyclopaedia of Aboriginal Australia*, vol 1, p 203, vol 2, p 1071.
49 B Arthur & F Morphy, *Macquarie Atlas of Indigenous Australia*, p 49.
50 J Rowley, 'Language of George's River, Cowpastures and Appin', in W Ridley, *Kamilaroi and other Australian Languages*, 2nd edn, NSW Government Printer, Sydney, 1875, p 105.
51 *Sydney Gazette*, 23 December 1804.
52 Arthur & Morphy, *Macquarie Atlas of Indigenous Australia*, pp 48–49; Horton, *Encyclopaedia of Aboriginal Australia*, vol 1, p 143.
53 Horton, *Encyclopaedia of Aboriginal Australia*, vol 1, p 285, 511; vol 2, pp 1167–68.
54 *Sydney Gazette*, 2 September 1804, 27 January 1805; R Knopwood, *The Diary of the Reverend Robert Knopwood 1803–1838: First Chaplain of Van Diemen's Land*, ed M Nicholls, Tasmanian Historical Research Association, Launceston, 1977, pp 128, 171.
55 Horton, *Encyclopaedia of Aboriginal Australia*, vol 1, p 985; vol 2, p 1167; Jose & Carter, *Australian Encyclopaedia*, vol 1, p 33.
56 Arthur & Morphy, *Macquarie Atlas of Indigenous Australia*, p 52.
57 *Sydney Morning Herald*, 16 & 25 August 1999.

2 Frontier warfare in Australia Jonathan Richards

1 See 'Conceptions of "frontier"' in A Nettelbeck and R Smandych, 'Policing Indigenous peoples on two colonial frontiers: Australia's Mounted Police and Canada's North-West Mounted Police', *Australian and New Zealand Journal of Criminology*, 43(2), 2010, p 358; and K Burns, 'Frontier conflict, contact, exchange: Re-imagining colonial architecture', *Imagining*, Society of Architectural Historians, 2010, p72.
2 B Buchan, *The Empire of Political Thought: Indigenous Australians and the Language of Colonial Government*, Pickering & Chatto, London, 2008, p 79; HP Willmott and MB Barrett, *Clausewitz Reconsidered*, ABC-CLIO, Santa Barbara, 2010, p 151.
3 J Hopkins-Weise, *Blood Brothers: The Anzac Genesis*, Penguin, London, 2009, p 14.
4 CE Callwell, *Small Wars: Their Principles and Practice*, Greenhill, London, 1906 (1990 facsimile).
5 G Harries-Jenkins, *The Army in Victorian Society*, Routledge & Kegan Paul, Toronto, 1977, p 184; D Whittington, '"Savage warfare": CE Callwell, the roots of counter-insurgency and the nineteenth-century context', *Small Wars & Insurgencies*, 23(4–5), p 591.
6 C Sturgill, *Low-Intensity Conflict in American History*, Praeger, Westport, 1993, p 23.

7   J Kociumbas, 'Genocide and modernity in colonial Australia 1788–1850', in AD Moses (ed), *Genocide and Settler Society: Frontier Violence and Stolen Indigenous Children in Australian History*, Berghahn Books, New York, 2004, pp 77–78; R Broome, *Aboriginal Australians: A History since 1788*, Allen & Unwin, Sydney, 2010, pp 37 & 55.
8   B Attwood, *Telling the Truth about Aboriginal History*, Allen & Unwin, Sydney, 2005, pp 114–115.
9   A Laurie, 'The Black War in Queensland', *Royal Historical Society of Queensland Journal*, 6(1), 1959, pp 155–73; J Woolmington, 'Early contacts: From the dreamtime to the nightmare', in P Stanbury (ed), *The Moving Frontier: Aspects of Aboriginal-European Interaction in Australia*, Reed, Sydney, 1977; F Robinson and B York, *The Black Resistance*, Widescope, Melbourne, 1977, PW Newbury (ed), *Aboriginal Heroes of the Resistance: From Pemulwuy to Mabo*, Action for World Development, Sydney, 1999.
10 C Williamson, 'Contact archaeology and the writing of Aboriginal history', in T Murray (ed), *The Archaeology of Contact in Settler Societies*, CUP, Cambridge, 2004, p 178.
11 Williamson, 'Contact archaeology', p 183; J Grey, *A Military History of Australia*, CUP, Melbourne, 2008, pp 28–29; Broome, *Aboriginal Australians*, pp 45 & 50 (quote).
12 N Cole, 'Painting the police: Aboriginal visual culture and identity in colonial Cape York Peninsula', *Australian Archaeology*, 71, 2010, p 26.
13 P Wolfe, 'Race and the trace of history: For Henry Reynolds', in Fiona Bateman & Lionel Pilkington (eds), *Studies in Settler Colonialism: Politics, Identity and Culture*, Palgrave Macmillan, Basingstoke, 2011, p 273.
14 B Vandervort, *Indian Wars of Canada, Mexico and the United States 1812–1900*, Routledge, London, p xiii.
15 L Ford, *Settler Sovereignty: Jurisdiction and Indigenous People in America and Australia 1788–1836*, Harvard University Press, Cambridge, 2010; K Harman, *Aboriginal Convicts: Australian, Khoisan and Māori Exiles*, UNSW Press, Sydney, 2012.
16 H Douglas & M Finnane, *Indigenous Crime and Settler Law: White Sovereignty after Empire*, Palgrave Macmillan, Basingstoke, 2012, p 9.
17 R Gott, *Britain's Empire: Resistance, Repression and Revolt*, Verso, London, 2011, p 3.
18 M Grewcock, *Border Crimes: Australia's War on Illicit Migrants*, Institute of Criminology Press, Sydney, 2006, p 21; R Davis, 'Introduction: Transforming the frontier in contemporary Australia', in D Bird Rose & R Davis (eds), *Dislocating the Frontier: Essaying the Mystique of the Outback*, ANU Press, Canberra, 2005, p 11.
19 N Finzsch, '"The Aborigines ... were never annihilated, and still they are becoming extinct": Settler imperialism and genocide in nineteenth-century America and Australia', in Moses (ed), *Empire, Colony, Genocide*, p 261.
20 AD Moses, *Genocide and Settler Society: Frontier Violence and Stolen Indigenous Children in Australian History*, OUP, Oxford, 2004.
21 K Roy, 'The hybrid military establishment of the East India Company in South Asia 1750–1849', *Journal of Global History*, 6, 2011, p 195.
22 KI Smith, 'The commandants: The leadership of the Natal native contingent

in the Anglo–Zulu War', MA thesis, University of Western Australia, 2005; Gott, *Britain's Empire*, p 6.
23 WE Lee, 'Projecting power in the early modern world', in WE Lee (ed), *Empires and Indigenes: Intercultural Alliance, Imperial Expansion, and Warfare in the Early Modern World*, New York University Press, New York, 2011, p 10.
24 H Bailes, 'Technology and imperialism: A case study of the Victorian army in Africa', *Victorian Studies*, 24(1), 1980, p 96.
25 J Connor, *The Australian Frontier Wars*, UNSW Press, Sydney, 2005.
26 Kociumbas, 'Genocide and modernity in colonial Australia', p 87; Buchan, *The Empire of Political Thought*, p 87.
27 N Wolski, 'All's not quiet on the western front: Rethinking resistance and frontiers in Aboriginal historiography', in L Russell (ed), *Colonial Frontiers: Indigenous-European Encounters in Settler Societies*, Manchester University Press, Manchester, 2001, pp 218–19.
28 Buchan, *The Empire of Political Thought*, p 88; Broome, *Aboriginal Australians*, p 41.
29 Buchan, *The Empire of Political Thought*, p 84.
30 B Thorpe, *Colonial Queensland: Perspectives on a Frontier Society*, UQP, Brisbane, 1996, p 184.
31 J Bou, *Light Horse: A History of Australia's Mounted Arm*, CUP, Cambridge, 2010, p 14.
32 B Casey, 'The Queensland Volunteers, the Queensland Rifle Association and Queensland's frontier war', *Crossroads*, 5(2), 2011, pp 87–96.
33 Notable exceptions are Connor, *The Australian Frontier Wars*; C Wilcox, *Red Coat Dreaming: How Colonial Australia Embraced the British Army*, CUP, Melbourne, 2009.
34 CD Rowley, *The Destruction of Aboriginal Society*, ANU Press, Canberra, 1970, and H Reynolds, *The Other Side of the Frontier: Aboriginal Resistance to the European Invasion of Australia*, Penguin, Melbourne, 1982, were among the first; but see also K Willey, *When the Sky Fell Down: The Destruction of the Tribes of the Sydney Region 1788–1850s*, Collins, Sydney, 1979; R Broome, 'The struggle for Australia: Aboriginal–European warfare 1770–1930', in M McKernan & M Browne (eds), *Australia: Two Centuries of War and Peace*, AWM, Canberra, 1988; B Attwood & SG Foster, *Frontier Conflict: The Australian Experience*, National Museum of Australia, Canberra, 2003.
35 B Morris, 'Frontier colonialism as a culture of terror', *Journal of Australian Studies*, 35, 1992; Kociumbas, 'Genocide and modernity in colonial Australia'.
36 E Willmot, *Pemulwuy: Rainbow Warrior*, Weldons, Sydney, 1987; KV Smith, *King Bungaree*, Kangaroo Press, Sydney, 1992; KV Smith, *Bennelong: The Coming in of the Eora Sydney Cove 1788–1792*, Kangaroo Press, Sydney 2001; Wilcox, *Red Coat Dreaming*, pp 11–22.
37 J Ferry, *Colonial Armidale*, UQP, Brisbane, 1999.
38 D Kent, 'Frontier conflict and Aboriginal deaths: How do we weigh the evidence?', *Journal of Australian Colonial History*, 8, 2006, p 42.
39 G Karskens, *The Colony: A History of Early Sydney*, Allen & Unwin, Sydney, 2009, pp 361, 374, 594; Kociumbas, 'Genocide and modernity in colonial Australia', pp 79–82.
40 Connor, *The Australian Frontier Wars*.

41 Legislative Council meeting, 5 March 1839, *Sydney Gazette*, 7 March 1839, p 2.
42 LE Skinner, 'The days of the Squatting Acts: Districts of Darling Downs and Moreton Bay', part 1, in *Queensland Heritage*, 3(6), 1977, p 3.
43 Letter from J Glennie, 18 Feb 1839, cited in *Australian*, 7 March 1839, p 2.
44 B Gammage, *Narrandera Shire*, Narrandera Shire Council, Narrandera, 1986, p 32.
45 Skinner, 'The days of the Squatting Acts', pp 9–10.
46 RHW Reece, *Aborigines and Colonists: Aborigines and Colonial Society in New South Wales in the 1830s and 1840s*, Sydney University Press, Sydney, 1974.
47 See also LE Skinner, *Police of the Pastoral Frontier: Native Police 1849–1859*, UQP, Brisbane, 1975.
48 L Armand, 'Et in Arcadia Ego: Landscapes of genocide', *Triquarterly*, 116, 2003, p 171.
49 JF McMahon, 'The British Army: Its role in counter-insurgency in the Black War in Van Diemen's Land', *Tasmanian Historical Studies*, 5(1), 1996.
50 R Manne (ed), *Whitewash: On Keith Windschuttle's "Fabrication of Aboriginal History"*, Black Inc, Melbourne, 2003; L Ryan, 'List of multiple killings of Aborigines in Tasmania 1804–1835', <www.massviolence.org>, accessed 12 January 2013.
51 L Ryan, '"Hard evidence': The debate about massacre in the Black War in Tasmania', in F Peters-Little, A Curthoys & J Docker, *Passionate Histories: Myth, Memory and Indigenous Australia*, ANU Press, Canberra, 2010; L Ryan, *Tasmanian Aborigines: A History since 1803*, Allen & Unwin, Sydney, 2012.
52 R Broome, *Aboriginal Victorians: A History since 1800*, Allen & Unwin, Sydney, 2005.
53 J Critchett, *'A 'Distant Field of Murder': Western District Frontiers 1834–1848*, MUP, Melbourne, 1990; I Clark, *Scars on the Landscape: A Register of Massacre Sites in Western Victoria*, Aboriginal Studies Press, Canberra, 1995.
54 M Fels, *Good Men and True: The Aboriginal Police of the Port Phillip District 1837–1853*, MUP, Melbourne, 1988; M Cannon, *Who Killed the Koories?*, William Heinemann Australia, Melbourne, 1990; I Clark, *'That's my Country Belonging to Me': Aboriginal Land Tenure and Dispossession in Nineteenth-Century Western Victoria*, Heritage Matters, Melbourne, 1998.
55 B Pascoe, *Convincing Ground: Learning to Fall in Love with Your Country*, Aboriginal Studies Press, Canberra, 2007; L Ryan, 'Settler massacres on the Australian colonial frontier 1836–1851', in PG Dwyer & L Ryan (eds), *Theatres of Violence: Massacre, Mass Killing and Atrocity throughout History*, Berghahn Books, New York, 2012, p 107.
56 Ryan, 'Settler massacres on the Australian colonial frontier', pp 104–108.
57 G Presland, *For God's Sake Send the Trackers: A History of Queensland Trackers and Victoria Police*, Victoria Press, Melbourne, 1998.
58 C Cormick, 'Ned Kelly dreaming', *Unwritten Histories*, Aboriginal Studies Press, Canberra, 1998, pp 109–115.
59 N Green, *Broken Spears: Aboriginals and Europeans in the South-West of Australia*, Focus, Perth, 1984; T Austen, *A Cry in the Wind: Conflict in Western Australia 1829–1929*, Darlington, Perth, 1998.
60 Austen, *A Cry in the Wind*, pp xi–x.

61 Connor, *The Australian Frontier Wars*, p 79; P Statham, 'James Stirling and Pinjarra: A battle in more ways than one', *Studies in Western Australian History*, 23, 2003.
62 N Green, 'The evidence for the Forrest River Massacre', *Quadrant*, 2003.
63 S Adams, *Murder and Hanging on Australia's Western Frontier*, UWA Press, Perth, 2009, pp 51–63.
64 A Gill, 'Aborigines, settlers and police in the Kimberleys 1887–1905', *Studies in Western Australian History*, 1, 1977; D Lewis, *A Wild History: Life and Death of the Victoria River Frontier*, Monash University Publishing, Melbourne, 2012.
65 H Pedersen & B Worunmurra, *Jandamarra and the Bunuba Resistance*, Magabala Books, Broome, 1995.
66 A Pope, *One Law for All: Aboriginal People and Criminal Law in Early South Australia*, Aboriginal Studies Press, Canberra, 2011, p 3.
67 R Foster, R Hosking & A Nettelbeck, *Fatal Collisions: The South Australian Frontier and the Violence of Memory*, Wakefield Press, Adelaide, 2001; R Foster & A Nettelbeck, *Out of the Silence: The History and Memory of South Australia's Frontier Wars*, Wakefield Press, Adelaide, 2012.
68 Broome, *Aboriginal Australians*, p 46.
69 P Read & J Read, *Long Time, Olden Time: Aboriginal Accounts of Northern Territory History*, Institute for Aboriginal Development Publications, Alice Springs, 1991; B Wilson, 'Police trackers: Myth and reality', in T Austin & S Parry (eds), *Connection and Disconnection: Encounters between Settlers and Indigenous People in the Northern Territory*, Northern Territory University, Darwin, 1998; A Nettelbeck, 'Writing and remembering frontier conflict: The rule of law in 1880s Central Australia', *Aboriginal History*, 28, 2004.
70 RG Kimber, *The End of the Bad Old Days: European Settlement in Central Australia 1871–1894*, State Library of the Northern Territory, Darwin, 1991.
71 P Vallee, *God, Guns and Government on the Central Australian Frontier*, Restoration, Canberra, 2004.
72 T Roberts, *Frontier Justice: A History of the Gulf Country to 1900*, UQP, Brisbane, 2005; NK Grguric, 'Fortified homesteads: The architecture of fear in frontier South Australia and the Northern Territory ca 1847–1885', PhD thesis, Flinders University, 2007.
73 A Nettelbeck & R Foster, *In The Name of the Law: William Willshire and the Policing of the Australian Frontier*, Wakefield Press, Adelaide, 2007.
74 A Laurie, 'The Black War in Queensland', *Royal Historical Society of Queensland Journal*, 6(1), 1959; Skinner, 'The days of the Squatting Acts'; J Richards, *The Secret War: A True History of Queensland's Native Police*, UQP, Brisbane, 2008.
75 R Evans, '"Plenty shoot 'em"; The destruction of Aboriginal societies along the Queensland frontier', in Moses (ed), *Genocide and Settler Society*; R Evans, 'The country has another past: Queensland and the History Wars', in Peters-Little et al (eds), *Passionate Histories*.
76 N Loos, *Invasion and Resistance: Aboriginal-European Relations on the North Queensland Frontier, 1861–1897*, ANU Press, Canberra, 1982.
77 Richards, *The Secret War*.

3 British soldiers in colonial Australia Peter Stanley

1. Journal of Alexander Huey, 73rd Regiment, 1809–1811, NLA, Ms 2830.
2. Memorial from Marines on the *Scarborough*, 1787, *Historical Records of New South Wales*, vol 1, pp 100–101.
3. J Easty, *Memorandum of the Transactions of a Voyage from England to Botany Bay 1787–1793: A First Fleet Journal*, Public Library of New South Wales, Sydney, 1965, p 100.
4. Macquarie to Bathurst, 31 July 1813, *Historical Records of Australia*, 1:8, p 4.
5. *Colburn's United Services Journal*, 1839, no 2, p 396.
6. Ll Cowper (ed), *The King's Own*, vol 3, *1814–1914*, King's Own Regiment, Oxford, 1939, p 56.
7. P Stanley, 'British infantry regiments of the line and the empire 1840–1869', *Sabretache: Journal of the Military Historical Society of Australia*, Jan–Mar 1984, pp 4–7.
8. *Sydney Herald*, 6 June 1831, p 2.
9. T Bunbury, *Reminiscences of a Veteran: Being personal and military adventures in Portugal, Spain, France, Malta, New South Wales, Norfolk Island, New Zealand, Andaman Islands, and India*, Charles Skeet, London, 1861, p 290.
10. HW Haygarth, *Recollections of Bush Life in Australia*, Murray, London, 1848, pp 37–39.
11. R Therry, *Reminiscences of Thirty Years' Residence in New South Wales and Victoria*, Sampson Low, Son & Co, London, 1863, p 39.
12. J Backhouse, *A Narrative of a Visit to the Australian Colonies*, Hamilton, Adams & Co, London, 1843, pp 308, 422–23.
13. Bunbury, *Reminiscences of a Veteran*, p 290.
14. General Order, 8 Feb 1796, *Historical Records of New South Wales*, vol 3, p 17.
15. P Stanley, 'A mere point of Military etiquette: The Norfolk Island mutiny of 1839', *The Push from the Bush: a bulletin of social history*, 7, Sept 1980, pp 1–12.
16. Gipps to Stanley, 9 Dec 1845, *Historical Records of Australia*, 1:24, pp 655–58.
17. J McCrea (ed), 'A transcript written by William Pidcock, a member of the 11th Regiment', <freepages.history.rootsweb.ancestry.com/~garter1/atranscr.htm> (viewed 18 Jan 2013).
18. WC Wentworth, *A Statistical, Historical and Political Description of the Colony of New South Wale*, G & WB Whittaker, London, 1819, p 35.
19. R Cannon, *Historical Record of the Forty-Sixth, or South Devonshire, Regiment of Foot*, Parker, Furnivall & Parker, London, 1851, pp 49–52.
20. Ensign McMahon to Major Stewart, 19 March 1817, *Historical Records of Australia*, 3:2, p 474.
21. Wentworth, *A Statistical, Historical and Political Description*, p 33.
22. T Barker, *A History of Bathurst*, vol 1, *The Early Settlement to 1862*, Crawford House, Bathurst, 1992, pp 80–83.
23. G Blake, *To Pierce the Tyrant's Heart: A Military History of the Battle for the Eureka Stockade 3 December 1854*, Australian Military History Publications, Loftus, 2009.
24. N Taylor (ed), *The Journal of Ensign Best 1837–1843*, New Zealand Government Printer, Wellington, 1966, p 164.
25. *Sydney Herald*, 18 July 1833.

26 'Penal servitude' (c 1830), in FG Clarke (ed), *The Land of Contrarieties: British Attitudes to the Australian Colonies 1828–1855*, MUP, Melbourne, 1977, p 5.
27 See the General Orders for the Bengal Army in the late 1840s, which reveal a distinct 'spike' in soldiers committing offences such as insubordination and striking NCOs in 1847: *Bengal, General Orders*, 1847–1849, BL, IOR/L/MIL/17/2/296-298.
28 E Beale, *Kennedy of Cape York*, Rigby, Adelaide, 1970, p 26.
29 P Hilton, 'Branded D on the left side: A study of former soldiers and marines transported to Van Diemen's Land 1804–1854', PhD thesis, University of Tasmania, 2010.
30 J Anderson, *Recollections of a Peninsular Veteran*, Arnold, London, 1913, p 163.
31 C Wright, *Wellington's Men in Australia: Peninsular War Veterans and the Making of Empire c. 1820-40*, Palgrave Macmillan, Basingstoke, 2011.
32 GC Mundy, *Our Antipodes*, Bentley, London, 1852, vol 3, pp 63–67.
33 J Byrne, *Twelve Years' Wanderings in the British Colonies*, Bentley, London, 1848, p 227.
34 J Dunmore Lang, *An Historical and Statistical Account of New South Wales*, Cochrane & M'Crone, London, 1834, p 112.
35 Backhouse, *Narrative of a Visit to the Australian Colonies*, pp 2–3.
36 The Indian station and regimental medical reports in WO 334, National Archives, UK, provide an opportunity to identify and track the fates of hundreds of individual men who had served in Australia and who became ill and died in India of illness or battle.
37 M Austin, *The Army in Australia 1840-50*, AGPS, Canberra, 1979.
38 *Sydney Herald*, 27 Aug 1838; G de Winton, *Soldiering Fifty Years Ago*, European Mail, London, 1898, p 81.
39 EAH Webb, *History of the 12th (The Suffolk) Regiment 1685-1913*, Spottiswoode, London, 1914, p 275.
40 Therry, *Reminiscences of Thirty Years' Residence*, p 59.
41 P Stanley, 'Heritage of strangers: The Australian Army's British legacy', *Australian Defence Force Journal*, Mar–Apr 1991, pp 21–26.
42 P Stanley, 'Remember me when this you see: Artefacts and records of the British Army in Australia held in British Museums', privately published, Canberra, 1996.
43 P Stanley, '"A horn to put your powder in": Interpreting artefacts of British soldiers in colonial Australia', *Journal of the Australian War Memorial*, Oct 1988, pp 13–29.
44 P Stanley, *The Remote Garrison: The British Army in Australia 1788-1870*, Kangaroo Press, Sydney, 1986.
45 C Sargent, *The Colonial Garrison 1817–1824: The 48th Foot, the Northamptonshire Regiment in the Colony of New South Wales*, TLC Publications, Canberra, 1996; G Blackburn, *Conquest and Settlement: The 21st Regiment of Foot (North British Fusiliers) in Western Australia 1833–1840*, Hesperian Press, Perth, 1999; K Larbalestier, *12th Regiment of Foot (East Suffolk) Service in Australia and New Zealand 1854–1867*, privately published, 2010.
46 O Leckbrandt, *The Mount Walker Stockade Cox's River*, privately published, c 1998; J Allen, *Port Essington: The Historical Archaeology of a North Australian*

Nineteenth-Century Military Outpost, Sydney University Press/Australasian Society for Historical Archaeology, 2008.
47 C Wilcox, *Red Coat Dreaming*, CUP, Melbourne, 2009.
48 'The journal of Captain Mason', King's Own Royal Regiment Museum, Lancaster, <www.kingsownmuseum.plus.com/mason01.htm> (viewed 18 Jan 2013).
49 J McCrea (ed), 'A transcript written by William Pidcock, a member of the 11th Regiment', <freepages.history.rootsweb.ancestry.com/~garter1/atranscr.htm> (viewed 18 Jan 2013).

4 The battle for the Eureka Stockade Gregory Blake

1   Indicative of the enduring resonance of the Eureka narrative for Australian audiences is the fact that Peter FitzSimon's recent book (*Eureka: The Unfinished Revolution*, Heinemann, Sydney, 2012) has at the time of writing sold in excess of 60 000 copies.
2   T Pierson, diaries, State Library of Victoria, MS 11646 Box 2178/4-5.
3   *Geelong Advertiser and Intelligencer*, 6 Dec 1854, p 4. This correspondent may have been Samuel Irwin, a member of the Ballarat Reform League and a significant player in the diggers' committees leading up to Eureka. He was hardly an objective observer.
4   HG Turner, *Our Own Little Rebellion: The Story of the Eureka Stockade*, Whitcombe & Tombs, Melbourne, 1913, p 94.
5   *Argus*, 21 Dec 1854, p 4.
6   HB Stoney, *Victoria: With a description of its principal cities, Melbourne and Geelong: and remarks on the present state of the colony; including an account of the Ballarat disturbances, and the death of Captain Wise, 40th Regiment*, Smith, Elder & Co, Dublin, 1856, p 123.
7   PF Gilbert, *Gold*, Jacaranda Press, Brisbane, 1970, p 26. For an examination of the role of women at Eureka see C Wright, '"New Brooms they say sweep clean": Women's political activism on the Ballarat Goldfields 1854', *Australian Historical Studies*, 39(3), Sept 2008, pp 305–21.
8   Pierson, diaries.
9   B O'Brien, *Massacre at Eureka, The Untold Story*, Sovereign Hill Museums Association, Ballarat, 1973, p 118; G Hocking, *The Red Ribbon Rebellion: The Bendigo Petition 3rd–27th of August 1853*, New Chum Press, Melbourne, 2001, p 38.
10 J Molony, *Eureka*, Viking, Melbourne, 1984, p 169.
11 W Bate, *Lucky City: The First Generation at Ballarat 1851–1901*, MUP, Melbourne, 1979, p 70.
12 G Serle, *The Golden Age: The History of the Colony of Victoria 1851–1861*, MUP, Melbourne, 1963, p 168.
13 L Blake, *Peter Lalor: The Man from Eureka*, Neptune Press, Melbourne, 1979, p 82.
14 J Keegan, *The Face of Battle: A Study of Agincourt, Waterloo and the Somme*, Barrie & Jenkins, London, 1976, p 103.
15 The exception is a monograph by this author: G Blake, *Eureka Stockade: A Ferocious and Bloody Battle*, Big Sky, Sydney, 2012.
16 R Carboni, *The Eureka Stockade*, Miegunyah Press, Melbourne, 2004.

17 Pierson, diaries; Samuel Lazarus, diary, 24 Sept 1853–21 Jan 1855, SLV, MS 11484 box 1777/4.
18 Charles Pasley, letters to his father 1853–1861, SLV, MS 6167 box 94/4 (b).
19 See Supreme Court of Victoria Library, 1855 Victoria, State Trials, *R v Hayes* & *R v Joseph*; PROV, Eureka Stockade: Depositions, VPRS 5527/P unit 2, item 2.
20 Hotham to Grey, PROV 1085/P0, Duplicate Despatches from the Governor to the Secretary of State, Unit 8, Duplicate Despatch no 162.
21 Pasley, letters to his father.
22 J Lynch, *Story of the Eureka Stockade, Epic Days of the Early Fifties at Ballarat*, facs edn, Goldfields Heritage Publications, Ballarat, 1999, p 30.
23 WB Withers, *History of Ballarat*, facs edn, orig 1887, Queensbury Hill Press, Melbourne, 1980, p 117; Rede to Wright, 2 December 1854, PROV 1189 Box 92, 54/J14462.
24 *Eureka Reminiscences*, Ballarat Heritage Services, Ballarat, 1998, p 64.
25 C Ferguson, *Experiences of a Forty-Niner in Australia and New Zealand*, Gaston Renard, Melbourne, 1979, p 60.
26 Hotham to Grey (see above n 20) reports that no shots were fired or any other military casualties inflicted prior to the death of the first soldier, which was Roney. Roney's wound is described in Thomas to Nickle, 3 Dec, 1854, PROV 1085/P Unit 8, Duplicate 162 Enclosure no 7. The muster rolls of the 40th record Roney being killed in action: UK National Archives, WO12/5365.
27 Thomas to Nickle, 3 Dec 1854.
28 Withers, *History of Ballarat*, p 124.
29 Supreme Court of Victoria Library, *R v. Hayes*, pp 76 & 83; *R v Joseph*, p 35.
30 *Argus*, 5 (blanks) and 9 Dec 1854 (Thompson); Knight in *Eureka Reminiscences*, p 47.
31 *Life in Victoria; or Victoria in 1853 and Victoria in 1858*, reprint of 1859 original, Lowden Publishing, Kilmore, 1977, vol 2, p 110.
32 *Argus*, 5 Dec 1854.
33 Kelly, *Life in Victoria*, p 111.
34 *Argus*, 10 April 1855, p 7.
35 Thomas to Nickle, PROV 1085/P Unit 8, Duplicate 162 Enclosure no 7.
36 Withers, *History of Ballarat*, p 124.
37 Supreme Court of Victoria Library, *R v Hayes*, p 76.
38 Lynch, *Story of the Eureka Stockade*, p 30.
39 Withers, *History of Ballarat*, p 124.
40 Keegan (*Face of Battle*, p 124) recounts how soldiers who fought at Waterloo reported that similar bullets made 'whizzing' and 'whistling' sounds. R Lorimer, who was boarding in a restaurant near the stockade recalled 'The bullets were whizzing about like mosquitoes' (in Withers, *History of Ballarat*, p 118). Personal experience firing a black-powder Enfield rifled-musket, and having a round from a black-powder Colt revolver fly close by my ear, confirms these phenomena.
41 *Eureka Reminiscences*, p 44.
42 Ferguson, *Experiences of a Forty-Niner in Australia and New Zealand*, p 60.
43 Withers, *History of Ballarat*, p 117.
44 *Eureka Reminiscences*, p 32; Serle, *Golden Age*, p 168.

45 H Anderson (ed), *Eureka: Victorian Parliamentary Papers, Votes and Proceedings 1854–1867*, Red Rooster Press, Melbourne, 1999, p 42; *Argus*, 11 April, 1917, p 11.
46 Ferguson, *Experiences of a Forty-Niner in Australia and New Zealand*, p 60.
47 Lynch, *Story of the Eureka Stockade*, p 30.
48 *Argus*, 11 April 1917, p 11.
49 Pasley, letters to his father.
50 Thomas to Nickle, 3 Dec, 1854, PROV 1085/P Unit 8, duplicate 162, enclosure no 7.
51 Carboni, *The Eureka Stockade*, p 96.
52 Ferguson, *Experiences of a Forty-Niner*, p 58; J Allan (ed), *The Eureka Uprising, by Eye-Witness Richard Allan*, Hobart, 2004, p 16.
53 Carboni, *The Eureka Stockade*, p 85.
54 Lynch, *Story of the Eureka Stockade*, p 31.
55 W Howitt, *Land, Labour and Gold: Or Two Years in Victoria with Visits to Sydney and Van Diemen's Land*, 1855, Lowden Publishing Company, Kilmore, 1972, pp 381–82.
56 Thomas to Nickle, 3 Dec, 1854, PROV 1085/P Unit 8, duplicate 162, enclosure no 7.
57 D Wickham, *Deaths at Eureka*, Wickham, Ballarat, 1996, p 29.
58 Carboni, *The Eureka Stockade*, p 96.
59 An informed estimate is that about 5 per cent of rounds fired during this era actually hit a target during battle: see BP Hughes, *Firepower: Weapons' Effectiveness on the Battlefield 1630–1850*, Arms & Armour Press, London, 1974.
60 Carboni, *The Eureka Stockade*, p 97.
61 Carboni, *The Eureka Stockade*, p 64.
62 Lynch, *Story of the Eureka Stockade*, p 30.
63 Journal of Samuel Huyghue, 'The Ballarat Riots 1854', SLV, MS7725 Box 646/9.
64 Withers, *History of Ballarat*, p 117.
65 Carboni, *The Eureka Stockade* , p 64.
66 Huyghue, journal.
67 Turner, *Our Own Little Rebellion*, p 72.
68 G Hocking, *Eureka Stockade: The Events Leading up to the Attack in the Pre-Dawn of 3 December 1854*, Five Mile Press, Melbourne, 2004, p 138.
69 See H Strachan, *From Waterloo to Balaclava: Tactics, Technology and the British Army 1815–1854*, CUP, Cambridge, 1985.
70 Pasley, letters to his father.
71 For a discussion of just what may have led to this action see: Blake, *Eureka Stockade*, pp 148–49.
72 Lynch, *Story of the Eureka Stockade*, p 30.
73 Carboni, *The Eureka Stockade*, p 64.
74 Huyghue, journal.
75 Supreme Court of Victoria Library, *R v Joseph*, pp 24 & 35; *R v Hayes*, p 76.
76 Thomas to Nickle, 3 Dec 1854, PROV 1085/P Unit 8, duplicate 162, enclosure no 7.
77 Supreme Court of Victoria Library, *R v Joseph*, pp 21 & 24; Carboni, *The*

Eureka Stockade, p 64.
78 Withers, *History of Ballarat*, p 124.
79 There is much conjecture about when Wise fell: see Blake, *Eureka Stockade*, pp 155–56.
80 Thomas to Nickle, 3 Dec 1854, PROV 1085/P Unit 8, duplicate 162, enclosure no 7.
81 Ferguson, *Experiences of a Forty-Niner*, p 60.
82 *Argus*, 5 Dec 1854, p 5. On the Canadians, see Blake, *Eureka Stockade*, pp 135–44 and 158–59.
83 Carboni, *The Eureka Stockade*, p 101. Ferguson (*Experiences of a Forty-Niner*, p 60) relates how he was standing next to Ross at the height of the battle when Ross was hit.
84 Withers, *History of Ballarat*, p 98.
85 UK National Archives, WO12/5365 and SLV AJCP M2580 notes the death of Private Denis Brien killed in action at Eureka. Brien's fate was not included in the original report sent by Thomas to Nickle and thus his death is overlooked by most Eureka story-tellers. *The Eureka Encyclopaedia* (J Corfield, D Wickham and C Gervasoni (eds), Ballarat Heritage Services, Ballarat, 2004, p 247) notes the case of Private James Hammond, who died while being taken to Geelong on a cart immediately after the batle.
86 Such stories can only be viewed with scepticism. Carboni (*The Eureka Stockade*, p 100) specifically mentions Thomas treating him with respect when he met him at that time. Pasley (letters to his father) describes using the threat of his pistol to restrain excited soldiery from mistreating prisoners post-battle. Given these actions and the respected service records of Thomas and Pasley, as well as police Sub-Inspector Carter, it is most unlikely that such officers would have tolerated for one moment the deliberate murder of diggers by burning them alive. For Thomas's service record in Afghanistan and India see RH Smythies, *Historical Records of the 40th (2nd Somersetshire) Regiment now 1st Battalion The Prince of Wales's Volunteers (South Lancashire Regiment) From its Formation, 1717, to 1893*, AH Swiss, Devonport (UK), 1894. For a critical examination of the Eureka massacre myth see Blake, *Eureka Stockade*, pp 175–90.
87 Huyghue, journal.
88 *Eureka Reminiscences*, p 70.

5 Australian naval defence Greg Swinden

1 C Jones, *Australian Colonial Navies*, AWM, Canberra, 1986, p 13.
2 B Nicholls, *Bluejackets and Boxers: Australia's Naval Expedition to the Boxer Uprising*, Allen & Unwin, Sydney, 1986, p 11.
3 Nicholls, *Bluejackets and Boxers*, p 37.

6 Australians in the New Zealand Wars Damien Fenton

1 For more detail on Māori traditional society and warfare and the impact that early European contact had on both, see A Ballara, *Taua: 'Musket Wars', 'Land Wars' or Tikanga? Warfare in Māori Society in the Early Nineteenth Century*, Penguin, Auckland, 2003.
2 RS Hill, *The History of Policing in New Zealand, Policing the Colonial Frontier:*

Part 1, Historical Publications Branch, Department of Internal Affairs, Wellington, 1986, pp 152–53.
3   For more on Māori entrepreneurship with early European traders, including organised prostitution, see J Belich, *Making Peoples: A History of the New Zealanders from Polynesian Settlement to the End of the Nineteenth Century*, Penguin, Auckland, 1996, pp 148–55.
4   Belich, *Making Peoples*, p 157; see also see Ballara, *Taua*; and R Crosby, *The Musket Wars: A History of Inter-Iwi Conflict 1806–1845*, Reed Books, Auckland, 1999.
5   See Elsdon Best, 'The Pa Māori', *Dominion Museum Bulletin*, no 6, New Zealand Government Printer, Wellington,1927; also I Knight, *Māori Fortifications*, Osprey, Oxford, 2009.
6   Belich, *Making Peoples*, pp 198–201.
7   See O Wilson, *Kororareka & Others Essays*, John McIndoe, Dunedin, 1990. For the darker side of early European contact in the Bay of Islands, see R Wolfe, *Hell-hole of the Pacific: The Story of Kororareka*, Penguin, Auckland, 2005.
8   P Adam, *Fatal Necessity: British Intervention in New Zealand 1830–1847*, Auckland University Press, Auckland, 1977.
9   Wolfe, *Hell-hole of the Pacific*, p 98.
10   For more detail and background to these events, see Adams, *Fatal Necessity*.
11   Hill, *History of Policing in New Zealand*, pp 125–27.
12   Adams, *Fatal Necessity*.
13   J Hopkins-Wiesse, *Blood Brothers: The Anzac Genesis*, Penguin, Auckland, 2009, p 26.
14   Hill, *History of Policing in New Zealand*, pp 125–30.
15   See Belich, *Making Peoples*, pp 29–70.
16   On the evolution of the name 'New Zealand Wars', see D Green, *Battlefields of the New Zealand Wars*, Penguin, Auckland, 2010, pp 12–13.
17   T Ryan & B Parham, *The Colonial New Zealand Wars*, Grantham House, Wellington, 1986, pp 159–61.
18   From I McGibbon (ed), *The Oxford Companion to New Zealand Military History*, OUP, Auckland, 2000, p 70. For a comparative listing of British infantry regiments in Australia, see P Dennis *et al* (eds), *The Oxford Companion to Australian Military History*, 2nd edn, OUP, Melbourne, 2008, p 108.
19   J Belich, *The New Zealand Wars and the Victorian Interpretation of Racial Conflict*, Auckland UP, Auckland, 1986, pp 75–80.
20   Green, *Battlefields*, p 88.
21   Belich, *New Zealand Wars*, pp 78–80.
22   Dennis, *Oxford Companion to Australian Military History*, p 552.
23   F Glen, *Australians at War in New Zealand*, Wilsonscott, Christchurch, 2011, p 28.
24   The key aspects of the Act in this regard are articles 14 and 17: see Victorian Historical Acts database on the Australasian Legal Information Institute website: <www.austlii.edu.au/au/legis/vic/hist_act/aatpftbradoavitsohmlgiv1193.pdf> (viewed 4 April 2013).
25   McGibbon, *Oxford Companion*, p 203.
26   Glen, *Australians at War*, pp 32–37, 41.
27   Glen, *Australians at War*, p 34.

28 Belich, *New Zealand Wars*, p 108.
29 Belich, *New Zealand Wars*, pp 47–52, 105–107.
30 Belich, *New Zealand Wars*, pp 108–113.
31 Belich, *New Zealand Wars*, pp 106, 114–16.
32 Glen, *Australians at War*, pp 37–38.
33 For more on Grey, see E Bohan, *To Be a Hero: A Biography of George Grey*, HarperCollins, Auckland, 1998.
34 Belich, *New Zealand Wars*, pp 129–30.
35 J Alexander, *Bush Fighting: The Māori War in New Zealand*, 1st pub 1875, Capper Press, Christchurch, 1973, appx 3, p 331; Belich, *New Zealand Wars*, p 126.
36 *Statistics of New Zealand for 1860 Compiled from Official Records*, Government Printer, Auckland, 1861, table 1. By comparison, the total Māori population of the North Island in 1861 is estimated to have been no more than 50 000: Green, *Battlefields*, p 14.
37 McGibbon, *Oxford Companion*, pp 331–32.
38 McGibbon, *Oxford Companion*, pp 331–32.
39 McGibbon, *Oxford Companion*, pp 103–104.
40 See Belich, *The New Zealand Wars*, pp 211–13; Stowers, *New Zealand Medal*, pp 63, 74–75.
41 See *The Royal New Zealand Fencibles 1847–1852*, Royal New Zealand Fencible Society, Auckland, 2009.
42 Glen, *Australians at War*, pp 61–62.
43 Hopkins-Wiesse, *Blood Brothers*, appx A & B, pp 245–46.
44 Belich, *New Zealand Wars*, p 18.
45 Hopkins-Wiesse, *Blood Brothers*, appx C, pp 250–51.
46 *Statistics of New Zealand for 1863 Compiled from Official Records*, Government Printer, Auckland, 1864, table 2, Immigration and Emigration (overseas).
47 Glen, *Australians at War*, pp 66–67.
48 Glen gives a total of 2400 enlistments in the military settler scheme, while Hopkins-Wiesse gives a figure of 2500 but estimates that up to 3000 Australian served if those who enlisted in other New Zealand colonial units (presumably including miners recruited in Otago) are taken in to account: see Glen, *Australians at War*, p 142; Hopkins-Wiesse, *Blood Brothers*, pp 236–37.
49 Glen, *Australians at War*, pp 134–35.
50 The *Argus* reporter was Howard Willoughby (born in England in 1839 and migrated to Victoria in 1857), who arrived in New Zealand onboard the troopship *Himalaya* in mid-November 1863. The identity of Willoughby's colleague from the *Sydney Morning Herald* remains unknown. Whoever it was began reporting from New Zealand in September 1863, two months before Willoughby's arrival, and was therefore Australia's first war correspondent: see Glen, *Australians at War*, pp 120–21; Hopkins-Weise, *Blood Brothers*, pp 118–19.
51 Belich, *New Zealand Wars*, p 133.
52 Glen, *Australians at War*, pp 83–97; Hopkins-Wiesse, *Blood Brothers*, pp 123–45.
53 The Great Southern Road exists today as State Highway 1, and the route between Auckland and Hamilton is largely unchanged (the odd spaghetti-

junction not withstanding): a measure of its importance to New Zealand then and in the intervening 150 years.
54 For the details of these campaigns see Belich, *The New Zealand Wars*, pp 142–200.
55 This compares to total British combat losses for 1863–1865 of 182 killed in action, 59 died of wounds and 506 wounded in action. Colonial troops accounted for 73 of these casualties, including 25 dead: see Alexander, *Bush Fighting*, appx 3, p 331. Alexander's figures do not include the years 1866 and 1867 so we shouldn't think that 21 of the 25 colonial dead were Australian military settlers as the former figure includes 1866–1867. Modern consensus suggests a figure of 750–800 total European war dead for the New Zealand Wars (including civilians) and approximately 2200–2300 Māori (both anti- and pro-government). Total figure re wounded or those who died of war-related disease and accidents is unknown: see Green, *Battlefields*, pp 13–14.
56 Hopkins-Wiesse, *Blood Brothers*, pp 254–55.
57 Glen, *Australians at War*, pp 221–22.
58 Glen, *Australians at War*, pp 75–76.
59 Glen, *Australians at War*, pp 186, 210–19; Hopkins-Wiesse, *Blood Brothers*, pp 166–67, 171–72.
60 Two more warrior-prophets, Titokawaru and Te Kooti, took up arms in 1868, respectively plunging Taranaki and an area comprising the east coast, Hawke's Bay and the Ureweras back into guerilla-style conflict yet again. Only in 1872 did the fighting end once and for all. For detailed accounts of these later campaigns see Belich, *The New Zealand Wars*, pp 203–90; J Belich, *'I Shall Not Die': Titokowaru's War 1868–1869*, Allen & Unwin, Wellington, 1989; J Cowan, *The New Zealand Wars: Volume 2: The Hauhau Wars 1864–1872*, Government Printer, Wellington, 1923; R Crosby, *Gilbert Mair: Te Kooti's Nemesis*, Reed, Auckland, 2004.
61 McGibbon, *Oxford Companion*, pp 3–36, 69–70.
62 Hopkins-Weise, *Blood Brothers*, pp 221–30.
63 Glen, *Australians at War*, p 223.
64 EM Hodder, 'Publicising the sources: Australians in the Waikato War', in *The Volunteers: The Journal of the New Zealand Military Historical Society*, 9(1), June 1982, pp 3–7; R Stowers, *New Zealand Medal to Colonials*, 8th edn, Richard Stowers, Hamilton, 2005.

7 **The rifle clubs** Andrew Kilsby

1 The Adelaide Rifle Company began in 1838, while the first recorded rifle club in NSW formed in Parramatta in 1843 and held its annual prize shoot each January from 1844. The Adelaide German Shooting Company (The Adelaider Deutsche Schuetzen Gesellshaft) was formed in 1853 with another formed in Tanunda in 1856, while some rifle clubs in Tasmania had formed as early as 1858. V Potezny, 'South Australian German shooting companies (kingship and ring target shooting)', unpublished MS provided to A Kilsby, Feb 2010. See also *Mercury*, 16 July 1858, p 2; 23 July 1858, p 2.
2 C Halls, *Guns in Australia*, Paul Hamlyn, Sydney, 1974, p 130.
3 J Hopkins-Weise, *Blood Brothers: The Anzac Genesis*, Wakefield Press, Adelaide,

2009, pp 105–109.
4   Anon, 'The National Rifle Association', *MacMillan's Magazine*, 93, July 1867, p 180.
5   For example, the committee of the Victorian Rifle Association (VRA), formed on 14 Dec 1860, was stacked with a formidable range of dignitaries and Volunteer officers. The president was the colonial governor, while the committee included the parliamentary speaker, the chief justice and a future chief justice, the chief secretary, the treasurer, nine Legislative Council and Assembly MPs and the Volunteer commander, his senior commanders and a host of junior staff officers. Rifle associations were formed in most colonies by the 1870s, except in Western Australia where its its population of just over 3000 men in the early 1860s was barely enough to keep a few small units of Volunteers in being. It would not form a single rifle association until 1910.
6   *Report of the Council of the Victorian Rifle Association for the eight months ending on 28th February 1871*, Govt Printer, Melbourne, 1871, p 19.
7   See *Australian Dictionary of Biography*, vol 4, p 130.
8   This was for all intents and purposes, the first intercolonial commandants' conference, and informally rifle clubs and associations were almost certainly discussed, for it is more than coincidence that from about 1892 commandants seemed to be sending the same message to associations to put more service-style matches into the annual prize meetings.
9   Edwards saw rifle clubs as the 'ready reserve' and recommended their extension across the country. For example in Queensland, Edwards strongly recommended that rifle clubs 'be placed on a more definite footing'. See 'Report of Major-General Edwards, CB, upon the local forces and defences of Queensland, with scheme for the organization of the military forces of the Australian colonies', *Queensland Parliament Report CA 99-1889, 9th October 1889*, Govt Printer, Brisbane, 1889.
10 *Australian Dictionary of Biography*, vol 9, pp 415–18.
11 *Report of the New South Wales National Rifle Association for the year 1895*, Govt Printer, Sydney, 1896, p 60.
12 PS Lang, *Index to the Minute Books of the Victorian Rifle Association 1873–1906*, Haase Printer, Melbourne, 1906, p 36.
13 Report of the Council of Defence [Victoria], Govt Printer, Melbourne, 1885, p 16; see also *Argus*, 7 Sept 1885, p 10.
14 *Report of the Victorian Rifle Association for the Year 1886*, Sloane collection, provided to the author by Alex Sloane, 2009.
15 Report of the Council of Defence [Victoria], Govt Printer, Melbourne, 1898, p 14; *Queensland Defence Scheme, Corrected to 4th January 1898*, Govt Printer, Brisbane, 1898, p 7.
16 *Report of the Victorian Rifle Association meeting 1900*, Hewitt, Melbourne, 1900.
17 *Argus*, 6 March 1902, p 6.
18 'Military Forces of the Commonwealth: Minute upon the defence of Australia by Major-General Hutton, Commandant', *Commonwealth of Australia Parliamentary Papers*, vol 2, Govt Printer, Melbourne, 1902, p 2; see also *Argus*, 24 April 1902, p 7.
19 'Report of the Council of Defence', *Victorian Parliamentary Papers*, vol 2, Govt Printer, Melbourne, 1900, p 9.

20 'Statement of strengths: Defence Forces of Commonwealth 18 July 1901', *Commonwealth Parliamentary Papers: House of Representatives*, vol 2, 1901.
21 As early as July 1902, only 100 Victorian riflemen were turning up for drill; numbers did not increase: see *Argus*, 9 July 1902, p 6.
22 *Argus*, 7 Nov 1904, p 6.
23 *Advertiser*, 16 Nov 1904, p 7.
24 'Military Forces: Return showing numbers in the several States, 21 Nov 1905', *Parliament of the Commonwealth of Australia*, session 1905, vol 2, report 57, Govt Printer Victoria, 1906, p 325.
25 This was Alexander Ferguson, also a member of the Queensland Rifle Association's council: 'Military Order 32 of 11th May 1905', *Index to Military Orders 1905*, Govt Printer Victoria, 1906.
26 General Order 162, 13 Sept 1902, *Military Forces of the Commonwealth: Index to General Orders for 1902*, Govt Printer, Melbourne, 1903.
27 H Dakin, 'The rifle clubs and national defence', *The Call*, 8 Aug 1906, p 13.
28 *Australian Dictionary of Biography*, vol 7, pp 548–49.
29 *Australian Dictionary of Biography*, vol 11, pp 344–45.
30 *Sydney Morning Herald*, 8 Nov 1906, p 7.
31 General Order 299, 11 Dec 1906, *Military Forces of the Commonwealth: General Orders for 1906*, Govt Printer, Melbourne, 1907.
32 C Stockings, *The Torch and the Sword*, UNSW Press, Sydney, 2007, p 51.
33 *Advertiser*, 20 March 1908, p 6.
34 *Argus*, 13 April 1908, p 9; 11 May 1908, p 5.
35 *West Australian*, 29 Jan 1909, p 9.
36 *Brisbane Courier*, 11 Sept 1909, p 4; *Argus*, 4 Oct 1909, p 5.
37 H Kitchener, *Memorandum on the Defence of Australia*, Govt Printer, Melbourne, 1910, pp 8–12.
38 *Advertiser*, 24 Aug 1912, p 7.
39 *Advertiser*, 28 March 1911, p 8.
40 I Hamilton, *Report on an Inspection of the Military Forces of the Commonwealth of Australia*, Govt Printer, Melbourne, 1913, pp 14–16.
41 *Sydney Morning Herald*, 14 July 1914, p 9.
42 *Sydney Morning Herald*, 13 July 1914, p 11.
43 Report on the State Rifle Associations, District Rifle Club Unions, and Rifle Clubs for the year ended 30 June 1914, *Parliament of the Commonwealth of Australia*, 2 Dec 1914, Govt Printer, Melbourne, 1914, pp 1–8.
44 Report on the State Rifle Associations, District Rifle Club Unions, and Rifle Clubs for the year ended 30 June 1914, p 7.

8 Australia's boy soldiers: The army cadet movement
Craig Stockings

1 P Kitney, 'The history of the Australian school cadet movement to 1893', *Defence Force Journal*, 12, Sept–Oct 1978, p 54.
2 *South Australian Government Gazette*, 4 Dec 1862, p 1007; CEW Bean, *Here, My Son*, Angus & Robertson, Sydney, 1950, p 56.
3 KW Bromham, 'A brief history of the school cadet corps in New South Wales: The first forty years', MEd thesis, University of Sydney, 1968, p 13; *Parramatta*

Advertiser, 19 March 1975.
4   PC Candy, *The Victorian Cadet Movement: An Outline History from 1867 to 1969*, priv pubn, Melbourne, 1969, pp 24-2 & 24-3.
5   Kitney, 'History of the Australian school cadet movement', p 54; N Pixley, 'Queensland: One hundred years of defence', *Royal Historical Society of Queensland Journal*, Sept 1959, p 102.
6   Aikenhead to Legge (1883), Archives Office of Tasmania (AOT), CSD13, item 67/1155; 'Notes on the history of the cadet corps in Tasmania', Headquarters Australian Army Cadets (HQAAC), file 123/1/32.
7   *WA Minutes, Votes & Proceedings of the Parliament* (*WAMV&P*), 1890–1891 & 1897: Reports of the Commandant of the Local Forces of Western Australia for the Years 1889, p 5 & 1897, p 4.
8   Report of the Military Acting Commandant for the Year 1899–1900, *South Australian Parliamentary Papers* (*SAPP*), 1900, vol 2, pp 3–4; DM Horner, *Prince Alfred College Cadet Unit: Extracts from Unit History*, Prince Alfred College, Adelaide, 1964, p 3; RM Gibbs, *A History of Prince Alfred College*, Peacock, Adelaide, 1984, p 137.
9   Maitland Boys High School, submission 433 to the Committee of Inquiry, in CA Laffin, 'The Australian Cadet Corps in secondary education', MEd (hons) thesis, University of Sydney, appx 2, p 289; *SMH*, 5 Aug 1873; Kitney, 'History of the Australian school cadet movement', p 55; RS Horan, *Fort Street*, Honeysett, Sydney, 1989, pp 69–70; DJ Jones, 'The military use of state schools 1872–1914', PhD thesis, La Trobe University, p 191; Deputy Chief Inspector to Commandant, 10 July 1889, State Records of NSW (SRNSW), CGS3038, item 20/12655.
10 Kitney, 'History of the Australian school cadet movement', p 56; DL Henry, 'The Victorian cadet system', *Journal of the Royal United Services Institute*, 3(7), Dec 1894, pp 5–6; Candy, *Victorian Cadet Movement*, p 24-10; C Daley, 'The story of the Victorian junior cadet corps 1855–1912', *The Victorian Historical Magazine*, 20(1), June 1943, pp 18–21; *Journal of the Australian Cadet Corps*, 2, 1951, p 51.
11 Report of the Minister for Public Instruction for the Year 1890–1891, *Victorian Parliamentary Papers* (*VPP*), 1891, vol 4, p xx & appx D(2); Report of the Minister for Public Instruction for the Year 1900–1901, *VPP*, 1901, vol 3, appx C, p 47.
12 Reports of the Commandant of the Queensland Defence Force, 1888–1889 & 1889–1890, *Qld Legislative Assembly Votes and Proceedings* (*QLAV&P*), 1889 (vol 1, p 2); 1890 (vol 3, p 278).
13 Report of the Secretary for Education for the Year 1905, *WAMV&P*, vol 2, 1906, p 71.
14 Bromham, 'Cadet corps in NSW', p 44; Report of the Minister of Public Instruction for the Year 1899, *NSW Legislative Assembly Votes & Proceedings* (*NSWLAV&P*), 1900, vol 4, p 407.
15 *Cadet Journal*, 2, 1951, pp 30 & 53; Report of the Minister for Public Instruction for the Year 1899–1900, *VPP*, 1900, vol 2, p 23.
16 Jones, 'Military use of state schools', p 299.
17 Officer Commanding Cadets to Battalion Commanders, 2 Feb 1893, SRNSW, CGS3864, item 1/2119.

18   J Kiddle & R Jukes, *Liber Melburniensis 1848–1936*, Griffin Press, Adelaide, 1965, p 740; Report of the Minister of Public Instruction for the Year 1884, *NSWJLC*, 1885, vol 34, p 15.
19   Kitney, 'History of the Australian school cadet movement', p 59; R Audley, 'New South Wales cadet encampment, August 1890', *Despatch*, vol 15, pp 64–65.
20   Candy, *Victorian Cadet Movement*, pp 24-13; Daley, 'Victorian Junior Cadet Corps', pp 18–28; Jones, 'Military use of state schools', p 299.
21   Candy, *Victorian Cadet Movement*, pp 24-13.
22   Sydney Grammar School, *The Sydneian*, 1957, p 49.
23   Bromham, 'Cadet corps in NSW', p 16.
24   Candy, *Victorian Cadet Movement*, p 24-11; Officer Commanding Cadets to Department of Education (Victoria), 18 Nov 1899, Public Records Office of Victoria (PROV), series 794, item 947.
25   Kitney, 'History of the Australian school cadet movement', pp 54–55.
26   Henry, 'Victorian cadet system', p 18.
27   Kitney, 'History of the Australian school cadet movement', p 556; Notes on the history of the cadet corps in Tasmania, HQAAC, file 123/1/32.
28   Report by the Commandant on the Reorganisation of the Defence Force, *Tasmania, Journals & Papers of Parliament* (*TJPP*), 1884, vol 3, p 3.
29   Bromham, 'Cadet corps in NSW', pp 3–5.
30   Aikenhead to Legge, 1883, AOT, CSD13, 67/1155.
31   MJ Lee and SJ Williams, 'A history of St Peter's College cadet unit', unpublished, 1963, p 1.
32   Candy, *Victorian Cadet Movement*, p 24-13.
33   GA French, *Federal Military Conference*, 1901, Government Printer, Sydney, 1901, pp 7 & 41.
34   Extract from *Regulations under the Defence Act* 1903–1912, National Archives of Australia (NAA), series A1194, item 12.11/4338; Notes on the *Defence Act* 1909, NAA, A5954, 1282/1; TW Tanner, 'The introduction of compulsory military training in Australia 1901–1914', *Armidale and District Historical Society Journal & Proceedings*, 10, 1967, p 21.
35   ETH Hutton, 'Minute upon the Defence of Australia', 7 April 1902, *Commonwealth Parliamentary Papers* (*CPP*), 1901–02, vol 2, p 58.
36   Report upon the military forces of the Commonwealth, 1 May 1903, *CPP*, 1903, vol 2, pp 62–64.
37   Department of Defence, Conference, 1905, p 1.
38   *Official Yearbook of the Commonwealth of Australia* (*Commonwealth Yearbook*), no 1 (1908), p 894; Report of the Minister for Public Instruction for the year 1906, *NSWLAV&P*, 1907, vol 1, p 50.
39   Report of the Minister of Public Instruction for the Year 1900, *NSWLAV&P*, 1901, vol 3, appx 17, p 101; A Fisher, *Commonwealth Parliamentary Debates* (*CPD*), vol 15, 7 Aug 1903, pp 3268–73.
40   Report of the Minister of Public Instruction for the Year 1893, *NSWJLC*, 1894, vol 52, p 24; Memoranda of the Minister of State for Defence on the Estimates for the Financial Years 1908–1909 & 1909–1910, *CPP*, 1908, vol 2, p 353 & 1909, vol 2, p 116.
41   'Report of the Inspector General Commonwealth Military Forces for 1907',

NAA, A1194, 20.15/6697; 'Report of the Director General of Cadets for 1908', NAA, MP84/1, 1832/1/296.
42 *Mercury*, 19 Aug 1907, NAA, MP84/1, 1532/1/14; 'Cadet weapon returns schedules (NSW) (1909)', NAA CP697/41, 1912/12; Army Headquarters, internal memo, Nov 1910, NAA, MP84/1, 332/14/14.
43 Report of the Director-General for the Year ending 30 June 1909, *CPP*, 1909, vol 2, p 468.
44 Jones, 'Military use of state schools', p 447.
45 A study of the Junior Cadet component of this scheme is outside the scope of this chapter since, as a non-uniformed, classroom-based activity they were positioned outside the definition of true cadets: see Notes on the Defence Act 1909, NAA, A5954, 1282/1; K White, 'Compulsory military training in Australia in 1914', *Sabretache*, 18, 18 Jan 1977, p 16.
46 Tanner, 'Compulsory military training', p 27; HH Kitchener, *Memorandum on the Defence of Australia*, Government Printer, p 11.
47 Staff and Regimental Lists of the Military Cadet Forces (1911), NAA, A1194, 03.06/1536.
48 Notes of lectures by Lieutenant Colonel JG Legge (1911), NAA, A1194, 12.11/4880; *Commonwealth Yearbook*, no 4 (1911), p 1085.
49 NM Brazier, *Australian Military Journal*, 5(3), 1914, p 450; 26th Senior Cadet Battalion Quarterly Training Program (1925), Australian War Memorial (AWM), series 62, item 55/3/226; Kitchener, *Memorandum*, p 6.
50 *CPD*, vol 42, 13 Dec 1907, p 7528.
51 *CPD*, vol 41, 7 Nov 1907, p 5683; Pearce & Carpenter to Cabinet, p 207. A similar social agenda would be enunciated during the 1950s National Service scheme: see Grey, *Australian Army*, p 182.
52 *CPD*, vol 41, 7 Nov 1907, p 5684.
53 Army Headquarters, Notes on Senior Cadet Training 1911–18 (table), NAA, A5954, 895/9; Ballarat High School, *The Minervan*, 1915, p 15; Senior Cadet Battalion Training Programs (various) (1925), AWM, 62, 55/3/226.
54 Army Headquarters to ANA, Aug 1911, NAA, MP84/1, 1964/1/7; *Commonwealth Yearbook*, no 9 (1916), p 977; Report on the progress of universal training (1912), NAA, A5954, 1208/7, p 8.
55 Department of Defence, Report of the Conference of Militia Officers 22–25 Oct 1912, Government Printer, 1912, p 10; Reports of the Inspector General of the Australian Military Forces, 1912, p 13 & 1913, p 13, NAA, A1194, 20.25/6698 & 20.15/6699.
56 Brighton Grammar School, *Grammarian*, 1912, p 48; JA Goldsmith, 'Suggestions for improvement in cadet training', *Australian Military Journal*, 5, July 1914, p 468.
57 Adjutant General to Military Board, Dec 1911, NAA, MP84/1, 1832/13/486; Goldsmith, 'Suggestions', pp 470–75.
58 Report of Senior Cadet Parade of 30 March 1912, NAA, MP84/1, 139/3/89.
59 Goldsmith, 'Suggestions', pp 479–80.
60 TW Tanner, *Compulsory Citizen Soldiers*, Maxwell Printing, Sydney, 1980, p 185.
61 Army Headquarters to Military Commandants, 18 Sept 1911, NAA, D845, 1911/28; *Commonwealth Yearbook*, no 9 (1916), p 983; Department of Defence,

Report of the Conference of Militia Officers 1912, Government Printer, 1912, p 11.
62 Army Headquarters to Attorney-General, Feb–March 1912, NAA, A6006, 1911/12/31; Minister for Defence to Attorney General, July–Sept 1912, NAA, MP84/1, 1939/3/130.
63 Army Headquarters to Military Commandants, Jan 1913, NAA, MP84/1, 1939/3/219; Report of Cadet Training in Area 5A, Nov 1918, NAA, MP376/1, 629/16/1176.
64 J Barrett, *Falling In: Australians and Boy Conscription 1911–1915*, Hale & Iremonger, Sydney, 1979, p 2.
65 Tanner, *Compulsory Citizen Soldiers*, pp 322 & 411.
66 Department of Defence, *Report of the Minister of Defence on the Progress of Universal Training (to 30 June, 1912)*, Government Printer, 1912, p. 7; 'Industrial Workers of the World' (pamphlet), 1912, NAA, MP84/1, 2020/1/41; Minutes of Meeting between Minister of Public Instruction and Women's Peace Army, 8 Feb 1917, Queensland State Archives, series RSI15191, item 1-430.
67 Military Board Order 146 of 1930, AWM, 61, 426/1/177.

9 Australians in the wars in Sudan and South Africa
Craig Wilcox

1 *Sydney Morning Herald*, 21 Feb 1885, p 11.
2 *Letters by the Late Lieut Colonel Coveny*, priv pubn, Sydney [1885?], pp 10, 33.
3 *Freeman's Journal*, 21 Feb 1885, p 14.
4 These attitudes are reflected in two folktale versions of history filmed at the time: *Breaker Morant*, directed by Bruce Beresford and released in March 1980, and *Gallipoli*, directed by Peter Weir and released in Aug 1981.
5 *Empire* (Sydney), 8 Sept 1851, p 3.
6 For the remount trade see MJ Kennedy, *Hauling the Loads: A History of Australia's Working Horses and Bullocks*, MUP, Melbourne, 1992, ch 9.
7 JM Epps (ed), *The Chambers Letters*, Quadcolour, Sydney, 1997, p 220.
8 E Hickson (ed), *Blanche: An Australian Diary*, John Ferguson, Sydney, 1980, p 225.
9 H Thring, *Suggestions for Colonial Reform*, Stevens & Haynes, London, 1865, p 23.
10 RA Preston, *Canada and Imperial Defense*, Duke University Press, Durham NC, 1967, p 23.
11 *Hansard's Parliamentary Debates* (UK), 3rd series, vol 165, col 1060, 4 March 1862.
12 G Bowen, *Thirty Years of Colonial Government*, Longman, London, 1889, vol 1, p 82.
13 BA Knox, 'Colonial influence on imperial policy 1856–1866', *Historical Studies*, 11(41), Nov 1963, p 77.
14 *Freeman's Journal*, 23 June 1883, p 13.
15 *Singleton Argus*, 21 Nov 1883, p 2; *Kilmore Free Press*, 10 Dec 1885, p 4; *Sydney Morning Herald*, 17 June 1885, p 5.
16 *Manchester Guardian*, 7 April 1884, p 5.

Notes to pages 211–19

17 *Argus* (Melbourne), 19 Sept 1882, p 5.
18 TE Kebbel, *Selected Speeches of the Late Right Honourable the Earl of Beaconsfield*, Longmans Green, London, 1882, vol 2, p 530.
19 GR Parkin, *Imperial Federation*, Macmillan, London, 1892, p 199.
20 JCR Colomb, *The Defence of Great and Greater Britain*, Stanford, London, 1880, pp 107–108.
21 T Walker, 'Oration on Mr Dalley's offer of troops for the Soudan campaign', Lee & Ross, Sydney, 1885, SLNSW, DSM 042/P28.
22 R Thomson, *Australian Nationalism*, Sydney, 1888, reprod in N Meaney (ed), *Australia and the World: A Documentary History from the 1870s to the 1970s*, Longman Cheshire, Melbourne, 1985, p 90.
23 KS Inglis, *The Rehearsal: Australians in the Sudan 1885*, Weldon, Sydney, 1985, p 25; see also *Argus* (Melbourne), 24 Dec 1879, p 6; 27 Dec 1879, p 8.
24 IFW Beckett, *The Amateur Military Tradition 1558–1945*, Manchester University Press, Manchester, 1991, p 183; P Pigott, *Canada in Sudan*, Dundurn, Toronto, 2009, ch 3.
25 *Sydney Morning Herald*, 2 March 1885, p 11.
26 M Saunders, *Britain, the Australian Colonies and the Sudan Campaigns of 1884–1885*, University of New England, Armidale, 1985, ch 5.
27 *Sydney Morning Herald*, 21 Feb 1885, p 11.
28 *Parliamentary Debates* (NSW), 1st series, vol 16, p 39, 17 March 1885.
29 *Sydney Morning Herald*, 29 April 1885, p 10.
30 *Sydney Morning Herald*, 28 April 1885, p 7.
31 'Further Employment of Sudan Contingent', *Legislative Assembly Votes & Proceedings* (NSW), 1885, vol 2, no 12; see also Inglis, *The Rehearsal*, pp 120–23.
32 Quoted in *Launceston Examiner*, 19 May 1885, p 2.
33 File note by R Herbert, 8 Nov 1890, National Archives (UK), f 475, CO 309/135.
34 Tryon to Loch, 27 March 1885, in NA Lambert, *Australia's Naval Inheritance: Imperial Maritime Strategy and the Australia Station 1880–1909*, RAN Maritime Studies Program, Canberra, 1998, pp 65–70.
35 M Hooper, 'The Naval Defence Agreement of 1887', *Australian Journal of Politics and History*, 14(1), April 1968, p 74.
36 On the commandants see SJ Clarke, 'Marching to their own drum: British Army officers as military commandants in the Australian colonies and New Zealand 1870–1901', doctoral thesis, University of NSW Australian Defence Force Academy, 1999, esp ch 6.
37 *Parliamentary Debates* (NSW), 1st series, vol 73, p 1363, 16 Oct 1894.
38 C Wilcox, *Red Coat Dreaming: How Colonial Australia Embraced the British Army*, CUP, Melbourne, 2009, ch 9.
39 Nathan, minute, 11 July 1898, National Archives (UK), WO 32/6365; Methuen to Roberts, 22 September 1900, WO 105/25; Mackay to NSW Governor, 18 July 1899, CO 201/625; Colonial Defence Committee memorandum, 30 March 1901, *Commonwealth Parliamentary Papers*, 1901–02, vol 2, no 31, pp 10–11.
40 JL Mordike, *An Army for a Nation: A History of Australian Military Developments 1880–1914*, Allen & Unwin, Sydney, 1992, p 53.

41 Proceedings of 1897 Colonial Conference, *Parliamentary Papers* (UK), 1897, vol 49, no C8596, p 8.
42 Report on 1897 Colonial Conference, in Meaney, *Australia and the World*, p 116.
43 Precis of papers on interchange of military units, 3 Aug 1898, National Archives (UK), cab 11/124.
44 C Wilcox, *The New South Wales Lancers in England and South Africa 1899: An Episode in Imperial Federation*, Menzies Centre for Australian Studies, London, 2000.
45 Chamberlain to NSW Governor, 3 Oct 1899, in 'First and other contingents to South Africa', 5 Dec 1901, *Legislative Assembly Votes & Proceedings* (NSW), 1901, vol 3, no 559, p 42.
46 See Davies' newspaper obituaries at the National Centre for Biography website, <www.oa.anu.edu.au>.
47 For longer accounts of Australian engagement in the war which this and subsequent passages condense see C Wilcox, 'Australia's involvement in the Boer War: Imperial pressure or colonial realpolitik?', in JA Moses and C Pugsley (eds), *The German Empire and Britain's Pacific Dominions 1871–1919*, Regina, Claremont CA, 2000, pp 197–220; and C Wilcox, *Australia's Boer War*, OUP, Melbourne, 2002.
48 The second of two requests, 3 Oct 1899, is reproduced in LM Field, *The Forgotten War: Australian Involvement in the South African Conflict of 1899–1902*, MUP, Melbourne, 1979, p 192.
49 A Griffith, 'The facts about the Transvaal', *Worker* (Sydney), 1902, pp 23–24.
50 CN Connolly, 'Manufacturing spontaneity: The Australian offers of troops for the Boer War', *Historical Studies*, 18(70), April 1978, pp 106–117; Field, *Forgotten War*, ch 1.
51 *Bulletin* (Sydney), 10 Feb 1900, p 6.
52 *Brisbane Courier*, 15 February 1900, pp. 5–6.
53 *Brisbane Courier*, 3 March 1900, p. 6.
54 Wilcox, 'Australia's Involvement in the Boer War', pp. 217–19.
55 See eg *Sydney Morning Herald*, 24 Oct 1900, p 7; *Mercury* (Hobart), 21 Nov 1900, p 2; *Daily Telegraph* (Sydney), 5 Dec 1901, p 5.
56 For the Australian contribution to the war in China see B Nicholls, *Bluejackets and Boxers*, Allen & Unwin, Sydney, 1986; and J Corfield (ed), *The Australian Illustrated Encyclopaedia of the Boxer Uprising 1899–1901*, Slouch Hat, Melbourne, 2001.
57 *The Times*, 4 Oct 1900, p 6.
58 A Deakin, *Federated Australia: Selections from Letters to the 'Morning Post' 1900–1910*, MUP, Melbourne, 1968, p 26.
59 Wilcox, *Australia's Boer War*, pp 87, 272–74.
60 Despatches on Boer prisoners, March–June 1901, National Archives, CO 418/9 and CO 418/14.
61 File on Imperial Light Horse recruiting, Dec 1901–June 1902, NAA, item 1902/25/154, series A8.
62 Wilcox, *Australia's Boer War*, pp 325–30, 336–41.
63 Wilcox, *Australia's Boer War*, pp 187–88, 314–16, 322–24.
64 The customary count of 16 000 or so volunteers double-counts Australians

who enlisted twice, and ignores the thousands of Australians who joined stateless 'irregular' regiments. For clear sketches of Australian contingents at war see M Chamberlain, *The Australians in the South African War 1899–1902: A Map History*, priv pubn, Melbourne, 1999; and, for soldiers' experiences, M Chamberlain and R Droogleever (eds), *The War with Johnny Boer: Australians in the Boer War 1899–1902*, Australian Military History Publications, Sydney, 2003.
65 JHM Abbott, *Tommy Cornstalk*, Longmans Green, London, 1902, p 213.
66 See eg *Chronicle* (Adelaide), 3 Nov 1900, p 11; *Northern Star* (Lismore), 15 Dec 1900, p 8; and *Cumberland Argus*, 13 Jan 1901, p 4. For a note of unease, or at least mockery of Cox, see Cox scrapbook, SLNSW, f. 43, ML MSS 7903.
67 G Souter, *Lion and Kangaroo: The Initiation of Australia 1901–1919*, Collins, Sydney, 1976, ch 3.
68 For typical comment on Morant see *Freeman's Journal*, 12 April 1902, p 19; on the accomplice see A Davey (ed), *Breaker Morant and the Bushveldt Carbineers*, Van Riebeeck Society, Cape Town, 1987, ch 7.
69 See esp P Dennis et al, *The Oxford Companion to Australian Military History*, 2nd edn, OUP, Melbourne, 2008, p 176.
70 AB Paterson, 'Our own flag', 1900, in R Campbell and P Harvie (eds), *Singer of the Bush: AB (Banjo) Paterson Complete Works 1885–1900*, Lansdowne, Sydney, 1983, pp 685–86.
71 Papers from 1902 Colonial Conference, *Commonwealth Parliamentary Papers* (Australia), 1903, vol 2, no 2, p 3.
72 P Kennedy, *The Rise and Fall of the Great Powers*, Hyman, London, 1989, pp 290–99 (quote p 295).
73 *Sydney Morning Herald*, 13 Oct 1902, p 7.

10 Radical nationalists and Australian invasion novels
Augustine Meaher IV

1 *Commonwealth Parliamentary Debates*, House of Representatives, vol 182, 27 Feb 1992, p 374.
2 J Curran, *The Power of Speech: Australian Prime Ministers Defining the National Image*, MUP, Melbourne, 2004, p 12.
3 M Connor, 'The secret plan to invade Sydney', *Quadrant*, Nov 2009.
4 Quoted in D Day, *The Politics of War*, HarperCollins, Sydney, 2003, p 270.
5 'Tasso Australasiatticus', *Sydney Delivered; or the Princely Buccaneer*, Australian Daily Journal, Sydney 1845, p 14.
6 AJ Morris, *The Scaremongers: The Advocacy of War and Rearmament 1896–1914*, Routledge, London, 1984, p 107.
7 None of these novels appear to have gone through a second printing, although this is not unusual in such a small publishing market.
8 William Lane, *White or Yellow? A Story of the Race War of AD 1908*, Little Darling, Sydney, 2011.
9 WH Walker, *The Invasion*, Turner and Henderson, Sydney, 1877.
10 Lane, *White or Yellow?*, p 14.
11 The best account of the effect of the Mount Rennie rape case on Australian invasion literature is D Walker, 'Shooting Mabel: Warrior masculinity and Asian invasion', *History Australia*, 2(3), 2005.

12   K Mackay, *The Yellow Wave: A Romance of the Asiatic Invasion of Australia*, Bentley, London, 1897.
13   CH Kirmess, *The Australian Crisis*, Walter Scott Publishing Co, London, 1909, p 45.
14   See entry for Mackay in *Australian Dictionary of Biography*, National Centre of Biography, ANU, <adb.anu.edu.au/biography/mackay-james-alexander-kenneth-7379/text12825>, (accessed 26 Aug 2012).
15   Rata, *The Coloured Conquest*, New South Wales Bookstall, Sydney, 1904.
16   *Examiner* (Launceston), 11 June 1909, *Register* (Adelaide), 19 June 1909, *Argus* (Melbourne), 28 May 1909, *Advertiser* (Adelaide), 28 May 1909.
17   See eg C Stockings, 'There is an idea that the Australian is a born soldier …' in Stockings (ed), *Zombie Myths of Australian Military History*, NewSouth, Sydney, 2010, p 94.
18   *Sunday Times* (Perth), 27 July 1913. *Mildura Cultivator*, 8 April 1914, *Sydney Morning Herald*, 21 July 1913, 2 Aug 1913.
19   *Barrier Miner* (Broken Hill), 8 Sept 1913.
20   'Australia looks to America', *Australian Worker*, 31 Dec 1941.

11 Edwardian transformation Craig Wilcox

1   The best recent accounts are J Grey, *A Military History of Australia*, 3d edition, CUP, Melbourne, 2008, ch 4; J Bou, 'Ambition and diversity: Developing an Australian military force 1901–1914', in P Dennis and J Grey (eds), *1911: Preliminary Moves*, Big Sky, Sydney, 2011, ch 9; and J Connor, *Anzac and Empire: George Foster Pearce and the Foundations of Australian Defence*, CUP, Melbourne, 2011, pp 13–44.
2   NK Meaney, *The Search for Security in the Pacific 1901–1914*, Sydney University Press, Sydney, 1976; JL Mordike, *An Army for a Nation: A History of Australian Military Developments 1880–1914*, Allen & Unwin, Sydney, 1992.
3   *Bulletin* (Sydney), 12 April 1902.
4   *Commonwealth Parliamentary Debates* (Australia), vol 14, p 1798, 7 July 1903.
5   See eg *Bulletin*, 5 April 1902, p 6.
6   Campbell Bannerman to Bryce, 26 Jan 1903, in JA Spender, *The Life of the Right Hon. Sir Henry Campbell-Bannerman*, Hodder & Stoughton, London, 1923, vol 2, p 88.
7   Report by the Committee of Imperial Defence, 1906, *Commonwealth Parliamentary Papers*, 1906, vol 2, no 62, p 13.
8   For rival interpretations of Hutton and resistance to his military reforms see Mordike, *Army for a Nation*, chs 7–8, and C Wilcox, 'Australia's citizen army 1889–1914', doctoral thesis, ANU, Canberra, 1993, chs 4–5.
9   *Australasian* (Melbourne), 24 May 1902, p 1199.
10   Clarke to Deakin, 1 June 1906, Deakin papers, NLA, MS1540/15/3588.
11   Meaney, *Search for Security in the Pacific*, p 64.
12   Papers from 1902 colonial conference, *Commonwealth Parliamentary Papers*, 1903, vol 2, no 2, p 3.
13   P Oliver, 'World wars and the anticipation of conflict: The impact on long-established Australian–Japanese relations 1904–1943', in P Dean (ed), *Australia 1942: In the Shadow of War*, CUP, Melbourne, 2012, pp 33–44.

14 *Herald* (Melbourne), 12 June 1905, p 3.
15 Jose to Deakin, 13 Jan 1908, Deakin papers, NLA, MS1540/15/3621-2.
16 *Commonwealth Parliamentary Debates*, vol 32, pp 2580-9, 9 Aug 1906.
17 *Sydney Morning Herald*, 8 Aug 1905, p 6.
18 On the militia between Hutton and compulsory service see C Stockings, *The Making and Breaking of the Post-Federation Army 1901–1909*, Land Warfare Studies Centre, Canberra, 2007, pp 25–27, 55–74.
19 Lyle to Campbell, 8 October 1905, NDL papers, AWM, 2DRL/1098/10.
20 *Lone Hand*, Oct 1908–Aug 1909, later published as 'CH Kirmess' [Fox], *The Australian Crisis*, Robertson, Melbourne, 1909. For the NDL see J Barrett, *Falling In: Australians and 'Boy Conscription' 1911–1915*, Hale & Iremonger, Sydney, 1979, pp 46–51.
21 Scheme for the defence of the Commonwealth of Australia, 4 Sept 1905, NAA, item S1905/181, series B173.
22 *Commonwealth Parliamentary Debates*, vol 41, p 5683, 7 Nov 1907.
23 *Commonwealth Parliamentary Debates*, vol 42, pp 7526–36, 13 Dec 1907.
24 *Argus* (Melbourne), 27 Jan 1908, p 4.
25 Neild to Campbell, 12 March 1908, NDL papers, AWM, 2DRL/1098/11.
26 *Sydney Morning Herald*, 13 June 1906, p 8.
27 *Mercury* (Hobart), 11 May 1907, p 4.
28 Fisher to Tweedmouth, 1 Oct 1907, in A Marder (ed), *Fear God and Dread Nought*, Cape, London, 1956, vol 2, p 139.
29 Fisher to Escher, 13 Sept 1909, in Marder, *Fear God and Dread Nought*, vol 2, p 266. For the Admiralty and the 1907 conference see NA Lambert (ed), *Australia's Naval Inheritance: Imperial Maritime Strategy and the Australia Station 1880–1909*, RAN Maritime Studies Program, Canberra, 1998, pp 139–51.
30 NK Meaney, 'The problem of Greater Britain and Australia's strategic crisis 1905–1914', in P Dennis and J Grey (eds) *1911: Preliminary Moves*, Big Sky, Sydney, 2011, p 64.
31 A point made by J Roger, 'The last word: The cult of the navy and the imperial age', in D Stevens and J Reeve (eds), *The Navy and the Nation: The Influence of the Navy on Modern Australia*, Allen & Unwin, Sydney, 2005, pp 62–64.
32 *Bulletin*, 27 Aug 1908, p 11; see also R Stone, 'Welcoming the fleets', *National Library of Australia News*, Aug 2004, pp 18–21, J Greenwood, 'The 1908 visit of the Great White Fleet', *History Australia*, 5(3), 2008.
33 Lord Mayor's Patriotic Dreadnought Fund cash book 1909–1919, SLNSW, A4987.
34 *Sydney Morning Herald*, 12 July 1909, p 7.
35 Meaney, *Search for Security in the Pacific*, pp 181–85.
36 Connor, *Anzac and Empire*, pp 21–22.
37 GLB Concanon, 'The psychology of a citizen company', *Commonwealth Military Journal*, Jan 1913, p 40.
38 Defence minister's report on universal training, 17 July 1912, *Commonwealth Parliamentary Papers*, 1912, vol 2, no 26, p 9.
39 For the first three years of the new militia see Wilcox, 'Australia's citizen army', ch 7.
40 GA Taylor, *Songs for Soldiers*, Building Ltd, Sydney, 1913, p 2.

41 RA Crouch, 'First steps in battalion training', *Commonwealth Military Journal*, July 1913, p 401.
42 RA Crouch, 'Richmond's early military history', *Victorian Historical Magazine*, Nov 1937, p 129.
43 C Wilcox, *For Hearths and Homes: Citizen Soldiering in Australia 1854–1945*, Allen & Unwin, Sydney, 1998, pp 65–68.
44 *Argus* (Melbourne), 27 Nov 1912, p 12.
45 GF Pearce, *Carpenter to Cabinet: Thirty Seven Years of Parliament*, Hutchinson, London, 1951, p 97.
46 W Murdoch, *The Australian Citizen: An Elementary Account of Civic Rights and Duties*, Whitcombe & Tombs, Melbourne, 1912, esp ch 20.
47 GM Kirkpatrick, portions of memoir for years 1909–1914, SLNSW, ML MSS 5708, p 276.
48 Connor, *Anzac and Empire*, p 27.
49 Watson to Campbell, 11 Sept 1911, NDL papers, AWM, 2DRL/1098/12.
50 *Commonwealth Parliamentary Debates*, vol 72, p 3644, 2 Dec 1913.
51 For a detailed account see Wilcox, 'Australia's citizen army', pp 332–39.
52 J Wattle, 'An open letter to the Honorable the Minister for Defence', *Lone Hand*, April 1911, p 442.
53 Wilcox, 'Australia's citizen army', pp 339, 342–44.
54 *Commonwealth Parliamentary Debates*, vol 72, p 4586, 17 Dec 1913.
55 Wilcox, 'Australia's citizen army', pp 339–42.
56 On the origins of Australia's air force see M Molkentin, *Fire in the Sky: The Australian Flying Corps in the First World War*, Allen & Unwin, Sydney, 2010, pp 2–11.
57 Police reports, July 1914–Jan 1915, NAA, item A4/2/183, series A2023.
58 Report on Australian military forces, 24 April 1914, *Commonwealth Parliamentary Papers*, 1914, vol 2, no 14, p 45.
59 The navy cost the federal government £1.9m in 1913-14; the military £2.7m: Meaney, *Search for Security in the Pacific*, p 277.
60 *The Times*, 10 Feb 1910, p 7.
61 *Scotsman* (Edinburgh), 26 Oct 1911, p 9.
62 *West Gippsland Gazette*, 25 March 1913, p 2.
63 *Sydney Morning Herald*, 2 Oct 1913, p 8. For the RAN's early years see memorandum by Pearce, 23 June 1913, in GL Macandie (ed), *The Genesis of the Royal Australian Navy: A Compilation*, Government Printer, Sydney, 1949, pp 278–85.
64 *Sydney Morning Herald*, 4 Oct 1913, p 9.
65 Connor, *Anzac and Empire*, p 1.
66 *Sydney Morning Herald*, 6 Oct 1913, p 8.
67 *Bairnsdale Advertiser*, 10 Oct 1913, p 3.
68 *Sydney Morning Herald*, 6 Oct 1913, p 7.
69 K Jeffrey, 'The Imperial Conference, the Committee of Imperial Defence and the continental commitment', in Dennis and Grey (eds), *1911*, pp 26–30 (quote p 27).
70 *Parliamentary Debates* (UK), 5th series, vol 59, cols 1931–35, 17 March 1914.
71 *Punch* (Melbourne), 2 April 1914, p 547.
72 *Sydney Morning Herald*, 27 Jan 1913, p 10.

73 *Commonwealth Parliamentary Debates*, vol 77, p 4100, 17 June 1915. For Australia's early munitions industry see CD Coulthard Clark, *Breaking Free: Transforming Australia's Defence Industry*, Australian Scholarly Publishing, Melbourne, 1999, pp 9–14.
74 Wilson diary, 30 May 1911, in K Jeffrey, 'The Imperial Conference', p 32. Contrasting interpretations of the 1911 conference discussions are in Meaney, *Search for Security*, ch 7; Mordike, *Army for a Nation*, pp 238–41; and Connor, *Anzac and Empire*, pp 33–34.
75 Legge to White, 25 July 1913, NAA, item 3A, series MP826/1.
76 Gordon to defence secretary, 16 June 1913, NAA, item 1855/1/6, series B197.
77 Pearce's annotations to defence scheme, c 2 August 1912, NAA, item 1856/4/156, series B197.
78 Argued in JL Mordike, *We Should Do this Thing Quietly: Japan and the Great Deception in Australian Defence Policy 1911–1914*, Aerospace Centre, Canberra, 2002.
79 Connor, *Anzac and Empire*, p 37.
80 Kirkpatrick, memoir, p 309.
81 Proceedings of conference between Godley and Gordon, 18 Nov 1912, NAA, item 1856/1/33, series MP84/1; E Scott, *Australia During the War*, 4th edn, Angus & Robertson, Sydney, 1938, p 200.
82 For pre-war military planning see C Wilcox, 'Relinquishing the past: John Mordike's *An Army for a Nation*', *Australian Journal of Politics and History*, 40(1), 1994, pp 59–62.
83 *West Australian*, 19 Aug 1914, p 8.
84 *Adelaide Register*, 14 Feb 1921, p 5.
85 Meaney, *Search for Security*, p 277.
86 C Wilcox, 'False start: The mobilisation of Australia's citizen army 1914', *Journal of the Australian War Memorial*, no 26, April 1995, pp 4–9.
87 *Nepean Times* (Sydney), 21 Nov 1914, p 2.

12 The capture of German New Guinea John Connor

1 See JMR Young, *Australia's Pacific Frontier: Economic and Cultural Expansion into the Pacific 1795–1885*, Cassell, Melbourne, 1967; DR Hainsworth, *The Sydney Traders: Simeon Lord and his Contemporaries 1788–1821*, MUP, Melbourne, 2nd edn, 1981; D Shineberg, *They Came for Sandalwood: A Study of the Sandalwood Trade in the South-West Pacific 1830–1865*, MUP, Melbourne, 1967.
2 D Munro, 'The origins of labourers in the South Pacific: Commentary and statistics', in C Moore, J Leckie & D Munro (eds), *Labour in the South Pacific*, James Cook University, Townsville, 1990, p xxxix.
3 Islanders worked on sugar plantations in Queensland and northern New South Wales until the system was banned after Federation in 1901 and the majority deported. Some remained to become the foundation of Australia's Pacific Islander community: see G Davison et al, *The Oxford Companion to Australian History*, OUP, Melbourne, 2nd edn, 2001, p 491.
4 See P Corris, *Passage, Port and Plantation: A History of Solomon Islands Labour Migration 1870–1914*, MUP, Melbourne, 1973; C Moore, *Kanaka: A History*

of Melanesian Mackay, Institute of Papua New Guinea Studies/University of Papua New Guinea Press, Port Moresby, 1985.

5   See N Gunson, *Messengers of Grace: Evangelical Missions in the South Seas 1797–1860*, OUP, Melbourne, 1978; D Hilliard, *A History of the Melanesian Mission 1849–1942*, UQP, Brisbane, 1978; D Langmore, *Missionary Lives: Papua 1874–1914*, University of Hawai'i Press, Honolulu, 1989.

6   C Newbury, 'Spoils of war: Sub-imperial collaboration in South-West Africa and New Guinea 1914-1920', *Journal of Imperial and Commonwealth History*, 16(3), 1988, pp 83–106; A Ross, *New Zealand Aspirations in the Pacific in the Nineteenth Century*, Clarendon Press, Oxford. 1964; R Hyam, *The Failure of South African Expansion 1908–1948*, Macmillan, London, 1972; PR Warhurst, 'Smuts and Africa: A study in sub-imperialism', *South African Historical Journal*, 16(1), 1984, pp 82–100.

7   R Thompson, *Australian Imperialism in the Pacific: The Expansionist Era 1820–1920*, MUP, Melbourne, 1980, pp 15–18, 23–32; R Aldrich, *The French Presence in the South Pacific*, Macmillan, Basingstoke, 1990, pp 23, 26.

8   JB Joyce, 'Australian interests in New Guinea before 1906', in WJ Hudson (ed), *Australia and Papua New Guinea*, Sydney University Press, Sydney, 1971, p 8; S Mullins, 'Queensland's quest for Torres Strait', *Journal of Pacific History*, 27(2), 1992, pp 174–79; Thompson, *Australian Imperialism in the Pacific*, pp 36–44.

9   HJ Ohff, 'Empires of enterprise: German and English commercial interests in East New Guinea 1884 to 1914', PhD thesis, Adelaide University, 2008, pp 25, 28; Thompson, *Australian Imperialism in the Pacific*, pp 49–50.

10 Thompson, *Australian Imperialism in the Pacific*, pp 51–67; SS Mackenzie, *The Australians at Rabaul: The Capture and Administration of the German Possessions in the Southern Pacific*, CEW Bean (ed), *The Official History of Australia in the War of 1914–1918*, vol 10, reprinted by UQP, Brisbane, 1993, pp 21–22.

11 See WR Louis, *Great Britain and Germany's Lost Colonies 1914–1919*, Clarendon Press, Oxford, 1967, pp 10–14.

12 P Sack & D Clark (eds & trans), *German New Guinea: The Draft Annual Report for 1913–1914*, Department of Law, ANU, Canberra, 1980, p 16; J Lyng, *Our New Possession (Late German New Guinea)*, Melbourne Publishing Company, Melbourne, 1919, pp 122–28.

13 Sack & Clark, *German New Guinea: Draft Annual Report 1913–1914*, pp 15, 17–18.

14 Louis, *Great Britain and Germany's Lost Colonies*, p 12; Lyng, *Our New Possession*, p 60; Sack & Clark, *German New Guinea: Draft Annual Report 1913–1914*, pp 26, 36, 153, 155–56.

15 The white population of Papua in 1911 was 1064, the indigenous population was estimated as 271 000: see WH Mercer et al, *The Colonial Office List for 1914*, Waterlow & Sons, London, 1914, p 88.

16 Mercer et al., *Colonial Office List 1914*, p 89; Lyng, *Our New Possession*, pp 60, 233.

17 Lyng, *Our New Possession*, p 218; JW Buxton, *The Call of the Pacific*, Charles Kelly, London, 1912, p 231; *Sydney Morning Herald*, 24 Nov 1914.

18 K Buckley & K Klugmanm, *The History of Burns Philp: The Australian Company in the South Pacific*, Burns, Philp & Co, Sydney, 1981, pp 254–55;

Sack & Clark, *German New Guinea: Draft Annual Report 1913–1914*, pp 23–24; Lyng, *Our New Possession*, pp 234–35.
19 Sack & Clark, *German New Guinea: Draft Annual Report 1913–1914*, p 130.
20 Vice Admiral Günther von Krosigk, 'Memorandum on the importance of cruiser warfare in the event of war against England', April 1911, and 'Most high orders to His Majesty's Ships abroad in case of war', 17 March 1914, in Jürgen Tampke (trans & ed), *'Ruthless Warfare': German Military Planning and Surveillance in the Australia-New Zealand Region before the Great War*, Southern Highlands Publishers, Canberra, 1998, pp 71, 178.
21 P Overlack, 'The force of circumstance: Graf Spee's options for the cruiser squadron in August 1914', *Journal of Military History*, 60(4), Oct 1996, p 680.
22 P Overlack, 'The Anglo-German struggle for the Australian airwaves before 1914: Marconi versus Telefunken', *Journal of the Australian Naval Institute*, 23(1), Jan–March 1997, pp 26–27. The Australian government dismantled the Telefunken radio station on King Island 'for defence reasons' following the outbreak of war in 1914: *Commonwealth Parliamentary Debates* (hereafter *CPD*), vol 76, p 2311.
23 Governor-General Lord Denman to UK Colonial Secretary Lord Harcourt, 17 Oct 1911, Harcourt Papers, Bodleian Library, Oxford (hereafter BL), dep 478, f 14; Major-General George Kirkpatrick, Inspector-General, to Senator George Pearce, Defence Minister, 30 Nov 1911, NAA, MP84/1, 1849/1/2. See also J Connor, 'Coronation conversations: The Dominions and military planning talks at the 1911 Imperial Conference', in P Dennis & J Grey (eds), *1911: Preliminary Moves*, Chief of Army History Conference, Big Sky Publishing, Sydney, 2011, pp 21–41.
24 'Proceedings of the conference between Major-General AJ Godley, CB, Commanding New Zealand Military Forces, and Brigadier-General JM Gordon, CB, Chief of the General Staff, CM Forces', 18 Nov 1912, NAA, MP84/1, 1856/1/33, pp 1–2, 4; 'Notes for conference 18:11:1912', Archives New Zealand/Te Rua Mahara o te Kāwanatanga, Wellington, AD10, 16/6.
25 See *Jane's Fighting Ships of World War I*, 1st pub 1919, reprint Studio Editions, London, 1990, pp 95, 111, 167.
26 Graf von Spee to wife, 18 Aug 1914, quoted in D Stevens, '1914–1918: World War I', in D Stevens (ed), *The Royal Australian Navy*, OUP, Melbourne, 2001, p 33.
27 JS Corbett, 'To the Battle of the Falklands, December 1914', in *History of the Great War: Naval Operations*, vol 1, Longmans, Green & Co, London, 1920, p 139, 141; AW Jose, *The Royal Australian Navy 1914–1918*, vol 9 in Bean (ed), *The Official History of Australia in the War of 1914–1918*, pp 5, 9–14.
28 Corbett, *Naval Operations*, pp 144; 341–57, 415–36.
29 'Proceedings of a Joint Naval and Military Sub-Committee for the Consideration of Combined Operations in Foreign Territory', [UK] National Archives, Committee of Imperial Defence Paper 113-C, 6 Oct 1914, CAB 5/3, f. 187.
30 SJ Smith, 'The seizure and occupation of Samoa', in HTB Drew (ed), *The War Effort of New Zealand*, Whitcombe & Tombs, Auckland, 1923, pp 25, 33–35; I McGibbon, 'The shaping of New Zealand's war effort, August–October 1914', in J Crawford & I McGibbon (eds), *New Zealand's Great War: New*

Zealand, the Allies and the First World War, Exisle Publishing, Auckland, 2007, pp 63–65.
31 CD Coulthard-Clark, *No Australian Need Apply: The Troubled Career of Lieutenant-General Gordon Legge*, Allen & Unwin, Sydney, 1988, pp 83–84; *Argus* (Melbourne), 10 Aug 1914.
32 R Mallett, 'The preparation and deployment of the Australian Naval and Military Expeditionary Force', in P Dennis & J Grey (eds), *Battles Near and Far: A Century of Operational Deployment*, The 2004 Chief of Army History Conference, Army History Unit, Canberra, 2005, pp 22, 24–25.
33 Legge to Senator Edward Millen, Defence Minister, 14 Aug 1914, NAA, B543, W170/1/15.
34 Mallett, 'Preparation and deployment', pp 25–26, 28; *Clarence and Richmond Examiner* (Grafton), 20 Aug 1914.
35 Mackenzie, *Australians at Rabaul*, pp 29–33; Jose, *Royal Australian Navy*, pp 76–78.
36 Jose, *Royal Australian Navy*, pp 78–81, 96–97; <www.awm.gov.au/units/unit_10759.asp> (accessed 7 Feb 2012).
37 Mackenzie, *Australians at Rabaul*, pp 39–40, 42, 48; Lyng, *Our New Possession*, pp 85–86.
38 Mackenzie, *Australians at Rabaul*, pp 50–53
39 Lt G Hill, quoted in K Meade, *Heroes before Gallipoli: Bita Paka and that One Day in September*, Wiley, Brisbane, 2005, p 39.
40 Mackenzie, *Australians at Rabaul*, pp 54–58, 64–67.
41 Mackenzie, *Australians at Rabaul*, pp 58, 59, 61, 63–64, 65, 73.
42 Mackenzie, *Australians at Rabaul*, p 74; Axtens to father, quoted in Meade, *Heroes before Gallipoli*, p 56; and see D Blair, *No Quarter: Unlawful Killing and Surrender in the Australian War Experience 1915–1918*, Ginninderra Press, Canberra, 2005.
43 *Sydney Morning Herald*, 7 Oct 1914, reprinted in FS Burnell, *Australia Versus Germany: The Story of the Taking of German New Guinea*, George Allen & Unwin, London, 1915, p 132.
44 Mackenzie, *Australians at Rabaul*, pp 78–85, 118–19; *CPD*, vol 76, p 2697; HJ Hiery, *The German South Pacific and the Influence of World War I*, University of Hawai'i Press, Honolulu, 1995, p 276.
45 *Sydney Morning Herald*, 16 Sept 1914.
46 Mackenzie, *Australians at Rabaul*, pp 105, 182–83, 189; Pearce to Legge, 22 Dec 1914, NAA, B543, W112/4/457
47 CD Rowley, *The Australians in German New Guinea*, MUP, Melbourne, 1958, pp 4–6; *Daily News* (Perth), 9 Jan 1915; *Sydney Morning Herald*, 16 Jan 1915.
48 *Sydney Morning Herald*, 2 Nov 1914; *CPD*, vol 75, pp 413, 510, 958.
49 *Sydney Morning Herald*, 7, 15 & 21 Oct, 28 Nov 1914. The flag appears to be now held by the Australian War Memorial.
50 Mackenzie, *Australians at Rabaul*, pp 120–24. Hiery claims Cox provided the ANMEF with military information, but there is no evidence for this: *German South Pacific*, p 36.
51 Mackenzie, *Australians at Rabaul*, pp 124–26; Holmes to Pearce, 30 Nov 1914, NAA, B543, W112/4/463; 'Bas' to Colonel RJ Travers, 24 Nov 1952, B Dovey to Travers, 24 Nov 1952, both AWM, PR84/202.

52 *Sydney Morning Herald*, 14 Dec 1914; *Argus*, 14 Dec 1914; *Clarence and Richmond Examiner*, 15 Dec 1914.
53 Munro-Ferguson to Harcourt, 23 Jan 1915, Harcourt Papers, British Library, dep 479, f 240; *CPD*, vol 76, p 1951.
54 Mackenzie, *Australians at Rabaul*, p 261; Munro-Ferguson to Harcourt, 28 Dec 1914, Harcourt Papers, BL, dep 479, f 230; Munro-Ferguson to Harcourt, 26 Jan 1915, NA, CO 418/132, f 153.
55 M Piggott, 'Stonewalling in German New Guinea', *Journal of the Australian War Memorial*, 12, April 1988, p 13.
56 Piggott, 'Stonewalling in German New Guinea', pp 11–12
57 CD Rowley, *The Australians in German New Guinea*, MUP, Melbourne, 1958, p 12.
58 Meade, *Heroes before Gallipoli*, p 95.
59 This force consisted of men aged between 30 and 50, preferably with tropical experience. It was initially recruited to occupy the German islands north of the Equator, but Japan had already captured these. Pearce decided that Pethebridge and the Tropical Force should replace Holmes and the ANMEF: see *Sydney Morning Herald*, 19 Nov 1914; Pethebridge to Pearce, 18 Dec 1914, NAA, B543, W112/4/553; Trumble to Pethebridge, 28 Dec 1914, NAA: B543, W112/4/457.
60 Mackenzie, *Australians at Rabaul*, p 195.
61 Mackenzie, *Australians at Rabaul*, pp 195–96; Meade, *Heroes before Gallipoli*, pp 101–105.
62 *McIvor Times and Rodney Advertiser* (Heathcote), 27 May 1915.
63 CEW Bean, *The Story of Anzac: From the Outbreak of War to the end of the First Phase of the Gallipoli Camapaign, May 4, 1915*, vol 1 in CEW Bean (ed), *The Official History of Australia in the War in 1914–1918*, pp 128–30.
64 *Sydney Morning Herald*, 15 Oct 1914.
65 See Louis, *Great Britain and Germany's Lost Colonies*.
66 C Bridge, *William Hughes, Australia: The Paris Peace Conferences of 1919–1923 and their Aftermath*, Haus, London, 2011, pp 55, 78, 83.
67 *Sydney Morning Herald*, 12 Nov 1914.
68 These words were written by journalist Conrad Eitel who served in the ANMEF machine gun section and published under the pseudonym 'Darnoc' ('Conrad' spelt backwards): *Sydney Morning Herald*, 7 Sept 1914.
69 *Sydney Morning Herald*, 15 Oct 1914.

Index

Note: Military personnel are listed in this index with the highest rank shown in the book.

1st Australian Horse regiment 247
1st Waikato Regiment (NZ) 142
2nd Infantry (Kennedy) Regiment 280, 293
4th (King's Own) Regiment (UK) 43–4, 53
11th Regiment of Foot (UK) 48
12th (East Suffolk) Regiment of Foot (UK) 58, 72, 125
14th Battalion (Australia) 271–2
14th (Buckinghamshire) Regiment of Foot (UK) 57–8, 125
18th (Royal Irish) Regiment of Foot (UK) 125
21st Fusiliers (UK) 58
39th Regiment of Foot (UK) 51
40th (Somersetshire) Regiment of Foot (UK) 62, 72, 81–3, 125
43rd (Monmouthshire) Light Infantry 125
46th Regiment of Foot (UK) 41, 49–50
48th Regiment of Foot (UK) 49–50
50th (Queen's Own) Regiment of Foot (UK) 47, 125
56th Battalion (Australia) 269–70
57th (West Middlesex) Regiment of Foot (UK) 125, 142
58th (Rutlandshire) Regiment of Foot 124–5
65th (Yorkshire North Riding) Regiment of Foot (UK) 125
68th (Durham) Light Infantry (UK) 125
70th (Surrey) Regiment of Foot 125
73rd Regiment of Foot (UK) 39–41, 49–50
80th (South Staffordshire) Regiment of Foot (UK) 44, 47, 123, 125
96th (Manchester) Regiment of Foot 125
99th (Lanarkshire) Regiment of Foot 44, 47–8, 124–5

Abbott, Corporal Jack 225
Abercrombie River, bushrangers captured at 51
Aboriginal Crafts stamp issue 9–10
Aboriginal Victorians 32
Aborigines *see* Indigenous Australians
Aborigines and Colonists 31–2
Acheron (torpedo boat) 97
Adams, Simon 34
AE1 and AE2, HMAS 112, 115, 294
Afghanistan Crisis 234–5
Ahmad, Mahdi Muhammad 214–15
Aikenhead, Major William 179, 190
Albany garrison 218
Albert, HMVS 101–2
Alfred Graving Dock 101
Allan, Richard 65
Allen, Jim 58
American War of Independence, militias in 72
Anderson, Joseph 54
Anglo-Japanese Alliance 242, 247
Anzac Day, neglect of history and 1
'Anzac spirit' in invasion novels 231
Argus newspaper, on Eureka Stockade 69, 75
Armed Constabulary Act 1867 (NZ) 145–6
Armed Vessels Regulation Act 1860 (Vic) 95, 128
army cadet movement *see* cadet movement
Arnoldian Tradition 189
Arthur, Richard 261
Asquith, Herbert 276

Index

Athens, Royal Navy blockade of 207
Atiawa tribe 127, 131
Auckland, perceived threat to 133
Austen, Tom 33–4
Austin, Maurice 56
Australasian Auxiliary Squadron proposal 103–4
Australasian Naval Defence Act 1887 (UK) 104
Australasian Naval Force 109 *see also* Royal Australian Navy
Australia, HMAS
  arrival in Sydney 274–5
  commissioned 115
  construction of ordered 112
  East Asiatic Squadron outgunned by 290
  New Guinea force escorted by 294
  Samoa force escorted by 292
Australia
  'betrayal' by Britain 230, 243–4
  cadet movement in 174–203
  colonial rebellions 50
  conditions in for servicemen 54–7
  firearm ownership in 148–9
  frontier conflicts in 21–38
  German New Guinea and 288–9
  invasion novels 6–7, 230–54
  martial values in 4
  military horses supplied by 207–8
  rifle clubs in 148–73
Australia Calls (movie) 251–2
Australian Citizen, The 270–1
Australian Commonwealth Horse 225, 255, 279
'Australian Corps' in South Africa 221
Australian Crisis, The 242, 245–6, 248–9
Australian Freedom League 201, 270
Australian Frontier Wars, The 30
Australian Imperial Force 1–2, 279–80, 300
Australian Joint Copying Project 59
Australian Labor Party
  defence policies 218–19, 271, 277
  NDL influence on 262
  radical nationalism in 232
  supports cadet scheme 191

Australian military forces *see also* colonial military forces; Royal Australian Navy
  auxiliary naval squadron 258, 260
  cadet movement and 190–203
  formation of 255–82
  in South African War 105–6, 206, 220–6, 255–8
Australian National Defence League 262
Australian Naval and Military Expeditionary Force 283, 292–3, 299–300
Australian Navy *see* Royal Australian Navy
Australian War Memorial, no Indigenous conflicts represented in 8
Avernus (torpedo boat) 97
Axtens, Private Jack 296

Backhouse, James 46–7, 55
Baden-Powell, Robert 223–4
Bakery Hill, Ballarat 72
Ballarat Reform League 71
Ballarat, unrest among miners in 70–1
Barkly, Sir Henry 132
Barkly, RA 200
Barney, George 48–9
Barr, John 252
Barton, Edmund
  becomes Prime Minister 224
  defence policies 258, 260
  on support for Sudan campaign 215
  'reasonable Imperialism' of 228–9
Bate, Weston 67
Bathurst rebellion 50
Battle of Dorking: Reminiscences of a Volunteer 236
Batumbil, Phyllis 11
Bay of Islands 124
Beagle, HMS 92
Bean, Charles 2
'Bennelong' (Aborigine) 29
Bentley, James 70
Beresford, Commander JAH 292
Berrima liner 293
Bibby, Richard 34
Bismarck Archipelago 285, 287

339

Bitapaka, defence of 283, 294
Black, Alfred 72
'Black Line' in Tasmania 32
'Black Week' in South African War 222–3
Blackburn, Geoff 58
Blake, Gregory 51
Blake, Les 67
Bligh, Governor William 39, 41
Boam, Major MM 167
Boer War *see* South African War
Boomerang, HMS 104, 217
boomerangs, Aboriginal use of 17–18
Border Police *see* Native Police forces
Bowen, Lieutenant Rowland 295
Boxer Rebellion
    Australian volunteers in 106–7, 223–4
    British suppression of 206
    naval forces in 103–4
Boy Scouts 271
Boyle, Private Felix 74
Bracegirdle, Midshipman Leighton Seymour 107
'Branded D on the Left Side' 54
Brassey, Governor Thomas 219
Brazier, Lieutenant-Colonel NM 195–6
Bremer, Captain James 91–2
Brighton Grammar School cadet corps 198
Brisbane Grammar School cadet corps 179, 184
Brisbane, HMAS 112
British Chartist companies 72
British Empire *see also* British military forces; Colonial Conferences; Imperial Conferences
    Australian dependence on 211–13
    colonial loyalties to 1–2, 204–6, 219
    force used by 25
    New Guinea claimed for 210–11
    radical opposition to 231–2
British military forces *see also* Royal Navy (UK)
    Australia lobbies to annex Pacific territories 284–5
    Australian volunteers in 225–6
    Australians copy uniform caps of 2
    bugle calls 76–7
    colonial opposition to 53
    colonial policies 218–20, 228, 264–5
    conditions for servicemen 53–4
    horses supplied to 207–8
    in colonial Australia 5, 29, 39–61
    in New Zealand 124–6, 133
    leave Australia 187, 208, 234
    moved to NZ from Australia 144–5
    relations with rifle clubs 154–8
    retirees from settle in Australia 53–6
    Royal Artillery 48
    Royal Engineers 48–9
    'small wars' fought by 23
    tactics used by 83–4
    UK bears costs of 258
British National Rifle Association 149–50
Broken Hill, Muslim butcher killed at 280
Broome, Richard 11, 24, 32
Brown, George 288
Browne, Governor Thomas Gore 127–8, 132
'Buchan Charley' (bushranger) 45
Bunbury, Major Thomas 44–5, 47, 123
'Bungaree' (Aborigine) 29
Burnell, Frederick 296
Burnette, Robert 73
Burns, James 220
Busby, James 121–2
bushrangers 44–5, 49, 51, 178
Butlin, Noel 13
Byrne, Joseph 55

cadet movement 6, 113, 174–203, 268–9
Call, The 262
Callwell, Charles 23
Cambrian, HMS 115
Cambridge settlement 144
Camden College cadet corps 185
Cameron, Major General Duncan 132–3, 135, 140–1, 144
Campbell, Colonel Gerald Ross 165, 262, 271

Index

Canada, British military forces in 208
Canadian War Museum 8
Cannon, Michael 33
Cape Regiment 27
capitalism, criticism of 245
Carboni, Rafaello 68–9, 76–7, 80–1
Carnarvon, Lord 285
Carrington, Lady 185
casualty figures
    Aboriginal deaths in Victoria 32–3
    Eureka Stockade 79–80, 88
    German New Guinea campaign 283, 295–6
    New Zealand Wars 129, 142
    Sudan campaign 204–5
    World War I 115, 283
cavalry *see* mounted troops
Cerberus, HMVS 96, 101, 108
ceremonial activities, in cadet movement 185–6
Chamberlain, Joseph 219–20, 222, 227–8, 260
Chesney, George Tomykns 236
Chester, Henry 285
Childers, HMVS 101–2, 108
China 237–42, 286 *see also* Boxer Rebellion
Choiseul Plantations Limited 288
Churchill, Winston 276
Citizen Military Forces 113, 195, 202–3 *see also* militias
civilian rifle clubs 150, 152–3
Clark, Ian 32–3
Clendinnen, Inga 29
Cloncurry conflict 36
Clubb, John 109
clubs, Indigenous use of 17–18
Cockatoo Island Dockyard 97, 112, 277
Colburn's United Service Journal 41
Collins, David 13
Colomb, John 212
Colonia Nueva Australia 241
Colonial Armidale 30
Colonial Conferences *see also* Imperial Conferences
    1887: 217
    1897: 219
    1902: 227–8, 260
    1907: 264
Colonial Defence Committee 217, 219
Colonial Defence Force Cavalry (NZ) 134, 137
Colonial Garrison, The 58
colonial military forces *see also* Australian military forces; British military forces
    cadet movement and 174–90
    in New Zealand 118–47
    naval forces 5, 93–108, 209, 217, 266–7
    relations with rifle clubs 168
    stamp issue shows uniforms of 2–3
colonisation 26, 28
Colony, The 30
Coloured Conquest, The 242, 247, 250–1
Colquhoun, Lieutenant William Jarvie 105–6
Commandants' Conferences 150, 156
Commonwealth Council of the Rifle Associations of Australia 159–62
'Commonwealth Crisis, The' 262
Commonwealth Defence Bill 1901 191
Commonwealth Director of Rifle Associations and Rifle Clubs position 167, 169–70
Commonwealth Military Cadet Corps 193
Commonwealth Military Forces *see* Australian military forces
Commonwealth Naval Forces 96–7, 99–100, 105–6, 109–10, 291 *see also* Royal Australian Navy
Commonwealth of Nations *see* British Empire
compulsory cadet scheme 195–202
compulsory militia scheme 263
Connor, John 30
Conquest and Settlement 58
contact zones 22
convicts, military supervision of 46, 52–3
Cook, Captain James 90
Cook, Joseph 266, 273, 275–7
Cordelia, HMS 128
Countess of Hopetoun, HMVS 101, 108

341

Coveny, Robert 204, 229
Cox, Captain Charles 226
Cox, Reverend William Henry 288, 298
Cox's River Stockade 58
Creswell, Captain William Rooke
  advocates independent navy 110, 258, 264, 267
  commands ANF 107–8
Crimean War, effect on Australia 48, 93
Critchett, Jan 32
Crouch, Major Richard 269–70
Curtain, Patrick 87
Curtin, John 253
Curtis, Commander GAH 113–14
Cutlack, Frederick 275

Dakin, Lieutenant Herbert 164–5
Dalmas, William 178
Darrell, George 214
Darug peoples 11–18
Darwin, attacks on 233, 273
Darwin, Charles 92
Davies, Walter 'Karri' 220–1, 224–5
Dawes Point battery 48
Deakin, Alfred
  as Defence minister 164–5
  compulsory military training inaugurated by 196
  defence policies 262–6
  on Japanese threat 261
  on South African War 224
  plans independent Navy 110
  supports cadet scheme 194
  supports Creswell 108
deaths *see* casualty figures
Deeds That Won the Empire 219
Defence Act 1903-4 (Cth) 159, 162–3, 191
Defence Act 1903 (Cth) 109
Defence Act 1909-10 (Cth) 113, 167
Defence Act 1911 (Cth) 194–5, 199–200
Defence Department (Cth), cadet movement and 183, 194
Defence Forces Rifle Association 156, 162
Defence League 201

defence reviews 150
Denison, Sir William 95
Denman, Lord 199
Derby, Lord 243
disease, deliberate use against Indigenous peoples 30
Disraeli, Benjamin 212
'divide and rule' strategy 26–7
Doris, HMS 106
Douglas, Heather 25
dreadnought construction 264–5
Duntroon military college 268

East Asiatic Squadron (Germany) 289–90
East Coast War (NZ) 145
East India Squadron (UK) 91
Easty, Private John 40
'educationalism' in cadet corps 175–6, 181–4
Edwards, General Sir James Bevan 153–4, 218
Egypt, British conquest of 211
Elwell, Lieutenant-Commander Charles 295
Emden cruiser 116, 280, 289
Encounter, HMAS 114, 293, 297
Endeavour, HMS 40
Entwistle, Ralph 51
Eureka Hotel, Ballarat 70
Eureka Stockade conflict 5, 50–2, 62–89
Eureka Stockade, The 68–9
Eureka Stockade: The Events Leading Up to the Attack in the Pre-Dawn of 3 December 1854 82–3
European settlers, conflict with Indigenous peoples
  in Australia 14, 21–38
  in New Zealand 118–47

Face of Battle, The 67–8
Facts About the Transvaal, The 222
Falkland Islands, Battle of 116, 291
Fargher, Philip 165
Federal Council of Rifle Associations of Australasia 153
Fels, Marie 33

Index

Ferguson, Alexander 168
Ferguson, Charles 73, 78, 86
Ferry, John 30
Fiji, annexed by Britain 210, 285
Finnane, Mark 25
firearm ownership in Australia 148–9
First Fleet 29–30
First Taranaki War *see* Taranaki Wars
Fisher, Andrew
   commits Australia to World War I 279
   Creswell supported by 108
   defence policies 266–7
   Holmes rebuked by 298
   naval policy 111
   supports cadet scheme 193
Fisher, Admiral Sir John 'Jacky' 110, 264
Fitzroy graving dock 97
Fleet Unit, construction of 112
Flinders, Commander Matthew 91
Flinders Naval Depot 96, 114
Flintoff, Harry 270
Ford, Lisa 25
Forlorn Hope, The 214
formal battles among Indigenous peoples 12–13
Fort Denison 48, 93
Fort Dundas 92
Fortescue, Ensign 43
fortifications
   at Eureka Stockade 72
   fortified homesteads 45
   in Australia 48
   in NSW 93–4, 96
   in South Australia 99–100
   in Victoria 151
   locations recommended for 153–4
   Māori *pa* 120, 129–31
   Royal Navy hands to civilian governments 208
Fortuna (schooner) 114
Foster, Robert 34–5
Fox, Frank 258, 262 *see also The Australian Crisis*
Foxton, Justin 266
France
   Pacific annexations 236, 285

   perceived threat from 121, 176, 187, 232–3
Franco-Prussian War 236
Freedom League 201, 270
Fremantle Naval Volunteers (WA) 101
French, Major General George Arthur 153, 155–6, 160
frontier warfare, defined 22–3
Fysh, Hudson 36

Gamble, WM 181–3
Gate Pa, Battle of 141
Gayundah gunboat (Qld) 97–8, 106–8, 110, 113–14
Geary, Peter 49
George, Duke of Edinburgh, inspects cadets 185–6
German New Guinea, Australian capture of 7, 115–16, 280, 283–303
Germany
   colonial empire 286
   naval forces in Pacific 116
   naval threat to Britain 264
   Pacific annexations 235–6
   perceived threat from 112, 187, 227, 278
Gipps, Governor Sir George 31, 122
Gneisenau cruiser 289
Gold, Colonel Charles 128
Good Men and True 33
Gordon, General Charles 214
Gordon, HMVS 101
Gordon, Joseph 263, 278
Gott, Richard 25
Gravel Pits diggings, riots at 71–2
'Great Southern Road' from Auckland 133, 140–2
Greater Public Schools athletic competitions 183
Green, Neville 33
Grewcock, Michael 25–6
Grey, Edward 277
Grey, Governor Sir George 132–7, 144
Grguric, Nicolas 35
Griffith, Arthur 219, 222, 277
'grog mutiny' 47–8
Grose Farm military camp 39
guerilla warfare

by Indigenous peoples 28
  in New Zealand 124
  in South Africa 158
  Kupapa forces in 136
Gulf of Carpentaria, conflict in 35

Haber, Eduard 294, 297
Hackett, Charles 74
Hale, Horatio 12
Hall, Ben 178
Hamilton, General Sir Ian 170, 273
Hamilton settlement 144
Handcock, Lieutenant Peter 226
Harcourt, Lord 299
Harman, Kristyn 25
Harriet (schooner) 114
Hauhau religion 145
Helidon settlement 42
Henderson, Admiral Sir Reginald 113
Henderson Naval Base 114
Herald, HMS 122
Herbertshöhe, landing at 295
Hilton, Philip 54
Hoad, Major General John 166, 193, 263
Hobson, Captain William 122–3, 134
Hocking, Geoffrey 82–3
Holmes, Colonel William 283–4, 292–3, 297–8
Hone Heke 124
Hordern, Samuel 266
horses, military use of 207–8 *see also* mounted troops
Hosking, Rick 34
Hotham, Governor Sir Charles 94
Howse, Neville, stamp issue commemorates 3
Huddart, Midshipman Cymberline Alonso Edric 106
Huey, Ensign Alexander 39
Hughes, William Morris
  defence policies 261–2
  on Anzac tradition 1, 90
  on new RAN 275
  supports cadet scheme 191
  supports retaining New Guinea 301
Humffray, John Basson 65
Huon, HMAS 112

Hutton, Major General Sir Edward Thomas Henry
  as ADF head 259–60
  as NSW Commandant 153–5, 218
  pressures rifle clubs to provide military training 159–63
  supports cadet scheme 192
Huyghue, Samuel 81, 85

Imperial Colonial Naval Defence Act 1865 (UK) 95
Imperial Commissariat Transport Service (UK) 140–2
Imperial Conferences 110–12, 276–7
  see also Colonial Conferences
Imperial Light Horse regiment 221
Improvised Explosive Devices 296
In the Name of the Law 35
'Independent California Rangers Revolver Brigade' 79
Indian Mutiny 206
Indigenous Australians
  colonial views of 26
  conflict with European settlers 21–38
  'criminalisation' of 25
  depicted in invasion novels 249
  military intelligence held by 27
  military response to resistance by 42
  traditional warfare 4, 8–20
  use of as trackers 33, 36
  warrior cultures among 11
  weapons used by 11, 15–19
Inglis, Ken 214
initiation ceremonies, weapons presented during 11
internal policing 23
invasion novels 6–7, 230–54
Invasion, The 238, 245–6, 249
Investigator, HMS 91
Irish convicts, alleged support for French invasion 233

Jandamarra and the Bunuba Resistance 34
Japan
  British alliance with 242, 260, 276
  Darwin bombed by 233

Index

'fifth columnists' from 245
perceived threat from 112, 247–8, 260–1, 278
Jeffries, CA 252
Jeffs, Private Henry 142
Johnston, Major George 50
Junction Stockade, Mount Victoria 47
Juniper, Private William 74

Kabakaul, landing at 295
Kaiser Wilhelmsland 286, 287
Kanowna transport vessel 293
Karrakatta, HMS 104
Karskens, Grace 29–30
Katoomba, HMS 104
Keating, Paul 230
Keegan, John 67–8
Kelly, William 75
Kempf, Lieutenant EE 295
Kennedy Regiment 280, 293
Kent, David 30
Kent, HMS 116
Kimber, Richard 35
King George Sound settlement 33, 42
King, Governor Philip Gidley 232
King-Hall, Admiral Sir George 115
King Island, claimed for Britain 232
King Movement 124, 126, 131–3, 141
King Ya-nup people 14
King's Own Royal Regiment Museum 60
Kipling, Rudyard 224
Kirkpatrick, George 271, 278
Kirmess, CH *see* Fox, Frank
Kitchener, Lord Herbert 167, 267
Knight, Charles 74–5
knives, use of by indigenous peoples 18
Kociumbas, Jan 29–30
Koheroa gunboat 140
Konishi, Shino 13
Kororareka settlement 120, 124
Ku Klux Klan, influence on Australian nationalism 239–40
Kupapa forces 135–6
Kurnai people 13

Labor Party *see* Australian Labor Party
Lalor, Peter 75, 86–7

Lambert, George 2
Lambing Flat riots 50, 52
Lane, William 238–44
Lang, John Dunmore 55
Larbalestier, Ken 58
Launceston Church Grammar School cadet corps 179, 189
Lazarus, Samuel 69
Leckbandt, Ollie 58
Lee-Enfield rifles 162, 166–8
Legge, Colonel (James) Gordon 195, 263, 278, 292
Legge, Lieutenant-Colonel WV 179
Legion of Frontiersmen 272
Leipzig cruiser 289
Leschen, Lieutenant Hugo 180
Life in Victoria 75
Lindsay, Norman 262
Lithgow rifle factory 167, 277
Lonsdale, HMVS 101
Loos, Noel 36
Louisiana, government of seized 240
Lyle, Marshall 262, 263
Lynch, John, account of Eureka conflict 65, 73, 76, 78–9, 85
Lyng, Jens 288
Lynn, John 10

Macarthur, Reverend GF 178, 188
Mackay, James Alexander Kenneth 219, 241–3, 247, 249–50
Macquarie Fields Corps 178
Macquarie, Governor Lachlan 39, 41
Madgwick, WM 300
Mafeking, relief of 223
Mahdi, The 214–15
Malay Corps 27
Mangatawhiri Stream 133
Manning, Captain Charles 298
Māori peoples *see also* New Zealand Wars
  as Crown auxiliaries 135–6
  conflicts with European settlers 124–5, 145
  culture of 19
  early European contacts with 118–20
  fortifications built by 120, 129–31

345

Marine Defence Force (Qld) 97–8
Martin, Michael 9
masculinity, violence connected with 30
Mason, Captain George 43–4, 60
Matarikoriko Pa 129–30
McCarthy, Corporal Justin 49
McCulloch, James 143
McIlwraith, Thomas 285–6
Mead, Margaret 13
media coverage of Eureka Stockade 64–7
Medic, SS 105
Melbourne, HMAS 112, 114, 294
Melbourne Rifle Club 157
Melville Island settlement 42
Midge picket boat (Qld) 98
Mildura, HMS 104
Military Board, rifle clubs and 164–5, 168
military engineering 48–9
military reserves, proposals for 272
Military Rifle Association (WA) 166
military settlements 42, 136–7, 145–6
Militia Act 1858 (NZ) 134
militias *see also* rifle clubs
   after Federation 258–9
   during South African War 223
   formation in Australia 208–9
   formation in New Zealand 134–5
   national, compulsory 267–73
   relations with rifle clubs 151–2, 157, 166–8, 170, 261–3, 272–3
   voluntary, formation of 149
Millen, Edward
   announces capture of German New Guinea 297
   announces creation of ANMEF 292
   as Defence minister 170, 273, 279
Mills Committee 95
Miner mine layer (Qld) 98–9
miners, unrest among *see* Eureka Stockade conflict
Ministry and Council of Defence (Vic) 181
Mitchell, Sir Thomas 207
Moffat, Signalman Robert 295
Molony, John 67
Morant, Lieutenant Harry 'Breaker' 226
Morinda passenger boat 299
Mosquito torpedo boat (Qld) 98
Mount Rennie rape case 239
Mount Victoria Junction Stockade 47
mounted troops *see also* Native Police forces
   at Eureka Stockade 72, 84–5
   in frontier wars 28–31
   in military forces 44–5
   in South African War 222–3
   sent to New Zealand 122
   Victorian Mounted Rifles 153, 157
Mundy, Colonel Geoffrey 55
Munro-Ferguson, Sir Ronald 299
Murdoch, Walter 270–1
Murray River peoples, revenge attacks by 15
Musket Wars 119–21
musketry training 149, 151, 166 *see also* rifle clubs
Myall Creek massacre 21, 31–2

National Defence League 164–5
National Rifle Association of Australia 155
national service proposals *see also* militias
   Deakin's support for 165, 194–6, 263
   under Pearce 278–9
Native Police forces
   in central and northern Australia 33, 35–6
   in NSW 31–2, 54
   in Victoria 32
   operations of 29
Nauru, as German colony 286, 294
Naval Agreement Acts (UK) 104, 108–9
Naval Artillery Volunteers (NSW) 97
Naval Brigades
   from NSW 94, 97, 102–3, 107
   from Queensland 97
   from Victoria 107, 128–9
Neill, Private John 76, 87
Nelson, HMS 96, 101
Nepean, HMVS 101
Nettelbeck, Amanda 34, 35

Index

Neu Pommern 287
New Caledonia 236, 285
New Guinea *see also* German New Guinea; Papua New Guinea
  annexation of 210–11, 235–6, 285–6
New Plymouth 127, 131
New South Wales
  cadet movement in 177–8, 180–6, 189, 192
  colonial naval defences 93–4, 96–8
  conflict between European settlers and Indigenous peoples 21–3
  National Defence League in 164–5
  New Zealand as part of 121–2
  offers to fund dreadnought construction 266
  Royal Navy's role in founding 91
  Sudan contingent from 6, 102, 204, 215–16
New South Wales Corps (UK) 39–41, 47, 50–1
New South Wales Rifle Association 154–6, 160, 168
New South Wales Torpedo and Signalling Corps 97
New Zealand *see also* Māori peoples; New Zealand Wars
  administrative separation from NSW 123
  British military forces in 208
  domestic regiments disbanded 146
  militias formed in 134–5
  offers to pay for dreadnought construction 266
  Samoa captured by 290, 292
  supports War Office proposals 228
  troops supplied to by Royal Navy 92–3
New Zealand Company 121
New Zealand Wars 118–47
  Australian military involvement 5–6, 149, 209–10
  medal awarded for 146–7
Newington College 185
Ngapuhi tribe 124
Ngaruawahia, Māori police force at 127
Ngati Ranganui tribe 141

Ngati Te Rangi tribe 141
Ngatiawa tribe 129
Nickle, Major General Sir Robert 75
Niger, HMS 128
non-lethal spearings 11
Norfolk Island, military government of 46–7
Norman, Captain William 94–5, 127
Norman River 94–5
Northern New Zealand War 92–3, 124–5
Northern Rifle Association 155
Nürnberg cruiser 289
Nyungar people, European settlers in conflict with 33–4

O'Connell, Major General Sir Maurice 123
O'Keefe, Private 86
On Darug Land 9
Orakau, Battle of 141
Osborne House naval college, Geelong 114, 274
Osborne, Major William Henry 169–70
Otago, gold rush in 138
Our Own Little Rebellion 82

pa (forts) 120, 129–31
Pacific Islanders working in Australia 284
Pai Marire movement 145
Paine, Daniel 12
Palmer, Sir Arthur 9
Paluma gunboat (Qld) 97–8, 107–8
Papua New Guinea 286–7, 301 *see also* German New Guinea; New Guinea
parade ground drill for cadets 198
Parkes, Henry 180
Parramatta, HMAS
  arrival in Australia 113
  ceremonial entry into Sydney 115
  construction of 111
  in World War I 291
  official launching 273–4
Pascoe, Bruce 33
Pasley, Captain Charles 62, 69, 78, 81
Paterson, AB 'Banjo' 226

Patey, Rear Admiral George 291, 293
Paton, Lieutenant Colonel John 300
Paul, Lieutenant William 86
Pax Britannica 207, 211
'payback' custom 11
Pearce, George Foster
    as Defence minister 267–9
    embarrassed by Holmes's administration 298–9
    on Australian support for imperial armies 278
    on lack of funds for cadets 193–4
    on new RAN 275
    supports Australian navy proposal 108
    supports compulsory militia 196–7, 200, 263, 270–2
Pedersen, Howard 34
Pelorus, HMS 128
'Pemulwuy' (Aborigine) 29
Penguin, HMAS 115
Permanent Artillery (NSW) 96
Péron, François 232–3
Perry, Samuel 78
Perth, settlement of 33
Peter Lalor: The Man From Eureka 67
Pethebridge, Samuel 297, 300
Phillimore, Lieutenant Colonel WG 179–80
Phillip, Governor Arthur 29, 40
Pidcock, William 60
Pierson, Thomas 65, 69
pikemen at Eureka Stockade 87
'Pinchgut' (Fort Denison) 48, 93
Pinjarra, conflict at 34
Pioneer gunboat 140
Pioneer, HMAS (cruiser) 114
Pitt, Lieutenant Colonel George Dean 139
Pockley, Captain Brian 295
Port Essington settlement 42, 58
Port Lincoln settlement 42–3
Port Moresby 293
Port Nicholson settlement 121
postage stamps 2–3, 9–10
Potatau Te Wherowhero 126
Pratt, General Thomas 130–1
Presland, Gary 33

Prince of Wales's Own Regiment of Yorkshire (UK) 57–8
privateering 127–8
prosecutions of truant cadets 199–200
Protector cruiser (SA) 99–100, 107–8
Prussia, invasion novels about 236
Public School Cadet Force (NSW) 185, 189, 193
Public Schools Athletic Association 183

Queensland
    Aboriginal trackers from 33
    cadet movement in 179, 182–4, 192
    colonial militia in 29
    colonial naval defences 97
    defence spending 151
    Native Police forces 33, 35–6
    New Guinea annexed by 235
    rifle clubs in 158
Quinn, Patrick 53

Rabaul 283, 286–7, 296, 298–9
radical nationalists 230–54
radio communications in World War I 289
raids for women by indigenous peoples 13–14
Rangiriri, Battle of 141
Rangiriri gunboat 140
Ranken, George 238, 245–6, 249
'Rata' pseudonym *see* Roydhouse, Thomas Richard
Rattlesnake, HMS 92
Reay, Lieutenant Colonel William Thomas 165
Red Coat Dreaming 59
Rede, Robert 75
Reece, RHW 31–2
Reid, George 219, 221
Restriction of Immigration Act 1901 (Cth) 240
revenge attacks by Indigenous peoples 14–15
Reynolds, Henry 32
Ribbon Gang 51
Richards, Lieutenant James 74, 76, 85
Richards, Jonathan 42

Index

Richards, RW 298
Ridgeway, Aden 19
rifle clubs
 after Federation 259
 based on UK model 6
 in Australia 148–73
 relations with militias 151–2, 157, 166–8, 170, 261–3, 272–3
rifle shooting by cadet corps 183–4
Ringarooma, HMS 104
ritual trials among Indigenous peoples 13
Roberts, Field Marshal Lord Frederick 164–5
Roberts, Tony 35
Roney, Private Michael 62
Ross, Charles (Henry) 80, 87
Rowley, Charles 300
Royal Artillery (UK), man Australian fortifications 48
Royal Australian Air Force 273
Royal Australian Navy (and precursors)
 'Australasian Naval Force' 109
 Cerberus in 96
 Churchill calls for transfer to Britain 276
 'Commonwealth Naval Forces' 96–7, 99–100, 105–6, 109–10, 291
 development of 5, 90, 108–16, 258, 273–6
 in World War I 290–1
 Royal Navy hands assets over to 115
Royal Engineers (UK) 48–9
Royal Navy (UK)
 Artillery Brigades 105
 Athens blockaded by 207
 Australian defence dependent on 90–2, 108–12, 233–4
 Australians donate to 257
 colonial policies 228, 264
 dreadnought construction 264–5
 hands assets over to RAN 115, 275
 Marines from 40, 91
 RAN crew trained by 274
 response to invasion fears 103, 236–7
 Sydney squadron 208, 216–18, 258, 260

Royal New Zealand Fencible Corps 137
Roydhouse, Thomas Richard 242, 247
rural Australia, nationalistic view of 248–50
Russia
 Afghanistan Crisis 234–5
 Japanese defeat of 242, 260
 perceived threat from 93, 152, 176, 187, 215–16, 260
 war with Turkey 234–5
Ryan, Lyndall 32, 33

Salvation Army 271
Samoa 104, 280, 290
Sargent, Clem 58
Sargood, Captain FT 178–9, 181, 188
Scharnhorst cruiser 289, 291
school cadet movement *see* cadet movement
school military drill 175–7
Scobie, James 70
Second Taranaki War *see* Taranaki Wars
self-government, and response to imperial policy 212–13
Serjeant, Able Seaman Henry 129
Serle, Geoffrey 67
Service, James 181
Shanahan, Edward 65
Shedden, Sir Frederick 233
Shellam, Tiffany 14–15
Shenandoah, CSS 235
shields, use of by Indigenous peoples 18–19
'shooting time' 22
Sirius, HMS 91
skirmish order 83–4
smallpox, deliberate use claims 30
Smart, Lieutenant Henry Dalton 123
Smith, John Thomas 132
SMLE rifles 162, 166–8
South African Constabulary 224
South African War
 Australian troops in 105–6, 206, 220–6, 255, 257–8
 effect on rifle clubs 157–8
South Australia

cadet movement in 177, 180, 190, 192
colonial naval defences 99–100
conflict between European settlers and Indigenous peoples 22, 34–5
rifle clubs in 151
Southern Cross flag 72, 244
Southwell, Daniel 13
spears, Indigenous use of 11, 15–17
Spectacle Island 97
Spitfire (ketch) 93–4
squatters 31
St Mark's Collegiate School cadet corps 177–8, 185, 188
Stack, Captain William 145
Stanley, Captain Owen 92
Stanley, Peter 58
State School Cadets (Qld) 183–4
Statistical, Historical and Political Description of NSW 51
Stirling, Captain James 92
Stirling, HMAS 114
Stockyard Hill 72–3
Street, Able Seaman Harry 295
Strickland, Sir George 193
Submarine Mining Corps (NSW) 97
submarines constructed for RAN 112
Sudan campaign
　Australian naval involvement 102
　casualties in 204–5
　NSW contingent 6, 214–16
Suggestions for Colonial Reform 208
Supply, HMS 91
Sutherland graving dock 97
Sutherland, Henry 73
Swan, HMAS 112
Swan Island mine depot 101
Swan River colony 92
Sydney
　as Royal Navy port 95–8
　fortifications built in 48
　military establishments in 46
　role in Pacific trade 284
Sydney Delivered; or, the Princely Buccaneer 232–3, 246
Sydney Grammar School cadet corps 185–6, 189
Sydney, HMAS

construction of 112
enters Simpsonhafen 291
in World War I 115–16
New Guinea force escorted by 293
sinks *Emden* 280
Sydney Naval Volunteers 93–4
Sydney Volunteer Rifles 139

Tahiti, French takeover of 285
Tainui confederation 126–7
Taranaki, military settlements in 138
Taranaki Regiment 138
Taranaki Wars
　First Taranaki War 124
　fortifications used in 130–2
　Second Taranaki War 133, 141
　Victoria used in 94
Tasmania
　attempts to clear Indigenous peoples from 21, 32
　cadet movement in 179, 189, 192
　colonial naval defences 100–1
　defence spending 151
　Indigenous warfare in 18
　pursuit of bushrangers in 49–50
　rifle clubs in 163–4
'Tasso Australiasiaticus' 232
Tauranga, HMS 104
Tauranga settlement 144
Tawhiao (Māori leader) 126
Taylor, George 269
Te Pahi 16
Te Ranga, Battle of 141–2
Telefunken stations 289–90
Tharrgari people, weapons used by 18
The Australian Citizen 270–1
The Australian Crisis 242, 245–6, 248–9
The Australian Frontier Wars 30
The Call 262
The Colonial Garrison 58
The Colony 30
The Coloured Conquest 242, 247, 250–1
'The Commonwealth Crisis' 262
The Eureka Stockade 68–9
The Face of Battle 67–8
The Facts About the Transvaal 222
The Forlorn Hope 214
The Invasion 238, 245–6, 249

Index

The Yellow Wave: A Romance of the Asiatic Invasion of Australia 241–3, 249–51
'The Young Queen' 224
Therry, Roger 45–6, 56–7
Thomas, Captain John Wellesley 72–4, 76, 81, 86
Thompson, Constable William 74
Thonen, Edmund 87
Thorpe, Bill 28
Thring, Henry 208
throwing sticks 17
Thursday Island 218, 273
Tingara, HMAS 114, 274
Titi Hill raid 142
Tiwi people, weapons used by 15, 17–18
To Pierce the Tyrant's Heart 51
Togo, as German colony 287
Toma, capture of 297
Torpedo Corps (Tas) 100–1
Torrens, HMAS 112
Torres Strait 19, 210, 285, 293
Torres Strait Islanders *see* Indigenous Australians
'transnational' history 59
Treaty of Waitangi 122–3
'trooping routes' 44
Tryon, Admiral Sir George 103, 216–17
Tulloch, Major General AB 188
Tuohy, Michael 89
Turkey, war with Russia 234–5
Turner, Henry 82

undersea telegraph cable 234
Union Shirt Factory, Perth 279
United Kingdom *see also* British Empire; British military forces
  'betrayal' of Australia by 230, 243–4
  cadet rifle shooting scheme 165
  invasion fears in 236–7
  National Archives 59
  partitions New Guinea with Germany 286
  rifle club movement in 149–50
  school cadet detachments 176
  seeks preference for exports 228

United States 92, 110–11, 244, 264
United Tribes of New Zealand 121
Universal Training Scheme 113

Vallee, Peter 35
Van Diemen's Land *see* Tasmania
Vandervort, Bruce 25
Vereeniging, Treaty of 255
Victoria
  Aboriginal deaths in 32–3
  bans recruitment of troops for NZ 143
  cadet movement in 178–83, 185–7, 190, 192
  colonial naval defences 94–6
  Defence Department formed in 151
  National Defence League in 165
  Native Police forces 21
  offers naval aid to NZ 127–8
  offers to fund dreadnought construction 266
  rifle clubs in 152, 157–9, 160–3, 262–3
Victoria Barracks 46
Victoria Crosses 3, 223
Victoria I, HMVS 94, 101, 127–8, 131–2
Victoria II, HMVS 101–2, 209–10
Victorian Mounted Rifles 153, 157
Victorian Rangers 153, 157
Victorian Rifle Association 150
Victorian Volunteer Cadet Corps 181
Vinegar Hill rebellion 50–1
volunteer forces in Australia 149, 175, 268–9 *see also* militias; rifle clubs
Volunteer Rifles (Vic) 157
von Clausewitz, Carl 11
von Klewitz, Captain KGA 294
von Spee, Admiral Maximilian 116, 290

Waikato regiments 138, 143–4, 210
Waikato War 5–6, 124, 132–3, 140–1
Waitangi, Treaty of 122–3
Waka Waka people 13
Wakefield, Edward 121
Walker, Frederick 32
Walker, Able Seaman John 295

Walker, WH 238, 245–6, 249
Wall, Private Joseph 80
Wallaroo, HMS 104, 217
war, frontier conflicts as instance of 22–3
War Office (UK) *see* British military forces
Warrego, HMAS
   ceremonial entry into Sydney 115
   construction of 111
   in World War I 291, 295
   launch of 113
Water Transport Corps (NZ) 140
Waterloo, Battle of 67–8
Watson, Chris 271
weapons used by Indigenous peoples 15–19
Weber, Gustav 298
Webster, Graeme 74, 85
Weigall, Albert Bythesea 189
Wellington, Duke of 67–8
Wellington's Men in Australia 55
Wentworth, William Charles 48, 50–1
Western Australia
   cadet movement in 179–80, 182, 192
   colonial naval defences 101
   conflict between European settlers and Indigenous peoples 21, 33–4
   Military Rifle Association 166
Western Desert peoples, weapons used by 16
Westminster, HMS 122
White Australia Policy, imperial attitudes to 261
White, Brudenell 263, 279
White League 240
White or Yellow? A Story of the Race War of AD 1908: 238–44, 248, 250–1
Who Killed the Koories? 33
Wickham, Captain John 92
Wilcox, Craig 58–9
Wilkes, Commodore Charles 92
Wilkes expedition ships 48
Willey, Keith 29
Williams, Able Seaman Billy 295
Williams, Henry 122
Williamstown Naval Base 101, 274
Willis, Ian Howie 10
Willshire, William 35
Wilson, Henry 278
Wilson, Woodrow 301
Windschuttle, Keith 32
Wiradjuri people 13–14
wireless telegraphy, naval use of 110
Wise, Captain Henry 81, 86
Wolfe, Patrick 24
Wollongong, stockade at 46–7
Wolseley, General Sir Garnet 214–15, 222
Wolverine (training ship) 97
women
   Indigenous, participation in warfare 12–13, 18
   Indigenous tribal raids for 13–14
wonga-wonga vine 16
Wood, Reader 143
woomeras 15–17
World War I
   Australian Imperial Force 1–2, 279–80, 300
   Australian response to 231
   capture of German New Guinea 7, 115–16, 280, 283–303
   effect on cadet corps 197, 201
   Fisher commits Australia to 279
   HMAS *Sydney* sinks *Emden* 115–16, 280
   rifle clubs overlooked in 171–2
Worunmurra, Banjo 34
Wright, Christine 55

Yarra, HMAS
   arrival in Australia 113
   ceremonial entry into Sydney 115
   construction of 111
   in World War I 291, 295
Yellow Wave, The 241–3, 249–51
Yolngu people, traditional warfare among 11
'Young Queen, The' 224